OXFORD

UNIVERSITY PRESS

OXFORD
UNIVERSITY PRESS

Great Clarendon Street, Oxford OX2 6DP

Oxford University Press is a department of the University of Oxford.
It furthers the University's objective of excellence in research, scholarship,
and education by publishing worldwide in

Oxford New York

Athens Auckland Bangkok Bogotá Buenos Aires Cape Town
Chennai Dar es Salaam Delhi Florence Hong Kong Istanbul Karachi
Kolkata Kuala Lumpur Madrid Melbourne Mexico City Mumbai Nairobi
Paris São Paulo Shanghai Singapore Taipei Tokyo Toronto Warsaw

with associated companies in Berlin Ibadan

Oxford is a registered trade mark of Oxford University Press
in the UK and in certain other countries

Database right Oxford University Press (makers)

First published 2001

British Library Cataloguing in Publication Data
Data available
ISBN 0–19–8603770

10 9 8 7 6 5 4 3 2 1

Designed by George Hammond
Typeset in Swift
by Kolam Information Services, India
Printed in Great Britain by Mackays of Chatham plc., Chatham, Kent

INTRODUCTION

FROM its beginnings in November 1982, Countdown has grown to become one of the most popular and enduring British TV game shows. The format is simple but effective, and the game itself is utterly compulsive. Of course, as with any word game, there has to be a final arbiter whose job it is to judge whether a word is allowed. Since the early days, when the 7th edition of the *Concise Oxford Dictionary* was first used on the programme, this role has fallen to Oxford dictionaries; this relationship has led to the adoption, in July 2000, of the *New Oxford Dictionary of English* as the dictionary officially used in Countdown.

The dictionary is the authority when it comes to verifying spelling or hyphenation, or indeed in deciding whether the word exists at all. If a word is not listed in the dictionary 'Bible', then it cannot be allowed. If a word is listed but with a different spelling, then, again, it cannot be allowed. Furthermore, it is up to the guardians of the dictionary in Dictionary Corner to use the dictionary to decide tricky and contentious issues such as whether, for example, a noun can have a plural. Some nouns obviously do take a plural (words like 'cat' and 'table') and some obviously don't (like 'wealth' and 'hubbub'). In between there are lots of words where the answer is not so obvious, and making a good lexicographical judgement can determine whether a contestant wins or loses.

The *Official Countdown Dictionary* has been compiled and checked by Oxford dictionary editors and contains all the 'Countdown' words listed in the *New Oxford Dictionary of English*, together with their allowable plurals and inflections. This means that, for example, it lists not only the verb 'excite', but also 'excites', 'excited', and 'exciting'. The dictionary shows whether a particular plural is allowed or not, and so can be used as an instant guide as to whether 'hubbubs' or 'wealths' is acceptable. Words that have more than nine letters are not listed – for example, the dictionary lists 'clutter', 'clutters', and 'cluttered', but not 'cluttering', as it has ten letters. Also excluded are words which are not allowed in the rules of Countdown, for example, abbreviations, proper names, hyphenated words, and partial forms. For a full explanation of the rules, see the supplement in this dictionary, pp. 334–5.

This dictionary is intended as a quick reference guide to Countdown words for use on or off screen, but it is also more than that. A special supplement is included, giving information about the programme and an explanation of the rules, plus lots of test-yourself letters, numbers, and conundrums. Interesting and unusual words are listed from previous series, and there is also a full list of past champions.

We are grateful to the team of Oxford lexicographers and others who helped to compile and check the *Official Countdown Dictionary*, and also of course to the Countdown team themselves, especially Michael Wylie, who provided the material for the supplement. We hope that this dictionary will be a useful and interesting companion for all Countdown enthusiasts, and that, moreover, it will make the game of Countdown even more enjoyable.

Judy Pearsall
FEBRUARY 2001

C|O|N|T|E|N|T|S

Note on trademarks and proprietary status

This dictionary contains some words which have, or are
asserted to have, proprietary status as trademarks or
otherwise. Their inclusion does not imply that they have
acquired for legal purposes a non-proprietary or general
significance, nor any other judgement concerning their
legal status.

A A

aa
aapa
aapas
aardvark
aardvarks
aardwolf
aargh

A B

abaca
abacas
aback
abacus
abacuses
abafana
abaft
abaht
abalone
abalones
abandon
abandoned
abandons
abase
abased
abasement
abases
abash
abashed
abashes
abashing
abashment
abasing
abatagati
abate
abated
abatement
abates
abating
abatis
abatises

abattis
abattises
abattoir
abattoirs
abaxial
abaya
abayas
abba
abbacies
abbacy
abbatial
abbé
abbés
abbess
abbesses
abbey
abbeys
abbot
abbots
abbotship
abdabs
abdicate
abdicated
abdicates
abdicator
abdomen
abdomens
abdominal
abduct
abducted
abductee
abductees
abducting
abduction
abductor
abductors
abducts
abeam
abed
abele
abeles
abelia

abelian
abelias
aberrance
aberrancy
aberrant
abet
abetment
abetments
abets
abetted
abetter
abetters
abetting
abettor
abettors
abeyance
abeyant
abhor
abhorred
abhorrent
abhorrer
abhorrers
abhorring
abhors
abidance
abidances
abide
abided
abides
abiding
abidingly
abigail
abilities
ability
abiogenic
abiotic
abitur
abject
abjection
abjectly
abjure
abjured

abjures
abjuring
ablate
ablated
ablates
ablating
ablation
ablations
ablative
ablatives
ablaut
ablauts
ablaze
able
abled
ableism
ableist
abler
ablest
ablism
abloom
ablution
ablutions
ably
abnegate
abnegated
abnegates
abnegator
abnormal
abo
aboard
abode
aboded
abodes
aboding
abolish
abolished
abolisher
abolishes
abolition
abomasa
abomasum

abominate
aboral
aborally
aborigine
aborning
abort
aborted
aborting
abortion
abortions
abortive
aborts
aboulia
abound
abounded
abounding
abounds
about
above
abrade
abraded
abrader
abraders
abrades
abrading
abrasion
abrasions
abrasive
abrasives
abrazo
abrazos
abreact
abreacted
abreacts
abreast
abridge
abridged
abridger
abridgers
abridges
abridging
abroad

abrogate
abrogated
abrogates
abrogator
abrupt
abruption
abruptly
abscess
abscessed
abscesses
abscise
abscised
abscises
abscising
abscissa
abscissae
abscissas
abscond
absconded
absconder
absconds
abseil
abseiled
abseiler
abseilers
abseiling
abseils
absence
absences
absent
absented
absentee
absentees
absenting
absently
absents
absinth
absinthe
absinthes
absinths
absolute
absolutes
absolve
absolved
absolves
absolving
absonant
absorb
absorbed
absorbent

absorber
absorbers
absorbing
absorbs
abstain
abstained
abstainer
abstains
abstinent
abstract
abstracts
abstruse
absurd
absurder
absurdest
absurdism
absurdist
absurdity
absurdly
abubble
abulia
abulic
abundance
abundant
abura
abuse
abused
abuser
abusers
abuses
abusing
abusive
abusively
abustle
abut
abutilon
abutilons
abutment
abutments
abuts
abutted
abutter
abutters
abutting
abuzz
abysm
abysmal
abysmally
abyss

abyssal
abysses

A C

acacia
acacias
academe
academia
academic
academics
academies
academism
academy
acajou
acajous
acalculia
acanthus
acara
acaras
acaricide
acarid
acarids
acarine
acarines
acaroid
acarology
acausal
acca
accaroid
accas
accede
acceded
accedes
acceding
accent
accented
accenting
accentor
accentors
accents
accentual
accept
acceptant
accepted
accepter
accepters
accepting
acceptor
acceptors

accepts
access
accessary
accessed
accesses
accessing
accession
accessory
accidence
accident
accidents
accidie
accipiter
acclaim
acclaimed
acclaims
acclimate
acclivity
accolade
accolades
accompany
accord
accordant
accorded
according
accordion
accords
accost
accosted
accosting
accosts
account
accounted
accounts
accouter
accouters
accoutre
accoutred
accoutres
accra
accras
accredit
accredits
accrete
accreted
accretes
accreting
accretion
accretive
accrual

accruals
accrue
accrued
accrues
accruing
accuracy
accurate
accursed
accurst
accusal
accusals
accuse
accused
accuser
accusers
accuses
accusing
accustom
accustoms
ace
aced
acedia
acellular
acentric
acer
acerb
acerbic
acerbity
acers
aces
acetabula
acetal
acetals
acetamide
acetate
acetates
acetone
acetous
acetyl
acetylate
acetylene
acetylide
ach
achaar
achalasia
achar
achcha
ache
ached
achene

achenes	aconitine	act	actuation	adaxial
aches	acorn	actable	actuator	add
achier	acorns	actant	actuators	adda
achiest	acouchi	actants	acuity	addas
achieve	acouchis	acted	aculeate	addax
achieved	acoustic	actin	aculeates	addaxes
achiever	acoustics	acting	acumen	added
achievers	acquaint	actinian	acuminate	addenda
achieves	acquaints	actinians	acushla	addendum
achieving	acquiesce	actinic	acushlas	adder
achillea	acquire	actinide	acutance	adders
achilleas	acquired	actinides	acute	addict
achimenes	acquiree	actinism	acutely	addicted
aching	acquirees	actinisms	acuteness	addiction
achingly	acquirer	actinium	acutes	addictive
achiote	acquirers	action	acyclic	addicts
achiral	acquires	actioned	acyclovir	adding
achkan	acquiring	actioner	acyl	addition
achkans	acquit	actioners	acylate	additions
achromat	acquits	actioning	acylated	additive
achromats	acquittal	actions	acylates	additives
achy	acquitted	activate	acylating	addle
acicular	acrasia	activated	acylation	addled
acid	acratic	activates		addles
acidic	acre	activator		addling
acidified	acreage	active	A D	addorsed
acidifies	acreages	actively		address
acidify	acred	activism	ad	addressed
acidity	acres	activist	adage	addressee
acidly	acrid	activists	adages	addresser
acidophil	acridine	activity	adagio	addresses
acidosis	acridity	actor	adagios	adds
acidotic	acridly	actors	adamance	adduce
acids	acrimony	actress	adamances	adduced
acidulate	acrobat	actresses	adamancy	adduces
acidulous	acrobatic	actressy	adamant	adducible
acidy	acrobats	acts	adamantly	adducing
acing	acrolect	actual	adapt	adduct
acini	acrolects	actualise	adaptable	adducted
acinus	acronym	actuality	adaptably	adducting
ackee	acronyms	actualize	adapted	adduction
ackees	acropetal	actually	adapter	adductor
acme	acropolis	actuarial	adapters	adductors
acmes	across	actuaries	adapting	adducts
acne	acrostic	actuarily	adaption	adenine
acned	acrostics	actuary	adaptions	adenoidal
acolyte	acrylate	actuate	adaptive	adenoids
acolytes	acrylates	actuated	adaptogen	adenoma
aconite	acrylic	actuates	adaptor	adenomas
aconites	acrylics	actuating	adaptors	adenomata
			adapts	

adenosine
adenylate
adept
adeptly
adeptness
adepts
adequacy
adequate
adhere
adhered
adherence
adherent
adherents
adheres
adhering
adhesion
adhesions
adhesive
adhesives
adhibit
adhibited
adhibits
adhocracy
adiabatic
adieu
adieus
adieux
adios
adioses
adipate
adipates
adipic
adipocere
adipocyte
adipose
adiposity
adit
adits
adjacency
adjacent
adjective
adjigo
adjigos
adjiko
adjikos
adjoin
adjoined
adjoining
adjoins
adjoint

adjourn
adjourned
adjourns
adjudge
adjudged
adjudges
adjudging
adjunct
adjuncts
adjure
adjured
adjures
adjuring
adjust
adjusted
adjuster
adjusters
adjusting
adjusts
adjutancy
adjutant
adjutants
adjuvant
adjuvants
adland
adman
admass
admen
admi
admin
adminicle
admirable
admirably
admiral
admirals
admiralty
admire
admired
admirer
admirers
admires
admiring
admis
admission
admit
admits
admitted
admitting
admix
admixed

admixes
admixing
admixture
admonish
admonitor
adnate
adnexa
adnexal
adnominal
ado
adobe
adobes
adopt
adoptable
adopted
adoptee
adoptees
adopter
adopters
adopting
adoption
adoptions
adoptive
adopts
adorable
adorably
adoral
adorally
adoration
adore
adored
adorer
adorers
adores
adoring
adoringly
adorn
adorned
adorner
adorners
adorning
adornment
adorns
adpressed
adrenal
adrenalin
adrenals
adret
adrets
adrift

adroit
adroiter
adroitest
adroitly
ads
adsorb
adsorbate
adsorbed
adsorbent
adsorbing
adsorbs
adstrata
adstrate
adstratum
aduki
adukis
adulate
adulated
adulates
adulating
adulation
adulator
adulators
adulatory
adult
adulterer
adultery
adulthood
adultly
adults
adumbrate
adust
advance
advanced
advancer
advancers
advances
advancing
advantage
advect
advected
advecting
advection
advective
advects
advent
advents
adventure
adverb
adverbial

adverbs
adversary
adverse
adversely
adversity
advert
adverted
adverting
advertise
adverts
advice
advices
advisable
advisably
advise
advised
advisedly
adviser
advisers
advises
advising
advisor
advisors
advisory
advocaat
advocaats
advocacy
advocate
advocated
advocates
advowson
advowsons
adyta
adytum
adz
adze
adzes
adzuki
adzukis

`A E`

aedile
aediles
aegis
aegrotat
aegrotats
aeolian
aeon
aeons

aepyornis
aerate
aerated
aerates
aerating
aeration
aerations
aerator
aerators
aerial
aerialist
aeriality
aerially
aerials
aerie
aeries
aero
aerobatic
aerobe
aerobes
aerobic
aerobics
aerobrake
aerodrome
aerofoil
aerofoils
aerogel
aerogels
aerogram
aerograms
aerolite
aerolites
aerology
aeronaut
aeronauts
aeronomy
aerophagy
aerophone
aeroplane
aeroshell
aerosol
aerosols
aerospace
aerostat
aerostats
aesthete
aesthetes
aesthetic
aestival
aestivate

aetatis
aether
aetiology

A F

afar
afara
afaras
afeared
afebrile
affable
affably
affair
affaire
affairé
affaires
affairs
affect
affected
affecting
affection
affective
affects
afferent
affiance
affianced
affiances
affiant
affiants
affidavit
affiliate
affinal
affine
affined
affines
affinity
affirm
affirmed
affirmer
affirmers
affirming
affirms
affix
affixed
affixes
affixing
afflatus
afflict
afflicted

afflicts
affluence
affluent
afflux
affluxes
afforce
afforced
afforces
afforcing
afford
afforded
affording
affords
afforest
afforests
affray
affrays
affricate
affright
affrights
affront
affronté
affronted
affronts
affronty
afghan
afghani
afghanis
afghans
afield
afire
aflame
aflatoxin
afloat
afoot
afore
aforesaid
afoul
afraid
afreet
afreets
afresh
afrit
afrits
aft
after
aftercare
afterdamp
afterdeck
afterglow

afterlife
aftermath
aftermost
afternoon
afters
aftersun
afterward
afterword

A G

ag
aga
again
against
agal
agals
agama
agamas
agamic
agamid
agamids
agape
agapes
agar
agarbatti
agaric
agarics
agarose
agas
agate
agates
agave
agaves
age
aged
ageing
ageism
ageist
ageless
agencies
agency
agenda
agendas
agent
agentive
agents
ages
aggravate
aggregate

aggressor
aggrieved
aggro
aghast
agile
agilely
agiler
agilest
agilities
agility
agin
aging
agism
agist
agisted
agister
agisters
agisting
agistment
agists
agitate
agitated
agitates
agitating
agitation
agitato
agitator
agitators
agitprop
agleam
aglet
aglets
agley
aglow
agma
agmas
agnail
agnails
agnate
agnates
agnathan
agnathans
agnatic
agnation
agnations
agnolotti
agnosia
agnostic
agnostics

ago
agog
agogic
agogics
agogo
agogos
agonies
agonise
agonised
agonises
agonising
agonism
agonisms
agonist
agonistic
agonists
agonize
agonized
agonizes
agonizing
agony
agora
agorae
agoras
agorot
agoroth
agouti
agoutis
agraphia
agraphias
agrarian
agrarians
agree
agreeable
agreeably
agreed
agreeing
agreement
agrees
agrestal
agrestic
agrimony
agrion
agrions
agrology
agronomic
agronomy
aground
ague
agued

agues
aguish

A H

ah
aha
ahead
ahem
ahimsa
aholehole
ahoy

A I

ai
aid
aida
aide
aided
aides
aiding
aids
aigrette
aigrettes
aiguille
aiguilles
aikido
ail
ailanthus
ailed
aileron
ailerons
ailing
ailment
ailments
ails
aim
aimed
aiming
aimless
aimlessly
aims
ainhum
aioli
air
airband
airbase
airbases
airboat

airboats
airborne
airbrick
airbricks
airbrush
airburst
airbursts
aircraft
aircrew
aircrews
airdrop
airdrops
aired
airer
airers
airfield
airfields
airflow
airflows
airfoil
airfoils
airframe
airframer
airframes
airglow
airhead
airheads
airier
airiest
airily
airiness
airing
airings
airless
airlift
airlifted
airlifts
airline
airliner
airliners
airlines
airlock
airlocks
airmail
airmailed
airmails
airman
airmen
airmiss
airmisses

airmobile
airplane
airplanes
airplay
airport
airports
airs
airscrew
airscrews
airship
airships
airsick
airside
airsides
airspace
airspeed
airspeeds
airstream
airstrip
airstrips
airtight
airtime
airwaves
airway
airways
airwoman
airwomen
airworthy
airy
ais
aisle
aisled
aisles
ait
aitch
aitchbone
aitches
aits

A J

ajar
ajuga
ajugas

A K

akara
akaras
akasha

akashic
akebia
akebias
akee
akees
akimbo
akin
akinesia
akinetic
akrasia
akratic
akvavit
akvavits

A L

alabaster
alack
alacrity
alameda
alamedas
alanine
alanna
alannah
alap
alaps
alar
alarm
alarmed
alarming
alarmism
alarmist
alarmists
alarms
alarum
alarums
alas
alate
alb
alba
albacore
albacores
albas
albatross
albedo
albedos
albeit
albert
alberts
albescent

albinism	aleck	aliased	alizarin	allegedly
albinisms	alecks	aliases	alkahest	alleges
albino	alecost	aliasing	alkahests	alleging
albinos	alecs	alibi	alkali	allegoric
albite	alee	alibied	alkalic	allegory
albizzia	alehouse	alibiing	alkaline	allegro
albizzias	alehouses	alibis	alkalis	allegros
albs	alembic	alick	alkalise	allele
album	alembics	alicks	alkalised	alleles
albumen	aleph	alicyclic	alkaliser	allelic
albumin	alephs	alidade	alkalises	alleluia
albums	alerce	alidades	alkalize	alleluias
alcahest	alerces	alien	alkalized	allemande
alcahests	alert	alienable	alkalizer	allergen
alcaic	alerted	alienage	alkalizes	allergens
alcaics	alerter	alienate	alkaloid	allergic
alcalde	alertest	alienated	alkaloids	allergies
alcaldes	alerting	alienates	alkalosis	allergist
alcazar	alertly	alienator	alkane	allergy
alcazars	alertness	alienee	alkanes	alleviate
alchemic	alerts	alienist	alkanet	alley
alchemise	ales	alienists	alkanets	alleys
alchemist	alethic	alienness	alkene	alleyway
alchemize	aleurone	alienor	alkenes	alleyways
alchemy	alevin	aliens	alkie	allheal
alchera	alevins	aliform	alkies	alliance
alcid	alewife	alight	alky	alliances
alcids	alewives	alighted	alkyd	allicin
alcohol	alexia	alighting	alkyds	allicins
alcoholic	alfalfa	alights	alkyl	allied
alcohols	alfisol	align	alkylate	allies
alcopop	alfisols	aligned	alkylated	alligator
alcopops	alfresco	aligning	alkylates	allium
alcove	alga	alignment	alkyne	alliums
alcoves	algae	aligns	alkynes	allocable
aldehyde	algal	alike	all	allocate
aldehydes	algebra	aliment	allamanda	allocated
aldehydic	algebraic	aliments	allanite	allocates
alder	algicide	alimonies	allantoic	allocator
alderfly	algicides	alimony	allantoid	allod
alderman	alginate	aliphatic	allantoin	allodial
aldermen	alginates	aliquot	allantois	allodium
alders	algology	aliquoted	allay	allods
aldicarb	algorithm	aliquots	allayed	allogamy
aldol	alguacil	aliteracy	allaying	allogenic
aldrin	alhaja	aliterate	allays	allograft
ale	alhajas	alive	allée	allograph
aleatoric	alhaji	aliveness	allées	allometry
aleatory	alhajis	aliyah	allege	allomorph
alec	alias	aliyoth	alleged	allopath

allopaths
allopathy
allopatry
allophone
allot
allotment
allotrope
allotropy
allots
allotted
allottee
allottees
allotting
allow
allowable
allowably
allowance
allowed
allowedly
allowing
allows
alloxan
alloxans
alloy
alloyed
alloying
alloys
allseed
allspice
allude
alluded
alludes
alluding
allure
allured
allures
alluring
allus
allusion
allusions
allusive
alluvial
alluvion
alluvium
ally
allying
allyl
allylic
allyls
almagest

almagests
almanac
almanack
almanacks
almanacs
almandine
almighty
almirah
almirahs
almond
almonds
almoner
almoners
almonries
almonry
almost
alms
almshouse
aloe
aloes
aloft
alogical
aloha
alone
aloneness
along
alongside
aloo
aloof
aloofly
aloofness
alopecia
aloud
alow
alp
alpaca
alpacas
alpargata
alpenglow
alpenhorn
alpha
alphabet
alphabets
alphas
alphonso
alphonsos
alphorn
alphorns
alpine
alpinist

alpinists
alps
already
alright
alsike
also
altar
altars
alter
alterable
altercate
altered
altering
alterity
alternant
alternate
alters
althorn
althorns
although
altimeter
altimetry
altiplano
altissimo
altitude
altitudes
alto
altos
altricial
altruism
altruist
altruists
alu
aludel
aludels
alula
alulae
alum
alumina
aluminise
aluminium
aluminize
aluminous
aluminum
alumna
alumnae
alumni
alumnus
alums
alus

alveolar
alveolars
alveolate
alveoli
alveolus
alway
always
alyssum
alyssums

A M

am
amadavat
amadavats
amadou
amah
amahs
amalgam
amalgams
amaranth
amaranths
amaretti
amaretto
amaryllis
amass
amassed
amasser
amassers
amasses
amassing
amateur
amateurs
amatol
amatory
amaurosis
amaurotic
amaze
amazed
amazement
amazes
amazing
amazingly
amazon
amazons
ambatch
ambatches
amber
ambergris
amberjack

ambers
ambiance
ambiances
ambience
ambiences
ambient
ambiguity
ambiguous
ambisonic
ambit
ambition
ambitions
ambitious
ambits
ambivert
ambiverts
amble
ambled
ambler
amblers
ambles
ambling
amblyopia
amblyopic
ambo
ambones
ambos
amboyna
ambries
ambrosia
ambrosial
ambry
ambulacra
ambulance
ambulant
ambulate
ambulated
ambulates
ambuscade
ambush
ambushed
ambushes
ambushing
ameba
amebae
amebas
amebiasis
amebic
ameboid
amen

amenable	ammeter	amosite	amrit	anagram
amenably	ammeters	amount	amrita	anagrams
amend	ammo	amounted	amster	anal
amendable	ammonia	amounting	amsters	analecta
amended	ammonite	amounts	amtrac	analects
amender	ammonites	amour	amtracs	analeptic
amenders	ammonium	amours	amtrak	analgesia
amending	ammonoid	amp	amtraks	analgesic
amendment	ammonoids	amperage	amuck	anally
amends	amnesia	ampere	amulet	analog
amenities	amnesiac	amperes	amulets	analogies
amenity	amnesiacs	ampersand	amuse	analogise
amens	amnesic	amphibian	amused	analogize
ament	amnestied	amphibole	amusedly	analogous
amentia	amnesties	amphiboly	amusement	analogs
aments	amnesty	amphioxus	amuses	analogue
amerce	amnia	amphipod	amusing	analogues
amerced	amnio	amphipods	amusingly	analogy
amerces	amnion	amphiuma	amygdala	analysand
amercing	amnions	amphora	amygdalae	analyse
americium	amnios	amphorae	amygdale	analysed
amethyst	amniote	amphoras	amygdales	analyser
amethysts	amniotes	ample	amygdalin	analysers
amiable	amniotic	ampleness	amyl	analyses
amiably	amoeba	ampler	amylase	analysing
amianthus	amoebae	amplest	amyloid	analysis
amicable	amoebas	amplexus	amylose	analyst
amicably	amoebic	amplified		analysts
amice	amoeboid	amplifier		analytic
amices	amok	amplifies	A N	analyze
amici	among	amplify	an	analyzed
amicus	amongst	amplitude	anabatic	analyzes
amid	amoral	amply	anabiosis	analyzing
amide	amoralism	ampoule	anabiotic	anamneses
amides	amoralist	ampoules	anabolic	anamnesis
amidship	amorality	amps	anabolism	ananda
amidships	amoretti	ampster	anabranch	anapaest
amidst	amoretto	ampsters	anaclitic	anapaests
amigo	amorist	ampul	anaconda	anapest
amigos	amorists	ampule	anacondas	anapests
amine	amoroso	ampules	anacruses	anaphase
amines	amorous	ampulla	anacrusis	anaphases
amino	amorously	ampullae	anaemia	anaphor
amir	amorphous	ampuls	anaemic	anaphora
amirs	amortise	amputate	anaerobe	anaphoric
amiss	amortised	amputated	anaerobes	anaphors
amitosis	amortises	amputates	anaerobic	anapsid
amitotic	amortize	amputator	anagen	anapsids
amity	amortized	amputee	anaglyph	anaptyxis
amma	amortizes	amputees	anaglyphs	anarch

anarchic	andouille	angled	animated	annatto
anarchism	andradite	angler	animates	annattos
anarchist	androecia	anglers	animateur	anneal
anarchs	androgen	angles	animati	annealed
anarchy	androgens	anglice	animatic	annealer
anathema	androgyne	anglicise	animating	annealers
anathemas	androgyny	anglicize	animation	annealing
anatomies	android	angling	animato	anneals
anatomise	androids	angora	animator	annelid
anatomist	andromeda	angoras	animators	annelidan
anatomize	anecdotal	angostura	animatos	annelids
anatomy	anecdote	angrez	anime	annex
anatto	anecdotes	angrezi	animism	annexe
anattos	anechoic	angrezlog	animist	annexed
ancestor	anele	angrier	animistic	annexes
ancestors	aneled	angriest	animists	annexing
ancestral	aneles	angrily	animosity	annotate
ancestry	aneling	angry	animus	annotated
ancho	anemia	angst	anion	annotates
anchor	anemic	angstrom	anionic	annotator
anchorage	anemone	angstroms	anions	announce
anchored	anemones	angsty	anis	announced
anchoress	anent	anguish	anise	announcer
anchoring	anergia	anguished	aniseed	announces
anchorite	anergy	anguishes	anises	annoy
anchorman	aneroid	angular	anisette	annoyance
anchormen	aneurism	angularly	anisogamy	annoyed
anchors	aneurisms	angulate	ankh	annoyer
anchos	aneurysm	angulated	ankhs	annoyers
anchoveta	aneurysms	angulates	ankle	annoying
anchovies	anew	anhedonia	ankled	annoys
anchovy	angel	anhedonic	ankles	annual
anchusa	angelfish	anhedral	anklet	annually
anchusas	angelic	anhinga	anklets	annuals
ancient	angelica	anhingas	ankling	annuitant
anciently	angelical	anhydride	ankus	annuities
ancients	angelicas	anhydrite	ankuses	annuity
ancillary	angels	anhydrous	ankylose	annul
ancon	angelus	ani	ankylosed	annular
ancones	anger	aniline	ankylosis	annularly
and	angered	anilingus	ankylotic	annulate
andante	angering	anima	anlage	annulated
andantes	angers	animal	anlagen	annulet
andantino	angina	animalise	anna	annulets
andesite	angiogram	animalism	annal	annuli
andesitic	angioma	animalist	annalist	annulled
andiron	angiomas	animality	annalists	annulling
andirons	angiomata	animalize	annals	annulment
andisol	angelicas	animals	annas	annuls
andisols	angle	animate	annates	annulus

anoa
anoas
anodal
anode
anodes
anodic
anodise
anodised
anodiser
anodisers
anodises
anodising
anodize
anodized
anodizer
anodizers
anodizes
anodizing
anodyne
anodynes
anoint
anointed
anointer
anointers
anointing
anoints
anole
anoles
anomalies
anomalous
anomaly
anomia
anomic
anomie
anomy
anon
anonym
anonymise
anonymity
anonymize
anonymous
anonyms
anopheles
anopluran
anorak
anoraks
anorectal
anorectic
anorexia
anorexic

anorexics
anorthite
anosmia
anosmic
another
anotherie
anothery
anovulant
anoxia
anoxic
ansatz
anserine
answer
answered
answering
answers
ant
antacid
antacids
antbear
antbears
antbird
antbirds
ante
anteater
anteaters
anted
antedate
antedated
antedates
anteing
antelope
antelopes
antenatal
antenna
antennae
antennal
antennary
antennas
antennule
anterior
antes
anthelia
anthelion
anthem
anthemia
anthemic
anthemion
anthems

anther
anthers
anthesis
anthill
anthills
anthology
anthozoan
anthrax
anthurium
anti
antibody
antic
anticline
anticodon
antics
antidotal
antidote
antidotes
antigen
antigenic
antigens
antilog
antilogs
antilogy
antimonic
antimony
anting
antinode
antinodes
antinomy
antipasti
antipasto
antipathy
antiphon
antiphons
antiphony
antipodal
antipode
antipodes
antipope
antipopes
antiquark
antiquary
antique
antiqued
antiques
antiquing
antiquity
antis

antisense
antisera
antiserum
antitoxic
antitoxin
antitrust
antitype
antitypes
antivenin
antivenom
antiviral
antivirus
antler
antlered
antlers
antonym
antonyms
antra
antral
antrum
ants
antsier
antsiest
antsy
anura
anuran
anurans
anuria
anuric
anus
anuses
anvil
anvils
anxieties
anxiety
anxious
anxiously
any
anybody
anyhow
anymore
anyone
anyplace
anything
anytime
anyway
anyways
anywhere
anywheres
anywise

A O

aorist
aoristic
aorists
aorta
aortas
aortic
aoudad
aoudads

A P

apace
apache
apaches
apanage
apanages
apart
apartheid
apartment
apartness
apartotel
apathetic
apathy
apatite
ape
aped
apeman
apemen
aperçu
aperçus
aperient
aperients
aperiodic
aperitif
aperitifs
aperture
apertures
apery
apes
apetalous
apex
apexed
apexes
apexing
aphasia
aphasic
aphelia
aphelion

apheresis
aphesis
aphetic
aphicide
aphicides
aphid
aphides
aphids
aphis
aphonia
aphony
aphorise
aphorised
aphorises
aphorism
aphorisms
aphorist
aphorists
aphorize
aphorized
aphorizes
aphtha
aphthae
aphthous
apian
apiarian
apiaries
apiarist
apiarists
apiary
apical
apices
apiece
aping
apish
apishly
apishness
aplanat
aplanatic
aplanats
aplasia
aplastic
aplenty
aplomb
apnea
apnoea
apocope
apocrine
apocrypha
apodictic

apodoses
apodosis
apodous
apogee
apogees
apolar
apollo
apollos
apologia
apologias
apologies
apologise
apologist
apologize
apologue
apologues
apology
apolune
apolunes
apomict
apomictic
apomicts
apomixis
apophatic
apophyses
apophysis
apoplexy
apoptosis
apoptotic
aporia
aporias
apostasy
apostate
apostates
apostle
apostles
apostolic
apothegm
apothegms
apothem
apothems
app
appal
appall
appalled
appalling
appalls
appals
appanage
appanages

apparat
apparatus
apparel
appareled
apparels
apparent
appeal
appealed
appealer
appealers
appealing
appeals
appear
appeared
appearing
appears
appease
appeased
appeaser
appeasers
appeases
appeasing
appellant
appellate
appellee
appellees
append
appendage
appendant
appended
appending
appendix
appends
appertain
appestat
appestats
appetency
appetiser
appetite
appetites
appetizer
applaud
applauded
applauds
applause
apple
applejack
apples
applet
applets

appley
appliance
applicant
applied
applier
appliers
applies
appliqué
appliquéd
appliqués
apply
applying
appoint
appointed
appointee
appointer
appoints
apport
apportion
apports
appose
apposed
apposes
apposing
apposite
appraisal
appraise
appraised
appraisee
appraiser
appraises
apprehend
appress
appressed
appresses
apprise
apprised
apprises
apprising
apprize
apprized
apprizes
apprizing
appro
approach
approbate
approval
approvals
approve
approved

approves
approving
apps
apraxia
apraxic
apricot
apricots
apriorism
apron
aproned
aprons
apropos
apsara
apsaras
apsarases
apse
apses
apsidal
apsides
apsis
apt
apter
apterous
aptest
aptitude
aptitudes
aptly
aptness

`A` `Q`

aqua
aquacade
aquacades
aqualung
aqualungs
aquanaut
aquanauts
aquaplane
aquarelle
aquaria
aquarist
aquarists
aquarium
aquariums
aquatic
aquatics
aquatint
aquatints
aquavit

aqueduct
aqueducts
aqueous
aquifer
aquifers
aquilegia
aquiline
aquiver

A R

arabesque
arabica
arabicas
arabinose
arabis
arabises
arable
aracari
aracaris
arachnid
arachnids
arachnoid
aragonite
arak
aralia
aralias
arame
araneid
araneids
arapaima
arapaimas
arational
araucaria
arb
arbalest
arbalests
arbiter
arbiters
arbitrage
arbitral
arbitrary
arbitrate
arblast
arblasts
arbor
arboreal
arboreta
arboretum
arbors

arbour
arboured
arbours
arbovirus
arbs
arbutus
arbutuses
arc
arcade
arcaded
arcades
arcading
arcana
arcane
arcanely
arcanum
arced
arch
archaea
archaean
archaic
archaism
archaisms
archangel
archboard
archducal
archduchy
archduke
archdukes
arched
archer
archers
archery
arches
archest
archetype
archil
archils
arching
architect
archival
archive
archived
archives
archiving
archivist
archivolt
archlute
archlutes
archly

archness
archon
archons
archosaur
archway
archways
arcing
arco
arcology
arcos
arcs
arcsin
arctan
arctic
arctics
arcuate
ardencies
ardency
ardent
ardently
ardor
ardors
ardour
ardours
arduous
arduously
are
area
areal
areas
areaway
areaways
areca
arecas
areg
arena
arenas
areola
areolae
areolar
areolate
areole
areoles
ares
arête
arêtes
arf
argali
argalis
argent

argentine
argh
argillite
arginine
argol
argols
argon
argonaut
argonauts
argosies
argosy
argot
argots
arguable
arguably
argue
argued
arguer
arguers
argues
argufied
argufies
argufy
argufying
arguing
argument
arguments
argus
arguses
argute
argyle
arhat
arhats
arhythmic
aria
arias
arid
aridisol
aridisols
aridity
aridly
aridness
ariel
ariels
aright
aril
arillate
arils
arioso
ariosos

arise
arisen
arises
arising
arisings
aristo
aristos
aristotle
ark
arkose
arkosic
arks
arm
armada
armadas
armadillo
armament
armaments
armature
armatures
armband
armbands
armchair
armchairs
armed
armful
armfuls
armhole
armholes
armies
armiger
armigers
arming
armistice
armless
armlet
armlets
armlock
armlocks
armoire
armoires
armor
armored
armorer
armorers
armorial
armories
armoring
armors
armory

armour	arrantly	arsenal	artifices	ascertain
armoured	arras	arsenals	artillery	ascesis
armourer	arrases	arsenate	artiness	ascetic
armourers	array	arsenates	artisan	ascetics
armouries	arrayed	arsenic	artisanal	asci
armouring	arraying	arsenical	artisans	ascidian
armours	arrays	arsenide	artist	ascidians
armoury	arré	arsenides	artiste	ascites
armpit	arrear	arsenious	artistes	ascitic
armpits	arrearage	arses	artistic	ascon
armrest	arrears	arsey	artistry	asconoid
armrests	arrest	arsie	artists	ascons
arms	arrested	arsine	artless	ascorbate
army	arrestee	arsing	artlessly	ascot
arnica	arrestees	arsis	arts	ascots
aroha	arrester	arson	artsier	ascribe
aroid	arresters	arsonist	artsiest	ascribed
aroids	arresting	arsonists	artsy	ascribes
arolla	arrestor	art	artwork	ascribing
arollas	arrestors	artefact	artworks	ascus
aroma	arrests	artefacts	arty	asdic
aromas	arris	artel	arugula	aseismic
aromatic	arrises	arteli	arum	asepsis
aromatics	arrival	artels	arums	aseptic
aromatise	arrivals	artemisia	arvo	asexual
aromatize	arrive	arterial	arvos	asexually
arose	arrived	arteries	aryl	ash
around	arrives	arteriole	arytenoid	ashamed
arousable	arriving	arteritis		ashamedly
arousal	arrivisme	artery		ashcan
arousals	arriviste	artesian		ashcans
arouse	arrogance	artful	as	ashed
aroused	arrogant	artfully	asafetida	ashen
arouses	arrogate	arthritic	asana	ashes
arousing	arrogated	arthritis	asanas	ashet
arpeggio	arrogates	arthropod	asbestos	ashets
arpeggios	arrow	artic	ascarid	ashier
arquebus	arrowed	artichoke	ascarids	ashiest
arrack	arrowhead	article	ascaris	ashine
arrah	arrowing	articled	ascend	ashing
arraign	arrowroot	articles	ascendant	ashlar
arraigned	arrows	articling	ascended	ashlaring
arraigns	arrowy	artics	ascendent	ashlars
arrange	arroyo	articular	ascender	ashore
arranged	arroyos	artier	ascenders	ashplant
arranger	arroz	artiest	ascending	ashplants
arrangers	arse	artifact	ascends	ashram
arranges	arsed	artifacts	ascension	ashrama
arranging	arsehole	artifice	ascent	ashramas
arrant	arseholes	artificer	ascents	ashrams

A S

ashtray
ashtrays
ashy
aside
asides
asinine
asininity
asities
asity
ask
askance
askant
askari
askaris
asked
asker
askers
askew
asking
asks
aslant
asleep
aslope
asocial
asp
asparagus
aspartame
aspartate
aspect
aspected
aspecting
aspects
aspectual
aspen
aspens
asperges
asperity
aspermia
asperse
aspersed
asperses
aspersing
aspersion
asphalt
asphalted
asphaltic
asphalts
aspheric
asphodel
asphodels

asphyxia
asphyxial
aspic
aspirant
aspirants
aspirate
aspirated
aspirates
aspirator
aspire
aspired
aspires
aspirin
aspiring
aspirins
asprawl
asps
asquint
ass
assagai
assagais
assai
assail
assailant
assailed
assailing
assails
assart
assarted
assarting
assarts
assassin
assassins
assault
assaulted
assaulter
assaults
assay
assayed
assayer
assayers
assaying
assays
assed
assegai
assegaied
assegaing
assegais
assemble
assemblé

assembled
assembler
assembles
assemblés
assembly
assent
assented
assenter
assenters
assenting
assentor
assentors
assents
assert
asserted
asserter
asserters
asserting
assertion
assertive
assertor
assertors
asserts
asses
assess
assessed
assesses
assessing
assessor
assessors
asset
assets
asshole
assholes
assiduity
assiduous
assign
assigned
assignee
assignees
assigner
assigners
assigning
assignor
assignors
assigns
assist
assistant
assisted
assister

assisters
assisting
assists
assize
assizes
associate
assonance
assonant
assonate
assonated
assonates
assort
assorted
assorting
assorts
assuage
assuaged
assuages
assuaging
assumable
assume
assumed
assumedly
assumes
assuming
assurance
assure
assured
assuredly
assurer
assurers
assures
assuring
astable
astatic
astatine
aster
asterisk
asterisks
asterism
asterisms
astern
asteroid
asteroids
asters
asthenia
asthenic
asthma
asthmatic
astilbe

astilbes
astir
astonish
astound
astounded
astounds
astraddle
astragal
astragali
astragals
astrakhan
astral
astrantia
astray
astride
astrocyte
astrodome
astroid
astroids
astrolabe
astrology
astronaut
astronomy
astute
astutely
astuter
astutest
astylar
asunder
asura
asuras
aswarm
aswim
aswirl
asylum
asylums
asymmetry
asymptote
asyndeta
asyndetic
asyndeton

A|T

at
atactic
ataman
atamans
atap
ataractic

ataraxia	atomisers	attached	attiring	audiobook
ataraxic	atomises	attaches	attitude	audiogram
ataraxy	atomising	attachés	attitudes	audiology
atavism	atomism	attaching	attorn	audiotape
atavisms	atomist	attack	attorned	audit
atavistic	atomistic	attacked	attorney	audited
ataxia	atomists	attacker	attorneys	auditing
ataxic	atomize	attackers	attorning	audition
ataxy	atomized	attacking	attorns	auditions
ate	atomizer	attacks	attract	auditive
atelier	atomizers	attagirl	attracted	auditor
ateliers	atomizes	attain	attractor	auditoria
atemporal	atomizing	attainder	attracts	auditors
atenolol	atoms	attained	attribute	auditory
athanor	atomy	attaining	attrit	audits
athanors	atonal	attains	attrition	auger
atheism	atonalism	attaint	attrits	augers
atheist	atonalist	attainted	attritted	aught
atheistic	atonality	attaints	attune	aughts
atheists	atone	attap	attuned	augite
atheling	atoned	attar	attunes	augment
athelings	atonement	attars	attuning	augmented
athematic	atones	attempt	atypical	augmenter
atheroma	atonic	attempted		augments
atheromas	atonies	attempts	`A` `U`	augur
athetesis	atoning	attend		augural
athetize	atony	attendant	aubade	augured
athetized	atop	attended	aubades	auguries
athetizes	atopic	attendee	auberge	auguring
athetoid	atopies	attendees	auberges	augurs
athetosis	atopy	attender	aubergine	augury
athetotic	atrazine	attenders	aubretia	august
athirst	atremble	attending	aubretias	augustly
athlete	atresia	attends	aubrietia	auk
athletes	atria	attention	auburn	auklet
athletic	atrial	attentive	auction	auklets
athletics	atrium	attenuate	auctioned	auks
athwart	atriums	attest	auctions	auld
atlantes	atrocious	attested	aucuba	aumbries
atlas	atrocity	attesting	aucubas	aumbry
atman	atrophic	attestor	audacious	aunt
atoll	atrophied	attestors	audacity	auntie
atolls	atrophies	attests	audial	aunties
atom	atrophy	attic	audible	aunts
atomic	atropine	atticism	audibles	aunty
atomicity	ats	atticisms	audibly	aura
atomies	attaboy	attics	audience	aurae
atomise	attacca	attire	audiences	aural
atomised	attach	attired	audile	aurally
atomiser	attaché	attires	audio	aurar

auras
aureate
aurei
aureola
aureolas
aureole
aureoles
aureus
auric
auricle
auricles
auricula
auricular
auriculas
auriscope
aurochs
aurochses
aurora
aurorae
auroral
auroras
auroscope
auspice
auspices
austenite
austere
austerely
austerer
austerest
austerity
austral
autarch
autarchic
autarchs
autarchy
autarkic
autarkies
autarky
auteur
auteurism
auteurist
auteurs
authentic
author
authored
authoress
authorial
authoring
authorise
authority

authorize
authors
autism
autistic
auto
autocar
autocars
autoclave
autocracy
autocrat
autocrats
autocross
autocue
autocues
autofocus
autogamy
autogenic
autogiro
autogiros
autograft
autograph
autogyro
autogyros
autoharp
autoharps
autolysis
autolytic
automat
automata
automate
automated
automates
automatic
automaton
automats
automize
automized
automizes
autonomic
autonomy
autopilot
autopista
autopsied
autopsies
autopsy
autoroute
autos
autosave
autosaved
autosaves

autosomal
autosome
autosomes
autotelic
autotomy
autotoxic
autotoxin
autotroph
autowind
autumn
autumnal
autumns
autunite
auxiliary
auxin
auxins
auxotroph

A V

avadavat
avadavats
avail
available
availed
availing
avails
avalanche
avarice
avascular
avast
avatar
avatars
avaunt
ave
avenge
avenged
avenger
avengers
avenges
avenging
avens
avenue
avenues
aver
average
averaged
averagely
averages
averaging

averment
averred
averring
avers
averse
aversion
aversions
aversive
avert
avertable
averted
averting
averts
aves
avgas
avian
avians
aviaries
aviary
aviate
aviated
aviates
aviating
aviation
aviator
aviatrix
avid
avider
avidest
avidin
avidins
avidity
avidly
avifauna
avifaunal
avionics
avirulent
avizandum
avo
avocado
avocados
avocation
avocet
avocets
avoid
avoidable
avoidably
avoidance
avoided
avoider

avoiders
avoiding
avoids
avos
avouch
avouched
avouches
avouching
avow
avowal
avowals
avowed
avowedly
avowing
avows
avulse
avulsed
avulses
avulsing
avulsion
avuncular

A W

aw
await
awaited
awaiting
awaits
awake
awaken
awakened
awakening
awakens
awakes
awaking
award
awarded
awardee
awardees
awarder
awarders
awarding
awards
aware
awareness
awash
away
aways
awe

aweary
awed
aweigh
awes
awesome
awesomely
awestruck
awful
awfully
awfulness
awhile
awhirl
awing
awkward
awkwardly
awl
awls
awn
awned
awning
awnings

awns
awoke
awoken
awry

| A | X |

ax
axe
axed
axel
axels
axeman
axemen
axenic
axes
axial
axially
axil
axilla
axillae

axillary
axils
axing
axiom
axiomatic
axioms
axion
axions
axis
axle
axles
axman
axmen
axolemma
axolotl
axolotls
axon
axonal
axonemal
axoneme
axonemes

axons
axoplasm

| A | Y |

ay
ayah
ayahs
ayahuasca
ayatollah
aye
ayes

| A | Z |

azalea
azaleas
azan
azans
azarole
azaroles

azeotrope
azide
azides
azimuth
azimuthal
azimuths
azine
azines
azoic
azonal
azoturia
azoturias
azulejo
azulejos
azure
azures
azurite
azygos
azygous

B

| B | A |

ba
baa
baaed
baaing
baap
baaps
baas
baases
baasie
baba
babaçú
babaçús
babalaas
babas
babassu

babassus
babbies
babble
babbled
babbler
babblers
babbles
babbling
babby
babe
babel
babes
babiche
babied
babies
babirusa
babirusas

baboon
baboons
babouche
babouches
babu
babul
babuls
babus
babushka
babushkas
baby
babyhood
babying
babyish
babyishly
babysat
babysit

babysits
bacalao
baccarat
bacchanal
bacchant
bacchante
bacchants
baccy
bachcha
bachchas
bachelor
bachelors
bacillary
bacilli
bacillus
back
backache

backaches
backacter
backbar
backbars
backbeat
backbeats
backbiter
backboard
backbone
backbones
backcast
backcasts
backchat
backcloth
backcomb
backcombs
backcourt

backcrawl	backrests	baddish	bagmen	baiza
backcross	backs	baddy	bagnio	baizas
backdate	backshift	bade	bagnios	baize
backdated	backside	badge	bagpipe	baizes
backdates	backsides	badged	bagpiper	bajada
backdown	backsight	badger	bagpipers	bajadas
backdowns	backslash	badgered	bagpipes	bajra
backdraft	backslid	badgering	bags	bake
backdrop	backslide	badgers	baguette	bakeapple
backdrops	backspace	badges	baguettes	baked
backed	backspin	badging	bagwash	bakehouse
backer	backstage	badinage	bagwashes	baker
backers	backstamp	badlands	bagworm	bakeries
backfield	backstay	badly	bagworms	bakers
backfill	backstays	badmash	bah	bakery
backfills	backstop	badmashes	bahada	bakes
backfire	backstops	badminton	bahadas	bakeshop
backfired	backswing	badness	bahadur	bakeshops
backfires	backsword	bafana	bahadurs	bakeware
backfist	backtrack	baffle	baht	baking
backfists	backveld	baffled	bahts	bakkie
backflip	backward	bafflegab	bai	bakkies
backflips	backwards	baffler	bail	baklava
backhand	backwash	bafflers	bailable	baksheesh
backhands	backwater	baffles	bailed	balaclava
backhoe	backwind	baffling	bailee	balafon
backhoes	backwinds	baft	bailees	balafons
backing	backwoods	bafta	bailer	balalaika
backland	backyard	bag	bailers	balance
backlands	backyards	bagasse	bailey	balanced
backlash	baclava	bagatelle	baileys	balancer
backless	baclavas	bagel	bailie	balancers
backlight	bacon	bagels	bailies	balances
backline	baconer	bagful	bailiff	balancing
backlines	baconers	bagfuls	bailiffs	balanda
backlist	bacons	baggage	bailing	balandas
backlists	bacteria	baggages	bailiwick	balander
backlit	bacterial	bagged	bailment	balanders
backload	bacterium	bagger	bailor	balanitis
backloads	bacula	baggers	bailors	balas
backlog	baculum	baggier	bailout	balata
backlogs	bad	baggies	bailouts	balatas
backlot	badam	baggiest	bails	balboa
backlots	badams	baggily	bairn	balboas
backmost	badass	bagginess	bairns	balconied
backpack	badasses	bagging	bais	balconies
backpacks	badder	baggy	bait	balcony
backplane	baddest	bagh	baited	bald
backplate	baddie	baghs	baiting	baldachin
backrest	baddies	bagman	baits	baldaquin

balder	ballets	balsa	bandies	banish
baldest	ballgirl	balsam	bandiest	banished
baldie	ballgirls	balsamic	banding	banishes
baldies	ballhawk	balsams	bandit	banishing
balding	ballhawks	balti	bandito	banister
baldish	balling	baltis	banditos	banisters
baldly	ballista	balun	banditry	banjax
baldmoney	ballistae	baluns	bandits	banjaxed
baldness	ballistas	baluster	banditti	banjaxes
baldpate	ballistic	balusters	bandog	banjaxing
baldpates	ballock	bam	bandogs	banjo
baldric	ballocked	bama	bandoleer	banjoes
baldrics	ballocks	bambini	bandolier	banjoist
baldy	ballon	bambino	bandoneon	banjoists
bale	ballons	bamboo	bandora	banjos
baled	balloon	bamboos	bandoras	bank
baleen	ballooned	bamboozle	bandore	bankable
balefire	balloons	ban	bandores	banked
balefires	ballot	banal	bandpass	banker
baleful	balloted	banality	bands	bankers
balefully	balloting	banally	bandsaw	banket
baler	ballots	banana	bandsaws	banking
balers	ballpark	bananas	bandshell	bankings
bales	ballparks	banausic	bandsman	banknote
baling	ballpoint	banco	bandsmen	banknotes
balk	ballroom	band	bandstand	bankroll
balked	ballrooms	bandage	bandura	bankrolls
balkier	balls	bandaged	banduras	bankrupt
balkiest	ballsed	bandages	bandwagon	bankrupts
balking	ballses	bandaging	bandwidth	banks
balks	ballsier	bandanna	bandy	banksia
balky	ballsiest	bandannas	bandying	banksias
ball	ballsing	bandbox	bane	banned
ballad	ballsy	bandboxes	baneberry	banner
ballade	bally	bandeau	baneful	bannered
balladeer	ballyhoo	bandeaux	bang	banneret
ballades	ballyhoos	banded	banged	bannerets
balladry	ballyrag	bander	banger	banners
ballads	ballyrags	banderol	bangers	banning
ballast	balm	banderole	banging	bannister
ballasted	balmier	banderols	bangle	bannock
ballasts	balmiest	banders	bangles	bannocks
ballboy	balmily	bandfish	bangs	banns
ballboys	balminess	bandh	bangtail	banquet
ballcock	balmoral	bandhs	bangtails	banqueted
ballcocks	balmorals	bandicoot	bani	banqueter
balled	balms	bandido	bania	banquets
ballerina	balmy	bandidos	banian	banquette
ballet	baloney	bandied	banians	bans
balletic	baloneys	bandier	banias	bansela

banselas	barbel	barest	barn	barré
banshee	barbell	barf	barnacle	barred
banshees	barbells	barfed	barnacled	barrel
bantam	barbels	barfi	barnacles	barreled
bantams	barber	barfing	barnbrack	barreling
banteng	barbered	barflies	barnet	barrelled
bantengs	barbering	barfly	barnets	barrels
banter	barberry	barfs	barney	barren
bantered	barbers	bargain	barneys	barrener
banterer	barbet	bargained	barns	barrenest
banterers	barbets	bargainer	barnstorm	barrenly
bantering	barbette	bargains	barnyard	barrens
banters	barbettes	barge	barnyards	barres
banyan	barbican	barged	barograph	barrette
banyans	barbicans	bargee	barometer	barrettes
banzai	barbie	bargees	barometry	barricade
baobab	barbies	bargepole	baron	barrier
baobabs	barbital	barges	baronage	barriers
bap	barbitone	barging	baronages	barring
baps	barbless	barilla	baroness	barrio
baptise	barbola	barillas	baronet	barrios
baptised	barbotine	baring	baronetcy	barrister
baptises	barbs	barite	baronets	barroom
baptising	barbule	barites	baronial	barrooms
baptism	barbules	baritone	baronies	barrow
baptismal	barbwire	baritones	barons	barrows
baptisms	barcarole	barium	barony	barry
baptist	barchan	bark	baroque	bars
baptistry	barchans	barkcloth	barotitis	bartender
baptists	bard	barked	barouche	barter
baptize	barded	barkeep	barouches	bartered
baptized	bardee	barkeeper	barque	barterer
baptizes	bardees	barkeeps	barques	barterers
baptizing	bardic	barker	barrack	bartering
bar	bardie	barkers	barracked	barters
barathea	bardies	barking	barracks	bartsia
baraza	barding	barks	barracoon	bartsias
barazas	bards	barley	barracuda	barwing
barb	bardy	barleymow	barrage	barwings
barbarian	bare	barm	barraged	baryon
barbaric	bareback	barmaid	barrages	baryonic
barbarise	bareboat	barmaids	barraging	baryons
barbarism	bared	barman	barranca	baryta
barbarity	barefaced	barmbrack	barrancas	baryte
barbarize	barefoot	barmen	barranco	barytes
barbarous	barege	barmier	barrancos	baryton
barbecue	barely	barmiest	barrator	barytons
barbecued	bareness	barmily	barrators	bas
barbecues	barer	barminess	barratry	basal
barbed	bares	barmy	barre	basalt

basaltic	basilar	bastardy	batistes	baueras
basanite	basilect	baste	batman	baulk
bascinet	basilects	basted	batmen	baulked
bascinets	basilica	bastes	baton	baulkier
bascule	basilican	bastide	batons	baulkiest
bascules	basilicas	bastides	bats	baulking
base	basilisk	bastinado	batsman	baulks
baseball	basilisks	basting	batsmen	baulky
baseballs	basin	bastings	batt	bauxite
baseboard	basinet	bastion	battalion	bauxitic
baseborn	basinets	bastions	batted	bavardage
based	basinful	basuco	battels	bavarois
basehead	basinfuls	bat	battement	bavaroise
baseheads	basing	batata	batten	bawbee
baseless	basins	batch	battened	bawbees
baseline	basipetal	batched	battening	bawd
baselines	basis	batches	battens	bawdier
baseload	bask	batching	batter	bawdiest
baseloads	basked	bate	battered	bawdily
basely	basket	bateau	batterer	bawdiness
baseman	basketful	bateaux	batterers	bawdry
basemen	basketry	bated	batterie	bawds
basement	baskets	bateleur	batteries	bawdy
basements	basking	bateleurs	battering	bawl
baseness	basks	bates	batters	bawled
basenji	basmati	batfish	battery	bawley
basenjis	basophil	batfishes	battier	bawleys
baseplate	basophils	bath	battiest	bawling
baser	basque	bathe	battily	bawls
bases	basques	bathed	battiness	bawn
basest	bass	bather	batting	bawns
bash	basses	bathers	battle	bay
basha	basset	bathes	battleaxe	baya
bashas	bassets	bathetic	battled	bayadère
bashed	bassi	bathhouse	battler	bayadères
bashes	bassinet	bathing	battlers	bayas
bashful	bassinets	batholith	battles	bayberry
bashfully	bassist	bathos	battling	bayed
bashing	bassists	bathrobe	batts	baying
bashment	basslet	bathrobes	battue	bayonet
bashments	basslets	bathroom	battues	bayoneted
basho	basso	bathrooms	batty	bayonets
bashos	bassoon	baths	batwing	bayou
basic	bassoons	bathtub	batwoman	bayous
basically	bassos	bathtubs	batwomen	bays
basicity	basswood	bathyal	bauble	baza
basics	basswoods	batik	baubles	bazaar
basidia	bast	batiks	baud	bazaars
basidium	bastard	bating	bauds	bazas
basil	bastards	batiste	bauera	bazoo

bazooka	beamer	beastlier	beckoned	bedight
bazookas	beamers	beastly	beckoning	bedim
bazoom	beamier	beasts	beckons	bedimmed
bazooms	beamiest	beat	becks	bedimming
bazoos	beaming	beatable	becloud	bedims
	beams	beatbox	beclouded	bedizen
B D	beamy	beatboxes	beclouds	bedizened
	bean	beaten	become	bedizens
bdellium	beanbag	beater	becomes	bedjacket
	beanbags	beaters	becoming	bedlam
B E	beaned	beatific	becquerel	bedlinen
be	beaneries	beatified	bed	bedload
beach	beanery	beatifies	bedabble	bedmaker
beached	beanfeast	beatify	bedabbled	bedmakers
beaches	beanie	beating	bedabbles	bedpan
beachhead	beanies	beatings	bedad	bedpans
beaching	beaning	beatitude	bedaub	bedplate
beachside	beano	beatnik	bedaubed	bedplates
beachwear	beanos	beatniks	bedaubing	bedpost
beacon	beanpole	beats	bedaubs	bedposts
beacons	beanpoles	beau	bedazzle	bedridden
bead	beans	beaus	bedazzled	bedrock
beaded	beanstalk	beaut	bedazzles	bedroll
beadier	bear	beauteous	bedbug	bedrolls
beadiest	bearable	beauties	bedbugs	bedroom
beadily	bearably	beautiful	beddable	bedrooms
beadiness	bearberry	beautify	bedded	beds
beading	bearcat	beauts	bedder	bedside
beadle	bearcats	beauty	bedders	bedsides
beadles	beard	beaux	bedding	bedsit
beads	bearded	beaver	bedeck	bedsits
beadsman	beardfish	beavered	bedecked	bedsitter
beadsmen	beardie	beavering	bedecking	bedskirt
beadwork	beardies	beavers	bedecks	bedskirts
beady	bearding	bebop	bedeguar	bedsock
beagle	beardless	bebopper	bedeguars	bedsocks
beagled	beards	beboppers	bedel	bedsore
beagler	bearer	becalm	bedell	bedsores
beaglers	bearers	becalmed	bedells	bedspread
beagles	beargrass	becalming	bedels	bedstead
beagling	bearing	becalms	bedevil	bedsteads
beak	bearings	became	bedeviled	bedstraw
beaked	bearish	becard	bedevils	bedstraws
beaker	bearishly	becards	bedew	bedtime
beakers	bears	because	bedewed	bedtimes
beaks	bearskin	béchamel	bedewing	bee
beaky	bearskins	beck	bedews	beech
beam	beast	becket	bedfellow	beeches
beamed	beastie	beckets	bedhead	beechmast
	beasties	beckon	bedheads	beedi

beedis	beetroots	beggaring	behemoths	belched
beef	beets	beggarly	behest	belches
beefalo	beeves	beggars	behests	belching
beefaloes	beezer	beggary	behind	beldam
beefcake	befall	begged	behinds	beldame
beefcakes	befallen	begging	behold	beldames
beefeater	befalling	begin	beholden	beldams
beefed	befalls	beginner	beholder	beleaguer
beefier	befell	beginners	beholders	belemnite
beefiest	befit	beginning	beholding	belfries
beefily	befits	begins	beholds	belfry
beefiness	befitted	begob	behoof	belie
beefing	befitting	begone	behoove	belied
beefs	befog	begonia	behooved	belief
beefsteak	befogged	begonias	behooves	beliefs
beefwood	befogging	begorra	behooving	belies
beefwoods	befogs	begot	behove	believe
beefy	befool	begotten	behoved	believed
beehive	befooled	begrime	behoves	believer
beehived	befooling	begrimed	behoving	believers
beehives	befools	begrimes	beige	believes
beeline	before	begriming	beiges	believing
beelines	befoul	begrudge	beignet	belittle
been	befouled	begrudged	beignets	belittled
beep	befouling	begrudges	being	belittler
beeped	befouls	begs	beings	belittles
beeper	befriend	beguile	beira	bell
beepers	befriends	beguiled	beiras	bellbird
beeping	befuddle	beguiler	beisa	bellbirds
beeps	befuddled	beguilers	beisas	bellboy
beer	befuddles	beguiles	bejabbers	bellboys
beerhouse	befur	beguiling	bejabers	belle
beerier	befurred	beguine	bejeezus	belled
beeriest	befurring	beguines	bejesus	belles
beerily	befurs	begum	bejeweled	bellhop
beeriness	beg	begums	bel	bellhops
beers	begad	begun	belabor	bellicose
beery	began	behalf	belabored	bellied
bees	begat	behave	belabors	bellies
beestings	begem	behaved	belabour	belling
beeswax	begemmed	behaves	belabours	bellman
beeswaxed	begemming	behaving	belated	bellmen
beeswaxes	begems	behavior	belatedly	bellow
beeswing	beget	behaviour	belay	bellowed
beet	begets	behead	belayed	bellowing
beetle	begetter	beheaded	belayer	bellows
beetled	begetters	beheading	belayers	bells
beetles	begetting	beheads	belaying	belly
beetling	beggar	beheld	belays	bellyache
beetroot	beggared	behemoth	belch	bellyband

bellyflop	benchmark	benzoates	berthed	bestrewed
bellyful	benchwork	benzoin	berthing	bestrewn
bellyfuls	bend	benzol	berths	bestrews
bellying	bendable	benzole	beryl	bestride
belong	bender	benzoyl	beryllium	bestrides
belonged	benders	benzyl	beryls	bestrode
belonging	bendier	bequeath	beseech	bests
belongs	bendiest	bequeaths	beseeched	bet
beloved	bendiness	bequest	beseeches	beta
beloveds	bending	bequests	beset	betaine
below	bendlet	berate	besets	betaines
bels	bendlets	berated	besetting	betake
belt	bends	berates	beside	betaken
belted	bendy	berating	besides	betakes
belter	beneath	berberine	besiege	betaking
belters	benefic	berberis	besieged	betas
belting	benefice	berceuse	besieger	betatron
beltings	beneficed	berceuses	besiegers	betatrons
beltman	benefices	bereave	besieges	betcha
beltmen	benefit	bereaved	besieging	betel
belts	benefited	bereaves	besmear	bethink
beltway	benefits	bereaving	besmeared	bethinks
beltways	bengaline	bereft	besmears	bethought
beluga	benighted	beret	besmirch	betide
belugas	benign	berets	besom	betided
belvedere	benignant	berg	besoms	betides
belying	benignity	bergamot	besotted	betiding
bema	benignly	bergamots	besought	betimes
bemas	benison	bergen	bespangle	bêtise
bemata	benisons	bergenia	bespatter	bêtises
bemire	benne	bergenias	bespeak	betoken
bemired	bennies	bergens	bespeaks	betokened
bemires	benny	bergère	bespoke	betokens
bemiring	benomyl	bergères	bespoken	betonies
bemoan	bens	bergs	best	betony
bemoaned	bent	beriberi	bested	betook
bemoaning	benthic	berk	bestial	betray
bemoans	benthos	berkelium	bestially	betrayal
bemuse	bentonite	berks	bestiary	betrayals
bemused	bents	berm	besting	betrayed
bemusedly	bentwood	berms	bestir	betrayer
bemuses	benumb	berried	bestirred	betrayers
bemusing	benumbed	berries	bestirs	betraying
ben	benumbing	berry	bestow	betrays
bench	benumbs	berrying	bestowal	betroth
benched	benzene	berserk	bestowals	betrothal
bencher	benzenoid	berserker	bestowed	betrothed
benchers	benzin	berth	bestowing	betroths
benches	benzine	bertha	bestows	bets
benching	benzoate	berthas	bestrew	betted

better
bettered
bettering
betters
betting
bettong
bettongs
bettor
bettors
between
betwixt
beurré
beurrés
bevatron
bevatrons
bevel
beveled
beveling
bevelled
bevelling
bevels
beverage
beverages
bevies
bevvied
bevvies
bevvy
bevy
bewail
bewailed
bewailer
bewailers
bewailing
bewails
beware
bewares
bewaring
bewdy
bewigged
bewilder
bewilders
bewitch
bewitched
bewitches
bey
beyond
beys
bezant
bezants
bezel

bezels
bezique
bezoar
bezoars

B H

bhai
bhais
bhajan
bhajans
bhaji
bhajia
bhajis
bhakti
bhang
bhangra
bharal
bharals
bhavan
bhelpuri
bhindi

B I

bialy
bialys
biannual
bias
biased
biases
biasing
biassed
biasses
biassing
biathlete
biathlon
biathlons
biaxial
bib
bibbed
bibber
bibbers
bibbing
bibelot
bibelots
bibi
bibis
bible
bibles

biblical
bibs
bibulous
bicameral
bicarb
bice
biceps
bichir
bichirs
bicker
bickered
bickerer
bickerers
bickering
bickers
bickies
bicky
bicolour
bicolours
biconcave
biconvex
bicuspid
bicuspids
bicycle
bicycled
bicycles
bicyclic
bicycling
bicyclist
bid
bidarka
bidarkas
biddable
bidden
bidder
bidders
biddies
bidding
biddy
bide
bided
bides
bidet
bidets
bidi
biding
bidis
bidri
bids
biennale

biennales
biennia
biennial
biennials
biennium
bienniums
bier
biers
biface
bifaces
bifacial
biff
biffed
biffing
biffs
bifid
bifilar
bifocal
bifocals
bifold
bifurcate
big
bigamist
bigamists
bigamous
bigamy
bigeneric
bigeye
bigeyes
bigged
bigger
biggest
biggie
biggies
bigging
biggish
bigha
bighas
bighorn
bighorns
bight
bights
bigness
bigot
bigoted
bigotedly
bigotry
bigots
bigs
biguanide

bigwig
bigwigs
bijection
bijective
bijou
bijoux
bike
biked
biker
bikers
bikes
bikeway
bikeways
bikie
bikies
biking
bikini
bikinis
bikkies
bikky
bilabial
bilabials
bilateral
bilayer
bilayers
bilberry
bilbies
bilbo
bilboes
bilbos
bilby
bile
bilge
bilged
bilges
bilging
bilharzia
biliary
bilinear
bilingual
bilious
biliously
bilirubin
bilk
bilked
bilker
bilkers
bilking
bilks
bill

billable	binder	biochips	biotins	biriani
billabong	binderies	biocidal	biotite	birianis
billboard	binders	biocide	biotope	biris
billed	bindery	biocides	biotopes	biriyani
billet	bindi	bioclast	biotype	biriyanis
billeted	binding	bioclasts	biotypes	birl
billeting	bindings	biodata	bipartite	birled
billets	bindis	bioethics	biped	birling
billfish	binds	biofuel	bipedal	birlinn
billfold	bindweed	biofuels	bipeds	birlinns
billfolds	bine	biog	biphasic	birls
billhook	bines	biogas	biphenyl	biro
billhooks	bing	biogases	biphenyls	biros
billiard	binge	biogenic	bipinnate	birr
billiards	binged	biography	biplane	birrs
billies	bingee	biogs	biplanes	birth
billing	bingees	biohazard	bipod	birthday
billings	bingeing	biolistic	bipods	birthdays
billion	binger	biologism	bipolar	birthed
billions	bingers	biologist	biracial	birthing
billionth	binges	biology	biramous	birthmark
billon	binghi	biomass	birch	births
billow	binghis	biome	birchbark	birthwort
billowed	bingies	biomes	birched	biryani
billowing	binging	biometric	birchen	biryanis
billows	bingle	biometry	birches	bis
billowy	bingles	biomorph	birching	biscotti
bills	bingo	biomorphs	bird	biscuit
billy	bingos	bionic	birdbrain	biscuits
billycan	bings	bionics	birdcage	biscuity
billycans	bingy	bionomic	birdcages	bisect
billycart	binman	bionomics	birder	bisected
billycock	binmen	biophilia	birders	bisecting
bilobate	binnacle	biopic	birdie	bisection
bilobed	binnacles	biopics	birdied	bisector
biltong	binned	biopsies	birdies	bisectors
bim	binning	biopsy	birding	bisects
bimanual	binocs	bioregion	birdlime	biserial
bimbette	binocular	biorhythm	birds	bisexual
bimbettes	binomial	bios	birdseed	bisexuals
bimbo	binomials	bioscope	birdshot	bish
bimbos	binominal	bioscopes	birdsong	bished
bimodal	bins	biosensor	birdwing	bishes
bimonthly	bint	biosocial	birdwings	bishing
bims	bints	biosolids	birdying	bishop
bin	binturong	biosphere	bireme	bishopric
binaries	bio	biota	biremes	bishops
binary	bioactive	biotech	biretta	bismillah
binaural	bioassay	biotic	birettas	bismuth
bind	biochip	biotin	biri	bison

bisons	bitting	blacken	blamed	blat
bisque	bitts	blackened	blameful	blatancy
bisques	bitty	blackens	blameless	blatant
bistable	bitumen	blacker	blames	blatantly
bistables	bitwise	blackest	blaming	blather
bister	bitzer	blackface	blanch	blathered
bistort	bitzers	blackfish	blanched	blathers
bistorts	bivalence	blackfly	blanches	blats
bistoury	bivalent	blackhead	blanching	blatted
bistre	bivalve	blacking	blanco	blatter
bistro	bivalved	blackish	blancoed	blattered
bistros	bivalves	blackjack	blancoes	blatters
bisulfate	bivariate	blacklead	blancoing	blatting
bit	bivouac	blackleg	bland	blaze
bitch	bivouaced	blacklegs	blander	blazed
bitched	bivouacs	blacklist	blandest	blazer
bitchen	bivvied	blackly	blandish	blazers
bitchery	bivvies	blackmail	blandly	blazes
bitches	bivvy	blackness	blandness	blazing
bitchier	bivvying	blackout	blank	blazingly
bitchiest	biweekly	blackouts	blanked	blazon
bitchily	biyearly	blackpoll	blanker	blazoned
bitching	biz	blacks	blankest	blazoning
bitchy	bizarre	blacktop	blanket	blazonry
bite	bizarrely	blacktops	blanketed	blazons
biter	bizarrer	blackwood	blankets	bleach
biternate	bizarrest	blackwork	blankety	bleached
biters	bizzies	bladder	blanking	bleacher
bites	bizzy	bladders	blankly	bleachers
biting		blade	blankness	bleaches
bitingly		bladed	blanks	bleaching
bitmap	B L	blades	blare	bleak
bitmapped	blab	blaeberry	blared	bleaker
bitmaps	blabbed	blag	blares	bleakest
bitonal	blabber	blagged	blaring	bleakly
bits	blabbered	blagger	blarney	bleakness
bitstream	blabbers	blaggers	blarneyed	bleaks
bitted	blabbing	blagging	blarneys	blear
bitten	blabs	blags	blasé	bleared
bitter	black	blague	blaspheme	blearier
bitterer	blackball	blagues	blasphemy	bleariest
bitterest	blackbird	blagueur	blast	blearily
bitterly	blackboy	blagueurs	blasted	blearing
bittern	blackboys	blah	blaster	blears
bitterns	blackbuck	blahs	blasters	bleary
bitters	blackbutt	blain	blasting	bleat
bittier	blackcap	blains	blasts	bleated
bittiest	blackcaps	blamable	blastula	bleater
bittily	blackcock	blame	blastulae	bleaters
bittiness	blacked	blameable	blastulas	bleating

bleats	blighter	blithest	blondish	blotchy
bleb	blighters	blitz	blondness	blots
blebs	blighting	blitzed	blood	blotted
bled	blights	blitzes	bloodbath	blotter
bleed	blimey	blitzing	blooded	blotters
bleeder	blimp	blizzard	bloodfin	blotting
bleeders	blimpish	blizzards	bloodfins	blotto
bleeding	blimps	bloat	bloodied	blouse
bleeds	blin	bloated	bloodier	bloused
bleep	blind	bloater	bloodies	blouses
bleeped	blinded	bloaters	bloodiest	blousing
bleeper	blinder	bloating	bloodily	blouson
bleepers	blinders	bloats	blooding	blousons
bleeping	blindest	bloatware	bloodless	blow
bleeps	blindfold	blob	bloodline	blowback
blemish	blinding	blobbed	bloodlust	blowbacks
blemished	blindly	blobbier	bloodroot	blowdown
blemishes	blindness	blobbiest	bloods	blowdowns
blench	blinds	blobbing	bloodshed	blowed
blenched	blindside	blobby	bloodshot	blower
blenches	blindworm	blobs	bloodwood	blowers
blenching	blini	bloc	bloodworm	blowfish
blend	blinis	block	bloody	blowflies
blende	blink	blockade	bloodying	blowfly
blended	blinked	blockaded	blooey	blowgun
blender	blinker	blockader	blooie	blowguns
blenders	blinkered	blockades	bloom	blowhard
blending	blinkers	blockage	bloomed	blowhards
blends	blinking	blockages	bloomer	blowhole
blennies	blinks	blocked	bloomers	blowholes
blenny	blintze	blocker	bloomery	blowie
blent	blintzes	blockers	blooming	blowier
bleomycin	bliny	blockhead	blooms	blowies
blesbok	blip	blockhole	bloop	blowiest
blesboks	blipped	blocking	blooped	blowing
bless	blipping	blockish	blooper	blowlamp
blessed	blips	blocks	bloopers	blowlamps
blessedly	bliss	blockship	blooping	blown
blesses	blissed	blocky	bloops	blowout
blessing	blisses	blocs	bloopy	blowouts
blessings	blissful	bloke	blossom	blowpipe
blest	blissing	blokeish	blossomed	blowpipes
blether	blister	blokes	blossoms	blows
blethered	blistered	blokey	blossomy	blowsier
blethers	blisters	blokish	blot	blowsiest
blew	blithe	blond	blotch	blowsily
blewit	blithely	blonde	blotched	blowsy
blewits	blither	blonder	blotches	blowtorch
blight	blithered	blondes	blotchier	blowy
blighted	blithers	blondest	blotching	blowzier

blowziest
blowzy
blub
blubbed
blubber
blubbered
blubberer
blubbers
blubbery
blubbing
blubs
bluchers
bludge
bludged
bludgeon
bludgeons
bludger
bludgers
bludges
bludging
blue
blueback
bluebacks
bluebell
bluebells
blueberry
bluebill
bluebills
bluebird
bluebirds
blued
bluefin
bluefins
bluefish
bluegill
bluegills
bluegrass
bluegum
bluegums
bluehead
blueheads
blueing
blueish
blueness
bluenose
bluenosed
bluenoses
blueprint
bluer
blues

bluest
bluestone
bluesy
bluet
bluets
bluey
blueys
bluff
bluffed
bluffer
bluffers
bluffing
bluffly
bluffness
bluffs
bluing
bluish
blunder
blundered
blunderer
blunders
blunge
blunged
blunger
blungers
blunges
blunging
blunt
blunted
blunter
bluntest
blunting
bluntly
bluntness
blunts
blur
blurb
blurbed
blurbing
blurbs
blurred
blurrier
blurriest
blurring
blurry
blurs
blurt
blurted
blurting
blurts

blush
blushed
blusher
blushers
blushes
blushing
bluster
blustered
blusterer
blusters
blustery

B O

bo
boa
boab
boabs
boak
boaked
boaking
boaks
boar
board
boarded
boarder
boarders
boarding
boardroom
boards
boardwalk
boarfish
boars
boart
boarts
boas
boast
boasted
boaster
boasters
boastful
boasting
boasts
boat
boatbill
boatbills
boated
boatel
boatels
boater

boaters
boatful
boatfuls
boathook
boathooks
boathouse
boatie
boaties
boating
boatload
boatloads
boatman
boatmen
boats
boatswain
boatyard
boatyards
bob
bobbed
bobber
bobbers
bobbies
bobbin
bobbinet
bobbinets
bobbing
bobbins
bobble
bobbled
bobbles
bobbling
bobbly
bobby
bobcat
bobcats
bobol
bobolink
bobolinks
bobolled
bobolling
bobols
bobotie
bobs
bobskate
bobskates
bobsled
bobsleds
bobsleigh
bobstay
bobstays

bobtail
bobtails
bobweight
bobwhite
bobwhites
bocage
bocce
boccia
bock
bocks
bod
bodach
bodachs
bodacious
bode
boded
bodega
bodegas
bodes
bodge
bodged
bodger
bodgers
bodges
bodgie
bodgies
bodging
bodhrán
bodhráns
bodice
bodices
bodied
bodies
bodiless
bodily
boding
bodkin
bodkins
bods
body
bodyboard
bodyguard
bodying
bodyline
bodyshell
bodyside
bodysides
bodysuit
bodysuits
bodysurf

bodysurfs	bogusly	bolero	bolting	boned
bodywork	bogusness	boleros	bolts	bonefish
boerbull	bogy	boles	bolus	bonehead
boerbulls	bogyman	bolete	boluses	boneheads
boerewors	bogymen	boletes	boma	boneless
boerie	bohea	boletus	bomas	bonemeal
boeuf	boheas	boletuses	bomb	boner
boff	bohemian	bolide	bombard	boners
boffed	bohemians	bolides	bombarde	bones
boffin	boho	bolivar	bombarded	boneset
boffing	bohos	bolivars	bombardes	bonesets
boffins	bohrium	boliviano	bombardon	boney
boffiny	bohunk	boll	bombards	boneyard
boffo	bohunks	bollard	bombast	boneyards
boffola	boil	bollards	bombastic	boneys
boffolas	boiled	bollix	bombazine	bonfire
boffos	boiler	bollixed	bombe	bonfires
boffs	boilers	bollixes	bombé	bong
bog	boilie	bollixing	bombed	bonged
bogan	boilies	bollock	bomber	bonging
bogans	boiling	bollocked	bombers	bongo
bogbean	boilover	bollocks	bombes	bongoes
bogbeans	boilovers	bollocky	bombinate	bongos
bogey	boils	bolls	bombing	bongs
bogeyed	boing	bollux	bomblet	bonhomie
bogeying	boinged	bolluxed	bomblets	bonhomous
bogeyman	boinging	bolluxes	bombora	boniato
bogeymen	boings	bolluxing	bomboras	boniatos
bogeys	boîte	bollworm	bombproof	bonier
boggart	boîtes	bollworms	bombs	bonies
boggarts	boke	bolo	bombshell	boniest
bogged	boked	bologna	bombsight	boniness
boggier	bokes	bolognas	bonanza	boning
boggiest	boking	bolometer	bonanzas	bonito
bogginess	bokken	boloney	bonbon	bonitos
bogging	bokkens	boloneys	bonbons	bonk
boggle	bolas	bolos	bonce	bonked
boggled	bolases	bolshie	bonces	bonkers
boggles	bold	bolshier	bond	bonking
boggling	bolder	bolshies	bondage	bonks
boggy	boldest	bolshiest	bondager	bonne
bogie	boldface	bolshy	bondagers	bonnes
bogies	boldfaced	bolster	bonded	bonnet
bogland	boldfaces	bolstered	bondi	bonneted
bogle	boldly	bolsterer	bonding	bonnets
bogles	boldness	bolsters	bonds	bonnie
bogong	boldo	bolt	bondsman	bonnier
bogongs	boldos	bolted	bondsmen	bonniest
bogs	bole	bolter	bondstone	bonnily
bogus	bolection	bolters	bone	bonniness

bonny	boojum	boon	boozy	borne
bonobo	boojums	boondocks	bop	bornite
bonobos	book	boong	bopped	boron
bonsai	bookable	boongs	bopper	boronia
bonsela	bookcase	boonies	boppers	boronias
bonselas	bookcases	boons	bopping	borough
bonsella	booked	boor	bops	boroughs
bonsellas	bookend	boorish	bora	borrow
bonspiel	bookended	boorishly	boracic	borrowed
bonspiels	bookends	boors	borage	borrower
bontebok	booker	boos	borages	borrowers
bonteboks	bookers	boost	borak	borrowing
bonus	bookie	boosted	borane	borrows
bonuses	bookies	booster	boranes	borsch
bonxie	booking	boosters	boras	borscht
bonxies	bookings	boosting	borate	borstal
bony	bookish	boosts	borates	borstals
bonze	bookishly	boot	borax	bort
bonzer	bookland	bootable	bordello	borzoi
bonzes	booklet	bootblack	bordellos	borzois
boo	booklets	bootboy	border	bos
booai	booklice	bootboys	bordered	boscage
booay	booklouse	booted	borderer	bosey
boob	bookmaker	bootee	borderers	boseys
boobed	bookman	bootees	bordering	bosh
boobies	bookmark	booth	borders	bosie
boobing	bookmarks	booths	bordure	bosies
booboisie	bookmen	bootie	bordures	boskage
boobook	bookplate	booties	bore	bosky
boobooks	bookrest	booting	boreal	bosom
boobs	bookrests	bootjack	bored	bosomed
booby	books	bootjacks	boredom	bosoms
boodie	bookshelf	bootlace	boreen	bosomy
boodies	bookstall	bootlaces	boreens	boson
boodle	booksy	bootleg	borehole	bosons
booed	bookwork	bootlegs	boreholes	boss
boofhead	bookworm	bootless	borer	bossed
boofheads	bookworms	boots	borers	bosses
boogaloo	boom	bootstrap	bores	bossier
boogaloos	boomed	booty	borescope	bossies
boogie	boomer	booze	boric	bossiest
boogied	boomerang	boozed	boride	bossily
boogieing	boomers	boozer	borides	bossiness
boogies	boominess	boozers	boring	bossing
boohai	booming	boozes	boringly	bossism
boohoo	boomlet	boozier	bork	bossy
boohooed	boomlets	booziest	borked	bosun
boohooing	booms	boozily	borking	bosuns
boohoos	boomslang	booziness	borks	bot
booing	boomy	boozing	born	botanic

botanical	boubous	bountiful	bowhead	boxier
botanise	bouchée	bounty	bowheads	boxiest
botanised	bouchées	bouquet	bowhunter	boxing
botanises	bouclé	bouquets	bowie	boxout
botanist	boudin	bourbon	bowies	boxouts
botanists	boudins	bourbons	bowing	boxroom
botanize	boudoir	bourdon	bowknot	boxrooms
botanized	boudoirs	bourdons	bowknots	boxthorn
botanizes	bouffant	bourgeois	bowl	boxthorns
botany	bouffants	bourn	bowled	boxty
botch	bough	bourne	bowler	boxy
botched	boughs	bournes	bowlers	boy
botcher	bought	bourns	bowlful	boyar
botchers	boughten	bourrée	bowlfuls	boyars
botches	bougie	bourréed	bowline	boycott
botching	bougies	bourrées	bowlines	boycotted
botel	bouilli	bourréing	bowling	boycotts
botels	bouillon	bourse	bowls	boyfriend
botflies	boulder	bourses	bowman	boyhood
botfly	boulders	bout	bowmen	boyhoods
both	bouldery	boutade	bows	boyish
bother	boule	boutades	bowsaw	boyishly
bothered	boules	boutique	bowsaws	boyla
bothering	boulevard	boutiques	bowser	boylas
bothers	boulle	bouton	bowsers	boyo
bothie	boult	boutons	bowshot	boyos
bothies	boulted	bouts	bowshots	boys
bothy	boulting	boutu	bowsie	bozo
boto	boults	boutus	bowsies	bozos
botos	bounce	bouvier	bowsprit	
botrytis	bounced	bouviers	bowsprits	
bots	bouncer	bouzouki	bowstring	B R
botte	bouncers	bouzoukis	bowstrung	
bottes	bounces	bovid	bowyang	bra
botties	bouncier	bovids	bowyangs	braai
bottle	bounciest	bovine	bowyer	braaied
bottled	bouncily	bovinely	bowyers	braaiing
bottler	bouncing	bovines	box	braaing
bottlers	bouncy	bovver	boxboard	braais
bottles	bound	bow	boxcar	braata
bottling	boundary	bowed	boxcars	braatas
bottom	bounded	bowel	boxed	brace
bottomed	bounden	bowels	boxer	braced
bottoming	bounder	bower	boxercise	bracelet
bottomry	bounders	bowerbird	boxers	bracelets
bottoms	bounding	bowered	boxes	bracer
botty	boundless	bowering	boxfish	bracers
botulin	bounds	bowers	boxfishes	braces
botulism	bounteous	bowfin	boxful	brachial
boubou	bounties	bowfins	boxfuls	brachiate
				bracing

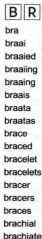

bracingly
brack
bracken
bracket
bracketed
brackets
brackish
bracks
braconid
braconids
bract
bracteate
bracts
brad
bradawl
bradawls
bradoon
bradoons
brads
brae
braes
brag
braggart
braggarts
bragged
bragger
braggers
bragging
brags
brahma
brahmas
braid
braided
braiding
braids
brail
brailed
brailing
brails
brain
brainbox
brained
brainiac
brainiacs
brainier
brainiest
brainily
braining
brainless
brainpan

brainpans
brains
brainstem
brainwash
brainwave
brainy
braise
braised
braises
braising
brak
brake
braked
brakeman
brakemen
brakes
brakesman
brakesmen
braking
braless
bramble
brambled
brambles
brambling
brambly
bran
branch
branched
branches
branchia
branchiae
branchial
branching
branchlet
branchy
brand
brandade
brandades
branded
brander
branders
brandies
branding
brandish
brandling
brands
brandy
branigan
branigans
branks

branle
branles
brannigan
brant
brants
bras
brash
brasher
brashest
brashly
brashness
brass
brassard
brassards
brasserie
brasses
brassica
brassicas
brassie
brassier
brassiere
brassies
brassiest
brassily
brassware
brassy
brat
brats
brattice
bratticed
brattices
brattish
brattle
brattled
brattles
brattling
bratty
bratwurst
bravado
brave
braved
bravely
braveness
braver
bravery
braves
bravest
braving
bravo
bravoes

bravos
bravura
braw
brawl
brawled
brawler
brawlers
brawling
brawls
brawly
brawn
brawnier
brawniest
brawny
braxy
bray
brayed
braying
brays
braze
brazed
brazen
brazened
brazening
brazenly
brazens
brazes
brazier
braziers
braziery
brazil
brazils
brazing
breach
breached
breaches
breaching
bread
breaded
breadline
breads
breadth
breadths
break
breakable
breakage
breakages
breakaway
breakdown
breaker

breakers
breakfast
breaking
breakneck
breakout
breakouts
breaks
breakwind
bream
breamed
breaming
breams
breast
breasted
breastfed
breasting
breastpin
breasts
breath
breathe
breathed
breather
breathers
breathes
breathier
breathily
breathing
breaths
breathy
breccia
brecciate
bred
bredie
bredies
breech
breeched
breeches
breeching
breed
breeder
breeders
breeding
breeds
breeks
breeze
breezed
breezes
breezeway
breezier
breeziest

breezily	brickyard	brightly	brisking	brochette
breezing	bricolage	brights	briskly	brochs
breezy	bricoleur	brigs	briskness	brochure
brei	bridal	brill	brisks	brochures
breid	bride	brilliant	brisling	brock
breiing	brides	brim	brislings	brocket
breis	bridewell	brimful	bristle	brockets
brekkie	bridge	brimless	bristled	brocks
brekky	bridged	brimmed	bristles	brogan
brethren	bridges	brimming	bristling	brogans
breve	bridging	brims	bristly	brogue
breves	bridie	brimstone	bristols	brogues
brevet	bridies	brindle	brittle	broil
breveted	bridle	brindled	brittlely	broiled
breveting	bridled	brindles	brittler	broiler
brevets	bridles	brine	brittlest	broilers
brevetted	bridleway	brined	brittly	broiling
breviary	bridling	brines	britzka	broils
brevity	bridoon	bring	britzkas	broke
brew	bridoons	bringer	britzska	broken
brewed	brief	bringers	britzskas	brokenly
brewer	briefcase	bringing	bro	broker
breweries	briefed	brings	broach	brokerage
brewers	briefer	brinier	broached	brokered
brewery	briefest	briniest	broaches	brokering
brewhouse	briefing	brining	broaching	brokers
brewing	briefings	brinjal	broad	broking
brewpub	briefless	brinjals	broadacre	brolga
brewpubs	briefly	brink	broadband	brolgas
brews	briefness	brinks	broadbill	brollies
briar	briefs	brinnies	broadcast	brolly
briars	brier	brinny	broaden	bromate
briary	briers	briny	broadened	bromates
bribable	brig	brio	broadens	brome
bribe	brigade	brioche	broader	bromeliad
bribed	brigaded	brioches	broadest	bromes
briber	brigades	briquet	broadleaf	bromide
bribers	brigadier	briquets	broadloom	bromides
bribery	brigading	briquette	broadly	bromidic
bribes	brigalow	brisé	broadness	bromine
bribing	brigalows	brisés	broads	bromism
brick	brigand	brisk	broadside	bronc
brickbat	brigandry	brisked	broadtail	bronchi
brickbats	brigands	brisken	broadway	bronchial
bricked	bright	briskened	brocade	bronchus
brickie	brighten	briskens	brocaded	bronco
brickies	brightens	brisker	brocades	broncos
bricking	brighter	briskest	brocading	broncs
bricks	brightest	brisket	broccoli	bronze
brickwork	brightish	briskets	broch	bronzed

bronzes
bronzing
bronzy
broo
brooch
brooches
brood
brooded
brooder
brooders
broodier
broodiest
broodily
brooding
broods
broody
brook
brooked
brooking
brooklet
brooklets
brooklime
brooks
brookweed
broom
broomie
broomies
broomrape
brooms
bros
brose
broses
broth
brothel
brothels
brother
brotherly
brothers
broths
brougham
broughams
brought
brouhaha
brow
browbeat
browbeats
browed
brown
browned
browner

brownest
brownie
brownies
browning
brownish
brownness
browns
browntop
browny
brows
browsable
browse
browsed
browser
browsers
browses
browsing
brrr
brubru
brubrus
brucite
bruin
bruins
bruise
bruised
bruiser
bruisers
bruises
bruising
bruit
bruited
bruiting
bruits
brumbies
brumby
brume
brummy
brumous
brunch
brunches
brunet
brunets
brunette
brunettes
brung
brunt
brush
brushback
brushed
brushes

brushing
brushless
brushtail
brushwood
brushwork
brushy
brusque
brusquely
brut
brutal
brutalise
brutalism
brutalist
brutality
brutalize
brutally
brute
brutes
brutish
brutishly
bruxism
bryology
bryonies
bryony
bryophyte
bryozoan
bryozoans

B U

bub
bubal
bubals
bubba
bubbas
bubble
bubbled
bubblegum
bubbler
bubblers
bubbles
bubblier
bubbliest
bubbling
bubbly
bubinga
bubo
buboes
bubonic
bubs

bucatini
buccal
buccaneer
buchu
buchus
buck
buckaroo
buckaroos
buckbean
buckbeans
buckboard
buckbrush
bucked
buckeen
buckeens
bucket
bucketed
bucketful
bucketing
buckets
buckeye
buckeyes
buckhorn
buckhorns
bucking
buckjump
buckjumps
buckle
buckled
buckler
bucklers
buckles
buckling
bucklings
bucko
buckoes
buckos
buckra
buckram
buckras
bucks
buckshee
buckshot
buckskin
buckskins
buckthorn
buckwheat
bucolic
bucolics
bud

budded
buddhu
buddhus
buddied
buddies
budding
buddle
buddleia
buddleias
buddles
buddy
buddying
budge
budged
budges
budget
budgetary
budgeted
budgeting
budgets
budgie
budgies
budging
buds
budstick
budsticks
budwood
budworm
budworms
buff
buffalo
buffaloed
buffaloes
buffed
buffer
buffered
buffering
buffers
buffet
buffeted
buffeting
buffets
buffing
buffo
buffoon
buffoons
buffos
buffs
bug
bugaboo

bugaboos	bulgy	bullion	bummers	bungholes
bugbane	bulimia	bullish	bumming	bunging
bugbanes	bulimic	bullishly	bump	bungle
bugbear	bulimics	bullock	bumped	bungled
bugbears	bulk	bullocked	bumper	bungler
bugged	bulked	bullocks	bumpers	bunglers
bugger	bulker	bullocky	bumph	bungles
buggered	bulkers	bullous	bumpier	bungling
buggering	bulkhead	bullpen	bumpiest	bungs
buggers	bulkheads	bullpens	bumpily	bunion
buggery	bulkier	bullring	bumpiness	bunions
buggier	bulkiest	bullrings	bumping	bunk
buggies	bulkily	bullrush	bumpkin	bunked
buggiest	bulkiness	bulls	bumpkins	bunker
bugging	bulking	bullseye	bumps	bunkered
buggy	bulks	bullseyes	bumptious	bunkering
bughouse	bulky	bullshit	bumpy	bunkers
bughouses	bull	bullshits	bums	bunkhouse
bugle	bulla	bullwhip	bun	bunking
bugled	bullace	bullwhips	bunch	bunks
bugler	bullaces	bully	bunched	bunkum
buglers	bullae	bullying	bunches	bunnies
bugles	bullate	bullyrag	bunching	bunny
bugleweed	bulldike	bullyrags	bunchy	buns
bugling	bulldikes	bulrush	bunco	bunt
bugloss	bulldog	bulrushes	buncoed	buntal
buglosses	bulldogs	bulwark	buncoes	bunted
bugs	bulldoze	bulwarks	buncoing	bunting
buhl	bulldozed	bum	buncombe	buntings
build	bulldozer	bumbag	buncos	buntline
builder	bulldozes	bumbags	bund	buntlines
builders	bulldyke	bumble	bundle	bunts
building	bulldyker	bumblebee	bundled	bunya
buildings	bulldykes	bumbled	bundler	bunyas
builds	bulled	bumbler	bundlers	bunyip
built	bullet	bumblers	bundles	bunyips
bulb	bulletin	bumbles	bundling	buoy
bulbil	bulletins	bumbling	bunds	buoyage
bulbils	bullets	bumboat	bundu	buoyancy
bulbous	bullfight	bumboats	bunfight	buoyant
bulbs	bullfinch	bumboy	bunfights	buoyantly
bulbul	bullfrog	bumboys	bung	buoyed
bulbuls	bullfrogs	bumf	bungalow	buoying
bulgar	bullhead	bumfluff	bungalows	buoys
bulge	bullheads	bumiputra	bunged	buppie
bulged	bullhorn	bummalo	bungee	buppies
bulges	bullhorns	bummaree	bungeed	bur
bulging	bullied	bummarees	bungeeing	burb
bulgingly	bullies	bummed	bungees	burble
bulgur	bulling	bummer	bunghole	burbled

burbler	burgraves	burpee	busbars	busks
burblers	burgs	burpees	busbies	busman
burbles	burgundy	burping	busboy	busmen
burbling	burial	burps	busboys	buss
burbot	burials	burr	busby	bussed
burbots	buried	burra	bused	busses
burbs	buries	burrawang	buses	bussing
burden	burin	burrawong	bush	bust
burdened	burins	burred	bushbaby	bustard
burdening	burk	burrfish	bushbuck	bustards
burdens	burka	burring	bushbucks	busted
burdock	burkas	burrito	bushchat	bustee
bureau	burke	burritos	bushchats	bustees
bureaus	burkes	burro	bushcraft	buster
bureaux	burkha	burros	bushed	busters
buret	burkhas	burrow	bushel	bustier
burets	burks	burrowed	bushelful	bustiers
burette	burl	burrower	bushels	bustiest
burettes	burlap	burrowers	bushes	bustiness
burfi	burlesque	burrowing	bushido	busting
burg	burley	burrows	bushier	bustle
burgage	burlier	burrs	bushies	bustled
burgages	burliest	burs	bushiest	bustles
burgee	burliness	bursa	bushily	bustling
burgees	burls	bursae	bushiness	busts
burgeon	burly	bursal	bushing	busty
burgeoned	burn	bursar	bushman	busway
burgeons	burned	bursarial	bushmen	busways
burger	burner	bursaries	bushtit	busy
burgers	burners	bursars	bushtits	busybody
burgess	burnet	bursary	bushveld	busying
burgesses	burnets	bursas	bushwa	busyness
burgh	burning	burse	bushwah	busywork
burghal	burningly	burses	bushwhack	but
burgher	burnish	bursitis	bushy	butadiene
burghers	burnished	burst	busied	butane
burghs	burnisher	burster	busier	butanoate
burghul	burnishes	bursters	busies	butanoic
burglar	burnoose	bursting	busiest	butanol
burglars	burnooses	bursts	busily	butch
burglary	burnous	bursty	business	butcher
burgle	burnouses	burthen	busing	butchered
burgled	burnout	burthens	busk	butchers
burgles	burns	burton	busked	butchery
burgling	burnside	burtons	busker	butches
burgonet	burnsides	bury	buskers	bute
burgonets	burnt	burying	buskin	buteo
burgoo	buroo	bus	buskined	buteos
burgrave	burp	busbar	busking	butler
	burped		buskins	butlers

buts
butt
butte
butted
butter
butterbur
buttercup
buttered
butterfat
butterfly
butteries
buttering
butternut
butters
buttery
buttes
buttie
butties
butting
buttle
buttled

buttles
buttling
buttock
buttocks
button
buttoned
buttoning
buttons
buttony
buttress
butts
butty
butut
bututs
butyl
butyrate
butyrates
butyric
buxom
buxomness
buy

buyer
buyers
buying
buyout
buyouts
buys
buzz
buzzard
buzzards
buzzed
buzzer
buzzers
buzzes
buzzing
buzzword
buzzwords

B W

bwana
bwanas

B Y

by
bye
byeline
byelines
byes
bygone
bygones
byline
bylines
byname
bynames
bypass
bypassed
bypasses
bypassing
bypath
bypaths
byplay

byre
byres
byroad
byroads
byssal
byssi
byssus
byssuses
bystander
byte
bytes
bytownite
byway
byways
byword
bywords

C

C A

caatinga
cab
cabal
cabaletta
cabalette
caballero
cabals
cabana
cabanas
cabaret
cabarets
cabbage
cabbages
cabbagy
cabbalism

cabbalist
cabbed
cabbie
cabbies
cabbing
cabby
caber
cabers
cabezon
cabezons
cabildo
cabildos
cabin
cabined
cabinet
cabinetry
cabinets

cabining
cabins
cable
cabled
cablegram
cables
cableway
cableways
cabling
cabman
cabmen
caboched
cabochon
cabochons
caboclo
caboclos
caboodle

caboose
cabooses
caboshed
cabossed
cabotage
cabover
cabovers
cabrio
cabriole
cabrioles
cabriolet
cabrios
cabs
cacao
cacaos
cachalot
cachalots

cache
cachectic
cached
cachepot
cachepots
caches
cachet
cachets
cachexia
caching
cachou
cachous
cachucha
cachuchas
cacique
caciques
cack

cacked	cadis	caique	calcanea	caliche
cacking	cadmium	caiques	calcanei	calico
cackle	cadre	cairn	calcaneum	calicoes
cackled	cadres	cairngorm	calcaneus	calicos
cackles	cads	cairns	calces	caliper
cackling	caducei	caisson	calcic	calipers
cacodemon	caduceus	caissons	calcicole	caliph
cacodyl	caducity	caitiff	calcific	caliphate
cacodylic	caducous	caitiffs	calcified	caliphs
cacoethes	caeca	cajeput	calcifies	calix
cacology	caecal	cajeputs	calcifuge	calixes
cacophony	caecilian	cajole	calcify	calk
cacti	caecitis	cajoled	calcimine	calked
cactus	caecum	cajolery	calcine	calking
cactuses	caesium	cajoles	calcined	calks
cacuminal	caesura	cajoling	calcines	call
cad	caesural	cajuput	calcining	calla
cadastral	caesuras	cajuputs	calcite	callaloo
cadaver	cafard	cake	calcitic	callaloos
cadaveric	cafe	caked	calcium	callalou
cadavers	cafes	cakehole	calcrete	callalous
caddie	cafeteria	cakeholes	calcretes	callas
caddied	cafetière	cakes	calculate	callback
caddies	caff	cakewalk	calculi	callbacks
caddis	caffeine	cakewalks	calculus	called
caddises	caffs	caking	caldaria	caller
caddish	caftan	calabash	caldarium	callers
caddishly	caftans	calabaza	caldera	calling
caddy	cage	calabazas	calderas	callings
caddying	caged	calaboose	caldron	calliope
cadelle	cages	calabrese	caldrons	calliopes
cadelles	cagey	caladium	caleche	calliper
cadence	cageyness	caladiums	caleches	callipers
cadenced	cagier	calamanco	calendar	callop
cadences	cagiest	calamares	calendars	callops
cadencies	cagily	calamari	calender	callosity
cadency	caginess	calami	calenders	callous
cadential	caging	calamine	calendric	calloused
cadenza	cagoule	calamint	calends	callouses
cadenzas	cagoules	calamints	calendula	callously
cadet	cagy	calamites	calenture	callow
cadets	cahier	calamity	calf	callower
cadetship	cahiers	calamus	calfskin	callowest
cadge	cahoots	calando	calfskins	callowly
cadged	cahoun	calandra	caliber	calls
cadger	cahouns	calandras	calibers	calluna
cadgers	cahow	calash	calibrate	callus
cadges	cahows	calashes	calibre	callused
cadging	caiman	calathea	calibred	calluses
cadi	caimans	calatheas	calibres	calm

calmative	cambered	campo	candidly	cannibals
calmed	cambers	camporee	candied	cannier
calmer	cambia	camporees	candies	canniest
calmest	cambial	campos	candiru	cannily
calming	cambium	camps	candirus	canniness
calmly	cambozola	campsite	candle	canning
calmness	cambric	campsites	candled	cannon
calms	camcorder	campus	candlelit	cannonade
calomel	came	campuses	candlenut	cannoned
calomels	camel	campy	candler	cannoneer
caloric	camelback	cams	candlers	cannoning
calorie	cameleer	camshaft	candles	cannons
calories	cameleers	camshafts	candling	cannot
calorific	camelid	camwood	candomblé	cannula
calotype	camelids	can	candor	cannulae
calque	camellia	canaille	candour	cannulas
calqued	camellias	canal	candy	cannulate
calques	camels	canalise	candying	canny
caltrap	cameo	canalised	candyman	canoe
caltraps	cameos	canalises	candymen	canoed
caltrop	camera	canalize	candytuft	canoeing
caltrops	cameraman	canalized	cane	canoeist
calumet	cameramen	canalizes	canebrake	canoeists
calumets	cameras	canals	caned	canoes
calumnied	cames	canapé	caner	canola
calumnies	camisole	canapés	caners	canon
calumny	camisoles	canard	canes	canoness
calutron	camo	canards	canid	canonic
calutrons	camomile	canaries	canids	canonical
calve	camomiles	canary	canine	canonise
calved	camp	canasta	canines	canonised
calves	campaign	cancan	caning	canonises
calving	campaigns	cancans	canings	canonist
calx	campanile	cancel	canister	canonists
calyces	campanula	cancelbot	canisters	canonize
calypso	campcraft	canceled	canker	canonized
calypsos	camped	canceling	cankered	canonizes
calyx	camper	cancelled	cankering	canonries
calyxes	campers	canceller	cankerous	canonry
calzone	campesino	cancels	cankers	canons
calzones	campfire	cancer	canna	canoodle
calzoni	campfires	cancerous	cannabis	canoodled
cam	camphor	cancers	cannas	canoodles
cama	campier	candela	canned	canopied
camarilla	campiest	candelas	cannelure	canopies
camas	campily	candid	canner	canopy
camass	campiness	candida	canneries	canopying
camasses	camping	candidacy	canners	canorous
cambazola	campion	candidas	cannery	cans
camber	campions	candidate	cannibal	canst

cant	canyons	caponiers	capsulise	carangid
cantabile	canzona	caponise	capsulize	carangids
cantal	canzone	caponised	captain	carapace
cantata	canzoni	caponises	captaincy	carapaces
cantatas	cap	caponize	captained	carat
canted	capable	caponized	captains	carats
canteen	capably	caponizes	captan	caravan
canteens	capacious	capons	caption	caravans
canter	capacitor	capos	captioned	caravel
cantered	capacity	capot	captions	caravels
cantering	caparison	capote	captious	caraway
canters	cape	capotes	captivate	caraways
canthari	caped	capots	captive	carb
cantharus	capelin	capotted	captives	carbamate
canthi	capelins	capotting	captivity	carbanion
canthic	caper	capped	captor	carbaryl
canthus	capered	capper	captors	carbazole
canticle	caperer	cappers	capture	carbene
canticles	caperers	capping	captured	carbenes
cantilena	capering	capri	capturer	carbide
cantina	capers	capriccio	capturers	carbides
cantinas	capes	caprice	captures	carbine
canting	capeskin	caprices	capturing	carbines
cantle	capful	caprine	capuchin	carbolic
cantles	capfuls	capriole	capuchins	carbon
canto	capias	caprioles	capybara	carbonado
canton	capiases	capris	capybaras	carbonara
cantonal	capillary	caproate	car	carbonate
cantons	caping	caproates	carabao	carbonic
cantor	capital	caproates	carabaos	carbonise
cantorial	capitally	caproic	carabid	carbonize
cantoris	capitals	caprylate	carabids	carbons
cantors	capitano	caps	carabiner	carbonyl
cantos	capitanos	capsaicin	caracal	carbonyls
cantrail	capitate	capsicum	caracals	carboxyl
cantrails	capitates	capsicums	caracara	carboxyls
cantrip	capitol	capsid	caracaras	carboy
cantrips	capitols	capsids	caracole	carboys
cants	capitula	capsize	caracoled	carbs
cantus	capitular	capsized	caracoles	carbuncle
canvas	capitulum	capsizes	caracul	carburise
canvased	caplet	capsizing	caraculs	carburize
canvases	caplets	capstan	carafe	carcajou
canvasing	caplin	capstans	carafes	carcajous
canvass	caplins	capstone	caragana	carcase
canvassed	capo	capstones	caraganas	carcases
canvasser	capoeira	capsular	caramba	carcass
canvasses	capon	capsulate	carambola	carcasses
canyon	caponata	capsule	caramel	carceral
canyoning	caponier	capsules	caramels	carcinoid

carcinoma	caress	carlins	carouser	carryall
card	caressed	carload	carousers	carryalls
cardamom	caresses	carloads	carouses	carrycot
cardamoms	caressing	carls	carousing	carrycots
cardamum	caret	carman	carp	carrying
cardamums	caretaker	carmen	carpaccio	cars
cardboard	carets	carmine	carpal	carse
carded	careworn	carnage	carpals	carses
carder	carex	carnal	carped	carsick
carders	carfare	carnality	carpel	cart
cardia	carful	carnally	carpels	cartage
cardiac	carfuls	carnation	carpenter	carte
cardias	cargador	carnauba	carpentry	carted
cardie	cargo	carnaubas	carper	cartel
cardies	cargoes	carnelian	carpers	cartelise
cardigan	cargos	carnet	carpet	cartelize
cardigans	carhop	carnets	carpeted	cartels
cardinal	carhops	carney	carpeting	carter
cardinals	cariama	carneys	carpets	carters
carding	cariamas	carnier	carpi	cartful
cardioid	caribou	carniest	carping	cartfuls
cardioids	caribous	carnival	carpology	carthorse
carditis	carices	carnivals	carpool	cartilage
cardoon	caries	carnivore	carpooled	carting
cardoons	carillon	carnosaur	carpooler	cartload
cardphone	carillons	carnotite	carpools	cartloads
cards	carina	carny	carport	cartogram
cardy	carinae	carob	carports	carton
care	carinal	carobs	carps	cartons
cared	carinas	carol	carpus	cartoon
careen	carinate	caroled	carr	cartooned
careened	carinated	caroling	carrack	cartoons
careening	caring	carolled	carracks	cartoony
careens	carioca	caroller	carrageen	cartouche
career	cariocas	carollers	carrel	cartridge
careered	cariole	carolling	carrels	carts
careering	carioles	carols	carriage	cartwheel
careerism	carious	carom	carriages	caruncle
careerist	caritas	caromed	carried	caruncles
careers	carjack	caroming	carrier	carve
carefree	carjacked	caroms	carriers	carved
careful	carjacker	carotene	carries	carvel
carefully	carjacks	carotid	carriole	carvels
caregiver	carking	carotids	carrioles	carven
careless	carl	carousal	carrion	carver
careline	carlin	carousals	carronade	carveries
carelines	carline	carouse	carrot	carvers
carer	carlines	caroused	carrots	carvery
carers	carling	carousel	carroty	carves
cares	carlings	carousels	carry	carving

carvings	casing	castrates	cataphors	catenary
caryatid	casings	castrati	cataplexy	catenas
caryatids	casino	castrato	catapult	catenated
caryopses	casinos	castrator	catapults	catenoid
caryopsis	cask	casts	cataract	cater
casaba	casket	casual	cataracts	cateran
casabas	caskets	casualise	catarrh	caterans
casareep	casks	casualize	catarrhal	catered
casbah	casque	casually	catatonia	caterer
casbahs	casques	casuals	catatonic	caterers
cascabel	cassareep	casualty	catawba	catering
cascabels	cassata	casuarina	catawbas	caters
cascade	cassation	casuist	catbird	caterwaul
cascaded	cassava	casuistic	catbirds	cates
cascades	cassavas	casuistry	catboat	catfish
cascading	casserole	casuists	catboats	catfishes
cascara	cassette	cat	catcall	catgut
cascaras	cassettes	catabolic	catcalled	catharsis
case	cassia	cataclysm	catcalls	cathartic
caseation	cassias	catacomb	catch	cathead
casebook	cassingle	catacombs	catchable	catheads
casebooks	cassis	catalase	catcher	cathectic
cased	cassock	catalases	catchers	cathedral
casein	cassocked	catalepsy	catches	catheter
caseload	cassocks	catalog	catchfly	catheters
caseloads	cassone	cataloged	catchier	cathexis
casemate	cassones	cataloger	catchiest	cathodal
casemates	cassoni	catalogs	catchily	cathode
casement	cassoulet	catalogue	catching	cathodes
casements	cassowary	catalpa	catchline	cathodic
caseous	cast	catalpas	catchment	catholic
cases	castanets	catalufa	catchup	catholics
casevac	castaway	catalufas	catchups	cathouse
casevaced	castaways	catalyse	catchword	cathouses
casevacs	caste	catalysed	catchy	cation
casework	casteism	catalyser	cate	cationic
cash	castellan	catalyses	catechin	cations
cashable	caster	catalysis	catechins	catkin
cashback	casters	catalyst	catechise	catkins
cashed	castes	catalysts	catechism	catlick
cashes	castigate	catalytic	catechist	catlicks
cashew	casting	catalyze	catechize	catlike
cashews	castle	catalyzed	catechol	catlinite
cashier	castled	catalyzes	catechols	catmint
cashiered	castles	catamaran	catechu	catmints
cashiers	castling	catamite	categoric	catnap
cashing	castor	catamites	category	catnapped
cashless	castors	catamount	catena	catnaps
cashmere	castrate	cataphor	catenae	catnip
cashpoint	castrated	cataphora	catenane	catnips

catoptric
cats
catseye
catseyes
catsuit
catsuits
catsup
catsups
cattail
cattails
catted
catteries
cattery
cattie
cattier
catties
cattiest
cattily
cattiness
catting
cattish
cattishly
cattle
cattleya
cattleyas
catty
catwalk
catwalks
caubeen
caubeens
caucus
caucused
caucuses
caucusing
caudal
caudally
caudate
caudex
caudices
caudillo
caudillos
caught
caul
cauldron
cauldrons
caulk
caulked
caulker
caulkers
caulking

caulks
cauls
causal
causalgia
causality
causally
causation
causative
cause
caused
causeless
causer
causerie
causeries
causers
causes
causeway
causeways
causey
causeys
causing
caustic
caustics
cauteries
cauterise
cauterize
cautery
caution
cautioned
cautions
cautious
cava
cavalcade
cavalier
cavaliers
cavalries
cavalry
cavatina
cavatine
cave
caveat
caveats
caved
cavefish
caveman
cavemen
cavendish
caver
cavern
cavernous

caverns
cavers
caves
cavesson
cavessons
cavewoman
cavewomen
caviar
caviare
cavies
cavil
caviled
caviling
cavilled
caviller
cavillers
cavilling
cavils
caving
cavitary
cavities
cavity
cavort
cavorted
cavorting
cavorts
cavy
caw
cawed
cawing
caws
cay
cayenne
cayman
caymans
cays
cayuse
cayuses

C E

ceanothus
cease
ceased
ceasefire
ceaseless
ceases
ceasing
cebid
cebids

ceca
cecitis
cecropia
cecropias
cecum
cedar
cedarn
cedars
cede
ceded
cedes
cedi
cedilla
cedillas
ceding
cedis
ceiba
ceibas
ceil
ceiled
ceilidh
ceilidhs
ceiling
ceilings
ceils
cel
celadon
celandine
celeb
celebrant
celebrate
celebrity
celebs
celeriac
celerity
celery
celesta
celestas
celeste
celestes
celestial
celiac
celiacs
celibacy
celibate
celibates
cell
cella
cellae
cellar

cellarage
cellared
cellarer
cellarers
cellaret
cellarets
cellaring
cellarman
cellarmen
cellars
celled
cellist
cellists
cello
cellos
cellphone
cells
cellular
cellulase
cellulite
celluloid
cellulose
celosia
celosias
celt
celts
cembalist
cembalo
cembalos
cement
cemented
cementer
cementers
cementing
cementite
cements
cementum
cemetery
cenacle
cenacles
cenobite
cenobites
cenotaph
cenotaphs
cense
censed
censer
censers
censes
censing

censor
censored
censorial
censoring
censors
censure
censured
censures
censuring
census
censuses
cent
centas
centaur
centaurea
centaurs
centaury
centavo
centavos
centenary
center
centered
centering
centers
centesimo
centigram
centile
centiles
centime
centimes
centimo
centimos
centipede
cento
centos
centra
central
centrally
centre
centred
centrepin
centres
centrex
centric
centrical
centring
centriole
centrism
centrist
centrists

centroid
centroids
centrum
centrums
cents
centuple
centupled
centuples
centurial
centuries
centurion
century
cep
cephalic
cephalin
cephalon
cephalons
cepheid
cepheids
ceps
ceramic
ceramics
cerastes
cerastium
ceratite
ceratites
cercaria
cercariae
cerci
cerclage
cercus
cere
cereal
cereals
cerebella
cerebra
cerebral
cerebrate
cerebrum
cerecloth
cerement
cerements
ceremony
cereology
ceres
ceresin
cerise
cerium
cermet
cermets

cero
ceros
cert
certain
certainly
certainty
certes
certified
certifies
certify
certitude
certs
cerulean
cerumen
ceruse
cervelat
cervical
cervices
cervid
cervids
cervix
cesium
cess
cessation
cesser
cesses
cession
cessions
cesspit
cesspits
cesspool
cesspools
cestode
cestodes
cetacean
cetaceans
cetane
cetrimide
ceviche

C|H

cha
chaat
chabazite
chacham
chachams
chack
chacked
chacking

chacks
chaconne
chaconnes
chad
chadar
chadars
chador
chadors
chaebol
chaebols
chaeta
chaetae
chafe
chafed
chafer
chafers
chafes
chaff
chaffed
chaffer
chaffered
chafferer
chaffers
chaffinch
chaffing
chaffs
chaffweed
chaffy
chafing
chagrin
chagrined
chai
chain
chaîné
chained
chaînés
chaining
chainring
chains
chainsaw
chainsaws
chair
chaired
chairing
chairlady
chairlift
chairman
chairmen
chairs
chaise

chaises
chakra
chakras
chal
chalaza
chalazae
chalazal
chalcid
chalcids
chalet
chalets
chalice
chalices
chalk
chalkdown
chalked
chalkface
chalkie
chalkier
chalkies
chalkiest
chalking
chalks
chalky
challah
challahs
challenge
challis
chalone
chalones
chals
chalumeau
chamber
chambered
chambers
chambray
chambrays
chambré
chamcha
chamchas
chameleon
chameli
chamelis
chametz
chamfer
chamfers
chamise
chamises
chamois
chamomile

champ	chanters	characins	charnel	chastity
champagne	chanteuse	character	charnels	chasuble
champaign	chantey	charade	charpoy	chasubles
champak	chanties	charades	charpoys	chat
champaks	chanting	charango	charr	chateau
champed	chantries	charangos	charred	chateaux
champers	chantry	charas	charring	chatelain
champerty	chants	charbroil	charro	chatline
champing	chanty	charcoal	charros	chatlines
champion	chaology	chard	chars	chatoyant
champions	chaos	chards	chart	chats
champlevé	chaotic	charge	charted	chatted
champs	chap	chargé	charter	chattel
chana	chaparral	charged	chartered	chattels
chance	chapatti	charger	charterer	chatter
chanced	chapattis	chargers	charters	chattered
chancel	chapbook	charges	charting	chatterer
chancels	chapbooks	chargés	chartism	chatters
chancer	chape	charging	charts	chattery
chancers	chapeau	chargrill	charwoman	chattier
chancery	chapeaux	charier	charwomen	chattiest
chances	chapel	chariest	chary	chattily
chancier	chapelry	charily	chase	chatting
chanciest	chapels	chariot	chased	chatty
chancily	chaperon	charioted	chaser	chaudhuri
chancing	chaperone	chariots	chasers	chauffeur
chancre	chaperons	charism	chases	chausses
chancres	chapes	charisma	chasing	chaw
chancroid	chaplain	charities	chasm	chawed
chancy	chaplains	charity	chasmic	chawing
chandelle	chaplet	charivari	chasms	chawl
chandler	chapleted	charka	chasse	chawls
chandlers	chaplets	charkas	chassé	chaws
chandlery	chapman	charkha	chasséd	chayote
change	chapmen	charkhas	chasséing	chayotes
changed	chappal	charlady	chasses	cheap
changeful	chappals	charlatan	chassés	cheapen
changer	chapped	charlie	chasseur	cheapened
changers	chappie	charlies	chasseurs	cheapens
changes	chappies	charlock	chassis	cheaper
changing	chapping	charlotte	chaste	cheapest
channa	chaprasi	charm	chastely	cheapie
channel	chaprasis	charmed	chasten	cheapies
channeled	chaps	charmer	chastened	cheapish
channels	chapter	charmers	chastener	cheapjack
chanson	chapters	charmeuse	chastens	cheaply
chansons	char	charming	chastise	cheapness
chant	charabanc	charmless	chastised	cheapo
chanted	characin	charmonia	chastiser	cheapos
chanter	characins	charms	chastises	cheat

cheated	cheese	cheroot	chews	chiefs
cheater	cheesed	cheroots	chewy	chieftain
cheaters	cheeses	cherries	chez	chiffon
cheating	cheesier	cherry	chi	chigger
cheats	cheesiest	chert	chiasma	chiggers
check	cheesing	cherts	chiasmata	chignon
checkable	cheesy	cherty	chiasmus	chignons
checkbox	cheetah	cherub	chiastic	chigoe
checked	cheetahs	cherubic	chibol	chigoes
checker	chef	cherubim	chibols	chihuahua
checkered	chefs	cherubs	chibouk	chikan
checkers	chela	chervil	chibouks	chilblain
checking	chelae	chess	chibouque	child
checklist	chelas	chessman	chic	childbed
checkmate	chelate	chessmen	chicane	childcare
checkout	chelated	chest	chicaned	childhood
checkouts	chelates	chested	chicanery	childish
checkroom	chelating	chestier	chicanes	childless
checks	chelation	chestiest	chicaning	childlike
checksum	chelator	chestily	chicer	children
checksums	chelators	chesting	chicest	chile
chedarim	chelicera	chestnut	chicha	chiles
cheder	chelonian	chestnuts	chichi	chili
cheders	chemical	chests	chick	chiliarch
cheechako	chemicals	chesty	chickadee	chiliasm
cheek	chemise	chetrum	chickaree	chiliast
cheekbone	chemises	chetrums	chicken	chiliasts
cheeked	chemist	chevalier	chickened	chilies
cheekier	chemistry	chevet	chickens	chill
cheekiest	chemists	chevets	chickpea	chilled
cheekily	chemo	chevied	chickpeas	chiller
cheeking	chemostat	chevies	chicks	chillers
cheeks	chempaka	cheviot	chickweed	chilli
cheeky	chempakas	cheviots	chicle	chillier
cheep	chemurgic	chèvre	chicly	chillies
cheeped	chemurgy	chevron	chicories	chilliest
cheeping	chenar	chevrons	chicory	chilling
cheeps	chenars	chevvys	chid	chillness
cheer	chenille	chevy	chidden	chills
cheered	cheongsam	chevying	chide	chillsome
cheerful	cheque	chevys	chided	chillum
cheerier	chequer	chew	chider	chillums
cheeriest	chequered	chewable	chiders	chilly
cheerily	chequers	chewed	chides	chilopod
cheering	cheques	chewer	chiding	chilopods
cheerio	cherimoya	chewers	chidingly	chimaera
cheerless	cherish	chewier	chief	chimaeras
cheerly	cherished	chewiest	chiefdom	chimb
cheers	cherishes	chewiness	chiefdoms	chimbs
cheery	chernozem	chewing	chiefly	chime

chimed	chipmunks	chiton	choice	cholos
chimer	chipolata	chitons	choicely	chometz
chimera	chipotle	chits	choicer	chomp
chimeras	chipotles	chitted	choices	chomped
chimeric	chipped	chitter	choicest	chomping
chimers	chipper	chittered	choil	chomps
chimes	chippers	chitters	choils	chondrite
chiming	chippie	chitties	choir	chondrule
chimney	chippies	chitting	choirboy	choof
chimneys	chipping	chitty	choirboys	choofed
chimp	chippings	chivalric	choirgirl	choofing
chimps	chippy	chivalry	choirman	choofs
chin	chips	chive	choirmen	chook
china	chipset	chives	choirs	chookie
chinar	chipsets	chivied	choisya	chookies
chinars	chiral	chivies	choisyas	chooks
chinas	chirality	chivvied	choke	choom
chinch	chirimoya	chivvies	choked	chooms
chinches	chiropody	chivvy	chokehold	choose
chine	chirp	chivvying	choker	chooser
chined	chirped	chivy	chokers	choosers
chines	chirper	chivying	chokes	chooses
ching	chirpers	chlamydia	chokey	choosier
chings	chirpier	chlamys	chokeys	choosiest
chining	chirpiest	chloasma	chokier	choosily
chink	chirpily	chloracne	chokies	choosing
chinkapin	chirping	chloral	chokiest	choosy
chinkara	chirps	chlorate	choking	chop
chinked	chirpy	chlorates	chokka	chophouse
chinking	chirr	chlordane	choko	chopped
chinks	chirred	chlorella	chokos	chopper
chinless	chirring	chloride	chokra	choppers
chinned	chirrs	chlorides	chokras	choppier
chinning	chirrup	chlorine	choky	choppiest
chino	chirruped	chlorines	chola	choppily
chinook	chirrups	chlorite	cholas	chopping
chinooks	chirrupy	chloritic	cholent	choppy
chinos	chiru	chlorosis	choler	chops
chins	chis	chlorotic	cholera	chopsocky
chinstrap	chisel	choc	choleraic	chopstick
chintz	chiseled	chocho	choleric	choral
chintzier	chiseling	chochos	choli	chorale
chintzily	chiselled	chock	choliamb	chorales
chintzy	chiseller	chocka	choliambs	chorally
chinwag	chisels	chocked	cholic	chord
chinwags	chit	chocker	choline	chordal
chip	chital	chocking	cholis	chordate
chipboard	chitals	chocks	cholla	chordates
chipmaker	chitin	chocolate	chollas	chorded
chipmunk	chitinous	chocolaty	cholo	chording

chords	chromatin	chugalugs	churchier	ciceroni
chore	chrome	chugged	churching	cichlid
chorea	chromed	chugging	churchman	cichlids
chores	chromic	chugs	churchmen	cicisbei
choriambi	chromide	chukar	churchy	cicisbeo
choric	chromides	chukars	churidar	cicisbeos
chorine	chromite	chukka	churidars	cider
chorines	chromites	chukkas	churinga	ciders
chorion	chromium	chukker	churingas	cig
chorionic	chromo	chukkers	churl	cigar
chorions	chromogen	chukor	churlish	cigaret
chorister	chromoly	chukors	churls	cigarets
chorizo	chromos	chum	churn	cigarette
chorizos	chromous	chumble	churned	cigarillo
choroid	chronic	chumbled	churning	cigars
choroidal	chronicle	chumbles	churns	ciggies
choroids	chrysalid	chumbling	churr	ciggy
chorten	chrysalis	chummed	churrasco	cigs
chortens	chrysanth	chummier	churred	ciguatera
chortle	chthonian	chummiest	churring	cilantro
chortled	chthonic	chummily	churrs	cilia
chortles	chub	chumming	chut	ciliary
chortling	chubbier	chummy	chute	ciliate
chorus	chubbiest	chump	chutes	ciliated
chorused	chubbily	chumps	chutist	ciliates
choruses	chubby	chums	chutists	ciliation
chorusing	chubs	chunder	chutney	cilice
chose	chuck	chundered	chutneys	cilices
chosen	chucked	chunders	chutzpah	cilium
chota	chucker	chunk	chyle	cill
chough	chuckers	chunked	chylous	cills
choughs	chuckhole	chunkier	chyme	cimbalom
chow	chucking	chunkiest	chymous	cimbaloms
chowder	chuckle	chunkily	chypre	cinch
chowed	chuckled	chunking		cinched
chowing	chuckler	chunks		cinches
chowk	chucklers	chunky	C|I	cinching
chowkidar	chuckles	chunni		cinchona
chows	chuckling	chunnis	ciabatta	cinchonas
chrism	chucks	chunter	ciao	cincture
chrisom	chuddar	chuntered	ciboria	cinctures
chrisoms	chuddars	chunters	ciborium	cinder
christen	chufa	chup	cicada	cinders
christens	chufas	chupatty	cicadas	cindery
chroma	chuff	chuppa	cicatrice	cine
chromakey	chuffed	chuppah	cicatrise	cineast
chromate	chuffing	chuppot	cicatrix	cineaste
chromates	chuffs	church	cicatrize	cineastes
chromatic	chug	churched	cicelies	cineasts
chromatid	chugalug	churches	cicely	cinema
			cicerone	

cinemas
cinematic
cinephile
cineplex
cineraria
cinereous
cingula
cingulate
cingulum
cinnabar
cinnamon
cinq
cinqs
cinque
cinques
cion
cions
cipher
ciphered
ciphering
ciphers
cipolin
circa
circadian
circinate
circle
circled
circles
circlet
circlets
circling
circlip
circlips
circs
circuit
circuited
circuitry
circuits
circular
circulars
circulate
circus
circuses
cire
cirque
cirques
cirrhosis
cirrhotic
cirri
cirriped

cirripede
cirripeds
cirrus
cis
cisalpine
cisco
ciscoes
cislunar
cisplatin
cissier
cissies
cissiest
cissing
cissus
cissy
cist
cistern
cisterns
cisticola
cistron
cistrons
cists
cistus
cistuses
citable
citadel
citadels
citation
citations
cite
cited
cites
cities
citified
citing
citizen
citizenry
citizens
citole
citoles
citral
citrate
citrates
citric
citril
citrils
citrine
citron
citrons
citrous

citrus
citruses
citrusy
cittern
citterns
city
cityfied
cityscape
cityward
citywards
civet
civets
civic
civically
civics
civil
civilian
civilians
civilise
civilised
civilises
civility
civilize
civilized
civilizer
civilizes
civilly
civvies
civvy

C L

clabber
clabbered
clabbers
clachan
clachans
clack
clacked
clacker
clackers
clacket
clacketed
clackets
clacking
clacks
clad
cladded
cladding
clade

clades
cladism
cladistic
cladode
cladodes
cladogram
clads
claggy
claim
claimable
claimant
claimants
claimed
claimer
claimers
claiming
claims
clam
clamant
clamantly
clambake
clambakes
clamber
clambered
clambers
clammed
clammier
clammiest
clammily
clamming
clammy
clamor
clamored
clamoring
clamorous
clamors
clamour
clamoured
clamours
clamp
clampdown
clamped
clamper
clampers
clamping
clamps
clams
clamshell
clan
clang

clanged
clanger
clangers
clanging
clangor
clangors
clangour
clangours
clangs
clank
clanked
clanking
clanks
clannish
clans
clanship
clansman
clansmen
clap
clapboard
clapped
clapper
clappers
clapping
claps
claptrap
claque
claques
claqueur
claqueurs
clarence
clarences
claret
clarets
claries
clarified
clarifier
clarifies
clarify
clarinet
clarinets
clarion
clarions
clarity
clarkia
clarkias
clarsach
clarsachs
clart
clartier

clartiest
clarts
clarty
clary
clash
clashed
clasher
clashers
clashes
clashing
clasp
clasped
claspers
clasping
clasps
class
classed
classes
classic
classical
classics
classier
classiest
classify
classily
classing
classism
classist
classless
classmate
classroom
classy
clast
clastic
clasts
clathrate
clatter
clattered
clatters
clausal
clause
clauses
claustral
clavate
clave
claves
clavicle
clavicles
clavier
claviers

claviform
claw
clawback
clawbacks
clawed
clawing
clawless
claws
clay
clayey
clayish
claymore
claymores
claypan
claypans
clays
clean
cleanable
cleaned
cleaner
cleaners
cleanest
cleaning
cleanish
cleanlier
cleanly
cleanness
cleans
cleanse
cleansed
cleanser
cleansers
cleanses
cleansing
cleanskin
cleanup
cleanups
clear
clearable
clearance
clearcole
cleared
clearer
clearers
clearest
clearing
clearings
clearly
clearness
clears

clearway
clearways
clearwing
cleat
cleated
cleats
cleavable
cleavage
cleavages
cleave
cleaved
cleaver
cleavers
cleaves
cleaving
clef
clefs
cleft
clefts
cleg
clegs
clematis
clemency
clement
clench
clenched
clenches
clenching
cleome
cleomes
cleopatra
clepsydra
clergies
clergy
clergyman
clergymen
cleric
clerical
clerics
clerihew
clerihews
clerisy
clerk
clerked
clerkess
clerking
clerkish
clerkly
clerks
clerkship

clever
cleverer
cleverest
cleverly
clevis
clevises
clew
clewed
clewing
clews
clianthus
cliche
cliched
cliches
click
clickable
clicked
clicker
clickers
clicking
clicks
clicky
client
clientele
clientism
clients
cliff
cliffs
cliffy
climactic
climate
climates
climatic
climax
climaxed
climaxes
climaxing
climb
climbable
climbdown
climbed
climber
climbers
climbing
climbs
clime
climes
clinal
clinch
clinched

clincher
clinchers
clinches
clinching
cline
clines
cling
clinger
clingers
clingfish
clingier
clingiest
clinging
clings
clingy
clinic
clinical
clinician
clinics
clink
clinked
clinker
clinkers
clinking
clinks
clint
clints
clip
clipboard
clipped
clipper
clippers
clippie
clippies
clipping
clippings
clips
clique
cliques
cliquey
cliquier
cliquiest
cliquish
clit
clitic
clitics
clitoral
clitoris
clitter
clittered

clitters
clivia
clivias
cloaca
cloacae
cloacal
cloak
cloaked
cloaking
cloakroom
cloaks
clobber
clobbered
clobbers
clochard
clochards
cloche
cloches
clock
clocked
clocker
clockers
clocking
clocks
clockwise
clockwork
clod
cloddish
clodpole
clodpoles
clods
clog
clogged
clogger
cloggers
cloggier
cloggiest
clogging
cloggy
clogs
cloisonné
cloister
cloisters
cloistral
clomp
clomped
clomping
clomps
clompy
clonal

clone
cloned
clones
clonic
cloning
clonk
clonked
clonking
clonks
clonky
clonus
clop
clopped
clopping
clops
cloqué
closable
close
closed
closely
closeness
closer
closers
closes
closest
closet
closeted
closeting
closets
closing
closish
closure
closured
closures
closuring
clot
clotbur
clotburs
cloth
clothe
clothed
clothes
clothier
clothiers
clothing
cloths
clots
clotted
clotting
cloture

clotures
clou
cloud
clouded
cloudier
cloudiest
cloudily
clouding
cloudless
cloudlet
cloudlets
clouds
cloudy
clough
cloughs
clous
clout
clouted
clouting
clouts
clove
cloven
clover
clovers
cloves
clown
clowned
clownfish
clowning
clownish
clowns
cloy
cloyed
cloying
cloyingly
cloys
clozapine
club
clubbable
clubbed
clubber
clubbers
clubbier
clubbiest
clubbing
clubby
clubhouse
clubland
clubman
clubmate

clubmates
clubmen
clubmoss
clubroot
clubrush
clubs
cluck
clucked
cluckier
cluckiest
clucking
clucks
clucky
clue
clued
clueing
clueless
clues
clump
clumped
clumpier
clumpiest
clumping
clumps
clumpy
clumsier
clumsiest
clumsily
clumsy
clunch
clung
clunk
clunked
clunker
clunkers
clunkier
clunkiest
clunking
clunks
clunky
clupeoid
clupeoids
cluster
clustered
clusters
clutch
clutched
clutches
clutching
clutter

cluttered
clutters
clypeal
clypei
clypeus
clyster
clysters

cnidarian

C O

coach
coached
coaches
coaching
coachload
coachman
coachmen
coachroof
coachwhip
coachwood
coachwork
coadjutor
coagula
coagulant
coagulase
coagulate
coagulum
coal
coaled
coaler
coalers
coalesce
coalesced
coalesces
coalface
coalfaces
coalfield
coalfish
coalhouse
coaling
coalition
coalman
coalmen
coals
coaly
coaming

coamings	cobbles	cockerels	cocotte	coeds
coarctate	cobbling	cockers	cocottes	coeliac
coarse	cobby	cockfight	cocoyam	coelom
coarsely	cobia	cockier	cocoyams	coelomata
coarsen	coble	cockies	cod	coelomate
coarsened	cobles	cockiest	coda	coeloms
coarsens	cobnut	cockily	codas	coelostat
coarser	cobnuts	cockiness	codded	coenobite
coarsest	cobra	cocking	codding	coenocyte
coarsish	cobras	cockle	coddle	coenzyme
coast	cobs	cocklebur	coddled	coenzymes
coastal	cobweb	cockled	coddler	coequal
coasted	cobwebbed	cockler	coddlers	coequals
coaster	cobwebby	cocklers	coddles	coerce
coasters	cobwebs	cockles	coddling	coerced
coasting	coca	cockling	code	coerces
coastland	cocaine	cockney	codec	coercible
coastline	cocas	cockneys	codecs	coercing
coasts	coccal	cockpit	coded	coercion
coastwise	cocci	cockpits	codeine	coercions
coat	coccidia	cockroach	coder	coercive
coated	coccidian	cocks	coders	coeternal
coatee	coccoid	cockscomb	codes	coeval
coati	coccolith	cocksfoot	codex	coevality
coating	coccus	cockshies	codexes	coevally
coatings	coccygeal	cockshy	codfish	coevals
coatis	coccyges	cocksman	codfishes	coexist
coatroom	coccyx	cocksmen	codger	coexisted
coatrooms	coccyxes	cockspur	codgers	coexists
coats	cochineal	cockspurs	codices	cofactor
coax	cochlea	cocksure	codicil	cofactors
coaxed	cochleae	cocktail	codicils	coffee
coaxer	cochlear	cocktails	codified	coffees
coaxers	cochoa	cocky	codifier	coffer
coaxes	cochoas	coco	codifiers	cofferdam
coaxial	cock	cocoa	codifies	coffered
coaxially	cockade	cocoanut	codify	cofferer
coaxing	cockaded	cocoanuts	codifying	coffers
coaxingly	cockades	cocoas	coding	coffin
cob	cockamamy	cocobolo	codling	coffined
cobalamin	cockatiel	cocobolos	codlings	coffining
cobalt	cockatoo	coconut	codomain	coffins
cobaltic	cockatoos	coconuts	codomains	coffle
cobaltous	cockboat	cocoon	codon	coffles
cobber	cockboats	cocooned	codons	coffret
cobbers	cockcrow	cocooner	codpiece	coffrets
cobble	cockcrows	cocooners	codpieces	cog
cobbled	cocked	cocooning	cods	cogencies
cobbler	cocker	cocoons	coecilian	cogency
cobblers	cockerel	cocos	coed	cogent

cogently	cohoes	colcannon	collator	colludes
cogged	cohort	colchicum	collators	colluding
cogitable	cohorts	cold	colleague	collusion
cogitate	cohos	colder	collect	collusive
cogitated	cohosh	coldest	collected	colluvial
cogitates	cohoshes	coldie	collector	colluvium
cogitator	cohune	coldies	collects	collyria
cogito	cohunes	coldish	colleen	collyrium
cognac	coif	coldly	colleens	colobine
cognacs	coifed	coldness	college	colobines
cognate	coiffed	colds	colleges	coloboma
cognately	coiffeur	cole	collegia	colobus
cognates	coiffeuse	colectomy	collegial	colobuses
cognisant	coiffing	coles	collegian	colocynth
cognise	coiffure	coleseed	collegium	cologne
cognised	coiffured	coleslaw	collet	colon
cognises	coiffures	coleus	collets	colón
cognising	coifing	coleuses	colliculi	colonel
cognition	coifs	colewort	collide	colonelcy
cognitive	coign	coleworts	collided	colonels
cognizant	coigns	coley	collider	colones
cognize	coil	coleys	colliders	colonial
cognized	coiled	colic	collides	colonials
cognizes	coiling	colicin	colliding	colonic
cognizing	coils	colicins	collie	colonies
cognomen	coin	colicky	collier	colonise
cognomens	coinage	colies	colliers	colonised
cogs	coinages	coliform	colliery	colonises
cogwheel	coincide	coliseum	collies	colonist
cogwheels	coincided	coliseums	colligate	colonists
cohabit	coincides	colitis	collimate	colonize
cohabited	coined	collage	collinear	colonized
cohabitee	coiner	collagen	collision	colonizer
cohabiter	coiners	collages	collocate	colonizes
cohabits	coining	collagist	collodion	colonnade
cohen	coins	collapsar	collogue	colons
cohens	coir	collapse	collogued	colony
cohere	coital	collapsed	collogues	colophon
cohered	coition	collapses	colloid	colophons
coherence	coitus	collar	colloidal	colophony
coherency	cojones	collard	colloids	color
coherent	coke	collards	collop	colorable
coherer	coked	collared	collops	colorant
coherers	cokes	collaring	colloquia	colorants
coheres	coking	collars	colloquy	colored
cohering	col	collate	collotype	coloreds
cohesion	cola	collated	collude	colorful
cohesive	colander	collates	colluded	colorific
coho	colanders	collating	colluder	coloring
cohoe	colas	collation	colluders	colorings

colorist
colorists
colorize
colorized
colorizer
colorizes
colorless
colors
colorway
colorways
colossal
colosseum
colossi
colossus
colostomy
colostrum
colour
colourant
coloured
coloureds
colourful
colouring
colourist
colourize
colours
colourway
cols
colt
colter
colters
coltish
coltishly
colts
coltsfoot
colubrid
colubrids
colubrine
colugo
colugos
columbine
columbite
columbium
columella
column
columnar
columned
columnist
columns
colure
colures

coly
colza
coma
comae
comas
comatose
comb
combat
combatant
combated
combating
combative
combats
combatted
combe
combed
comber
combers
combes
combfish
combi
combine
combined
combines
combing
combings
combining
combis
combo
combos
combs
combust
combusted
combusts
come
comeback
comebacks
comedian
comedians
comedic
comedies
comedo
comedones
comedown
comedowns
comedy
comelier
comeliest
comely
comer

comers
comes
comess
comesses
comet
cometary
comets
comfier
comfiest
comfily
comfiness
comfit
comfits
comfort
comforted
comforter
comforts
comfrey
comfreys
comfy
comic
comical
comically
comics
coming
comings
comital
comities
comity
comm
comma
command
commanded
commander
commando
commandos
commands
commas
commence
commenced
commences
commend
commended
commends
commensal
comment
commented
commenter
comments
commerce

commère
commères
commingle
commis
commish
commissar
commit
commits
committal
committed
committee
committer
commix
commixed
commixes
commixing
commo
commode
commodes
commodify
commodity
commodore
common
commonage
commoner
commoners
commonest
commonly
commons
commotion
comms
communal
communard
commune
communed
communes
communing
communion
communise
communism
communist
community
communize
commutate
commute
commuted
commuter
commuters
commutes
commuting

comp
compact
compacted
compactly
compactor
compacts
compadre
compadres
compand
companded
compander
compandor
compands
companied
companies
companion
company
compare
compared
compares
comparing
compass
compassed
compasses
comped
compeer
compeers
compel
compelled
compels
compendia
comper
compère
compèred
compères
compèring
compers
compete
competed
competent
competes
competing
compile
compiled
compiler
compilers
compiles
compiling
comping
complain

complains	computes	conchs	condone	confetti
complaint	computing	concierge	condoned	confidant
compleat	comrade	conciliar	condoner	confide
complete	comradely	concise	condoners	confided
completed	comrades	concisely	condones	confident
completes	con	conciser	condoning	confides
complex	conacre	concisest	condor	confiding
complexed	conacres	concision	condors	configure
complexes	conation	conclave	condos	confine
complexly	conative	conclaves	conduce	confined
compliant	concave	conclude	conduced	confines
complicit	concavely	concluded	conduces	confining
complied	concavity	concludes	conducing	confirm
complies	conceal	concoct	conducive	confirmed
compline	concealed	concocted	conduct	confirms
complines	concealer	concocter	conducted	confit
comply	conceals	concocts	conducti	conflab
complying	concede	concord	conductor	conflabs
compo	conceded	concordat	conducts	conflate
component	conceder	concords	conductus	conflated
compony	conceders	concours	conduit	conflates
comport	concedes	concourse	conduits	conflict
comported	conceding	concrete	condylar	conflicts
comports	conceit	concreted	condyle	confluent
compos	conceited	concretes	condyles	conflux
compose	conceits	concubine	condyloid	confluxes
composed	conceive	concur	condyloma	confocal
composer	conceived	concurred	cone	conform
composers	conceives	concurs	coned	conformal
composes	concenter	concuss	conehead	conformed
composing	concentre	concussed	coneheads	conformer
composite	concept	concusses	cones	conforms
compost	concepts	condemn	coney	confound
composted	conceptus	condemned	coneys	confounds
composts	concern	condemns	confab	confrère
composure	concerned	condense	confabbed	confrères
compote	concerns	condensed	confabs	confront
compotes	concert	condenser	confect	confronts
compound	concerted	condenses	confected	confuse
compounds	concerti	condign	confects	confused
comprador	concerto	condignly	confer	confuses
compress	concertos	condiment	conferee	confusing
comprise	concerts	condition	conferees	confusion
comprised	conch	condo	conferral	confute
comprises	concha	condole	conferred	confuted
comps	conchae	condoled	confers	confutes
compute	conches	condoles	confess	confuting
computed	conchie	condoling	confessed	conga
computer	conchies	condom	confesses	congaed
computers	conchoid	condoms	confessor	congaing

congas
congé
congeal
congealed
congeals
congee
congener
congeners
congenial
conger
congeries
congers
congested
congii
congius
congrats
congress
congruent
congruity
congruous
coni
conic
conical
conically
conics
conidia
conidium
conies
conifer
conifers
coniform
coniine
coning
conjoin
conjoined
conjoins
conjoint
conjugacy
conjugal
conjugate
conjunct
conjuncts
conjure
conjured
conjurer
conjurers
conjures
conjuring
conjuror
conjurors

conk
conked
conker
conkers
conking
conks
conn
connate
connect
connected
connector
connects
conned
connexion
conning
connive
connived
conniver
connivers
connives
conniving
connote
connoted
connotes
connoting
conns
connubial
conodont
conodonts
conoid
conoidal
conoids
conquer
conquered
conqueror
conquers
conquest
conquests
cons
conscious
conscript
consensus
consent
consented
consents
conserve
conserved
conserves
consider
considers

consign
consigned
consignee
consignor
consigns
consist
consisted
consists
console
consoled
consoler
consolers
consoles
consoling
consommé
consommés
consonant
consort
consorted
consortia
consorts
conspire
conspired
conspires
constable
constancy
constant
constants
constrain
constrict
construal
construct
construe
construed
construes
consul
consular
consulate
consuls
consult
consulted
consultee
consults
consume
consumed
consumer
consumers
consumes
consuming
contact

contacted
contactee
contacts
contadina
contadine
contadini
contadino
contagion
contain
contained
container
contains
contango
contangos
conte
contemn
contemned
contemner
contemns
contempt
contend
contended
contender
contends
content
contented
contents
contes
contessa
contessas
contest
contested
contester
contests
context
contexts
continent
continua
continual
continue
continued
continuer
continues
continuo
continuos
continuum
contort
contorted
contorts
contour

contoured
contours
contra
contract
contracts
contrail
contrails
contralto
contrary
contras
contrast
contrasts
contrasty
contrite
contrive
contrived
contriver
contrives
control
contrôlée
controls
contumacy
contumely
contuse
contused
contuses
contusing
contusion
conundrum
conure
conures
conus
convect
convected
convector
convects
convene
convened
convener
conveners
convenes
convening
convenor
convenors
convent
convents
converge
converged
converges
converse

conversed	cookable	coop	coppering	coralitas
converser	cookbook	cooped	coppernob	coralline
converses	cookbooks	cooper	coppers	corallita
convert	cooked	cooperage	coppery	corallite
converted	cooker	cooperant	coppice	coralloid
converter	cookeries	cooperate	coppiced	coralroot
convertor	cookers	coopered	coppices	corals
converts	cookery	cooperies	coppicing	corbeil
convex	cookhouse	coopering	copping	corbeille
convexity	cookie	coopers	copra	corbeils
convexly	cookies	coopery	coprolite	corbel
convey	cooking	cooping	cops	corbeled
conveyed	cookout	coops	copse	corbeling
conveyer	cookouts	coos	copses	corbelled
conveyers	cooks	coot	copter	corbels
conveying	cookshop	cooter	copters	corbicula
conveyor	cookshops	cooters	copula	corbie
conveyors	cooktop	cootie	copular	corbies
conveys	cooktops	cooties	copulas	cord
convict	cookware	coots	copulate	cordage
convicted	cool	cop	copulated	cordate
convicts	coolabah	copacetic	copulates	corded
convince	coolabahs	copal	copy	cordgrass
convinced	coolant	cope	copybook	cordial
convincer	coolants	copeck	copybooks	cordially
convinces	cooldrink	copecks	copycat	cording
convivial	cooled	coped	copycats	cordite
convoke	cooler	copepod	copydesk	cordless
convoked	coolers	copepods	copydesks	cordoba
convokes	coolest	coper	copyhold	cordobas
convoking	coolibah	copers	copying	cordon
convolve	coolibahs	copes	copyist	cordoned
convolved	coolie	copestone	copyists	cordoning
convolves	coolies	copiable	copyread	cordons
convoy	cooling	copied	copyreads	cordovan
convoyed	coolish	copier	copyright	cords
convoying	coolly	copiers	coquetry	corduroy
convoys	coolness	copies	coquette	corduroys
convulse	cools	coping	coquettes	cordwood
convulsed	coolth	copings	coquina	core
convulses	coomb	copious	coquinas	cored
cony	coombe	copiously	coquito	corella
coo	coombes	copita	coquitos	corellas
cooed	coombs	copitas	cor	coreopsis
cooee	coon	coplanar	coracle	corer
cooeed	cooncan	copolymer	coracles	corers
cooeeing	coonhound	copped	coracoid	cores
cooees	coons	copper	coracoids	corf
cooing	coonskin	copperas	coral	corgi
cook	coonskins	coppered	coralita	corgis

coriander	cornetts	corpus	cortile	cosmology
coring	cornflour	corpuscle	cortiles	cosmonaut
corium	cornice	corpuses	cortili	cosmos
cork	corniced	corral	cortina	cosmoses
corkage	cornices	corralled	cortinas	cosset
corked	corniche	corrals	cortinate	cosseted
corker	corniches	correct	cortisol	cosseting
corkers	cornicing	corrected	cortisone	cossets
corkier	cornier	correctly	corundum	cossie
corkiest	corniest	corrector	coruscant	cossies
corking	cornily	corrects	coruscate	cost
corks	corniness	correlate	corvée	costa
corkscrew	cornmeal	corrida	corvées	costae
corkwood	cornrows	corridas	corves	costal
corkwoods	corns	corridor	corvette	costate
corky	cornstone	corridors	corvettes	costed
corm	cornu	corrie	corvid	coster
cormel	cornua	corries	corvids	costers
cormels	cornual	corrode	corvina	costing
cormlet	cornus	corroded	corvinas	costings
cormlets	cornuses	corrodes	corvine	costive
cormorant	corny	corrodies	corydalis	costively
corms	corolla	corroding	corymb	costlier
corn	corollary	corrody	corymbose	costliest
cornball	corollas	corrosion	corymbs	costly
cornballs	corona	corrosive	coryphée	costmary
cornbrash	coronach	corrugate	coryphées	costs
cornbread	coronachs	corrupt	coryza	costume
corncrake	coronae	corrupted	cos	costumed
cornea	coronal	corrupter	cosecant	costumer
corneal	coronals	corruptly	cosecants	costumers
corneas	coronary	corrupts	coset	costumes
corned	coronas	corsage	cosets	costumier
cornel	coroner	corsages	cosh	costuming
cornelian	coroners	corsair	coshed	cosy
cornels	coronet	corsairs	coshes	cosying
corneous	coroneted	corse	coshing	cot
corner	coronets	corselet	cosied	cotangent
cornered	corpora	corselets	cosier	cote
cornering	corporal	corses	cosies	coterie
cornerman	corporals	corset	cosiest	coteries
cornermen	corporate	corseted	cosily	cotes
corners	corporeal	corsetry	cosine	cotillion
cornet	corposant	corsets	cosines	cotinga
cornetcy	corps	cortège	cosiness	cotingas
cornetist	corpse	cortèges	cosmetic	cotise
cornets	corpsed	cortex	cosmetics	cotises
cornett	corpses	cortical	cosmic	cots
cornetti	corpsing	corticate	cosmical	cotta
cornetto	corpulent	cortices	cosmogony	cottage

cottaged	coulters	courante	coven	cowered
cottager	coumarin	courantes	covenant	cowering
cottagers	coumarone	courbette	covenants	cowers
cottages	council	courgette	covens	cowfish
cottagey	councilor	courier	cover	cowfishes
cottaging	councils	couriered	coverable	cowgirl
cottar	counsel	couriers	coverage	cowgirls
cottars	counseled	courol	coverall	cowherd
cottas	counselor	courols	coveralls	cowherds
cotter	counsels	course	covered	cowhide
cotters	count	coursed	covering	cowhides
cottier	countable	courser	coverings	cowing
cottiers	countback	coursers	coverlet	cowl
cottise	countdown	courses	coverlets	cowled
cottised	counted	coursing	covers	cowlick
cottises	counter	court	coverslip	cowlicks
cotton	countered	courted	covert	cowling
cottoned	counters	courteous	covertly	cowlings
cottoning	countess	courtesan	coverts	cowls
cottons	countian	courtesy	coverture	cowman
cottony	countians	courtier	coves	cowmen
cotyledon	counties	courtiers	covet	cowpat
coucal	counting	courting	covetable	cowpats
coucals	countless	courtlier	coveted	cowpea
couch	countries	courtly	coveting	cowpeas
couchant	country	courtroom	covetous	cowpoke
couched	counts	courts	covets	cowpokes
couches	countship	courtship	covey	cowpox
couchette	county	courtyard	coveys	cowrie
couching	coup	couscous	covin	cowries
coudé	coupe	cousin	covine	cowry
coudés	coupé	cousinly	coving	cows
cougar	couped	cousins	cow	cowshed
cougars	coupes	couth	cowabunga	cowsheds
cough	coupés	couthie	coward	cowslip
coughed	couple	couthy	cowardice	cowslips
coughing	coupled	couture	cowardly	cox
coughs	coupledom	couturier	cowards	coxa
could	coupler	couvade	cowardy	coxae
coulee	couplers	couvades	cowbane	coxal
coulees	couples	couvert	cowbanes	coxcomb
coulibiac	couplet	couverts	cowbell	coxcombry
coulis	couplets	covalence	cowbells	coxcombs
coulisse	coupling	covalency	cowberry	coxed
coulisses	couplings	covalent	cowbird	coxes
couloir	coupon	covariant	cowbirds	coxing
couloirs	coupons	cove	cowboy	coxless
coulomb	coups	coved	cowboys	coxswain
coulombs	courage	covelline	cowed	coxswains
coulter	courant	covellite	cower	coy

coydog
coydogs
coyer
coyest
coyly
coyness
coyote
coyotes
coypu
coypus
coz
cozen
cozenage
cozened
cozener
cozeners
cozening
cozens
cozied
cozier
cozies
coziest
cozy
cozying
cozzie
cozzies

C R

crab
crabbed
crabbedly
crabber
crabbers
crabbier
crabbiest
crabbily
crabbing
crabby
crabgrass
crablike
crabmeat
crabs
crabwise
crack
crackdown
cracked
cracker
crackers
crackhead

cracking
crackle
crackled
crackles
cracklier
crackling
crackly
cracknel
cracknels
crackpot
crackpots
cracks
cracksman
cracksmen
cracky
cradle
cradled
cradles
cradling
craft
crafted
crafter
crafters
craftier
craftiest
craftily
crafting
crafts
craftsman
craftsmen
craftwork
crafty
crag
craggier
craggiest
craggily
craggy
crags
cragsman
cragsmen
craic
crake
crakes
cram
crambo
crammed
crammer
crammers
cramming
cramp

cramped
cramping
crampon
crampons
cramps
crams
cran
cranage
cranberry
crane
craned
cranes
crania
cranial
craniate
craniates
craning
cranium
craniums
crank
crankcase
cranked
crankier
crankiest
crankily
cranking
crankpin
crankpins
cranks
cranky
crannied
crannies
crannog
crannogs
cranny
crans
crap
crape
crapes
crapped
crapper
crappers
crappest
crappie
crappier
crappies
crappiest
crapping
crappy
craps

crapshoot
crapulent
crapulous
crapy
crases
crash
crashed
crashes
crashing
crasis
crass
crasser
crassest
crassly
crassness
cratch
cratches
crate
crated
crateful
cratefuls
crater
cratered
cratering
craters
crates
crating
craton
cratonic
cratons
cratur
craturs
cravat
cravats
cravatted
crave
craved
craven
cravenly
cravens
craver
cravers
craves
craving
cravings
craw
crawdad
crawdads
crawfish
crawl

crawled
crawler
crawlers
crawling
crawls
crawly
craws
cray
crayfish
crayon
crayoned
crayoning
crayons
crays
craze
crazed
crazes
crazier
crazies
craziest
crazily
craziness
crazing
crazy
creak
creaked
creakier
creakiest
creakily
creaking
creaks
creaky
cream
creamed
creamer
creamers
creamery
creamier
creamiest
creamily
creaming
creams
creamware
creamy
creance
creances
crease
creased
creases
creasing

create	creese	cresols	cricks	crippled
created	creeses	cress	cricoid	crippler
creates	cremaster	cresset	cricoids	cripplers
creatine	cremate	cressets	cried	cripples
creating	cremated	crest	crier	crippling
creation	cremates	crested	criers	crips
creations	cremating	crestfish	cries	crises
creative	cremation	cresting	crikey	crisis
creatives	cremator	crestless	crim	crisp
creator	cremators	crests	crime	crispate
creators	crematory	cresyl	crimed	crisped
creature	crenate	cretic	crimes	crisper
creatures	crenated	cretics	criminal	crispers
crèche	crenation	cretin	criminals	crispest
crèches	crenel	cretinism	criming	crispier
cred	crenelate	cretinous	crimp	crispiest
credal	crenelle	cretins	crimped	crisping
credence	crenelles	cretonne	crimper	crisply
credenza	crenels	cretonnes	crimpers	crispness
credenzas	crenulate	crevasse	crimping	crisps
credible	creodont	crevasses	crimplene	crispy
credibly	creodonts	crevice	crimps	crista
credit	creole	crevices	crimpy	cristae
credited	creoles	crew	crims	cristate
crediting	creolise	crewed	crimson	crit
creditor	creolised	crewel	crimsoned	criteria
creditors	creolises	crewels	crimsons	criterial
credits	creolize	crewing	cringe	criterion
credo	creolized	crewman	cringed	critic
credos	creolizes	crewmen	cringer	critical
credulity	creosol	crews	cringers	criticise
credulous	creosote	crib	cringes	criticism
creed	creosoted	cribbage	cringing	criticize
creedal	creosotes	cribbed	cringle	critics
creeds	crêpe	cribber	cringles	critique
creek	crêperie	cribbers	crinkle	critiqued
creeks	crêperies	cribbing	crinkled	critiques
creel	crêpes	cribella	crinkles	critter
creels	crêpey	cribellum	crinklier	crits
creep	crepitant	cribo	crinkling	critters
creeper	crepitate	cribos	crinkly	croak
creepers	crepitus	cribs	crinoid	croaked
creepie	crépon	cribwork	crinoidal	croaker
creepier	crept	cribworks	crinoids	croakers
creepies	crêpy	crick	crinoline	croakier
creepiest	crescendi	cricked	criollo	croakiest
creepily	crescendo	cricket	criollos	croakily
creeping	crescent	cricketer	crip	croaking
creeps	crescents	crickets	cripes	croaks
creepy	cresol	cricking	cripple	croaky

croc
crochet
crocheted
crocheter
crochets
croci
crock
crocked
crockery
crocket
crockets
crocking
crocks
crocodile
crocoite
crocosmia
crocs
crocus
crocuses
croft
crofted
crofter
crofters
crofting
crofts
croissant
crombec
crombecs
cromlech
cromlechs
crone
crones
croneyism
cronies
cronk
crony
cronyism
crook
crookback
crooked
crookeder
crookedly
crookery
crooking
crookneck
crooks
croon
crooned
crooner
crooners

crooning
croons
crop
cropped
cropper
croppers
cropping
crops
croquet
croqueted
croquets
croquette
crore
crores
crosier
crosiers
cross
crossbar
crossbars
crossbill
crossbow
crossbows
crosse
crossed
crosser
crossers
crosses
crossfire
crossflow
crossing
crossings
crossly
crossness
crossover
crossroad
crosstalk
crosswalk
crossways
crosswind
crosswise
crossword
crosswort
crostini
crotal
crotale
crotales
crotals
crotch
crotches
crotchet

crotchets
crotchety
croton
crotons
crottle
crottles
crouch
crouched
crouches
crouching
croup
croupade
croupades
croupier
croupiers
croups
croupy
croustade
croute
croutes
crouton
croutons
crow
crowbait
crowbaits
crowbar
crowbars
crowberry
crowd
crowded
crowdie
crowdies
crowding
crowds
crowdy
crowed
crowfoot
crowfoots
crowing
crown
crowned
crowning
crowns
crows
croze
crozes
crozier
croziers
cru
cruces

crucial
crucially
crucian
crucians
cruciate
crucible
crucibles
crucifer
crucifers
crucified
crucifier
crucifies
crucifix
cruciform
crucify
cruck
crucks
crud
cruddier
cruddiest
cruddy
crude
crudely
crudeness
cruder
crudest
crudités
crudities
crudity
cruel
crueler
cruelest
cruelled
crueller
cruellest
cruelling
cruelly
cruels
cruelties
cruelty
cruet
cruets
cruise
cruised
cruiser
cruisers
cruises
cruisie
cruisies
cruising

cruller
crullers
crumb
crumbed
crumbier
crumbiest
crumbing
crumble
crumbled
crumbles
crumblier
crumblies
crumbling
crumbly
crumbs
crumby
crumhorn
crumhorns
crummier
crummiest
crummily
crummy
crump
crumped
crumpet
crumpets
crumping
crumple
crumpled
crumples
crumplier
crumpling
crumply
crumps
crunch
crunched
cruncher
crunchers
crunches
crunchie
crunchier
crunchies
crunchily
crunching
crunchy
crupper
cruppers
crura
crural
crus

crusade
crusaded
crusader
crusaders
crusades
crusading
cruse
cruses
crush
crushable
crushed
crusher
crushers
crushes
crushing
crusie
crusies
crust
crustacea
crustal
crusted
crustie
crustier
crusties
crustiest
crustily
crusting
crustose
crusts
crusty
crutch
crutches
crux
cruxes
cry
crybabies
crybaby
cryer
cryers
crying
cryogen
cryogenic
cryogens
cryolite
cryonic
cryonics
cryostat
cryostats
crypt
cryptic

cryptogam
cryptonym
cryptozoa
crypts
crystal
crystals

C S

csardas

C T

ctenidia
ctenidium
ctenoid

C U

cuadrilla
cuatro
cuatros
cub
cubage
cubature
cubbed
cubbies
cubbing
cubby
cubbyhole
cube
cubeb
cubebs
cubed
cubes
cubic
cubical
cubically
cubicle
cubicles
cubiform
cubing
cubism
cubist
cubists
cubit
cubital
cubits
cubitus
cuboid
cuboidal

cuboids
cubs
cuckold
cuckolded
cuckoldry
cuckolds
cuckoo
cuckoos
cucumber
cucumbers
cucurbit
cucurbits
cud
cuddies
cuddle
cuddled
cuddles
cuddlier
cuddliest
cuddling
cuddly
cuddy
cudgel
cudgeled
cudgeling
cudgelled
cudgels
cudweed
cue
cueca
cuecas
cued
cueing
cueist
cueists
cues
cuesta
cuestas
cuff
cuffed
cuffing
cufflink
cufflinks
cuffs
cuing
cuirass
cuirasses
cuish
cuishes
cuisine

cuisse
cuisses
cuke
cukes
culch
culchie
culchies
culex
culices
culicine
culinary
cull
culled
culler
cullers
cullet
cullies
culling
culls
cully
culm
culmen
culmina
culminant
culminate
culms
culottes
culpable
culpably
culprit
culprits
cult
cultch
cultic
cultigen
cultigens
cultish
cultism
cultist
cultists
cultivar
cultivars
cultivate
cults
cultural
culture
cultured
cultures
culturing
cultus

cultuses
culverin
culverins
culvert
culverted
culverts
cum
cumber
cumbered
cumbering
cumbers
cumbia
cumbrous
cumene
cumin
cummin
cumquat
cumquats
cumulate
cumulated
cumulates
cumuli
cumulus
cuneate
cuneiform
cunjevoi
cunjevois
cunner
cunners
cunning
cunningly
cunt
cunts
cup
cupboard
cupboards
cupcake
cupcakes
cupel
cupeled
cupeling
cupelled
cupelling
cupels
cupful
cupfuls
cupid
cupidity
cupids
cupola

cupolaed	curdles	currency	curtsied	cussed
cupolas	curdling	current	curtsies	cussedly
cuppa	curds	currently	curtsy	cusses
cuppas	curdy	currents	curtsying	cussing
cupped	cure	curricle	curule	custard
cupping	curé	curricles	curvature	custards
cuppy	cured	curricula	curve	custodial
cupreous	curer	curried	curved	custodian
cupric	curers	currier	curves	custody
cuprite	cures	curriers	curvet	custom
cuprous	curés	curries	curveted	customal
cups	curettage	currish	curveting	customals
cupule	curette	currishly	curvets	customary
cupules	curetted	curry	curvetted	customer
cur	curettes	currying	curvier	customers
curable	curetting	curs	curviest	customise
curacao	curfew	curse	curviness	customize
curacaos	curfews	cursed	curving	customs
curacies	curie	cursedly	curvy	custumal
curacy	curies	curser	cuscus	custumals
curandera	curing	cursers	cuscuses	cut
curandero	curio	curses	cusec	cutaneous
curare	curios	cursillo	cusecs	cutaway
curassow	curiosa	cursillos	cush	cutaways
curassows	curiosity	cursing	cushat	cutback
curate	curious	cursive	cushats	cutbacks
curated	curiously	cursively	cushaw	cutch
curates	curium	cursor	cushaws	cute
curating	curl	cursorial	cushes	cutely
curation	curled	cursorily	cushier	cuteness
curative	curler	cursors	cushiest	cuter
curatives	curlers	cursory	cushiness	cutest
curator	curlew	curst	cushion	cutesy
curators	curlews	curt	cushioned	cuticle
curb	curlicue	curtail	cushions	cuticles
curbed	curlicues	curtailed	cushiony	cuticular
curbing	curlier	curtails	cushy	cutie
curbs	curliest	curtain	cusimanse	cuties
curbside	curliness	curtained	cusk	cutin
curbsides	curling	curtains	cusks	cutins
curbstone	curls	curtal	cusp	cutis
curculio	curly	curtals	cuspate	cutlass
curculios	currach	curtana	cusped	cutlasses
curcuma	currachs	curtanas	cuspid	cutler
curcumas	curragh	curtilage	cuspidate	cutlers
curd	curraghs	curtly	cuspidor	cutlery
curdle	currajong	curtness	cuspidors	cutlet
curdled	currant	curtsey	cuspids	cutlets
curdler	currants	curtseyed	cusps	cutline
curdlers	currawong	curtseys	cuss	cutlines

cutover
cutovers
cutpurse
cutpurses
cuts
cutscene
cutscenes
cutter
cutters
cutties
cutting
cuttingly
cuttings
cuttle
cuttles
cutty
cutwater
cutwaters
cutwork
cutworm
cutworms
cuvée
cuvées
cuvette
cuvettes

C W

cwm
cwms

C Y

cyan
cyanamide
cyanate
cyanates
cyanic
cyanide
cyanides
cyanogen
cyanogens
cyanosis
cyanotic
cyathia
cyathium
cyber
cybercafe
cybernaut
cyberpunk
cybersex
cyborg
cyborgs
cycad
cycads
cyclamate
cyclamen
cyclamens
cycle
cycled
cycles
cycleway

cycleways
cyclic
cyclical
cyclin
cycling
cyclins
cyclise
cyclised
cyclises
cyclising
cyclist
cyclists
cyclize
cyclized
cyclizes
cyclizing
cycloid
cycloidal
cycloids
cyclone
cyclones
cyclonic
cyclopean
cyclopian
cyclops
cyclopses
cyclorama
cyclotron
cyder
cygnet
cygnets

cylinder
cylinders
cylindric
cymbal
cymbalist
cymbals
cymbidium
cyme
cymes
cymose
cynic
cynical
cynically
cynicism
cynicisms
cynics
cynodont
cynodonts
cynosure
cynosures
cyphel
cyphels
cypher
cyphered
cyphering
cyphers
cypress
cypresses
cyprinid
cyprinids
cyprinoid

cypsela
cypselae
cyst
cysteine
cystic
cystine
cystitis
cystotomy
cysts
cytidine
cytisus
cytokine
cytokines
cytokinin
cytology
cytolysis
cytolytic
cytoplasm
cytosine
cytosol
cytosolic
cytotoxic

C Z

czar
czardas
czarevich
czarina
czarinas
czars

D

D A

dab
dabbed
dabber
dabbers
dabbing
dabble

dabbled
dabbler
dabblers
dabbles
dabbling
dabchick
dabchicks

dabs
dace
dacha
dachas
dachshund
dacite
dacites

dacitic
dacoit
dacoities
dacoits
dacoity
dactyl
dactylic

dactylics
dactyls
dad
dada
daddies
daddy
dado

dados	dainties	dammar	dances	danseuses
dads	daintiest	dammars	dancetté	danthonia
daemon	daintily	dammed	dancetty	dap
daemonic	dainty	damming	dancing	daphne
daemons	daiquiri	damn	danda	daphnes
daff	daiquiris	damna	dandas	daphnia
daffier	dairies	damnable	dandelion	dapped
daffiest	dairy	damnably	dander	dapper
daffiness	dairying	damnation	dandered	dapperly
daffodil	dairymaid	damnatory	dandering	dapping
daffodils	dairyman	damned	danders	dapple
daffs	dairymen	damnedest	dandiacal	dappled
daffy	dais	damnified	dandier	dapples
daft	daises	damnifies	dandies	dappling
dafter	daisies	damnify	dandiest	daps
daftest	daisy	damning	dandified	dapsone
dag	dak	damningly	dandiprat	darbies
dagga	daks	damns	dandle	dare
daggas	dal	damnum	dandled	daredevil
dagged	dalasi	damp	dandles	darer
dagger	dalasis	damped	dandling	darers
daggers	dale	dampen	dandruff	dares
daggier	dalek	dampened	dandruffy	darg
daggiest	daleks	dampener	dandy	dargah
dagging	dales	dampeners	dandyish	dargahs
daggy	dalliance	dampening	dandyism	dargs
dago	dallied	dampens	danewort	daring
dagoes	dallies	damper	daneworts	daringly
dagos	dally	dampers	dang	dariole
dags	dallying	dampest	danger	darioles
dah	dalmatic	damping	dangerous	dark
dahabeah	dalmatics	dampish	dangers	darken
dahabeahs	dalton	damply	dangle	darkened
dahi	daltonism	dampness	dangled	darkener
dahlia	daltons	damps	dangler	darkeners
dahlias	dam	dams	danglers	darkening
dahs	damage	damsel	dangles	darkens
dai	damaged	damselfly	dangling	darker
daikon	damages	damsels	dangly	darkest
daikons	damaging	damson	danio	darkie
dailies	damar	damsons	danios	darkies
daily	damascene	dan	dank	darkish
daimio	damask	danaid	danker	darkling
daimios	damasked	danaids	dankest	darkly
daimon	damasking	dance	dankly	darkness
daimonic	damasks	danceable	dankness	darkroom
daimons	dame	danced	dans	darkrooms
daimyo	dames	dancehall	danseur	darksome
daimyos	damfool	dancer	danseurs	darky
daintier	damfools	dancers	danseuse	darling

darlings
darn
darned
darnedest
darnel
darnels
darner
darners
darning
darns
darshan
darshans
dart
dartboard
darted
darter
darters
darting
darts
dash
dashboard
dashed
dasheen
dasher
dashers
dashes
dashiki
dashikis
dashing
dashingly
dashpot
dashpots
dassie
dassies
dastard
dastardly
dastards
dastoor
dastoors
dastur
dasturs
dasyure
dasyures
data
databank
databanks
database
databases
datable
datacomms

datacoms
dataglove
datcha
datchas
date
dateable
datebook
datebooks
dated
dateless
dates
dating
dative
datives
datum
datura
daturas
daub
daube
daubed
dauber
daubers
daubes
daubing
daubs
daughter
daughters
daunt
daunted
daunting
dauntless
daunts
dauphin
dauphins
daven
davened
davening
davenport
davens
davit
davits
daw
dawdle
dawdled
dawdler
dawdlers
dawdles
dawdling
dawn
dawned

dawning
dawnings
dawns
day
dayan
dayanim
daybed
daybeds
dayboat
dayboats
daybook
daybooks
daybreak
daybreaks
daycare
daycares
daydream
daydreams
dayglo
daylight
daylights
daymare
daymares
daypack
daypacks
days
daysack
daysacks
daysail
daysailed
daysailer
daysailor
daysails
dayside
daysides
dayspring
daytime
daytimes
daywear
daywork
dayworker
daze
dazed
dazedly
dazes
dazibao
dazing
dazzle
dazzled
dazzler

dazzlers
dazzles
dazzling

| D | B |

dbx

| D | E |

deacon
deaconed
deaconess
deaconing
deacons
dead
deadbeat
deadbeats
deadbolt
deadbolts
deaden
deadened
deadener
deadeners
deadening
deadens
deader
deadest
deadeye
deadeyes
deadfall
deadfalls
deadhead
deadheads
deadlier
deadliest
deadlight
deadline
deadlines
deadlock
deadlocks
deadly
deadman
deadmen
deadness
deadpan
deadpans
deadrise
deadstock
deaerate

deaerated
deaerates
deaf
deafen
deafened
deafening
deafens
deafer
deafest
deafness
deal
dealer
dealers
dealfish
dealign
dealigned
dealigns
dealing
dealings
deals
dealt
dean
deaneries
deanery
deans
dear
dearer
dearest
dearie
dearies
dearly
dearness
dears
dearth
dearths
deasil
death
deathbed
deathbeds
deathless
deathlier
deathlike
deathly
deaths
deb
debacle
debacles
debag
debagged
debagging

debags	debriefed	decaf	decencies	deckhands
deballast	debriefer	decaff	decency	deckhead
debar	debriefs	decagon	decennia	deckheads
debark	debris	decagonal	decennial	deckhouse
debarked	debruise	decagons	decennium	deckie
debarking	debruised	decahedra	decent	deckies
debarks	debruises	decal	decenter	decking
debarment	debs	decaliter	decenters	deckle
debarred	debt	decalitre	decently	deckles
debarring	debtor	decals	decentre	decks
debars	debtors	decameter	decentred	decky
debase	debts	decametre	decentres	declaim
debased	debug	decamp	deception	declaimed
debaser	debugged	decamped	deceptive	declaimer
debasers	debugger	decamping	decertify	declaims
debases	debuggers	decamps	decibel	declarant
debasing	debugging	decan	decibels	declare
debatable	debugs	decanal	decidable	declared
debatably	debunk	decane	decide	declarer
debate	debunked	decani	decided	declarers
debated	debunker	decans	decidedly	declares
debater	debunkers	decant	decider	declaring
debaters	debunkery	decanted	deciders	declass
debates	debunking	decanter	decides	déclassé
debating	debunks	decanters	deciding	declassed
debauch	debur	decanting	decidua	déclassée
debauched	deburr	decants	decidual	declasses
debauchee	deburred	decapod	deciduous	decline
debaucher	deburring	decapods	decile	declined
debauches	deburrs	decastyle	deciles	decliner
debby	deburs	decathlon	deciliter	decliners
debeak	debus	decay	decilitre	declines
debeaked	debuses	decayed	decimal	declining
debeaking	debussed	decaying	decimally	declivity
debeaks	debussing	decays	decimals	declutch
debenture	debut	decease	decimate	deco
debility	debutant	deceased	decimated	decoct
debit	debutante	deceases	decimates	decocted
debitage	debutants	deceasing	decimator	decocting
debited	debuted	decedent	decimeter	decoction
debiting	debuting	decedents	decimetre	decocts
debits	debuts	deceit	decipher	decodable
deblur	debye	deceitful	deciphers	decode
deblurred	debyes	deceits	decision	decoded
deblurs	decadal	deceive	decisions	decoder
debonair	decade	deceived	decisive	decoders
debouch	decadence	deceiver	deck	decodes
debouched	decadent	deceivers	deckchair	decoding
debouches	decadents	deceives	decked	decoke
debrief	decades	deceiving	deckhand	decoked

decokes	dedendum	defacer	defends	deflators
decoking	dedicate	defacers	defense	deflect
decollate	dedicated	defaces	defenses	deflected
décolleté	dedicatee	defacing	defensive	deflector
decompose	dedicates	defaecate	defer	deflects
decongest	dedicator	defalcate	deference	deflexed
decontrol	deduce	defame	deferent	deflexion
decor	deduced	defamed	deferents	deflower
decorate	deduces	defamer	deferment	deflowers
decorated	deducible	defamers	deferral	defocus
decorates	deducing	defames	deferrals	defocused
decorator	deduct	defaming	deferred	defocuses
decorous	deducted	defang	deferrer	defogger
decorum	deducting	defanged	deferrers	defoliant
decoupage	deduction	defanging	deferring	defoliate
decouple	deductive	defangs	defers	deforce
decoupled	deducts	defat	defiance	deforced
decouples	dee	defats	defiant	deforces
decoy	deed	defatted	defiantly	deforcing
decoyed	deeded	defatting	deficient	deforest
decoying	deeding	default	deficit	deforests
decoys	deeds	defaulted	deficits	deform
decrease	deedy	defaulter	defied	deformed
decreased	deejay	defaults	defier	deforming
decreases	deejays	defeat	defiers	deformity
decree	deem	defeated	defies	deforms
decreed	deemed	defeating	defilade	defraud
decreeing	deeming	defeatism	defiladed	defrauded
decrees	deems	defeatist	defilades	defrauder
decrement	deemster	defeats	defile	defrauds
decrepit	deemsters	defecate	defiled	defray
decretal	deep	defecated	defiler	defrayal
decretals	deepen	defecates	defilers	defrayals
decried	deepened	defecator	defiles	defrayed
decrier	deepening	defect	defiling	defraying
decriers	deepens	defected	definable	defrays
decries	deeper	defecting	define	defrock
decry	deepest	defection	defined	defrocked
decrying	deeply	defective	definer	defrocks
decrypt	deepness	defector	definers	defrost
decrypted	deeps	defectors	defines	defrosted
decrypts	deer	defects	definiens	defroster
decubitus	deergrass	defence	defining	defrosts
decumbent	deerhound	defences	definite	deft
decurrent	deerskin	defend	deflate	defter
decurved	deerskins	defendant	deflated	defterdar
decussate	dees	defended	deflates	deftest
decyl	def	defender	deflating	deftly
decyls	deface	defenders	deflation	deftness
dedans	defaced	defending	deflator	defunct

defuse	deicide	delator	delisting	demanders
defused	deicides	delators	delists	demanding
defuses	deictic	delay	deliver	demands
defusing	deictics	delayed	delivered	demantoid
defy	deid	delayer	deliverer	demarcate
defying	deified	delayered	delivers	démarche
dégagé	deifies	delayers	delivery	démarches
dégagés	deify	delaying	dell	demark
degas	deifying	delays	dells	demarkate
degases	deign	dele	delouse	demarked
degassed	deigned	deled	deloused	demarking
degassing	deigning	delegable	delouses	demarks
degauss	deigns	delegacy	delousing	demassify
degaussed	deil	delegate	dels	deme
degausser	deils	delegated	delta	demean
degausses	deionise	delegates	deltaic	demeaned
deglaze	deionised	delegator	deltas	demeaning
deglazed	deionises	deleing	deltoid	demeanor
deglazes	deionize	deles	delude	demeanour
deglazing	deionized	delete	deluded	demeans
degrade	deionizer	deleted	deludedly	dement
degraded	deionizes	deletes	deluder	demented
degrader	deisal	deleting	deluders	démenti
degraders	deism	deletion	deludes	dementia
degrades	deist	deletions	deluding	démentis
degrading	deistic	delexical	deluge	demerara
degrease	deistical	delft	deluged	demerge
degreased	deists	delftware	deluges	demerged
degreaser	deities	deli	deluging	demerger
degreases	deity	delicacy	delusion	demergers
degree	deixis	delicate	delusions	demerges
degrees	deject	delicates	delusive	demerging
degu	dejected	delicious	delusory	demerit
degus	dejecting	delict	deluster	demerits
degust	dejection	delicts	delusters	demersal
degusted	dejects	delight	delustre	demes
degusting	dekaliter	delighted	delustred	demesne
degusts	dekameter	delights	delustres	demesnes
dehisce	deke	delimit	delve	demigod
dehisced	deked	delimited	delved	demigods
dehiscent	dekes	delimiter	delver	demijohn
dehisces	deking	delimits	delvers	demijohns
dehiscing	dekko	delineate	delves	demilune
dehorn	del	deliriant	delving	demilunes
dehorned	delate	delirious	demagogic	demirep
dehorning	delated	delirium	demagogue	demireps
dehorns	delates	delis	demagogy	demise
dehors	delating	delish	demand	demised
dehydrate	delation	delist	demanded	demises
deicidal	delations	delisted	demander	demising

demission	demulcent	denning	denudes	deploy
demist	demur	denominal	denuding	deployed
demisted	demure	denote	deny	deploying
demister	demurely	denoted	denying	deploys
demisters	demurer	denotes	deodar	deplume
demisting	demurest	denoting	deodars	deplumed
demists	demurrage	denounce	deodorant	deplumes
demit	demurral	denounced	deodorise	depluming
demitasse	demurred	denouncer	deodorize	deponent
demits	demurrer	denounces	deontic	deponents
demitted	demurrers	dens	deoxidize	deport
demitting	demurring	dense	depart	deported
demiurge	demurs	densely	departed	deportee
demiurges	demy	denseness	departing	deportees
demiurgic	demystify	denser	departs	deporting
demo	den	densest	departure	deports
demob	denar	densified	depasture	depose
demobbed	denarii	densifies	dépaysé	deposed
demobbing	denarius	densify	dépaysée	deposes
demobs	denars	densities	depend	deposing
democracy	denary	density	dependant	deposit
democrat	denature	dent	depended	deposited
democrats	denatured	dental	dependent	depositor
démodé	denatures	dentalise	depending	deposits
demoed	dendrite	dentalium	depends	depot
demoing	dendrites	dentalize	depict	depots
demolish	dendritic	dentally	depicted	depower
demon	dendroid	dentaries	depicter	depowered
demoniac	dendroids	dentary	depicters	depowers
demoniacs	dendron	dentate	depicting	deprave
demonic	dendrons	dented	depiction	depraved
demonise	dene	dentelle	depicts	depraves
demonised	denervate	denticle	depigment	depraving
demonises	denes	denticles	depilate	depravity
demonism	dengue	dentil	depilated	deprecate
demonize	deniable	dentils	depilates	depress
demonized	deniably	dentin	depilator	depressed
demonizes	denial	dentinal	deplane	depresses
demons	denials	dentine	deplaned	depressor
demos	denied	denting	deplanes	deprival
demote	denier	dentist	deplaning	deprivals
demoted	deniers	dentistry	deplete	deprive
demotes	denies	dentists	depleted	deprived
demotic	denigrate	dentition	depletes	deprives
demoting	denim	dents	depleting	depriving
demotion	denims	denture	depletion	deprogram
demotions	denitrify	dentures	deplore	depth
demount	denizen	denturist	deplored	depthless
demounted	denizens	denude	deplores	depths
demounts	denned	denuded	deploring	depurate

depurated	derma	deseeded	desktops	destinies
depurates	dermal	deseeder	desman	destining
depurator	dermatome	deseeders	desmans	destiny
depute	dermestid	deseeding	desmid	destitute
deputed	dermic	deseeds	desmids	destock
deputes	dermis	deselect	desmoid	destocked
deputies	dermoid	deselects	desmosome	destocks
deputing	derogate	desert	desolate	destrier
deputize	derogated	deserted	desolated	destriers
deputized	derogates	deserter	desolates	destroy
deputizes	derrick	deserters	desolator	destroyed
deputy	derricks	deserting	desorb	destroyer
déraciné	derrière	desertion	desorbed	destroys
déracinés	derrières	deserts	desorbent	destruct
derail	derringer	deserve	desorber	destructs
derailed	derris	deserved	desorbers	desuetude
derailing	derrises	deserves	desorbing	desultory
derails	derry	deserving	desorbs	detach
derange	derv	desex	despair	detached
deranged	dervish	desexed	despaired	detaches
deranges	dervishes	desexes	despairs	detaching
deranging	desalt	desexing	despatch	detail
derate	desalted	deshi	desperado	detailed
derated	desalting	desi	desperate	detailing
derates	desalts	desiccant	despise	details
derating	descale	desiccate	despised	detain
deration	descaled	design	despiser	detained
derations	descaler	designate	despisers	detainee
derbies	descalers	designed	despises	detainees
derby	descales	designer	despising	detainer
derelict	descaling	designers	despite	detainers
derelicts	descant	designing	despoil	detaining
derepress	descanted	designs	despoiled	detains
deride	descants	desirable	despoiler	detangle
derided	descend	desirably	despoils	detangled
derider	descended	desire	despond	detangles
deriders	descender	desired	desponded	detect
derides	descends	desires	desponds	detected
deriding	descent	desiring	despot	detecting
derisible	descents	desirous	despotic	detection
derision	describe	desist	despotism	detective
derisive	described	desisted	despots	detector
derisory	describer	desisting	dessert	detectors
derivable	describes	desists	desserts	detects
derivate	descried	desk	destain	detent
derive	descries	deskill	destained	detente
derived	descry	deskilled	destains	detention
derives	descrying	deskills	destine	detents
deriving	desecrate	desks	destined	deter
derm	deseed	desktop	destines	deterge

deterged
detergent
deterges
deterging
determine
deterred
deterrent
deterring
deters
detest
detested
detester
detesters
detesting
detests
dethrone
dethroned
dethrones
detinue
detonate
detonated
detonates
detonator
detorsion
detour
detoured
detouring
detours
detox
detoxed
detoxes
detoxify
detoxing
detract
detracted
detractor
detracts
detrain
detrained
detrains
detriment
detrital
detrition
detritus
detrusor
detrusors
detumesce
detune
detuned
detunes

detuning
deuce
deuced
deucedly
deuces
deuteric
deuterium
deuteron
deuterons
deutzia
deutzias
deva
devadasi
devadasis
devalue
devalued
devalues
devaluing
devas
devastate
devein
deveined
deveining
deveins
develop
developed
developer
développé
develops
deverbal
deverbals
devi
deviance
deviancy
deviant
deviants
deviate
deviated
deviates
deviating
deviation
deviator
deviators
device
devices
devil
deviled
devilfish
deviling
devilish

devilled
devilling
devilment
devilry
devils
deviltry
devious
deviously
devis
devisable
devise
devised
devisee
devisees
deviser
devisers
devises
devising
devisor
devisors
devitrify
devoice
devoiced
devoices
devoicing
devoid
devoir
devoirs
devolve
devolved
devolves
devolving
dévot
devote
dévote
devoted
devotedly
devotee
devotees
devotes
dévotes
devoting
devotion
devotions
dévots
devour
devoured
devourer
devourers
devouring

devours
devout
devoutly
dew
dewan
dewans
dewar
dewars
dewater
dewatered
dewaters
dewberry
dewclaw
dewclaws
dewdrop
dewdrops
dewed
dewfall
dewier
dewiest
dewily
dewiness
dewing
dewlap
dewlaps
deworm
dewormed
dewormer
dewormers
deworming
deworms
dews
dewy
dex
dexies
dexter
dexterity
dexterous
dexters
dextral
dextrally
dextrals
dextran
dextrans
dextrin
dextrins
dextrose
dextrous
dexy

D H

dhaba
dhabas
dhal
dhamma
dhansak
dharma
dharmsala
dharna
dhikr
dhobi
dhobis
dhol
dholak
dholaks
dhole
dholes
dhols
dhoney
dhoneys
dhoti
dhotis
dhow
dhows
dhurrie
dhurries
dhyana

D I

diabase
diabetes
diabetic
diabetics
diablerie
diabolic
diabolise
diabolism
diabolist
diabolize
diabolo
diabolos
diachrony
diaconal
diaconate
diacritic
diadem
diademed
diadems

diaeresis
diagnose
diagnosed
diagnoses
diagnosis
diagonal
diagonals
diagram
diagramed
diagrams
diagrid
diagrids
dial
dialect
dialectal
dialectic
dialects
dialed
dialer
dialers
dialing
dialled
dialler
diallers
dialling
dialog
dialoged
dialogic
dialoging
dialogism
dialogs
dialogue
dialogued
dialogues
dials
dialysate
dialyse
dialysed
dialyses
dialysing
dialysis
dialytic
dialyzate
dialyze
dialyzed
dialyzes
dialyzing
diamagnet
diamanté
diameter

diameters
diametral
diametric
diamine
diamines
diamond
diamonds
diana
dianas
dianthus
diapason
diapasons
diapause
diapaused
diapauses
diaper
diapered
diapering
diapers
diaphone
diaphones
diaphragm
diaphyses
diaphysis
diapir
diapiric
diapirism
diapirs
diapsid
diapsids
diarchal
diarchic
diarchies
diarchy
diaries
diarise
diarised
diarises
diarising
diarist
diaristic
diarists
diarize
diarized
diarizes
diarizing
diarrhea
diarrhoea
diary
diaspora

diaspore
diaspores
diastase
diastases
diastema
diastole
diastolic
diathermy
diatheses
diathesis
diatom
diatomic
diatomite
diatoms
diatonic
diatreme
diatremes
diatribe
diatribes
diazepam
diazinon
diazo
diazonium
diazos
diazotype
dib
dibasic
dibatag
dibatags
dibbed
dibber
dibbers
dibbing
dibble
dibbled
dibbler
dibblers
dibbles
dibbling
diborane
dibs
dice
diced
dicentra
dicentras
dicentric
dicer
dicers
dices
dicey

dichasia
dichasium
dichogamy
dichotic
dichotomy
dichroic
dichroism
dicier
diciest
dicing
dick
dicked
dicken
dickens
dicker
dickered
dickerer
dickerers
dickering
dickers
dickey
dickeys
dickhead
dickheads
dickier
dickies
dickiest
dicking
dicks
dicky
dicot
dicots
dicrotic
dicta
dictamnus
dictate
dictated
dictates
dictating
dictation
dictator
dictators
diction
dictum
dictums
dicty
did
didactic
diddicoy
diddicoys

diddies
diddle
diddled
diddler
diddlers
diddles
diddling
diddums
diddy
didi
didicoi
didicois
didis
didjeridu
dido
didoes
didos
didst
didymium
die
dieback
died
diegeses
diegesis
diegetic
diehard
diehards
diel
dieldrin
diene
dienes
dieresis
dies
diesel
dieselise
dieselize
diestock
diestocks
diestrus
diet
dietaries
dietary
dieted
dieter
dieters
dietetic
dietetics
dietician
dieting
dietitian

diets	digitalis	dilator	dimissory	dingoes
diff	digitally	dilators	dimity	dingos
differ	digitate	dilatory	dimly	dings
differed	digitise	dildo	dimmed	dingus
different	digitised	dildoes	dimmer	dinguses
differing	digitises	dildos	dimmers	dingy
differs	digitize	dilemma	dimmest	dining
difficult	digitized	dilemmas	dimming	dink
diffident	digitizer	diligence	dimmish	dinked
diffract	digitizes	diligent	dimness	dinkier
diffracts	digitoxin	dill	dimnesses	dinkies
diffs	digits	dillier	dimorphic	dinkiest
diffuse	diglossia	dillies	dimple	dinking
diffused	diglossic	dilliest	dimpled	dinks
diffusely	dignified	dills	dimples	dinkum
diffuser	dignifies	dilly	dimplier	dinky
diffusers	dignify	dillybag	dimpliest	dinna
diffuses	dignitary	dillybags	dimpling	dinnae
diffusing	dignities	diluent	dimply	dinned
diffusion	dignity	diluents	dims	dinner
diffusive	digoxin	dilute	dimwit	dinners
diffusor	digraph	diluted	dimwits	dinning
diffusors	digraphic	diluter	din	dinosaur
dig	digraphs	diluters	dinar	dinosaurs
digamma	digress	dilutes	dinars	dins
digammas	digressed	diluting	dine	dint
digastric	digresser	dilution	dined	dinted
digenean	digresses	dilutions	diner	dinting
digerati	digs	dilutive	dinero	dints
digest	dihedral	diluvial	diners	diocesan
digested	dihedrals	diluvian	dines	diocesans
digester	dihybrid	dim	dinette	diocese
digesters	dihybrids	dime	dinettes	dioceses
digestif	dihydric	dimension	ding	dioch
digestifs	dike	dimer	dingbat	diochs
digesting	diked	dimeric	dingbats	diode
digestion	dikes	dimerise	dinged	diodes
digestive	diking	dimerised	dinger	dioecies
digests	dikkop	dimerises	dingers	dioecious
digger	dikkops	dimerize	dinges	dioecy
diggers	diktat	dimerized	dinghies	dioestrus
digging	diktats	dimerizes	dinghy	diogenite
diggings	dilatable	dimerous	dingier	diol
dight	dilatancy	dimers	dingiest	diols
dighted	dilate	dimes	dingily	diopside
dighting	dilated	dimeter	dinginess	dioptase
dights	dilates	dimeters	dinging	diopter
digit	dilating	dimetric	dingle	diopters
digital	dilation	dimidiate	dingles	dioptre
digitalin	dilations	diminish	dingo	dioptres

dioptric
dioptrics
diorama
dioramas
diorite
dioritic
diosgenin
dioxan
dioxane
dioxide
dioxides
dioxin
dioxins
dip
dipeptide
diphthong
diplegia
diploid
diploids
diploidy
diploma
diplomacy
diplomas
diplomat
diplomate
diplomats
diplont
diplontic
diplonts
diplopia
diplopias
diplopod
diplopods
diplotene
dipluran
diplurans
dipolar
dipole
dipoles
dipped
dipper
dippers
dippier
dippiest
dipping
dippy
dips
dipshit
dipshits
dipso

dipsos
dipstick
dipsticks
diptera
dipteral
dipteran
dipterans
dipterist
dipterous
diptych
diptyches
diptychs
diquat
dire
direct
directed
directing
direction
directive
directly
director
directors
directory
directrix
directs
direful
direfully
direly
direness
direr
direst
dirge
dirgeful
dirges
dirham
dirhams
dirigible
dirigisme
dirigiste
dirk
dirks
dirndl
dirndls
dirt
dirtied
dirtier
dirties
dirtiest
dirtily
dirtiness

dirty
dirtying
dis
disable
disabled
disables
disabling
disablist
disabuse
disabused
disabuses
disaccord
disaffirm
disagree
disagreed
disagrees
disallow
disallows
disappear
disapply
disarm
disarmed
disarmer
disarmers
disarming
disarms
disarray
disarrays
disaster
disasters
disavow
disavowal
disavowed
disavows
disband
disbanded
disbands
disbar
disbarred
disbars
disbelief
disbound
disbud
disbudded
disbuds
disburden
disbursal
disburse
disbursed
disburser

disburses
disc
discalced
discard
discarded
discards
discern
discerned
discerner
discerns
discharge
disciple
disciples
disclaim
disclaims
disclose
disclosed
discloser
discloses
disco
discoboli
discoed
discoes
discoid
discoidal
discoing
discolor
discolors
discolour
discomfit
discord
discorded
discords
discos
discount
discounts
discourse
discover
discovers
discovery
discredit
discreet
discrete
discs
discus
discuses
discuss
discussed
discusser
discusses

disdain
disdained
disdains
disease
diseased
diseases
disembark
disembody
disendow
disendows
disengage
disentail
disentomb
disesteem
diseuse
diseuses
disfavor
disfavors
disfavour
disfigure
disforest
disfrock
disfrocks
disgorge
disgorged
disgorger
disgorges
disgrace
disgraced
disgraces
disguise
disguised
disguises
disgust
disgusted
disgusts
dish
dishcloth
dishdash
dishdasha
dished
dishes
dishevel
dishevels
dishful
dishfuls
dishier
dishiest
dishing
dishonest

dishonor	dismissed	disposal	dissent	distrains
dishonors	dismisses	disposals	dissented	distraint
dishonour	dismount	dispose	dissenter	distrait
dishpan	dismounts	disposed	dissents	distraite
dishpans	disobey	disposer	disses	distress
dishrag	disobeyed	disposers	dissever	district
dishrags	disobeyer	disposes	dissevers	districts
dishwater	disobeys	disposing	dissident	distrust
dishy	disoblige	dispraise	dissing	distrusts
disinfect	disomic	disproof	dissipate	disturb
disinfest	disomy	disprove	dissolute	disturbed
disinter	disorder	disproved	dissolve	disturber
disinters	disorders	disproves	dissolved	disturbs
disinvent	disorient	disputant	dissolves	disulfide
disinvest	disown	dispute	dissonant	disunion
disinvite	disowned	disputed	dissuade	disunited
disjoin	disowner	disputer	dissuaded	disunity
disjoined	disowners	disputers	dissuader	disuse
disjoins	disowning	disputes	dissuades	disused
disjoint	disowns	disputing	distaff	disuses
disjoints	disparage	disquiet	distaffs	dit
disjunct	disparate	disquiets	distal	ditch
disjuncts	disparity	disrate	distally	ditched
disk	dispatch	disrated	distance	ditcher
diskette	dispel	disrates	distanced	ditchers
diskettes	dispelled	disrating	distances	ditches
diskless	dispeller	disregard	distant	ditching
disks	dispels	disrelish	distantly	diterpene
dislike	dispense	disrepair	distaste	ditheism
disliked	dispensed	disrepute	distemper	ditheist
dislikes	dispenser	disrobe	distend	ditheists
disliking	dispenses	disrobed	distended	dither
dislocate	dispersal	disrobes	distends	dithered
dislodge	disperse	disrobing	distich	ditherer
dislodged	dispersed	disrupt	distiches	ditherers
dislodges	disperser	disrupted	distichs	dithering
disloyal	disperses	disrupter	distil	dithers
dismal	dispirit	disruptor	distill	dithery
dismally	dispirits	disrupts	distilled	dithizone
dismantle	displace	diss	distiller	dithyramb
dismast	displaced	dissaver	distills	dits
dismasted	displaces	dissavers	distils	ditsier
dismasts	display	dissaving	distinct	ditsiest
dismay	displayed	dissect	distingué	ditsy
dismayed	displayer	dissected	distort	dittany
dismaying	displays	dissector	distorted	ditties
dismays	displease	dissects	distorts	ditto
dismember	disport	dissed	distract	ditty
dismiss	disported	dissemble	distracts	ditz
dismissal	disports	dissensus	distrain	ditzes

ditzier
ditziest
ditziness
ditzy
diuresis
diuretic
diuretics
diurnal
diurnally
diva
divagate
divagated
divagates
divalent
divan
divans
divas
dive
dived
diver
diverge
diverged
divergent
diverges
diverging
divers
diverse
diversely
diverser
diversest
diversify
diversion
diversity
divert
diverted
diverting
diverts
dives
divest
divested
divesting
divests
divesture
divi
divide
divided
dividend
dividends
divider
dividers

divides
dividing
divine
divined
divinely
diviner
diviners
divines
divinest
diving
divining
divinise
divinised
divinises
divinity
divinize
divinized
divinizes
divis
divisi
divisible
division
divisions
divisive
divisor
divisors
divorce
divorcé
divorced
divorcee
divorces
divorcing
divot
divots
divulge
divulged
divulges
divulging
divvied
divvies
divvy
divvying
diwan
diwans
dixie
dixies
diya
diyas
dizygotic
dizygous

dizzied
dizzier
dizzies
dizziest
dizzily
dizziness
dizzy
dizzying

D J

djebel
djebels
djellaba
djellabah
djellabas
djibba
djibbah
djibbahs
djibbas
djinn
djinns

D O

do
doable
dob
dobbed
dobbies
dobbin
dobbing
dobby
dobe
dobes
dobra
dobras
dobro
dobros
dobs
dobsonfly
docent
docents
docile
docilely
docility
dock
dockage
docked
docken
dockens

docker
dockers
docket
docketed
docketing
dockets
docking
dockland
docklands
docks
dockside
dockyard
dockyards
doctor
doctoral
doctorate
doctored
doctoring
doctorly
doctors
doctrinal
doctrine
doctrines
docudrama
document
documents
dodder
doddered
dodderer
dodderers
doddering
dodders
doddery
doddle
dodecagon
dodge
dodgeball
dodged
dodgem
dodgems
dodger
dodgers
dodges
dodgier
dodgiest
dodging
dodgy
dodo
dodoes
dodos

doe
doek
doeks
doer
doers
does
doeskin
doest
doeth
dof
doff
doffed
doffing
doffs
dog
dogana
doganas
dogbane
dogbanes
dogberry
dogbox
dogboxes
dogdom
doge
doges
dogface
dogfaces
dogfight
dogfights
dogfish
dogfishes
dogged
doggedly
dogger
doggerel
doggers
doggie
doggies
dogginess
dogging
doggish
doggo
doggone
doggoned
doggy
doghouse
doghouses
dogie
dogies
doglike

dogma	dollhouse	domicils	donkey	doomwatch
dogman	dollied	dominance	donkeyman	doomy
dogmas	dollier	dominancy	donkeymen	door
dogmatic	dollies	dominant	donkeys	doorbell
dogmatics	dolliest	dominants	donna	doorbells
dogmatise	dolling	dominate	donnas	doorcase
dogmatism	dollop	dominated	donné	doorcases
dogmatist	dolloped	dominates	donned	doored
dogmatize	dolloping	dominator	donnée	doorknob
dogmen	dollops	dominee	données	doorknobs
dognap	dolls	domineer	donnés	doorknock
dognapped	dolly	domineers	donning	doorman
dognapper	dollying	doming	donnish	doormat
dognaps	dolma	dominical	donnishly	doormats
dogs	dolmades	dominie	donor	doormen
dogsbody	dolman	dominies	donors	doornail
dogshore	dolmans	dominion	dons	doornails
dogshores	dolmas	dominions	donship	doorpost
dogskin	dolmen	dominium	donut	doorposts
dogstail	dolmens	dominiums	donuts	doors
dogtrot	dolmus	domino	doodad	doorstep
dogtrots	dolomite	dominoes	doodads	doorsteps
dogwatch	dolomitic	don	doodah	doorstop
dogwood	dolor	dona	doodahs	doorstops
doh	dolorous	donah	doodle	doorway
dohs	dolostone	donahs	doodlebug	doorways
doilies	dolour	donas	doodled	dooryard
doily	dolphin	donate	doodler	dooryards
doing	dolphins	donated	doodlers	doozie
doings	dolt	donates	doodles	doozies
doit	doltish	donating	doodling	doozy
dojo	doltishly	donation	doodly	dop
dojos	dolts	donations	doofus	dopa
dolce	domain	donative	doofuses	dopamine
doldrums	domaine	donatives	doohickey	dopant
dole	domaines	donator	doojigger	dopants
doled	domains	donators	doolally	dope
doleful	domal	done	doolie	doped
dolefully	domanial	donee	doolies	doper
dolerite	dome	donees	doom	dopers
doles	domed	dong	doomed	dopes
dolina	domes	donga	doomier	dopester
dolinas	domesday	dongas	doomiest	dopesters
doline	domestic	donged	doomily	dopey
dolines	domestics	donging	dooming	dopiaza
doling	domical	dongle	dooms	dopier
doll	domicil	dongles	doomsayer	dopiest
dollar	domicile	dongs	doomsday	dopily
dollars	domiciled	donjon	doomster	dopiness
dolled	domiciles	donjons	doomsters	doping

doppe	doss	doubloons	dovekies	downier
doppie	dossal	doublure	dovelike	downiest
doppies	dossed	doublures	doves	downily
dops	dosser	doubly	dovetail	downiness
dopy	dosseret	doubt	dovetails	downing
dor	dosserets	doubtable	dovish	downland
dorado	dossers	doubted	dowager	downlands
dorados	dosses	doubter	dowagers	downlight
doré	dosshouse	doubters	dowd	downlink
dorés	dossier	doubtful	dowdier	downlinks
dories	dossiers	doubting	dowdies	download
dorje	dossing	doubtless	dowdiest	downloads
dorjes	dost	doubts	dowdily	downmost
dork	dot	douce	dowdiness	downpipe
dorks	dotage	douceur	dowds	downpipes
dorm	dotard	douceurs	dowdy	downplay
dormancy	dotards	douche	dowel	downplays
dormant	dote	douched	doweled	downpour
dormer	doted	douches	doweling	downpours
dormers	doter	douching	dowelled	downrate
dormice	doters	dough	dowelling	downrated
dormitory	dotes	doughboy	dowels	downrates
dormouse	doth	doughboys	dower	downright
dorms	doting	doughier	dowered	downriver
dormy	dotingly	doughiest	dowering	downs
doronicum	dotish	doughnut	dowers	downscale
dorp	dots	doughnuts	dowitcher	downshift
dorps	dotted	doughtier	down	downside
dors	dotter	doughtily	downbeat	downsides
dorsa	dotterel	doughty	downbeats	downsize
dorsal	dotterels	doughy	downcast	downsized
dorsally	dotters	dour	downcasts	downsizes
dorsiflex	dottier	dourer	downcomer	downslope
dorsum	dottiest	dourest	downcut	downspout
dory	dottily	dourly	downcuts	downstage
doryphore	dottiness	dourness	downdraft	downstate
dos	dotting	douse	downdrift	downswing
dosa	dottle	doused	downed	downthrew
dosage	dottles	douses	downer	downthrow
dosages	dotty	dousing	downers	downtown
dosai	double	dout	downfall	downturn
dosas	doubled	douted	downfalls	downturns
dose	doubler	douting	downfield	downward
dosed	doublers	douts	downforce	downwards
dosemeter	doubles	dove	downgrade	downwarp
doses	doublet	dovecot	downhaul	downwarps
dosh	doubleton	dovecote	downhauls	downwash
dosimeter	doublets	dovecotes	downhill	downwind
dosimetry	doubling	dovecots	downhills	downy
dosing	doubloon	dovekie	downhole	downzone

downzoned
downzones
dowries
dowry
dowse
dowsed
dowser
dowsers
dowses
dowsing
dowt
dowted
dowting
dowts
doxastic
doxies
doxology
doxy
doyen
doyenne
doyennes
doyens
doze
dozed
dozen
dozens
dozenth
dozer
dozers
dozes
dozier
doziest
dozily
doziness
dozing
dozy

D R

drab
drabber
drabbest
drabble
drabbled
drabbles
drabbling
drably
drabness
drabs
dracaena

dracaenas
drachm
drachma
drachmae
drachmas
drachms
drack
dracks
dracone
dracones
draconian
draconic
draff
draft
drafted
draftee
draftees
drafter
drafters
draftier
draftiest
drafting
drafts
draftsman
draftsmen
drafty
drag
dragée
dragées
dragged
dragger
draggers
draggier
draggiest
dragging
draggle
draggled
draggles
draggling
draggy
dragline
draglines
dragnet
dragnets
dragoman
dragomans
dragomen
dragon
dragonet
dragonets

dragonfly
dragons
dragoon
dragooned
dragoons
drags
dragster
dragsters
drail
drails
drain
drainage
draincock
drained
drainer
drainers
draining
drainpipe
drains
drake
drakes
dram
drama
dramas
dramatic
dramatics
dramatise
dramatist
dramatize
dramaturg
drams
drank
drape
draped
draper
draperies
drapers
drapery
drapes
draping
drastic
drat
dratted
draught
draughted
draughts
draughty
draw
drawback
drawbacks

drawbar
drawbars
drawcard
drawcards
drawcord
drawcords
drawdown
drawdowns
drawee
drawees
drawer
drawerful
drawers
drawing
drawings
drawknife
drawl
drawled
drawler
drawlers
drawling
drawls
drawly
drawn
draws
dray
drayman
draymen
drays
dread
dreaded
dreadful
dreading
dreads
dream
dreamboat
dreamed
dreamer
dreamers
dreamful
dreamier
dreamiest
dreamily
dreaming
dreamland
dreamless
dreamlike
dreams
dreamt
dreamtime

dreamwork
dreamy
drear
drearier
dreariest
drearily
dreary
dreck
dreckish
drecky
dredge
dredged
dredger
dredgers
dredges
dredging
dree
dreed
dreeing
drees
dreggy
dregs
dreich
dreidel
dreidels
dreidl
dreidls
drek
drench
drenched
drenches
drenching
dress
dressage
dressed
dresser
dressers
dresses
dressier
dressiest
dressily
dressing
dressings
dressy
drew
drey
dreys
dribble
dribbled
dribbler

dribblers
dribbles
dribbling
dribbly
driblet
driblets
driech
dried
drier
driers
dries
driest
drift
drifted
drifter
drifters
driftfish
drifting
drifts
driftway
driftways
driftwood
drifty
drill
drilled
driller
drillers
drilling
drills
drily
drink
drinkable
drinker
drinkers
drinking
drinks
drip
dripped
drippier
drippiest
drippily
dripping
drippings
drippy
drips
dripstone
drivable
drive
driveable
drivel

driveled
driveler
drivelers
driveline
driveling
drivelled
driveller
drivels
driven
driver
drivers
drives
driveway
driveways
driving
drizzle
drizzled
drizzles
drizzlier
drizzling
drizzly
drogue
drogues
droid
droids
droit
droits
droll
droller
drollery
drollest
drollness
drolls
drolly
drome
dromedary
dromes
dromoi
dromond
dromonds
dromos
drone
droned
drones
drongo
drongoes
drongos
droning
droob
droobs

droog
droogs
drool
drooled
drooling
drools
droop
drooped
droopier
droopiest
droopily
drooping
droops
droopy
drop
drophead
dropheads
droplet
droplets
dropout
dropouts
droppable
dropped
dropper
droppers
dropping
droppings
drops
dropseed
dropsical
dropside
dropsies
dropsy
dropwort
dropworts
drosera
droseras
droshkies
droshky
dross
drossier
drossiest
drossy
drought
droughts
droughty
drouth
drouths
drouthy
drove

droved
drover
drovers
droves
droving
drown
drowned
drowning
drowns
drowse
drowsed
drowses
drowsier
drowsiest
drowsily
drowsing
drowsy
drub
drubbed
drubbing
drubs
drudge
drudged
drudgery
drudges
drudging
drug
drugged
drugget
druggets
druggie
druggies
drugging
druggist
druggists
druggy
drugs
drugstore
drum
drumbeat
drumbeats
drumfire
drumfish
drumhead
drumheads
drumlin
drumlins
drummed
drummer
drummers

drumming
drums
drumstick
drunk
drunkard
drunkards
drunken
drunkenly
drunker
drunkest
drunks
drupe
drupel
drupelet
drupelets
drupels
drupes
druse
druses
drusy
druther
druthers
dry
dryad
dryads
dryas
dryases
dryer
dryers
drying
dryish
drylands
dryly
dryness
drys
drystone
drysuit
drysuits
drywall

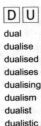

D U

dual
dualise
dualised
dualises
dualising
dualism
dualist
dualistic

dualists	duckwalk	duettists	dulness	dumpy
dualities	duckwalks	duff	dulosis	dun
duality	duckweed	duffed	dulotic	dunam
dualize	ducky	duffel	dulse	dunams
dualized	duct	duffer	duly	dunce
dualizes	ducted	duffers	dum	dunces
dualizing	ducti	duffest	dumb	dune
dualled	ductile	duffing	dumbed	dunes
dualling	ductility	duffle	dumber	dung
dually	ducting	duffles	dumbest	dungaree
duals	ductless	duffs	dumbfound	dungarees
dub	ducts	dufus	dumbhead	dunged
dubbed	ductular	dufuses	dumbheads	dungeon
dubbin	ductule	dug	dumbing	dungeoned
dubbined	ductules	dugite	dumbly	dungeons
dubbing	ductus	dugong	dumbness	dungheap
dubbining	ductwork	dugongs	dumbo	dungheaps
dubbins	dud	dugout	dumbos	dunghill
dubby	dude	dugouts	dumbs	dunghills
dubiety	duded	dugs	dumbshow	dunging
dubious	dudes	duiker	dumbshows	dungs
dubiously	dudgeon	duikers	dumbsize	dungworm
dubitable	duding	duke	dumbsized	dungworms
dubnium	dudish	dukedom	dumbsizes	dunite
dubs	duds	dukedoms	dumdum	dunk
ducal	due	dukes	dumdums	dunked
ducat	duel	dulcamara	dumfound	dunker
ducats	dueled	dulcet	dumfounds	dunkers
duces	dueler	dulcian	dumka	dunking
duchess	duelers	dulciana	dumkas	dunks
duchesse	dueling	dulcianas	dumky	dunlin
duchesses	duelist	dulcians	dummied	dunlins
duchies	duelists	dulcified	dummies	dunnage
duchy	duelled	dulcifies	dummy	dunnart
duck	dueller	dulcify	dummying	dunnarts
duckbill	duellers	dulcimer	dump	dunned
duckbills	duelling	dulcimers	dumped	dunnies
duckboard	duellist	dulcitone	dumper	dunning
ducked	duellists	dulia	dumpers	dunno
ducker	duels	dull	dumpier	dunnock
duckers	duende	dullard	dumpies	dunnocks
duckies	duendes	dullards	dumpiest	dunny
ducking	duenna	dulled	dumpily	duns
duckling	duennas	duller	dumpiness	dunt
ducklings	dues	dullest	dumping	dunted
duckpin	duet	dulling	dumpling	dunting
duckpins	duets	dullish	dumplings	dunts
ducks	duetted	dullness	dumps	duo
ducktail	duetting	dulls	dumpster	duodecimo
ducktails	duettist	dully	dumpsters	duodena

duodenal
duodenary
duodenum
duodenums
duologue
duologues
duomo
duomos
duopolies
duopoly
duos
duotone
duotones
dupable
dupatta
dupattas
dupe
duped
duper
duperies
dupers
dupery
dupes
duping
dupion
dupions
duple
duplet
duplets
duplex
duplexes
duplicate
duplicity
dupondii
dupondius
duppies
duppy
dura
durable
durables
durably
dural
duramen
durance
duras
duration
durative
durbar
durbars
duress

durgon
durgons
durian
durians
duricrust
during
durn
durned
durning
durns
durra
durras
durrie
durries
durst
durum
durzi
durzis
dusk
dusked
duskier
duskiest
duskily
duskiness
dusking
dusks
dusky
dust
dustball
dustballs
dustbin
dustbins
dustcart
dustcarts
dustcoat
dustcoats
dusted
duster
dusters
dustheap
dustheaps
dustier
dustiest
dustily
dustiness
dusting
dustless
dustman
dustmen
dustoor

dustoors
dustpan
dustpans
dusts
dusty
dutch
duteous
duteously
dutiable
duties
dutiful
dutifully
duty
duumvir
duumvirs
duvet
duvets
dux
duxelles

D W

dwaal
dwaals
dwale
dwam
dwams
dwarf
dwarfed
dwarfing
dwarfish
dwarfism
dwarfs
dwarves
dweeb
dweebish
dweebs
dweeby
dwell
dwelled
dweller
dwellers
dwelling
dwellings
dwells
dwelt
dwindle
dwindled
dwindles
dwindling

D Y

dyad
dyadic
dyads
dyarchies
dyarchy
dybbuk
dybbukim
dybbuks
dye
dyeable
dyed
dyeing
dyeline
dyelines
dyer
dyers
dyes
dyestuff
dyestuffs
dying
dyke
dyked
dykes
dykey
dyking
dynamic
dynamical
dynamics
dynamise
dynamised
dynamises
dynamism
dynamist
dynamists
dynamite
dynamited
dynamiter
dynamites
dynamize
dynamized
dynamizes
dynamo
dynamos
dynast
dynastic
dynasties
dynasts
dynasty

dyne
dynes
dyno
dynode
dynodes
dynoed
dynoing
dynos
dyscrasia
dyscrasic
dysentery
dysgenic
dyslalia
dyslectic
dyslexia
dyslexic
dyslexics
dyspepsia
dyspeptic
dysphagia
dysphasia
dysphasic
dysphonia
dysphoria
dysphoric
dysplasia
dyspnea
dyspnoea
dyspnoeic
dyspraxia
dysthymia
dysthymic
dystocia
dystonia
dystonic
dystopia
dystopian
dystopias
dystrophy
dysuria
dytiscid
dytiscids

D Z

dzho
dzhos
dzo
dzos

E

E A

each
eager
eagerly
eagerness
eagle
eagled
eagles
eaglet
eaglets
eagling
eagre
eagres
ear
earache
earaches
earbash
earbashed
earbasher
earbashes
eardrum
eardrums
eared
earful
earfuls
earhole
earholes
earl
earldom
earldoms
earless
earlier
earlies
earliest
earliness
earlock
earlocks
earls
early
earmark
earmarked
earmarks

earmuffs
earn
earned
earner
earners
earnest
earnestly
earning
earnings
earns
earphone
earphones
earpiece
earpieces
earplug
earplugs
earring
earrings
ears
earshot
earth
earthed
earthen
earthier
earthiest
earthily
earthing
earthlier
earthling
earthly
earthnut
earthnuts
earths
earthstar
earthward
earthwork
earthworm
earthy
earwax
earwig
earwigs
ease

eased
easeful
easel
easels
easement
easements
easer
easers
eases
easier
easiest
easily
easiness
easing
east
eastbound
easterly
eastern
easterner
easting
eastings
eastward
eastwards
easy
eat
eatable
eatables
eaten
eater
eateries
eaters
eatery
eating
eats
eaves
eavesdrop

E B

ebb
ebbed
ebbing
ebbs

ebon
ebonies
ebonise
ebonised
ebonises
ebonising
ebonite
ebonize
ebonized
ebonizes
ebonizing
ebony
ebullient

E C

ecad
ecads
écarté
ecbolic
eccentric
ecclesial
eccrine
ecdysial
ecdysiast
ecdysis
ecdysone
échappé
echelon
echeloned
echelons
echeveria
echidna
echidnas
echinacea
echinoid
echinoids
echinus
echinuses
echiuran
echiurans
echiuroid
echo

echoed
echoer
echoers
echoes
echoey
echogram
echograms
echograph
echoic
echoing
echolalia
echoless
echovirus
echt
eclair
eclairs
eclampsia
eclamptic
éclat
eclectic
eclipse
eclipsed
eclipses
eclipsing
ecliptic
ecliptics
eclogite
eclogue
eclogues
eclose
eclosed
ecloses
eclosing
eclosion
ecocide
ecocline
ecoclines
ecologist
ecology
economic
economics
economies

economise
economism
economist
economize
economy
écorché
écorchés
ecosphere
ecossaise
ecosystem
ecotage
ecotonal
ecotone
ecotones
ecotour
ecotours
ecotype
ecotypes
ecru
ecstasies
ecstasise
ecstasize
ecstasy
ecstatic
ecstatics
ectoderm
ectoderms
ectogene
ectogenes
ectomorph
ectopic
ectopics
ectoplasm
ectoproct
ectotherm
ectropion
ecu
ecumenism
ecus
eczema

E D

edacious
edacities
edacity
edaphic
eddied
eddies
eddo

eddoes
eddy
eddying
edelweiss
edema
edentate
edentates
edge
edged
edgeless
edger
edgers
edges
edgeways
edgewise
edgier
edgiest
edgily
edginess
edging
edgings
edgy
edh
edhs
edibility
edible
edibles
edict
edictal
edicts
edifice
edifices
edified
edifies
edify
edifying
edit
editable
edited
editing
edition
editions
editor
editorial
editors
editress
editrice
editrices
editrix
edits

educable
educate
educated
educates
educating
education
educative
educator
educators
educe
educed
educes
educible
educing
eduction

E E

ee
eejit
eejits
eek
eel
eelgrass
eelpout
eelpouts
eels
eelworm
eelworms
eely
eensy
eerie
eerier
eeriest
eerily
eeriness

E F

eff
effable
efface
effaced
effaces
effacing
effect
effected
effecting
effective
effector

effectors
effects
effectual
effendi
effendis
efferent
effete
efficacy
efficient
effigies
effigy
effing
effluence
effluent
effluents
effluvia
effluvium
efflux
effluxes
effluxion
effort
effortful
efforts
effs
effulgent
effuse
effused
effuses
effusing
effusion
effusions
effusive
eft
efts

E G

egad
egg
eggar
eggars
egged
egger
egghead
eggheads
eggier
eggiest
egging
eggless
eggplant

eggplants
eggs
eggshell
eggshells
eggy
eglantine
ego
egoism
egoist
egoistic
egoists
egoless
egomania
egomaniac
egos
egotise
egotised
egotises
egotising
egotism
egotist
egotistic
egotists
egotize
egotized
egotizes
egotizing
egregious
egress
egressed
egresses
egressing
egressive
egret
egrets

E H

eh

E I

eider
eiderdown
eiders
eidetic
eidola
eidolon
eidolons
eidos

eight
eighteen
eightfold
eighth
eighthly
eighthman
eighthmen
eighties
eightieth
eights
eightsome
eighty
eina
einas
einkorn
eirenic
eirenicon
eirenics
either
eiusdem

E J

ejaculate
eject
ejecta
ejected
ejecting
ejection
ejections
ejective
ejectment
ejector
ejectors
ejects
ejido
ejidos

E K

ekdam
eke
eked
ekes
eking
ekka
ekkas

E L

elaborate
elaichi

elan
eland
elands
elapse
elapsed
elapses
elapsing
elasipod
elasipods
elastane
elastase
elastic
elastin
elastomer
elate
elated
elatedly
elates
elating
elation
elbow
elbowed
elbowing
elbows
eld
elder
elderly
elders
eldership
eldest
eldorado
eldorados
eldritch
elect
electable
elected
electing
election
elections
elective
electives
elector
electoral
electors
electress
electret
electrets
electric
electrics
electrify

electro
electrode
electron
electrons
electros
electrum
elects
electuary
elegance
elegant
elegantly
elegiac
elegiacs
elegies
elegise
elegised
elegises
elegising
elegist
elegists
elegize
elegized
elegizes
elegizing
elegy
element
elemental
elements
elemi
elenchi
elenchus
elephant
elephants
elevate
elevated
elevates
elevating
elevation
elevator
elevators
elevatory
eleven
elevenses
eleventh
elevon
elevons
elf
elfin
elfish
elicit

elicited
eliciting
elicitor
elicitors
elicits
elide
elided
elides
eliding
eligible
eligibly
eliminate
elision
elisions
elite
elites
elitism
elitist
elitists
elixir
elixirs
elk
elks
ell
ellipse
ellipses
ellipsis
ellipsoid
elliptic
ells
elm
elms
elmy
elocution
elodea
elongate
elongated
elongates
elope
eloped
elopement
eloper
elopers
elopes
eloping
eloquence
eloquent
else
elsewhere
eluant

eluants
eluate
eluates
elucidate
elude
eluded
eludes
eluding
eluent
elusion
elusive
elusively
elute
eluted
elutes
eluting
elution
elutriate
elvan
elven
elver
elvers
elves
elvish
elytra
elytron

E M

em
emaciated
emanate
emanated
emanates
emanating
emanation
embalm
embalmed
embalmer
embalmers
embalming
embalms
embank
embanked
embanking
embanks
embargo
embargoed
embargoes
embark

embarked	embossers	emersed	emotively	emptied
embarking	embosses	emersion	emotivism	emptier
embarks	embossing	emery	emotivist	empties
embarrass	embowed	emesis	emotivity	emptiest
embassage	embowel	emetic	empanada	emptily
embassies	embowels	emetics	empanadas	emptiness
embassy	embower	emetine	empanel	empty
embattle	embowered	emic	empaneled	emptying
embattled	embowers	emigrant	empanels	empurple
embattles	embrace	emigrants	empath	empurpled
embay	embraced	emigrate	empathic	empurples
embayed	embracer	emigrated	empathise	empyema
embaying	embracers	emigrates	empathize	empyreal
embayment	embraces	émigré	empaths	empyrean
embays	embracing	émigrés	empathy	ems
embed	embrasure	eminence	empennage	emu
embedded	embrittle	eminences	emperor	emulate
embedding	embroider	eminent	emperors	emulated
embedment	embroil	eminently	emphases	emulates
embeds	embroiled	emir	emphasis	emulating
embellish	embroils	emirate	emphasise	emulation
ember	embryo	emirates	emphasize	emulative
embers	embryonal	emirs	emphatic	emulator
embezzle	embryonic	emissary	emphysema	emulators
embezzled	embryos	emission	empire	emulous
embezzler	embus	emissions	empires	emulously
embezzles	embused	emissive	empiric	emulsify
embitter	embuses	emit	empirical	emulsion
embitters	embusing	emits	emplane	emulsions
emblazon	embussed	emitted	emplaned	emulsive
emblazons	embussing	emitter	emplanes	emus
emblem	emcee	emitters	emplaning	
emblems	emceed	emitting	employ	
embodied	emceeing	emmer	employed	E N
embodies	emcees	emmet	employee	
embody	emend	emmets	employees	en
embodying	emended	emollient	employer	enable
embolden	emending	emolument	employers	enabled
emboldens	emends	emote	employing	enabler
emboli	emerald	emoted	employs	enablers
embolic	emeralds	emoter	empolder	enables
embolism	emerge	emoters	empolders	enabling
embolisms	emerged	emotes	emporia	enact
embolus	emergence	emoticon	emporium	enactable
embosom	emergency	emoticons	emporiums	enacted
embosomed	emergent	emoting	empower	enacting
embosoms	emerges	emotion	empowered	enaction
emboss	emerging	emotional	empowers	enactions
embossed	emeritus	emotions	empress	enactive
embosser	emerse	emotive	empresses	enactment
				enactor

enactors	encipher	endear	endoscope	enervate
enacts	enciphers	endeared	endoscopy	enervated
enamel	encircle	endearing	endosperm	enervates
enameled	encircled	endears	endospore	enfeeble
enameling	encircles	endeavor	endotherm	enfeebled
enamelled	enclasp	endeavors	endotoxin	enfeebles
enameller	enclasped	endeavour	endow	enfeoff
enamels	enclasps	ended	endowed	enfeoffed
enamor	enclave	endemic	endower	enfeoffs
enamored	enclaves	endemics	endowers	enfetter
enamoring	enclitic	endemism	endowing	enfetters
enamors	enclitics	endgame	endowment	enfevered
enamour	enclose	endgames	endows	enfilade
enamoured	enclosed	endgate	endpaper	enfiladed
enamours	encloses	endgates	endpapers	enfilades
enanthema	enclosing	ending	endplay	enflesh
enargite	enclosure	endings	endplayed	enfleshed
enation	encode	endite	endplays	enfleshes
enations	encoded	endites	endrin	enflurane
encage	encoder	endive	ends	enfold
encaged	encoders	endives	endue	enfolded
encages	encodes	endless	endued	enfolding
encaging	encoding	endlessly	endues	enfolds
encamp	encomia	endmember	enduing	enforce
encamped	encomiast	endmost	endurable	enforced
encamping	encomium	endnote	endurance	enforcer
encamps	encomiums	endnotes	endure	enforcers
encase	encompass	endocarp	endured	enforces
encased	encore	endocarps	endures	enforcing
encases	encored	endocrine	enduring	engage
encash	encores	endoderm	enduro	engagé
encashed	encoring	endoderms	enduros	engaged
encashes	encounter	endogamy	endways	engages
encashing	encourage	endogenic	endwise	engaging
encasing	encroach	endolymph	enema	engender
encaustic	encrust	endomorph	enemas	engenders
enceinte	encrusted	endophora	enemata	engine
enceintes	encrusts	endophyte	enemies	engined
enchain	encrypt	endoplasm	enemy	engineer
enchained	encrypted	endopod	energetic	engineers
enchains	encrypts	endopods	energies	enginery
enchant	encumber	endorphin	energise	engines
enchanted	encumbers	endorse	energised	engird
enchanter	encyst	endorsed	energises	engirded
enchants	encysted	endorsee	energize	engirding
enchase	encysting	endorsees	energized	engirdle
enchased	encysts	endorser	energizer	engirdled
enchases	end	endorsers	energizes	engirdles
enchasing	endanger	endorses	energumen	engirds
enchilada	endangers	endorsing	energy	englacial

englobe	enjoyably	enplane	ensiform	entangles
englobed	enjoyed	enplaned	ensign	entases
englobes	enjoyer	enplanes	ensigns	entasis
englobing	enjoyers	enplaning	ensilage	entelechy
engorge	enjoying	enprint	ensilaged	entellus
engorged	enjoyment	enprints	ensilages	entente
engorges	enjoys	enquire	ensile	ententes
engorging	enkindle	enquired	ensiled	enter
engraft	enkindled	enquirer	ensiles	enteral
engrafted	enkindles	enquirers	ensiling	enterally
engrafts	enlace	enquires	enslave	entered
engrailed	enlaced	enquiries	enslaved	enteric
engrain	enlaces	enquiring	enslaver	entering
engrained	enlacing	enquiry	enslavers	enteritis
engrains	enlarge	enrage	enslaves	enters
engram	enlarged	enraged	enslaving	entertain
engrams	enlarger	enrages	ensnare	enthalpy
engrave	enlargers	enraging	ensnared	enthral
engraved	enlarges	enrapt	ensnares	enthrall
engraver	enlarging	enrapture	ensnaring	enthralls
engravers	enlighten	enrich	ensnarl	enthrals
engraves	enlist	enriched	ensnarled	enthrone
engraving	enlisted	enriches	ensnarls	enthroned
engross	enlister	enriching	ensorcel	enthrones
engrossed	enlisters	enrobe	ensorcell	enthuse
engrosses	enlisting	enrobed	ensorcels	enthused
engulf	enlists	enrobes	ensoul	enthuses
engulfed	enliven	enrobing	ensouled	enthusing
engulfing	enlivened	enrol	ensouling	enthymeme
engulfs	enlivener	enroll	ensouls	entice
enhance	enlivens	enrolled	enstatite	enticed
enhanced	enmesh	enrollee	ensue	enticer
enhancer	enmeshed	enrollees	ensued	enticers
enhancers	enmeshes	enrolling	ensues	entices
enhances	enmeshing	enrolls	ensuing	enticing
enhancing	enmities	enrolment	ensure	entire
enigma	enmity	enrols	ensured	entirely
enigmas	ennead	ens	ensures	entirety
enigmatic	enneads	ensconce	ensuring	entisol
enisle	enneagram	ensconced	enswathe	entisols
enisled	ennoble	ensconces	enswathed	entities
enisles	ennobled	ensemble	enswathes	entitle
enisling	ennobles	ensembles	entail	entitled
enjambed	ennobling	ensheath	entailed	entitles
enjoin	ennui	ensheaths	entailing	entitling
enjoined	enology	enshrine	entails	entity
enjoining	enormity	enshrined	entameba	entomb
enjoins	enormous	enshrines	entamoeba	entombed
enjoy	enosis	enshroud	entangle	entombing
enjoyable	enough	enshrouds	entangled	entombs

entoproct
entoptic
entourage
entrails
entrain
entrained
entrains
entrammel
entrance
entranced
entrances
entrant
entrants
entrap
entrapped
entraps
entreat
entreated
entreats
entreaty
entrechat
entrecôte
entrée
entrées
entremets
entrench
entrepôt
entrepôts
entresol
entresols
entries
entrism
entrist
entropic
entropion
entropy
entrust
entrusted
entrusts
entry
entryism
entryist
entryists
entryway
entryways
entwine
entwined
entwines
entwining

enucleate
enumerate
enunciate
enure
enured
enures
enuresis
enuretic
enuring
enurn
enurned
enurning
enurns
envelop
envelope
enveloped
envelopes
envelops
envenom
envenomed
envenoms
enviable
enviably
envied
envier
enviers
envies
envious
enviously
environ
environed
environs
envisage
envisaged
envisages
envision
envisions
envoi
envois
envoy
envoys
envy
envying
enwrap
enwrapped
enwraps
enwreathe
enzootic
enzymatic
enzyme

enzymes
enzymic

E O

eohippus
eolian
eolith
eoliths
eon
eons
eosin

E P

epact
eparch
eparchies
eparchs
eparchy
épater
epaulet
epaulets
epaulette
epaxial
épée
épéeist
épéeists
épées
ependyma
ependymal
epergne
epergnes
ephah
ephahs
ephebe
ephebes
ephebic
ephedra
ephedras
ephedrine
ephemera
ephemeral
ephemeris
ephod
ephods
ephor
ephorate
ephorates
ephors

ephyra
ephyrae
epiblast
epiblasts
epic
epical
epically
epicedia
epicedian
epicedium
epicene
epicenes
epicenter
epicentre
epicormic
epicotyl
epicotyls
epicritic
epics
epicure
epicurean
epicures
epicurism
epicycle
epicycles
epicyclic
epidemic
epidemics
epidermal
epidermic
epidermis
epidote
epidural
epidurals
epifauna
epifaunal
epigeal
epigene
epigone
epigones
epigoni
epigram
epigrams
epigraph
epigraphs
epigraphy
epigynies
epigynous
epigyny
epilate

epilated
epilates
epilating
epilation
epilator
epilators
epilepsy
epileptic
epilimnia
epilithic
epilog
epilogs
epilogue
epilogues
epimedium
epimer
epimera
epimeric
epimerise
epimerism
epimerize
epimeron
epimerons
epimers
epimysium
epinician
epiphanic
epiphany
epiphora
epiphoras
epiphyses
epiphysis
epiphytal
epiphyte
epiphytes
epiphytic
episcopal
episcope
episcopes
episode
episodes
episodic
episome
episomes
epistasis
epistatic
epistaxis
epistemic
episterna
epistle

epistles
epistyle
epistyles
epitaph
epitaphs
epitaxial
epitaxy
epithelia
epithet
epithetic
epithets
epitome
epitomes
epitomise
epitomist
epitomize
epitope
epitopes
epizoa
epizoic
epizoite
epizoites
epizoon
epizootic
epoch
epochal
epochs
epode
epodes
eponym
eponymous
eponyms
epoxide
epoxides
epoxied
epoxies
epoxy
epoxying
epsilon
epsilons
epyllia
epyllion

E Q

equable
equably
equal
equaled
equaling

equalise
equalised
equaliser
equalises
equality
equalize
equalized
equalizer
equalizes
equalled
equalling
equally
equals
equant
equants
equatable
equate
equated
equates
equating
equation
equations
equative
equator
equators
equerries
equerry
eques
equid
equids
equifinal
equine
equines
equinox
equinoxes
equip
equipage
equipment
equipoise
equipped
equipper
equippers
equipping
equips
equiseta
equisetum
equitable
equitably
equitant
equites

equities
equity
equivocal
equivoke
equivokes
equivoque

E R

er
era
eradicant
eradicate
eras
erasable
erase
erased
eraser
erasers
erases
erasing
erasure
erasures
erbium
ere
erect
erectable
erected
erectile
erecting
erection
erections
erectly
erectness
erector
erectors
erects
eremite
eremites
eremitic
erethism
erewhile
erf
erfs
erg
ergative
ergatives
ergo
ergodic
ergometer

ergonomic
ergot
ergotism
ergots
ergs
erhu
erhus
erica
ericas
erigeron
erigerons
eristic
eristics
erk
erks
ermine
ermined
ermines
erminois
erne
ernes
erode
eroded
erodes
erodible
eroding
erogenous
erosion
erosional
erosions
erosive
erotic
erotica
eroticise
eroticism
eroticize
erotism
erotology
err
errancies
errancy
errand
errands
errant
errantry
errata
erratic
erratum
erred
erring

erroneous
error
errorless
errors
errs
ersatz
erst
erstwhile
erudite
eruditely
erudition
erupt
erupted
erupting
eruption
eruptions
eruptive
erupts
eruv
eruvim
erven
eryngium
eryngiums
eryngo
eryngoes
eryngos
erythema
erythemal
erythrism
erythroid

E S

escalade
escalades
escalate
escalated
escalates
escalator
escallop
escallops
escalope
escalopes
escapable
escapade
escapades
escape
escaped
escapee
escapees

escaper
escapers
escapes
escaping
escapism
escapist
escapists
escargot
escargots
escarole
eschar
eschars
eschaton
escheat
escheated
escheats
eschew
eschewal
eschewed
eschewing
eschews
escolar
escolars
escort
escorted
escorting
escorts
escrow
escrowed
escrowing
escrows
escudo
escudos
esculent
esculents
eserine
esker
eskers
esophagus
esoteric
esoterica
espada
espalier
espaliers
esparto
espartos
especial
espial
espied
espies

espionage
esplanade
espousal
espousals
espouse
espoused
espouser
espousers
espouses
espousing
espresso
espressos
esprit
espy
espying
esquire
esquires
ess
essay
essayed
essaying
essayist
essayists
essays
esse
essence
essences
essential
esses
est
establish
estaminet
estancia
estancias
estate
estates
esteem
esteemed
esteeming
esteems
ester
esterase
esterases
esterify
esters
esthete
esthetes
esthetic
esthetics
estimable

estimably
estimate
estimated
estimates
estimator
estival
estivate
estivated
estivates
estoile
estoiles
estop
estopped
estoppel
estopping
estops
estovers
estradiol
estrange
estranged
estranges
estreat
estreated
estreats
estriol
estrogen
estrogens
estrone
estrus
estuarial
estuaries
estuarine
estuary
estufa
estufas
esurient

E T

eta
etagere
etageres
etalon
etalons
etas
etcetera
etceteras
etch
etchant
etchants

etched
etcher
etchers
etches
etching
etchings
eternal
eternally
eternise
eternised
eternises
eternity
eternize
eternized
eternizes
eth
ethanal
ethane
ethanoate
ethanol
ethene
ether
ethereal
etherial
etheric
etherise
etherised
etherises
etherize
etherized
etherizes
ethers
ethic
ethical
ethically
ethicist
ethicists
ethics
ethmoid
ethmoidal
ethmoids
ethnic
ethnicity
ethnics
ethnocide
ethnology
ethogram
ethograms
ethology
ethos

eths
ethyl
ethylene
ethyne
etic
etics
etiolated
etiology
etiquette
étouffée
étouffées
etrier
etriers
étude
études
etui
etuis
etyma
etymology
etymon
etymons

E U

eucalypt
eucalypti
eucaryote
euchre
euchred
euchres
euchring
eucrite
eucryphia
eudemonic
eugenic
eugenics
eugenist
eugenists
eugenol
euglena
euglenas
euglenoid
euhedral
eukaryote
eulachon
eulachons
eulogia
eulogies
eulogise
eulogised

eulogises
eulogist
eulogists
eulogium
eulogiums
eulogize
eulogized
eulogizes
eulogy
eunuch
eunuchoid
eunuchs
euonymus
eupeptic
euphemise
euphemism
euphemize
euphonic
euphonies
euphonise
euphonium
euphonize
euphony
euphorbia
euphoria
euphoric
euphrasia
euphuism
euphuist
euphuists
eureka
eurhythmy
euro
europium
euros
euryapsid
eurythmy
eurytopic
eusocial
eusol
eustasy
eustatic
eutectic
eutectoid
euthanise
euthanize
eutherian
euthyroid
eutrophic

E V

evacuant
evacuants
evacuate
evacuated
evacuates
evacuee
evacuees
evadable
evade
evaded
evader
evaders
evades
evading
evaginate
evaluate
evaluated
evaluates
evaluator
evanesce
evanesced
evanesces
evangel
evangelic
evangels
evaporate
evaporite
evasion
evasions
evasive
evasively
eve
evection
even
evened
evening
eveninger
evenings
evenly
evenness
evens
evensong
event
eventer
eventers
eventful
eventide
eventides

eventing
eventive
eventless
events
eventual
eventuate
ever
evergreen
evermore
eversible
eversion
eversions
evert
everted
everting
everts
every
everybody
everyday
everyone
eves
evict
evicted
evicting
eviction
evictions
evictor
evictors
evicts
evidence
evidenced
evidences
evident
evidently
evil
evilly
evilness
evils
evince
evinced
evinces
evincing
eviternal
evocation
evocative
evoke
evoked
evoker
evokers
evokes

evoking
evolute
evolutes
evolution
evolutive
evolvable
evolve
evolved
evolves
evolving
evzone
evzones

E W

ewe
ewer
ewers
ewes

E X

ex
exact
exacta
exactable
exacted
exacting
exaction
exactions
exactly
exactness
exactor
exactors
exacts
exalt
exalté
exalted
exaltedly
exaltés
exalting
exalts
exam
examen
examens
examine
examined
examinee
examinees
examiner
examiners

examines
examining
example
exampled
examples
exams
exanthema
exarch
exarchate
exarchs
excavate
excavated
excavates
excavator
exceed
exceeded
exceeding
exceeds
excel
excelled
excellent
excelling
excels
excelsior
excentric
except
excepted
excepting
exception
excepts
excerpt
excerpted
excerpts
excess
excesses
excessive
exchange
exchanged
exchanger
exchanges
exchequer
excimer
excimers
excipient
excise
excised
exciseman
excisemen
excises
excising

excision	excuses	exergues	existence	exotoxins
excisions	excusing	exert	existent	expand
excitable	exeat	exerted	existing	expanded
excitably	exeats	exerting	exists	expander
excitant	exec	exertion	exit	expanders
excitants	execrable	exertions	exited	expanding
excite	execrably	exerts	exiting	expands
excited	execrate	exes	exits	expanse
excitedly	execrated	exeunt	exocarp	expanses
exciter	execrates	exfoliant	exocarps	expansile
exciters	execs	exfoliate	exocrine	expansion
excites	executant	exhalable	exodermis	expansive
exciting	execute	exhale	exodus	expat
exciton	executed	exhaled	exoduses	expatiate
excitons	executes	exhales	exoenzyme	expats
exclaim	executing	exhaling	exogamous	expect
exclaimed	execution	exhaust	exogamy	expectant
exclaims	executive	exhausted	exogenic	expected
exclave	executor	exhauster	exogenous	expecting
exclaves	executors	exhausts	exon	expects
exclosure	executory	exhibit	exonerate	expedient
exclude	executrix	exhibited	exons	expedite
excluded	exedra	exhibitor	exophora	expedited
excluder	exedrae	exhibits	exophoric	expediter
excluders	exegeses	exhort	exopod	expedites
excludes	exegesis	exhorted	exopodite	expeditor
excluding	exegete	exhorter	exopods	expel
exclusion	exegetes	exhorters	exorcise	expelled
exclusive	exegetic	exhorting	exorcised	expellee
excoriate	exempla	exhorts	exorcises	expellees
excrement	exemplar	exhume	exorcism	expeller
excreta	exemplars	exhumed	exorcisms	expellers
excrete	exemplary	exhumes	exorcist	expelling
excreted	exemplify	exhuming	exorcists	expels
excreter	exemplum	exigence	exorcize	expend
excreters	exempt	exigences	exorcized	expended
excretes	exempted	exigency	exorcizes	expending
excreting	exempting	exigent	exordia	expends
excretion	exemption	exigible	exordial	expense
excretive	exempts	exiguity	exordium	expensed
excretory	exequatur	exiguous	exordiums	expenses
exculpate	exequies	exile	exosphere	expensing
excurrent	exequy	exiled	exostoses	expensive
excursion	exercise	exiles	exostosis	expert
excursive	exercised	exilic	exoteric	expertise
excursus	exerciser	exiling	exotic	expertize
excusable	exercises	exine	exotica	expertly
excusably	exercycle	exines	exoticism	experts
excuse	exergonic	exist	exotics	expiable
excused	exergue	existed	exotoxin	expiate

expiated	expose	extensive	extropy	eyecups
expiates	exposé	extensor	extrorse	eyed
expiating	exposed	extensors	extrovert	eyeful
expiation	exposer	extent	extrude	eyefuls
expiator	exposers	extents	extruded	eyeglass
expiators	exposes	extenuate	extrudes	eyehole
expiatory	exposés	exterior	extruding	eyeholes
expire	exposing	exteriors	extrusile	eyeing
expired	expositor	extern	extrusion	eyelash
expires	exposure	external	extrusive	eyelashes
expiring	exposures	externals	exuberant	eyeless
expiry	expound	externs	exudate	eyelet
explain	expounded	extinct	exudates	eyeleted
explained	expounder	extirpate	exudation	eyeleting
explainer	expounds	extol	exudative	eyelets
explains	express	extolled	exude	eyelid
explanans	expressed	extoller	exuded	eyelids
explant	expresser	extollers	exudes	eyeline
explanted	expresses	extolling	exuding	eyeliner
explants	expressly	extolment	exult	eyeliners
expletive	expresso	extols	exultancy	eyelines
explicans	expressos	extort	exultant	eyepatch
explicate	expulsion	extorted	exulted	eyepiece
explicit	expulsive	extorter	exulting	eyepieces
explode	expunge	extorters	exults	eyes
exploded	expunged	extorting	exurb	eyeshade
exploder	expunger	extortion	exurban	eyeshades
exploders	expungers	extortive	exurbia	eyeshadow
explodes	expunges	extorts	exurbs	eyeshot
exploding	expunging	extra	exuviae	eyesight
exploit	expurgate	extract	exuvial	eyesore
exploited	exquisite	extracted	exuviate	eyesores
exploiter	exsert	extractor	exuviated	eyespot
exploits	exserted	extracts	exuviates	eyespots
explore	exserting	extradite		eyestalk
explored	exserts	extrados	E Y	eyestalks
explorer	exsolve	extras		eyestripe
explorers	exsolved	extravert	eyas	eyewash
explores	exsolves	extrema	eyasses	eyewater
exploring	exsolving	extreme	eye	eyewear
explosion	extant	extremely	eyeball	eying
explosive	extempore	extremes	eyeballed	eyot
exponent	extend	extremism	eyeballs	eyots
exponents	extended	extremist	eyebath	eyra
export	extender	extremity	eyebaths	eyras
exported	extenders	extremum	eyeblack	eyre
exporter	extending	extremums	eyebright	eyres
exporters	extends	extricate	eyebrow	eyrie
exporting	extensile	extrinsic	eyebrows	eyries
exports	extension	extropian	eyecup	eyrir

FA

fa
fab
fabbo
fabby
fable
fabled
fabler
fablers
fables
fabliau
fabliaux
fabling
fabric
fabricate
fabrics
fabulate
fabulated
fabulates
fabulator
fabulist
fabulists
fabulous
facade
facades
face
faceache
faceaches
facecloth
faced
faceless
facelift
facelifts
faceplate
facer
facers
faces
facet
faceted
facetiae
facetious
facets

facia
facial
facially
facials
facias
facies
facile
facilely
facility
facing
facings
facsimile
fact
facta
facticity
faction
factional
factions
factious
factitive
factive
factoid
factoids
factor
factorage
factored
factorial
factories
factoring
factorise
factorize
factors
factory
factotum
factotums
facts
factual
factually
factum
factums
facture
factures

facula
faculae
facular
faculties
faculty
fad
faddier
faddiest
faddily
faddiness
faddish
faddishly
faddism
faddist
faddists
faddy
fade
faded
fadeless
fader
faders
fades
fadge
fadges
fading
fado
fados
fads
faecal
faeces
faerie
faery
faff
faffed
faffing
faffs
fag
fagged
fagging
faggot
faggoted
faggoting

faggots
faggoty
faggy
fagot
fagoted
fagoting
fagots
fags
fah
fahlerz
fahs
faience
fail
failed
failing
failings
faille
fails
failure
failures
fain
fainéant
fainéants
faint
fainted
fainter
faintest
fainting
faintly
faintness
faints
fair
faired
fairer
fairest
fairies
fairing
fairings
fairish
fairlead
fairleads
fairly

fairness
fairs
fairwater
fairway
fairways
fairy
fairyland
fairylike
faisandé
faith
faithful
faithless
faiths
fajitas
fake
faked
faker
fakeries
fakers
fakery
fakes
fakie
fakies
faking
fakir
fakirs
falafel
falcate
falchion
falchions
falciform
falcon
falconer
falconers
falconet
falconets
falconry
falcons
falderal
falderals
faldstool
fale

fales	families	fanning	faring	fasciated
fall	familist	fanny	farl	fascicle
fallacies	famille	fannying	farls	fascicled
fallacy	family	fans	farm	fascicles
fallaway	famine	fantail	farmable	fascicule
fallaways	famines	fantails	farman	fasciitis
fallback	famished	fantasia	farmans	fascinate
fallbacks	famous	fantasias	farmed	fascine
fallen	famously	fantasied	farmer	fascines
faller	famuli	fantasies	farmers	fascism
fallers	famulus	fantasise	farmhand	fascist
fallfish	fan	fantasist	farmhands	fascistic
fallible	fanatic	fantasize	farmhouse	fascists
fallibly	fanatical	fantast	farming	fash
falling	fanatics	fantastic	farmland	fashed
fallopian	fanciable	fantasts	farmlands	fashes
fallout	fancied	fantasy	farms	fashing
fallow	fancier	fantod	farmstead	fashion
fallowed	fanciers	fantods	farmyard	fashioned
fallowing	fancies	fanzine	farmyards	fashioner
fallows	fanciest	fanzines	faro	fashions
falls	fanciful	faquir	farouche	fast
false	fancily	faquirs	farrago	fastback
falsehood	fanciness	far	farragoes	fastbacks
falsely	fancy	farad	farragos	fastball
falseness	fancying	faradaic	farrier	fastballs
falser	fandangle	faraday	farriers	fasted
falsest	fandango	faradays	farriery	fasten
falsetto	fandangos	faradic	farrow	fastened
falsettos	fandom	farads	farrowed	fastener
falsework	fane	farandole	farrowing	fasteners
falsies	fanes	farang	farrows	fastening
falsified	fanfare	farangs	farruca	fastens
falsifies	fanfares	faraway	farrucas	faster
falsify	fang	farce	farse	fastest
falsities	fanged	farces	fart	fasting
falsity	fangless	farceur	farted	fastness
falter	fango	farceurs	farther	fasts
faltered	fangs	farcical	farthest	fat
falterer	fankle	farcy	farthing	fatal
falterers	fankled	fardel	farthings	fatalism
faltering	fankles	fardels	farting	fatalist
falters	fankling	fare	fartlek	fatalists
fame	fanlight	fared	farts	fatality
famed	fanlights	fares	fas	fatally
familia	fanned	farewell	fasces	fatback
familiae	fanner	farewells	fascia	fatbacks
familial	fanners	farfalle	fasciae	fate
familiar	fannied	farina	fascial	fated
familiars	fannies	farinas	fascias	fateful

fatefully
fates
fathead
fatheads
father
fathered
fathering
fatherly
fathers
fathom
fathomed
fathoming
fathoms
fatigable
fatigue
fatigued
fatigues
fatiguing
fatless
fatling
fatlings
fatly
fatness
fats
fatso
fatsoes
fatstock
fatted
fatten
fattened
fattening
fattens
fatter
fattest
fattier
fatties
fattiest
fattiness
fatting
fattish
fattism
fattist
fattists
fatty
fatuities
fatuity
fatuous
fatuously
fatwa
fatwas

faubourg
faubourgs
fauces
faucet
faucets
faucial
faugh
fault
faulted
faultier
faultiest
faultily
faulting
faultless
faults
faulty
faun
fauna
faunal
faunas
faunistic
fauns
fauteuil
fauteuils
fauvism
fauvist
fauvists
faux
fave
favela
favelas
faves
favor
favorable
favored
favoring
favorite
favorites
favors
favour
favoured
favourer
favourers
favouring
favourite
favours
fawn
fawned
fawning
fawningly

fawns
fax
faxed
faxes
faxing
fay
fayalite
fayre
fayres
fays
faze
fazed
fazenda
fazendas
fazes
fazing

F E

fealties
fealty
fear
feared
fearful
fearfully
fearing
fearless
fears
fearsome
feart
feasible
feasibly
feast
feasted
feaster
feasters
feasting
feasts
feat
feather
feathered
feathers
feathery
feats
feature
featured
features
featuring
febrifuge
febrile

febrility
feces
feckless
feculence
feculent
fecund
fecundate
fecundity
fed
fedayeen
federal
federally
federate
federated
federates
fedora
fedoras
fee
feeb
feeble
feebler
feeblest
feebly
feebs
feed
feedback
feeder
feeders
feeding
feedlot
feedlots
feeds
feedstock
feedstuff
feeing
feel
feeler
feelers
feeling
feelingly
feelings
feels
fees
feet
feign
feigned
feigning
feigns
feijoa
feijoada

feijoas
feint
feinted
feinting
feints
feistier
feistiest
feistily
feisty
felafel
feldspar
felicific
felicity
felid
felids
feline
felines
felinity
fell
fella
fellah
fellahin
fellahs
fellate
fellated
fellates
fellating
fellatio
fellator
fellators
felled
feller
fellers
fellies
felling
felloes
fellow
fellows
fells
felon
felonies
felonious
felons
felony
felsic
felspar
felt
felted
felting
felts

felty	fenland	ferret	festering	fetus
felucca	fenlands	ferreted	festers	fetuses
feluccas	fennec	ferreter	festival	feu
felwort	fennecs	ferreters	festivals	feud
felworts	fennel	ferreting	festive	feudal
fem	fenny	ferrets	festively	feudalise
female	fens	ferrety	festivity	feudalism
females	fenugreek	ferriage	festoon	feudalist
feminal	feodaries	ferric	festooned	feudality
femineity	feodary	ferried	festoons	feudalize
feminine	feoffee	ferries	feta	feudally
feminines	feoffees	ferrite	fetal	feudatory
feminise	feoffment	ferritic	fetch	feuded
feminised	feoffor	ferritin	fetched	feuding
feminises	feoffors	ferrocene	fetcher	feudist
feminism	feral	ferrous	fetchers	feudists
feminist	ferberite	ferrule	fetches	feuds
feminists	feria	ferrules	fetching	feued
feminity	ferial	ferry	fête	feuing
feminize	ferias	ferrying	fêted	feus
feminized	feringhee	ferryman	fêtes	fever
feminizes	feringhi	ferrymen	fetich	fevered
femme	feringhis	fertile	fetiches	feverfew
femmes	fermata	fertilise	feticide	feverfews
femora	fermatas	fertility	fetid	fevering
femoral	ferment	fertilize	fetidly	feverish
fems	fermented	ferula	fetidness	feverous
femur	fermenter	ferulas	fêting	fevers
femurs	fermentor	ferule	fetish	few
fen	ferments	ferules	fetishes	fey
fenberry	fermi	fervency	fetishise	feyly
fence	fermion	fervent	fetishism	feyness
fenced	fermions	fervently	fetishist	fez
fenceless	fermium	fervid	fetishize	fezzed
fencer	fern	fervidly	fetlock	fezzes
fencerow	fernbird	fervor	fetlocks	
fencerows	fernbirds	fervour	fetor	F|I
fencers	fernbrake	fescue	fetors	
fences	ferneries	fescues	fetta	fiacre
fencible	fernery	fess	fetter	fiacres
fencibles	ferns	fesse	fettered	fiancé
fencing	ferny	fessed	fettering	fiancée
fend	ferocious	fesses	fetters	fiancées
fended	ferocity	fessing	fettle	fiancés
fender	ferox	festa	fettled	fiasco
fenders	feroxes	festal	fettler	fiascos
fending	ferrate	festally	fettlers	fiat
fends	ferrates	festas	fettles	fiats
fenestra	ferrel	fester	fettling	fib
fenestrae	ferrels	festered	fettucini	fibbed

fibber	fiddler	fiesta	filariae	fillis
fibbers	fiddlers	fiestas	filarial	fills
fibbing	fiddles	fife	filature	filly
fiber	fiddlier	fifed	filatures	film
fibers	fiddliest	fifer	filbert	filmed
fibre	fiddling	fifers	filberts	filmi
fibred	fiddly	fifes	filch	filmic
fibrefill	fideism	fifing	filched	filmier
fibreless	fideist	fifteen	filcher	filmiest
fibres	fideistic	fifteenth	filchers	filmily
fibril	fideists	fifth	filches	filminess
fibrillar	fidelity	fifthly	filching	filming
fibrils	fidget	fifties	file	films
fibrin	fidgeted	fiftieth	filé	filmset
fibrinoid	fidgeter	fifty	filed	filmsets
fibrinous	fidgeters	fiftyfold	filefish	filmstrip
fibro	fidgeting	fig	filer	filmy
fibroid	fidgets	figbird	filers	filo
fibroids	fidgety	figbirds	files	filopodia
fibroin	fids	figged	filet	filoselle
fibrolite	fiducial	figging	filets	filovirus
fibroma	fiduciary	fight	filial	fils
fibromas	fie	fightback	filially	filter
fibromata	fief	fighter	filiation	filtered
fibros	fiefdom	fighters	filibeg	filtering
fibrosis	fiefdoms	fighting	filibegs	filters
fibrotic	fiefs	fights	filicide	filth
fibrous	field	figment	filicides	filthier
fibrously	fielded	figments	filiform	filthiest
fibs	fielder	figs	filigree	filthily
fibula	fielders	figura	filigreed	filthy
fibulae	fieldfare	figurae	filing	filtrable
fibular	fielding	figural	filings	filtrate
fibulas	fields	figurant	fill	filtrated
fiche	fieldsman	figurante	filled	filtrates
fiches	fieldsmen	figure	filler	fimbria
fichu	fieldwork	figured	fillers	fimbriae
fichus	fiend	figures	fillet	fimbrial
fickle	fiendish	figurine	filleted	fimbriate
fickler	fiendlike	figurines	filleter	fin
ficklest	fiends	figuring	filleters	finagle
fickly	fierce	figwort	filleting	finagled
fictile	fiercely	figworts	fillets	finagler
fiction	fiercer	filabeg	fillies	finaglers
fictional	fiercest	filabegs	filling	finagles
fictive	fierier	filagree	fillings	finagling
ficus	fieriest	filagreed	fillip	final
fid	fierily	filament	filliped	finale
fiddle	fieriness	filaments	filliping	finales
fiddled	fiery	filaria	fillips	finalise

finalised	fingertip	firearms	firestorm	fishes
finalises	fingle	fireback	firethorn	fisheye
finalism	fingled	firebacks	firewall	fisheyes
finalist	fingles	fireball	firewalls	fishier
finalists	fingling	fireballs	firewater	fishiest
finality	finial	firebomb	fireweed	fishily
finalize	finials	firebombs	firewood	fishiness
finalized	finical	firebox	firework	fishing
finalizes	finically	fireboxes	fireworks	fishlike
finally	finicking	firebrand	firing	fishmeal
finals	finicky	firebrat	firings	fishnet
finance	fining	firebrats	firkin	fishplate
financed	finings	firebreak	firkins	fishtail
finances	finis	firebrick	firm	fishtails
financial	finish	firebug	firmament	fishway
financier	finished	firebugs	firman	fishways
financing	finisher	fireclay	firmans	fishwife
finback	finishers	firecrest	firmed	fishwives
finbacks	finishes	fired	firmer	fishy
finca	finishing	firedamp	firmest	fisk
fincas	finite	firedog	firming	fisks
finch	finitely	firedogs	firmly	fissile
finches	finitism	firedrake	firmness	fissility
find	finitist	firefight	firms	fission
findable	finitists	firefinch	firmware	fissioned
finder	finito	firefish	firn	fissions
finders	finitude	fireflies	firni	fissure
finding	fink	firefly	firry	fissured
findings	finked	fireguard	firs	fissures
finds	finking	firehall	first	fissuring
fine	finks	firehalls	firstborn	fist
fineable	finless	firehouse	firstling	fisted
fined	finnan	fireless	firstly	fistful
finely	finned	firelight	firsts	fistfuls
fineness	finnesko	firelock	firth	fisting
finer	finning	firelocks	firths	fists
fineries	finny	fireman	fisc	fistula
finery	fino	firemen	fiscal	fistulae
fines	finocchio	fireplace	fiscally	fistular
finesse	finos	fireplug	fiscs	fistulas
finessed	fins	fireplugs	fish	fistulous
finesses	fiord	firepower	fishbowl	fit
finessing	fiords	fireproof	fishbowls	fitch
finest	fioritura	firer	fished	fitché
finfoot	fioriture	firers	fisher	fitched
finfoots	fipple	fires	fisheries	fitches
finger	fipples	fireship	fisherman	fitchew
fingered	fir	fireships	fishermen	fitchews
fingering	fire	fireside	fishers	fitchy
fingers	firearm	firesides	fishery	fitful

fitfully
fitly
fitment
fitments
fitness
fits
fitted
fitter
fitters
fittest
fitting
fittingly
fittings
five
fivefold
fiver
fivers
fives
fix
fixable
fixate
fixated
fixates
fixating
fixation
fixations
fixative
fixatives
fixed
fixedly
fixedness
fixer
fixers
fixes
fixing
fixings
fixit
fixity
fixture
fixtures
fizgig
fizgigs
fizz
fizzed
fizzer
fizzers
fizzes
fizzier
fizziest
fizzily

fizziness
fizzing
fizzle
fizzled
fizzles
fizzling
fizzog
fizzogs
fizzy

F J

fjord
fjords

F L

flab
flabbier
flabbiest
flabbily
flabby
flaccid
flaccidly
flack
flacked
flackery
flacking
flacks
flacon
flacons
flag
flagella
flagellar
flagellum
flageolet
flagfish
flagged
flagger
flaggers
flagging
flagman
flagmen
flagon
flagons
flagpole
flagpoles
flagrancy
flagrant
flags

flagship
flagships
flagstaff
flagstone
flail
flailed
flailing
flails
flair
flak
flake
flaked
flakes
flakier
flakiest
flakily
flakiness
flaking
flaky
flam
flambé
flambeau
flambeaus
flambeaux
flambéed
flambéing
flambés
flame
flamed
flameless
flamen
flamenco
flamens
flameout
flameouts
flamer
flamers
flames
flamier
flamiest
flamines
flaming
flamingo
flamingos
flammable
flams
flamy
flan
flânerie
flâneur

flâneurs
flange
flanged
flanger
flangers
flanges
flanging
flank
flanked
flanker
flankers
flanking
flanks
flannel
flanneled
flannels
flans
flap
flapjack
flapjacks
flapped
flapper
flappers
flappier
flappiest
flapping
flappy
flaps
flapshell
flare
flared
flarepath
flares
flaring
flash
flashback
flashbulb
flashcard
flashcube
flashed
flasher
flashers
flashes
flashest
flashgun
flashguns
flashier
flashiest
flashily
flashing

flashings
flashover
flashy
flask
flasks
flat
flatbed
flatbeds
flatbill
flatbills
flatboat
flatboats
flatbread
flatbug
flatbugs
flatcar
flatcars
flatfeet
flatfish
flatfoot
flatfoots
flathead
flatheads
flatland
flatlands
flatlet
flatlets
flatline
flatlined
flatliner
flatlines
flatly
flatmate
flatmates
flatness
flats
flatted
flatten
flattened
flattener
flattens
flatter
flattered
flatterer
flatters
flattery
flattest
flattie
flatties
flatting

flattish	fleas	flesh	flickers	flirtier
flatty	fleawort	fleshed	flicking	flirtiest
flatulent	fleaworts	flesher	flicks	flirting
flatus	flèche	fleshers	flics	flirts
flatware	flèches	fleshes	flier	flirty
flatworm	flechette	fleshier	fliers	flit
flatworms	fleck	fleshiest	flies	flitch
flaunt	flecked	fleshing	flight	flitches
flaunted	flecking	fleshings	flighted	flits
flaunter	flecks	fleshless	flightier	flitted
flaunters	flection	fleshlier	flightily	flitter
flaunting	fled	fleshly	flighting	flittered
flaunts	fledge	fleshpots	flights	flitters
flaunty	fledged	fleshy	flighty	flitting
flautist	fledges	fletch	flimflam	flivver
flautists	fledging	fletched	flimflams	flivvers
flavin	fledgling	fletcher	flimsier	flixweed
flavins	flee	fletchers	flimsies	float
flavone	fleece	fletches	flimsiest	floatable
flavonoid	fleeced	fletching	flimsily	floated
flavor	fleeces	fleuron	flimsy	floatel
flavored	fleecier	fleurons	flinch	floatels
flavoring	fleeciest	fleury	flinched	floater
flavorous	fleecily	flew	flincher	floaters
flavors	fleecing	flews	flinchers	floating
flavour	fleecy	flex	flinches	floats
flavoured	fleeing	flexed	flinching	floaty
flavours	fleer	flexes	flinders	floc
flaw	fleered	flexible	fling	flocci
flawed	fleering	flexibly	flinger	floccose
flawless	fleers	flexile	flingers	floccule
flaws	flees	flexility	flinging	floccules
flax	fleet	flexing	flings	flocculi
flaxen	fleeted	flexion	flint	flocculus
flaxseed	fleeter	flexitime	flintier	floccus
flay	fleetest	flexo	flintiest	flock
flayed	fleeting	flexor	flintily	flocked
flayer	fleetly	flexors	flintlock	flockier
flayers	fleetness	flextime	flints	flockiest
flaying	fleets	flexuous	flinty	flocking
flays	flench	flexural	flip	flocks
flea	flenched	flexure	flippancy	flocky
fleabag	flenches	flexures	flippant	flocs
fleabags	flenching	flexwing	flipped	floe
fleabane	flense	flexwings	flipper	floes
fleabanes	flensed	flic	flippers	flog
fleadh	flenser	flick	flipping	flogged
fleadhs	flensers	flicked	flips	flogger
fleapit	flenses	flicker	flirt	floggers
fleapits	flensing	flickered	flirted	flogging

flogs	florist	flowery	flukier	flutier
flokati	floristic	flowing	flukiest	flutiest
flokatis	floristry	flowingly	flukily	fluting
flood	florists	flowmeter	flukiness	flutings
flooded	floruit	flown	fluking	flutist
floodgate	flory	flows	fluky	flutists
flooding	floss	flowsheet	flume	flutter
floodlit	flossed	flowstone	flumes	fluttered
floods	flosses	flu	flummery	flutterer
floor	flossier	flub	flummox	flutters
floored	flossiest	flubbed	flummoxed	fluttery
flooring	flossing	flubbing	flummoxes	fluty
floorings	flossy	flubs	flump	fluvial
floorpan	flotation	fluctuant	flumped	flux
floorpans	flotel	fluctuate	flumping	fluxed
floors	flotels	flue	flumps	fluxes
floosie	flotilla	fluellen	flung	fluxgate
floosies	flotillas	fluellens	flunk	fluxgates
floozie	flotsam	fluence	flunked	fluxing
floozies	flounce	fluency	flunkey	fluxion
floozy	flounced	fluent	flunkeys	fluxional
flop	flounces	fluently	flunkies	fluxions
flophouse	flouncier	flues	flunking	fly
flopped	flouncing	fluff	flunks	flyable
flopperoo	flouncy	fluffed	flunky	flyaway
floppier	flounder	fluffier	fluoresce	flyback
floppies	flounders	fluffiest	fluoride	flyblow
floppiest	flour	fluffily	fluorine	flyblown
floppily	floured	fluffing	fluorite	flybridge
flopping	flourier	fluffs	fluorosis	flyer
floppy	flouriest	flufftail	fluorspar	flyers
flops	flouring	fluffy	flurried	flyest
floptical	flourish	fluid	flurries	flying
flor	flours	fluidic	flurry	flyleaf
flora	floury	fluidics	flurrying	flyleaves
florae	flout	fluidise	flus	flyman
floral	flouted	fluidised	flush	flymen
florally	flouting	fluidises	flushed	flyness
floras	flouts	fluidity	flusher	flyover
floreat	flow	fluidize	flushers	flyovers
floret	flowed	fluidized	flushes	flypaper
florets	flower	fluidizes	flushing	flys
floriated	flowered	fluidly	flushness	flysch
florican	flowerer	fluidram	fluster	flysheet
floricans	flowerers	fluidrams	flustered	flysheets
florid	floweret	fluids	flusters	flyspeck
floridity	flowerets	fluke	flute	flyspecks
floridly	flowering	fluked	fluted	flytrap
florin	flowerpot	flukes	flutes	flytraps
florins	flowers	flukey	flutey	flyway

flyways	foes	folder	folly	footbath
flyweight	foetal	folderol	foment	footbaths
flywheel	foeticide	folderols	fomented	footbed
flywheels	foetid	folders	fomenter	footbeds
	foetus	folding	fomenters	footboard
F O	foetuses	folds	fomenting	footbrake
	fog	foley	foments	footed
foal	fogbound	folia	fomites	footer
foaled	fogbow	foliage	fond	footered
foaling	fogey	foliar	fondant	footering
foals	fogeydom	foliate	fondants	footers
foam	fogeyish	foliated	fonder	footfall
foamed	fogeyism	foliates	fondest	footfalls
foaming	fogeys	foliating	fondle	footgear
foamless	fogged	foliation	fondled	foothill
foams	foggier	folio	fondler	foothills
foamy	foggiest	folios	fondlers	foothold
fob	fogginess	foliose	fondles	footholds
fobbed	fogging	folium	fondling	footie
fobbing	foggy	folivore	fondly	footing
fobs	foghorn	folivores	fondness	footings
focaccia	foghorns	folivory	fondu	footle
focal	fogies	folk	fondue	footled
focalise	fogou	folkie	fondues	footles
focalised	fogous	folkier	font	footless
focalises	fogs	folkies	fontal	footling
focalize	fogy	folkiest	fontanel	footloose
focalized	fogyish	folkiness	fontanels	footman
focalizes	fogyism	folkish	fontina	footmark
foci	föhn	folklife	fonts	footmarks
focus	föhns	folklore	food	footmen
focused	foible	folkloric	foodie	footnote
focuser	foibles	folks	foodies	footnoted
focusers	foil	folksier	foods	footnotes
focuses	foiled	folksiest	foodstuff	footpad
focusing	foiling	folksy	foody	footpads
focussed	foilist	folkways	fool	footpath
focusser	foilists	folkweave	fooled	footpaths
focussers	foils	folky	foolery	footplate
focusses	foist	folles	foolhardy	footprint
focussing	foisted	follicle	fooling	footrest
fodder	foisting	follicles	foolish	footrests
foddered	foists	follies	foolishly	foots
foddering	folacin	follis	foolproof	footsie
fodders	folate	follow	fools	footslog
fodies	folates	followed	foolscap	footslogs
fody	fold	follower	foot	footsore
foe	foldable	followers	footage	footstalk
foehn	foldaway	following	football	footstep
foehns	folded	follows	footballs	footsteps

footstool	forbye	foredooms	fores	forfeits
footsure	force	foredune	foresail	forfend
footwall	forceable	foredunes	foresails	forfended
footwalls	forced	forefeet	foresaw	forfends
footway	forceful	forefend	foresee	forgather
footways	forcemeat	forefends	foreseen	forgave
footwear	forceps	forefoot	foreseer	forge
footwell	forcer	forefront	foreseers	forgeable
footwells	forcers	forego	foresees	forged
footwork	forces	foregoer	foresheet	forger
footy	forcible	foregoers	foreshock	forgeries
foozle	forcibly	foregoes	foreshore	forgers
foozled	forcing	foregoing	foreshow	forgery
foozles	ford	foregone	foreshown	forges
foozling	fordable	foregut	foreshows	forget
fop	forded	foreguts	foresight	forgetful
fopperies	fordid	forehand	foreskin	forgets
foppery	fording	forehands	foreskins	forgetter
foppish	fordless	forehead	forest	forging
foppishly	fordo	foreheads	forestall	forgive
fops	fordoes	forehock	forestay	forgiven
for	fordoing	forehocks	forestays	forgiver
fora	fordone	foreign	forested	forgivers
forage	fords	foreigner	forester	forgives
foraged	fore	foreknew	foresters	forgiving
forager	forearm	foreknow	foresting	forgo
foragers	forearmed	foreknown	forestry	forgoes
forages	forearms	foreknows	forests	forgoing
foraging	forebear	foreland	foretaste	forgone
foramen	forebears	forelands	foretell	forgot
foramina	forebode	forelock	foretells	forgotten
forastero	foreboded	forelocks	foretoken	forint
foray	forebodes	foreman	foretold	forints
forayed	forebrain	foremast	foretop	fork
forayer	forecabin	foremasts	foretops	forkball
forayers	forecast	foremen	forever	forkballs
foraying	forecasts	foremost	forewarn	forked
forays	forecheck	forename	forewarns	forkful
forb	foreclose	forenames	forewent	forkfuls
forbad	forecourt	forenoon	forewing	forking
forbade	foredawn	forensic	forewings	forklift
forbear	foredawns	forensics	forewoman	forklifts
forbears	foredeck	forepeak	forewomen	forks
forbid	foredecks	forepeaks	foreword	forktail
forbidden	foredid	foreplay	forewords	forktails
forbids	foredo	foreran	foreyard	forlorn
forbore	foredoes	forerib	foreyards	forlornly
forborne	foredoing	foreribs	forfeit	form
forbs	foredone	forerun	forfeited	forma
forby	foredoom	foreruns	forfeiter	formable

formae	forsooth	fossorial	foveae	frag
formal	forswear	foster	foveal	fragged
formalin	forswears	fosterage	fowl	fragging
formalise	forswore	fostered	fowler	fragile
formalism	forsworn	fosterer	fowlers	fragilely
formalist	forsythia	fosterers	fowling	fragility
formality	fort	fostering	fowls	fragment
formalize	fortalice	fosters	fox	fragments
formally	forte	fou	foxed	fragrance
formant	fortes	fouetté	foxes	fragrancy
formants	forth	fouettés	foxfire	fragrant
formas	forthwith	fought	foxglove	frags
format	forties	foul	foxgloves	frail
formate	fortieth	foulard	foxhole	frailer
formates	fortified	foulards	foxholes	frailest
formation	fortifier	fouled	foxhound	frailly
formative	fortifies	fouler	foxhounds	frailness
formats	fortify	foulest	foxie	frails
formatted	fortis	fouling	foxier	frailties
forme	fortitude	foully	foxies	frailty
formed	fortnight	foulness	foxiest	fraise
former	fortress	fouls	foxily	fraises
formerly	forts	foumart	foxiness	framable
formes	fortuity	foumarts	foxing	frambesia
forming	fortunate	found	foxlike	framboise
formless	fortune	founded	foxtail	frame
formol	fortunes	founder	foxtails	framed
forms	forty	foundered	foxtrot	frameless
formula	fortyfold	founders	foxtrots	framer
formulae	forum	founding	foxy	framers
formulaic	forums	foundling	foyer	frames
formulary	forward	foundress	foyers	frameset
formulas	forwarded	foundries		framesets
formulate	forwarder	foundry		framework
formwork	forwardly	founds		framing
formyl	forwards	fount		franc
fornenst	forwent	fountain	frabjous	franchise
fornent	fossa	fountains	fracas	francise
fornicate	fossae	founts	fracases	francised
fornices	fossas	four	fractal	francises
fornix	fosse	fourfold	fractals	francium
forrader	fosses	fourpenny	fraction	francize
forrard	fossick	fours	fractions	francized
forsake	fossicked	fourscore	fractious	francizes
forsaken	fossicker	foursome	fracture	francolin
forsaker	fossicks	foursomes	fractured	francs
forsakers	fossil	fourteen	fractures	frangible
forsakes	fossilise	fourth	frae	franglais
forsaking	fossilize	fourthly	fraenulum	frank
forsook	fossils	fovea	fraenum	franked

F R

fraenums

franker	free	frenetic	fribbles	frippery
frankers	freebase	frenulum	fricassee	frippet
frankest	freebased	frenum	fricative	frippets
franking	freebases	frenums	friction	frisbee
franklin	freebie	frenzied	frictions	frisbees
franklins	freebies	frenzies	fridge	frisée
frankly	freeboard	frenzy	fridges	frisk
frankness	freeboot	freon	fried	frisked
franks	freeboots	frequency	friend	frisker
frantic	freeborn	frequent	friended	friskers
frap	freed	frequents	friending	frisket
frappé	freedman	fresco	friendly	friskets
frapped	freedmen	frescoed	friends	friskier
frappés	freedom	frescoes	frier	friskiest
frapping	freedoms	frescos	friers	friskily
fraps	freehand	fresh	fries	frisking
frass	freehold	freshen	frieze	frisks
frat	freeholds	freshened	friezes	frisky
frater	freeing	freshens	frig	frisson
fraternal	freelance	fresher	frigate	frissons
fraters	freeload	freshers	frigates	frit
frats	freeloads	freshest	frigged	frites
fraud	freely	freshet	frigging	frith
frauds	freeman	freshets	fright	friths
fraudster	freemen	freshie	frighted	frits
fraught	freeness	freshly	frighten	frittata
fray	freer	freshman	frightens	frittatas
frayed	freeride	freshmen	frightful	fritted
fraying	freerides	freshness	frighting	fritter
frays	freerode	freshy	frights	frittered
frazil	frees	fresnel	frigid	fritters
frazzle	freesia	fresnels	frigidity	fritting
frazzled	freesias	fret	frigidly	fritz
frazzles	freest	fretboard	frigs	frivol
frazzling	freestone	fretful	frijoles	frivoled
freak	freestyle	fretfully	frikkadel	frivoling
freaked	freeware	fretless	frill	frivolity
freakier	freeway	frets	frilled	frivolled
freakiest	freeways	fretsaw	frillery	frivolous
freakily	freewheel	fretsaws	frillier	frivols
freaking	freezable	fretted	frillies	frizz
freakish	freeze	fretting	frilliest	frizzante
freaks	freezer	fretwork	frilling	frizzed
freaky	freezers	friable	frills	frizzes
freckle	freezes	friar	frilly	frizzier
freckled	freezing	friarbird	fringe	frizziest
freckles	freight	friaries	fringed	frizzing
frecklier	freighted	friars	fringes	frizzle
freckling	freighter	friary	fringing	frizzled
freckly	freights	fribble	fringy	frizzles

frizzling	frontiers	frowsier	frumpier	fudged
frizzly	fronting	frowsiest	frumpiest	fudges
frizzy	frontless	frowst	frumpily	fudging
fro	frontlet	frowsted	frumpish	fuehrer
frock	frontlets	frowster	frumps	fuehrers
frocked	frontman	frowsters	frumpy	fuel
frocks	frontmen	frowstier	frusemide	fueled
froe	fronton	frowsting	frusta	fueling
froes	frontons	frowsts	frustrate	fuelled
frog	fronts	frowsty	frustule	fuelling
frogbit	frontside	frowsy	frustules	fuels
frogbits	frontward	frowzier	frustum	fuelwood
frogfish	frore	frowziest	frustums	fufu
frogged	frost	frowzy	fruticose	fug
froggies	frostbite	froze	fry	fugacious
frogging	frosted	frozen	fryer	fugacity
froggy	frostier	frozenly	fryers	fugal
froglet	frostiest	fructify	frying	fugally
froglets	frostily	fructose	frypan	fugato
frogman	frosting	fructuous	frypans	fugatos
frogmarch	frostless	frug		fuggier
frogmen	frosts	frugal		fuggiest
frogmouth	frosty	frugality	**F U**	fuggy
frogs	froth	frugally		fugitive
frogspawn	frothed	frugged	fubsier	fugitives
froideur	frothier	frugging	fubsiest	fugleman
frolic	frothiest	frugivore	fubsy	fuglemen
frolicked	frothily	frugs	fuchsia	fugu
frolicker	frothing	fruit	fuchsias	fugue
frolics	froths	fruitage	fuchsin	fugues
from	frothy	fruitcake	fuchsine	fuguist
frond	frottage	fruitcrow	fuci	führer
frondage	frottages	fruited	fuck	führers
frondages	frotteur	fruiter	fuckable	fulcra
fronded	frotteurs	fruiterer	fucked	fulcrum
frondeur	frottola	fruiters	fucker	fulcrums
frondeurs	frottolas	fruitful	fuckers	fulfil
frondose	frottole	fruitier	fuckhead	fulfill
fronds	frottoles	fruitiest	fuckheads	fulfilled
frons	frounce	fruitily	fucking	fulfiller
front	frow	fruiting	fucks	fulfills
frontage	froward	fruition	fuckwit	fulfils
frontager	frowardly	fruitless	fuckwits	fulgent
frontages	frown	fruitlet	fucoid	fulgurant
frontal	frowned	fruitlets	fucoids	fulgurate
frontally	frowner	fruits	fucus	fulgurite
frontals	frowners	fruitwood	fuddle	fulgurous
fronted	frowning	fruity	fuddled	full
frontes	frowns	frumenty	fuddles	fullback
frontier	frows	frump	fuddling	fullbacks
			fudge	

fulled	funboards	funking	furless	fusariums
fuller	function	funks	furling	fuscous
fullered	functions	funkster	furlong	fuse
fullerene	functor	funksters	furlongs	fused
fullering	functors	funky	furlough	fusee
fullers	fund	funned	furloughs	fusees
fullest	fundal	funnel	furls	fuselage
fulling	fundament	funneled	furmety	fuselages
fullness	funded	funneling	furnace	fuseless
fulls	fundi	funnelled	furnaces	fuses
fully	fundie	funnels	furnish	fuseway
fulmar	fundies	funnier	furnished	fuseways
fulmars	funding	funnies	furnisher	fusible
fulminant	fundis	funniest	furnishes	fusiform
fulminate	funds	funnily	furniture	fusil
fulness	fundus	funniness	furor	fusileer
fulsome	funeral	funning	furore	fusileers
fulsomely	funerals	funny	furores	fusilier
fulvous	funerary	funs	furors	fusiliers
fumarate	funereal	funster	furphies	fusillade
fumarates	funfair	funsters	furphy	fusilli
fumarole	funfairs	fur	furred	fusils
fumaroles	fungal	furan	furrier	fusimotor
fumarolic	fungi	furans	furriers	fusing
fumble	fungible	furbelow	furriery	fusion
fumbled	fungicide	furbelows	furriest	fusional
fumbler	fungiform	furbish	furriness	fusionism
fumblers	fungo	furbished	furring	fusionist
fumbles	fungoes	furbisher	furrow	fusions
fumbling	fungoid	furbishes	furrowed	fuss
fume	fungos	furca	furrowing	fussed
fumed	fungous	furcae	furrows	fusser
fumes	fungus	furcal	furrowy	fussers
fumet	funguses	furcate	furry	fusses
fumets	funhouse	furcated	furs	fussier
fumier	funhouses	furcates	further	fussiest
fumiest	funicle	furcating	furthered	fussily
fumigant	funicles	furcation	furtherer	fussiness
fumigants	funicular	furcula	furthers	fussing
fumigate	funiculi	furculae	furthest	fusspot
fumigated	funiculus	furcular	furtive	fusspots
fumigates	funk	furfural	furtively	fussy
fumigator	funked	furies	furuncle	fustian
fuming	funkia	furioso	furuncles	fustic
fumingly	funkias	furious	fury	fustier
fumitory	funkier	furiously	furze	fustiest
fumy	funkiest	furl	furzy	fustily
fun	funkily	furlable	fusain	fustiness
funboard	funkiness	furled	fusarium	

fusty
futhark
futharks
futhorc
futhorcs
futhork
futhorks
futile
futilely
futility
futon

futons
futtock
futtocks
future
futures
futurism
futurist
futurists
futurity
futz
futzed

futzes
futzing
fuze
fuzed
fuzee
fuzees
fuzes
fuzing
fuzz
fuzzbox
fuzzboxes

fuzzed
fuzzes
fuzzier
fuzziest
fuzzily
fuzziness
fuzzing
fuzzy

F Y

fyke
fykes
fylfot
fylfots
fynbos
fyrd
fyrds
fytte
fyttes

G

G A

gab
gabardine
gabba
gabbas
gabbed
gabbier
gabbiest
gabbing
gabble
gabbled
gabbler
gabblers
gabbles
gabbling
gabbro
gabbroic
gabbroid
gabbros
gabby
gaberdine
gabfest
gabfests
gabion
gabionage
gabions

gable
gabled
gables
gaboon
gaboons
gabs
gad
gadabout
gadabouts
gadded
gadding
gadflies
gadfly
gadget
gadgeteer
gadgetry
gadgets
gadgety
gadid
gadids
gadoid
gadoids
gadroon
gadrooned
gadroons
gads
gadwall

gadwalls
gadzooks
gaff
gaffe
gaffed
gaffer
gaffers
gaffes
gaffing
gaffs
gag
gaga
gage
gaged
gages
gagged
gagging
gaggle
gaggles
gaging
gags
gagster
gagsters
gaieties
gaiety
gaijin
gaily

gain
gainable
gained
gainer
gainers
gainful
gainfully
gaining
gains
gainsaid
gainsay
gainsayer
gainsays
gait
gaita
gaitas
gaiter
gaitered
gaiters
gaits
gal
gala
galactic
galactose
galaed
galago
galagos

galah
galahs
galaing
galangal
galant
galantine
galas
galaxies
galaxy
galbanum
gale
galea
galeae
galeas
galena
galenic
galenical
galère
galères
gales
galette
galettes
gali
galilee
galilees
galingale
galipot

galis	gallop	gamboled	gammons	gaoled
galjoen	galloped	gamboling	gammy	gaoler
gall	galloper	gambolled	gamp	gaolers
galla	gallopers	gambols	gamps	gaoling
gallaed	galloping	gambrel	gams	gaols
gallah	gallops	gambrels	gamut	gap
gallahed	gallous	gambusia	gamuts	gape
gallahing	galloway	game	gamy	gaped
gallahs	galloways	gamecock	ganache	gaper
gallaing	gallows	gamecocks	gander	gapers
gallant	galls	gamed	ganders	gapes
gallanted	gallstone	gamefowl	gang	gapeworm
gallantly	gallus	gamefowls	gangboard	gapeworms
gallantry	galluses	gamelan	ganged	gaping
gallants	galoot	gamelans	ganger	gapingly
gallas	galoots	gamely	gangers	gapped
gallate	galop	gameness	ganging	gappier
gallates	galops	gameplay	gangland	gappiest
gallberry	galore	gamer	ganglia	gapping
galled	galosh	gamers	ganglier	gappy
galleon	galoshes	games	gangliest	gaps
galleons	gals	gamesman	gangling	gar
galleria	galumph	gamesmen	ganglion	garage
gallerias	galumphed	gamesome	ganglions	garaged
galleried	galumphs	gamest	gangly	garages
galleries	galvanic	gamester	gangplank	garaging
gallery	galvanise	gamesters	gangrene	garb
gallet	galvanism	gamete	gangrened	garbage
gallets	galvanize	gametes	gangrenes	garbanzo
galley	galvo	gametic	gangs	garbanzos
galleys	gam	gamey	gangsta	garbed
galliard	gamba	gamgee	gangstas	garbing
galliards	gambade	gamier	gangster	garble
galliass	gambades	gamiest	gangsters	garbled
gallice	gambado	gamily	gangue	garbler
galling	gambadoes	gamin	gangway	garblers
gallingly	gambados	gamine	gangways	garbles
gallinule	gambas	gamines	ganister	garbling
galliot	gambier	gaminess	ganja	garbo
galliots	gambiers	gaming	gannet	garboard
gallipot	gambit	gamins	gannetry	garboards
gallipots	gambits	gamma	gannets	garbology
gallium	gamble	gammas	ganoid	garbos
gallivant	gambled	gammer	gantlet	garbs
galliwasp	gambler	gammers	gantlets	garçon
gallon	gamblers	gammier	gantline	garçons
gallonage	gambles	gammiest	gantries	garden
gallons	gambling	gammon	gantry	gardened
galloon	gamboge	gammoned	ganzfeld	gardener
galloons	gambol	gammoning	gaol	gardeners

gardenia	garrote	gasps	gaudies	gawkiest
gardenias	garroted	gassed	gaudiest	gawkily
gardening	garrotes	gasser	gaudily	gawkiness
gardens	garroting	gassers	gaudiness	gawking
garderobe	garrotte	gasses	gauds	gawkish
garfish	garrotted	gassier	gaudy	gawks
garfishes	garrottes	gassiest	gauge	gawky
garganey	garrulity	gassiness	gaugeable	gawp
garganeys	garrulous	gassing	gauged	gawped
garget	garryowen	gassy	gauger	gawper
gargle	garter	gastric	gaugers	gawpers
gargled	gartered	gastrin	gauges	gawping
gargles	garters	gastrins	gauging	gawps
gargling	garth	gastritis	gault	gay
gargoyle	garths	gastropod	gaunt	gayal
gargoyles	gas	gastrula	gaunter	gayals
garibaldi	gasbag	gastrulae	gauntest	gayelle
garish	gasbags	gasworks	gauntlet	gayelles
garishly	gascon	gat	gauntlets	gayer
garland	gasconade	gate	gauntly	gayest
garlanded	gascons	gateau	gauntness	gayeties
garlands	gaseous	gateaus	gaur	gayety
garlic	gases	gateaux	gaurs	gayness
garlicky	gash	gatecrash	gauss	gaynesses
garment	gashed	gated	gausses	gays
garments	gashes	gatefold	gauze	gazania
garner	gashing	gatefolds	gauzier	gazanias
garnered	gasholder	gatehouse	gauziest	gaze
garnering	gasified	gatepost	gauzily	gazebo
garners	gasifies	gateposts	gauziness	gazeboes
garnet	gasify	gates	gauzy	gazebos
garnets	gasifying	gateway	gavage	gazed
garnish	gasket	gateways	gave	gazelle
garnished	gaskets	gather	gavel	gazelles
garnishee	gaskin	gathered	gaveled	gazer
garnishes	gaskins	gatherer	gaveling	gazers
garniture	gaslight	gatherers	gavelkind	gazes
garotte	gaslights	gathering	gavelled	gazette
garotted	gaslit	gathers	gavelling	gazetted
garottes	gasman	gating	gavels	gazetteer
garotting	gasmen	gator	gavial	gazettes
garpike	gasohol	gators	gavials	gazetting
garret	gasolene	gats	gavotte	gazillion
garrets	gasoline	gauche	gavottes	gazing
garrick	gasometer	gauchely	gawk	gazpacho
garricks	gasp	gaucherie	gawked	gazpachos
garrison	gasped	gaucho	gawker	gazump
garrisons	gasper	gauchos	gawkers	gazumped
garron	gaspers	gaud	gawkier	gazumper
garrons	gasping	gaudier		gazumpers

gazumping
gazumps

G E

gean
geans
gear
gearbox
gearboxes
geared
gearing
gears
gearstick
gearwheel
gecko
geckoes
geckos
gee
geebung
geebungs
geed
geeing
geek
geekier
geekiest
geeks
geeky
gees
geese
geezer
geezers
geisha
geishas
gel
gelada
geladas
gelati
gelatin
gelatine
gelation
gelato
gelcoat
gelcoats
geld
gelded
gelding
geldings
gelds
gelid

gelignite
gelled
gelling
gelly
gels
gelsemium
gelt
gem
gematria
geminal
geminally
geminate
geminated
geminates
gemma
gemmae
gemmation
gemmed
gemming
gemmology
gemmule
gemmules
gemology
gems
gemsbok
gemsboks
gemstone
gemstones
gemütlich
gen
gena
genae
genal
gendarme
gendarmes
gender
gendered
genders
gene
genealogy
genera
generable
general
generally
generals
generate
generated
generates
generator
generic

generous
genes
genesis
genet
genetic
genetical
genetics
genets
geneva
genever
genial
geniality
genially
genic
genie
genii
genip
genipap
genipapo
genipapos
genipaps
genips
genista
genistas
genital
genitalia
genitals
genitival
genitive
genitives
genitor
genitors
geniture
genius
geniuses
genlock
genlocked
genlocks
genned
genning
genoa
genoas
genocidal
genocide
genome
genomes
genomic
genotype
genotypes
genotypic

genre
genres
gens
gent
genteel
genteelly
gentes
gentian
gentians
gentile
gentiles
gentility
gentle
gentled
gentleman
gentlemen
gentler
gentles
gentlest
gentling
gently
gentoo
gentoos
gentrify
gentry
gents
genu
genua
genuflect
genuine
genuinely
genus
geo
geobotany
geode
geodes
geodesic
geodesist
geodesy
geodetic
geodic
geoduck
geoducks
geography
geoid
geoids
geologic
geologise
geologist
geologize

geology
geomancy
geomantic
geometer
geometers
geometric
geometrid
geometry
geophagy
georgette
georgic
georgics
geos
geotactic
geotaxis
geotropic
geranial
geraniol
geranium
geraniums
gerbera
gerberas
gerbil
gerbils
gerenuk
gerenuks
geriatric
germ
german
germander
germane
germanely
germanium
germicide
germier
germiest
germinal
germinate
germs
germy
gerontic
gerund
gerundive
gerunds
gesneriad
gesso
gessoes
gestalt
gestalts
gestate

gestated
gestates
gestating
gestation
gestural
gesture
gestured
gestures
gesturing
get
getaway
getaways
gets
gettable
getter
gettering
getters
getting
geum
geums
gewgaw
gewgaws
geyser
geysered
geysering
geyserite
geysers

G H

gharana
gharanas
gharara
ghararas
gharial
gharials
gharries
gharry
ghastlier
ghastly
ghat
ghats
ghazal
ghazals
ghee
gherao
gheraos
gherkin
gherkins
ghetto

ghettoed
ghettoes
ghettoing
ghettoise
ghettoize
ghettos
ghibli
ghillie
ghillies
ghost
ghosted
ghosting
ghostlier
ghostlike
ghostly
ghosts
ghoul
ghoulish
ghouls
ghyll
ghylls

G I

gi
giant
giantess
giantism
giantlike
giants
giaour
giaours
gibber
gibbered
gibbering
gibberish
gibbers
gibbet
gibbeted
gibbeting
gibbets
gibbon
gibbons
gibbosity
gibbous
gibbously
gibbsite
gibe
gibed
gibes

gibing
giblets
gibus
gibuses
gid
giddap
giddied
giddier
giddies
giddiest
giddily
giddiness
giddy
giddying
gidgee
gidgees
gie
gied
gies
gift
gifted
gifting
gifts
giftware
gig
gigabyte
gigabytes
gigaflop
gigaflops
gigantic
gigantism
gigged
gigging
giggle
giggled
giggler
gigglers
giggles
giggling
giggly
gigolo
gigolos
gigot
gigots
gigs
gigue
gigues
gild
gilded
gilder

gilders
gilding
gilds
gilet
gilets
gilgai
gilgais
gill
gilled
gillie
gillies
gilling
gills
gilt
gilts
gimbal
gimballed
gimbals
gimcrack
gimcracks
gimlet
gimlets
gimme
gimmick
gimmickry
gimmicks
gimmicky
gimp
gimped
gimping
gimps
gimpy
gin
ginger
gingered
gingering
gingerly
gingers
gingery
gingham
gingili
gingival
gingko
gingkoes
gingkos
ginglymi
ginglymus
gink
ginkgo
ginkgoes

ginkgos
ginks
ginned
ginnel
ginnels
ginner
ginneries
ginners
ginnery
ginning
ginormous
gins
ginseng
ginsengs
ginzo
ginzos
gip
gippo
gippos
gips
gipsies
gipsy
gipsywort
giraffe
giraffes
girandole
girasol
girasole
girasoles
girasols
gird
girded
girder
girders
girding
girdle
girdled
girdler
girdlers
girdles
girdling
girds
girl
girlhood
girlie
girlier
girlies
girliest
girlish
girlishly

girls
girly
girn
girned
girning
girns
giro
giros
girt
girth
girthed
girthing
girths
gis
gismo
gismos
gist
git
gîte
gîtes
gits
gittern
gitterns
give
giveaway
giveaways
giveback
givebacks
given
giver
givers
gives
giving
gizmo
gizmos
gizzard
gizzards

G L

glabella
glabellae
glabellar
glabrous
glacé
glacial
glacially
glaciated
glacier
glaciers

glacis
glad
gladded
gladden
gladdened
gladdens
gladder
gladdest
gladdie
gladdies
gladding
gladdon
gladdons
glade
glades
gladiator
gladioli
gladiolus
gladly
gladness
glads
gladsome
glaikit
glair
glairy
glaive
glaives
glam
glammed
glamming
glamor
glamorise
glamorize
glamorous
glamour
glams
glance
glanced
glances
glancing
gland
glanders
glandes
glands
glandular
glans
glare
glared
glares
glaring

glaringly
glary
glasnost
glass
glassed
glasses
glassfish
glassful
glassfuls
glassie
glassier
glassies
glassiest
glassily
glassine
glassing
glassless
glassware
glasswort
glassy
glaucoma
glaucous
glaze
glazed
glazer
glazers
glazes
glazier
glaziers
glazing
gleam
gleamed
gleaming
gleams
gleamy
glean
gleaned
gleaner
gleaners
gleaning
gleanings
gleans
glebe
glebes
glee
gleeful
gleefully
gleeman
gleemen
glees

gleesome
gleet
gleety
glen
glengarry
glens
gley
gleys
glia
glial
glias
glib
glibber
glibbest
glibly
glibness
glide
glided
glider
gliders
glides
gliding
glim
glimmer
glimmered
glimmers
glimpse
glimpsed
glimpses
glimpsing
glint
glinted
glinting
glints
glioma
gliomas
gliomata
glissade
glissaded
glissades
glissandi
glissando
glissé
glissés
glisten
glistened
glistens
glister
glistered
glisters

glitch
glitched
glitches
glitching
glitchy
glitter
glittered
glitters
glittery
glitz
glitzed
glitzier
glitziest
glitzily
glitzing
glitzy
gloaming
gloat
gloated
gloater
gloaters
gloating
gloats
glob
global
globalise
globalist
globalize
globally
globe
globed
globefish
globes
globetrot
globing
globoid
globose
globs
globular
globule
globules
globulin
globulins
globulous
glochid
glochidia
glom
glomeruli
glommed
glomming

gloms
gloom
gloomed
gloomier
gloomiest
gloomily
glooming
glooms
gloomy
gloop
gloopy
glop
gloppy
glops
gloried
glories
glorified
glorifier
glorifies
glorify
glorious
glory
glorying
gloss
glossal
glossary
glossator
glossed
glosser
glossers
glosses
glossier
glossies
glossiest
glossily
glossing
glossitis
glossy
glost
glottal
glottic
glottis
glottises
glove
glovebox
gloved
gloveless
glover
glovers
gloves

gloving
glow
glowed
glower
glowered
glowering
glowers
glowing
glowingly
glows
gloxinia
gloze
glozed
glozes
glozing
glucagon
glucan
glucans
glucose
glucoside
glue
glued
glueing
glues
gluey
glug
gluggable
glugged
glugging
glugs
gluing
glum
glume
glumes
glumly
glummer
glummest
glumness
gluon
gluons
glut
glutamate
glutamine
glute
gluteal
glutei
gluten
glutes
gluteus
glutinous

gluts
glutted
glutting
glutton
gluttons
gluttony
glyceride
glycerin
glycerine
glycerins
glycerol
glycerols
glyceryl
glycine
glycogen
glycol
glycoside
glyph
glyphic
glyphs
glyptic

GN

gnamma
gnammas
gnarl
gnarled
gnarlier
gnarliest
gnarls
gnarly
gnash
gnashed
gnashers
gnashes
gnashing
gnat
gnathic
gnats
gnaw
gnawed
gnawing
gnawingly
gnaws
gneiss
gneissic
gneissose
gnocchi
gnome

gnomes
gnomic
gnomish
gnomon
gnomonic
gnomons
gnosis
gnostic
gnostics
gnu
gnus

GO

go
goad
goaded
goading
goads
goal
goalball
goalie
goalies
goalless
goalmouth
goalpost
goalposts
goals
goanna
goannas
goat
goatee
goateed
goatees
goatfish
goatherd
goatherds
goatier
goatiest
goatish
goats
goatskin
goatskins
goaty
gob
gobbed
gobbet
gobbets
gobbing
gobble

gobbled
gobbler
gobblers
gobbles
gobbling
gobdaw
gobdaws
gobi
gobies
goblet
goblets
goblin
goblins
gobo
gobony
gobos
gobs
gobshite
gobshites
goby
god
godchild
goddam
goddamn
goddamned
goddess
goddesses
godet
godetia
godetias
godets
godfather
godhead
godheads
godhood
godless
godlier
godliest
godlike
godliness
godly
godmother
godown
godowns
godparent
gods
godsend
godsends
godship
godson

godsons
godward
godwards
godwit
godwits
goer
goers
goes
goest
goeth
goethite
gofer
gofers
goffer
goffered
goffering
goffers
gogga
goggas
goggle
goggled
goggles
goggling
going
goings
goiter
goiters
goitre
goitred
goitres
goitrous
gold
goldbug
goldbugs
goldcrest
golden
goldeneye
goldenly
goldenrod
goldfield
goldfinch
goldfish
goldsmith
goldwork
golem
golems
golf
golfball
golfballs
golfed

golfer
golfers
golfing
golfs
golgappa
golgappas
gollies
golliwog
golliwogs
gollop
golloped
golloping
gollops
golly
gombeen
gombeens
gonad
gonadal
gonads
gondola
gondolas
gondolier
gone
goner
goners
gonfalon
gonfalons
gong
gonged
gonging
gongs
goniatite
gonif
goniff
goniffs
gonifs
gonna
gonococci
gonolek
gonoleks
gonorrhea
gonzo
goo
good
goodby
goodbye
goodbyes
goodbys
goodfella
goodie

goodies
goodish
goodlier
goodliest
goodly
goodman
goodmen
goodness
goodnight
goodo
goods
goodwife
goodwill
goodwives
goody
gooey
gooeyness
goof
goofball
goofballs
goofed
goofier
goofiest
goofily
goofiness
goofing
goofs
goofus
goofuses
goofy
goog
googlies
googly
googol
googols
googs
gooier
gooiest
gook
gooks
goolie
goolies
gooly
goombah
goombahs
goombay
goombays
goon
goonda
goondas

goons
goop
goopier
goopiest
goopiness
goops
goopy
goos
goosander
goose
goosed
goosefish
goosefoot
goosegog
goosegogs
gooseneck
gooses
gooseskin
goosey
goosier
goosiest
goosing
goosy
gopak
gopaks
gopher
gophers
gopik
gopiks
goral
gorals
gorblimey
gorcock
gorcocks
gordo
gordos
gore
gored
gores
gorge
gorged
gorgeous
gorger
gorgers
gorges
gorget
gorgets
gorging
gorgio
gorgios

gorgon
gorgoneia
gorgonian
gorgons
gorier
goriest
gorilla
gorillas
gorily
goriness
goring
gormless
gorp
gorse
gorsier
gorsiest
gorsy
gory
gos
gosh
goshawk
goshawks
gosht
gosling
goslings
gospel
gospeler
gospelers
gospelise
gospelize
gospeller
gospels
goss
gossamer
gossamery
gossan
gossip
gossiped
gossiper
gossipers
gossiping
gossips
gossipy
gossoon
gossoons
gossypol
gossypols
got
gotcha
gotchas

gotcher
gotchers
goth
gothic
goths
gotta
gotten
gouache
gouaches
gouge
gouged
gouger
gougers
gouges
gouging
goujons
goulash
goulashes
goura
gourami
gouramis
gouras
gourd
gourde
gourdes
gourdful
gourdfuls
gourds
gourmand
gourmands
gourmet
gourmets
gout
goutier
goutiest
goutiness
gouts
goutweed
gouty
govern
governed
governess
governing
governor
governors
governs
gowan
gowans
gowk
gowks

gown
gowned
gowning
gowns
goy
goyim
goyish
goys

GR

grab
grabbed
grabber
grabbers
grabbier
grabbiest
grabbing
grabble
grabbled
grabbles
grabbling
grabby
graben
grabens
grabs
grace
graced
graceful
graceless
graces
gracile
gracilis
gracility
gracing
gracious
grackle
grackles
grad
gradable
gradate
gradated
gradates
gradating
gradation
grade
graded
gradely
grader
graders

grades
gradience
gradient
gradients
gradin
gradine
gradines
grading
gradins
grads
gradual
gradually
graduals
graduand
graduands
graduate
graduated
graduates
gradus
graduses
graffiti
graffito
graft
grafted
grafter
grafters
grafting
grafts
graham
grain
grained
grainer
grainers
grainier
grainiest
graining
grainless
grains
grainy
gralloch
grallochs
gram
gramma
grammar
grammars
gramme
grammes
gramp
grampies
gramps

grampses
grampus
grampuses
grampy
grams
gran
grana
granaries
granary
grand
grandad
grandads
grandam
grandame
grandames
grandams
granddad
granddads
grandee
grandees
grander
grandest
grandeur
grandiose
grandly
grandma
grandmama
grandmas
grandness
grandpa
grandpapa
grandpas
grands
grandsire
grandson
grandsons
grange
granges
granita
granite
granitic
granitise
granitize
granitoid
granivore
grannie
grannies
granny
granola
grans

grant
grantable
granted
grantee
grantees
granter
granters
granting
grantor
grantors
grants
granular
granulate
granule
granules
granulite
granuloma
granum
grape
grapes
grapeshot
grapevine
grapey
graph
graphed
grapheme
graphemes
graphemic
graphic
graphical
graphics
graphing
graphite
graphitic
graphs
grapier
grapiest
grapnel
grapnels
grappa
grapple
grappled
grappler
grapplers
grapples
grappling
grapy
grasp
graspable
grasped

grasper	gravelled	greasing	greensand	griddled
graspers	gravelly	greasy	greenware	griddles
grasping	gravels	great	greenway	griddling
grasps	gravely	greatcoat	greenways	gridiron
grass	graven	greater	greenwood	gridirons
grassbird	graveness	greatest	greeny	gridlock
grassbox	graver	greatly	greet	gridlocks
grassed	gravers	greatness	greeted	grids
grasses	graves	greats	greeter	grief
grassier	graveside	greave	greeters	griefs
grassiest	gravest	greaves	greeting	grievance
grassing	graveyard	grebe	greetings	grieve
grassland	gravid	grebes	greets	grieved
grassless	gravies	grebo	gregarine	griever
grassquit	graving	grebos	greisen	grievers
grassveld	gravitas	greed	gremlin	grieves
grassy	gravitate	greedier	gremlins	grieving
grate	graviton	greediest	grenade	grievous
grated	gravitons	greedily	grenades	griff
grateful	gravity	greedy	grenadier	griffin
grater	gravlax	greegree	grenadine	griffins
graters	gravure	greegrees	grevillea	griffon
grates	gravy	green	grew	griffons
graticule	gray	greenback	grey	grift
gratified	graybeard	greenbul	greybeard	grifted
gratifier	grayed	greenbuls	greyed	grifter
gratifies	graying	greened	greyer	grifters
gratify	graylag	greener	greyest	grifting
gratin	graylags	greenery	greyhen	grifts
gratiné	grayling	greenest	greyhens	grig
gratinée	graylings	greeneye	greyhound	grigs
gratinéed	grays	greeneyes	greying	grike
grating	grayscale	greenfeed	greyish	grikes
gratingly	graywacke	greenfly	greylag	grill
gratings	graze	greengage	greylags	grillade
gratins	grazed	greenhead	greyly	grillades
gratis	grazer	greenhide	greyness	grillage
gratitude	grazers	greenhorn	greys	grillages
gratuity	grazes	greenie	greyscale	grille
graunch	grazier	greenies	greywacke	grilled
graunched	graziers	greening	gribble	griller
graunches	grazing	greenings	gribbles	grillers
gravadlax	grease	greenish	gricer	grilles
gravamen	greased	greenlet	gricers	grilling
gravamina	greaser	greenlets	grid	grills
grave	greasers	greenling	gridded	grilse
graved	greases	greenly	gridder	grilses
gravel	greasier	greenmail	gridders	grim
graveled	greasiest	greenness	gridding	grimace
graveling	greasily	greens	griddle	grimaced

grimacer	grips	grockle	grossly	grousing
grimacers	grisaille	grockles	grossness	grout
grimaces	grisette	grog	grossular	grouted
grimacing	grisettes	groggier	grosz	grouter
grimalkin	griskin	groggiest	grosze	grouters
grime	griskins	groggily	groszy	grouting
grimed	grislier	groggy	grot	grouts
grimes	grisliest	grogram	grotesque	grove
grimier	grisly	groin	grots	grovel
grimiest	grison	groined	grottier	groveled
grimily	grisons	groins	grottiest	groveling
griminess	grissini	grok	grotto	grovelled
griming	grist	grokked	grottoed	groveller
grimly	gristle	grokking	grottoes	grovels
grimmer	gristlier	groks	grottos	groves
grimmest	gristly	grommet	grotty	grovy
grimness	gristmill	grommets	grouch	grow
grimoire	grit	gromwell	grouched	growable
grimoires	grits	gromwells	grouches	growbag
grimy	gritstone	groom	grouchier	growbags
grin	gritted	groomed	grouchily	grower
grind	gritter	grooming	grouching	growers
grinder	gritters	grooms	grouchy	growing
grinders	grittier	groomsman	ground	growl
grinding	grittiest	groomsmen	grounded	growled
grinds	grittily	groove	grounder	growler
gringo	gritting	grooved	grounders	growlers
gringos	gritty	grooves	groundhog	growling
grinned	grivet	groovier	grounding	growls
grinner	grivets	grooviest	groundnut	growmore
grinners	grizzle	groovily	groundout	grown
grinning	grizzled	grooving	grounds	grows
grins	grizzler	groovy	groundsel	growth
griot	grizzlers	grope	group	growths
griots	grizzles	groped	grouped	groyne
grip	grizzlies	groper	grouper	groynes
gripe	grizzling	gropers	groupers	grub
griped	grizzly	gropes	groupie	grubbed
griper	groan	groping	groupies	grubber
gripers	groaned	gropingly	grouping	grubbers
gripes	groaner	grosbeak	groupings	grubbier
griping	groaners	grosbeaks	groups	grubbiest
grippe	groaning	groschen	groupset	grubbily
gripped	groans	grosgrain	groupsets	grubbing
gripper	groat	gross	groupware	grubby
grippers	groats	grossed	grouse	grubs
grippier	grocer	grosser	groused	grubstake
grippiest	groceries	grosses	grouser	grudge
gripping	grocers	grossest	grousers	grudged
grippy	grocery	grossing	grouses	grudger

grudgers
grudges
grudging
gruel
grueling
gruelling
gruesome
gruff
gruffer
gruffest
gruffly
gruffness
grumble
grumbled
grumbler
grumblers
grumbles
grumbling
grumbly
grump
grumped
grumpier
grumpiest
grumpily
grumping
grumpish
grumps
grumpy
grunge
grungier
grungiest
grungy
grunion
grunions
grunt
grunted
grunter
grunters
grunting
gruntled
grunts
gryke
grykes
gryphon
gryphons
grysbok
grysboks

G U

guacamole
guacharo
guacharos
guaiac
guaiacol
guaiacum
guaiacums
guan
guanaco
guanacos
guanidine
guanine
guano
guanos
guanosine
guans
guar
guarache
guaraches
guarani
guarantee
guarantor
guaranty
guard
guardant
guarded
guardedly
guardee
guardees
guardian
guardians
guarding
guardroom
guards
guardsman
guardsmen
guars
guava
guavas
guayule
guayules
gubbins
guck
guddle
guddled
guddler
guddlers
guddles

guddling
gudgeon
gudgeons
guenon
guenons
guerdon
guerdoned
guerdons
guerilla
guerillas
guernsey
guernseys
guerrilla
guess
guessable
guessed
guesser
guessers
guesses
guessing
guesswork
guest
guested
guesting
guests
guff
guffaw
guffawed
guffawing
guffaws
guid
guidable
guidance
guide
guidebook
guided
guideline
guidepost
guider
guiders
guides
guideway
guideways
guiding
guidon
guidons
guild
guilder
guilders
guildhall

guilds
guile
guileful
guileless
guillemot
guilloche
guilt
guiltier
guiltiest
guiltily
guiltless
guilty
guimp
guimpe
guimpes
guimps
guinea
guineas
guinep
guineps
guipure
guiro
guiros
guise
guiser
guisers
guises
guitar
guitarist
guitars
guiver
gulag
gulags
gular
gulars
gulch
gulches
gulden
guldens
gules
gulf
gulfs
gulfweed
gull
gulled
gulleries
gullery
gullet
gullets
gulley

gulleyed
gulleying
gulleys
gullible
gullibly
gullied
gullies
gulling
gulls
gully
gullying
gulp
gulped
gulper
gulpers
gulping
gulps
gulpy
gum
gumbo
gumboil
gumboils
gumboot
gumboots
gumbos
gumdrop
gumdrops
gumma
gummas
gummata
gummatous
gummed
gummier
gummies
gummiest
gummily
gumminess
gumming
gummosis
gummy
gumption
gums
gumshield
gumshoe
gumshoes
gun
gunboat
gunboats
guncotton
gundi

gundis
gundy
gunfight
gunfights
gunfire
gunge
gunged
gungeing
gunges
gungy
gunite
gunk
gunkhole
gunkholed
gunkholes
gunless
gunlock
gunlocks
gunmaker
gunmakers
gunman
gunmen
gunmetal
gunned
gunnel
gunnels
gunner
gunnera
gunneras
gunners
gunnery
gunnies
gunning
gunny
gunplay
gunpoint
gunpowder
gunroom
gunrooms
gunrunner
guns
gunsel
gunsels
gunship
gunships
gunshot

gunshots
gunsight
gunsights
gunsmith
gunsmiths
gunstock
gunstocks
gunter
gunters
gunwale
gunwales
gunyah
gunyahs
guppies
guppy
gur
gurdwara
gurdwaras
gurgle
gurgled
gurgles
gurgling
gurjun
gurjuns
gurn
gurnard
gurnards
gurned
gurner
gurners
gurney
gurneys
gurning
gurns
gurry
guru
gurus
gush
gushed
gusher
gushers
gushes
gushier
gushiest
gushily
gushiness

gushing
gushingly
gushy
gusset
gusseted
gussets
gussied
gussies
gussy
gussying
gust
gustation
gustative
gustatory
gusted
gustier
gustiest
gustily
gustiness
gusting
gusto
gusts
gusty
gut
gutbucket
gutless
gutlessly
guts
gutser
gutsier
gutsiest
gutsily
gutsiness
gutsy
guttate
guttation
gutted
gutter
guttered
guttering
gutters
guttier
gutties
guttiest
gutting
guttural

gutturals
gutty
gutzer
gutzers
guv
guy
guyed
guying
guyot
guyots
guys
guyver
guzzle
guzzled
guzzler
guzzlers
guzzles
guzzling

| G | W |

gwyniad
gwyniads

| G | Y |

gybe
gybed
gybes
gybing
gym
gymkhana
gymkhanas
gymnasia
gymnasial
gymnasium
gymnast
gymnastic
gymnasts
gymnogene
gymnure
gymnures
gymp
gymps
gyms
gymslip
gymslips

gynaecea
gynaeceum
gynarchy
gynoecia
gynoecium
gyp
gypped
gypping
gyppo
gyppos
gyps
gypsies
gypsum
gypsy
gypsyish
gypsywort
gyral
gyrate
gyrated
gyrates
gyrating
gyration
gyrations
gyrator
gyrators
gyratory
gyre
gyred
gyres
gyrfalcon
gyri
gyring
gyro
gyron
gyronny
gyrons
gyropilot
gyroplane
gyros
gyroscope
gyrus
gyttja
gyve
gyved
gyver
gyves

H

ha
haaf
haar
haars
habanera
habaneras
habdabs
habendum
habendums
habergeon
habile
habit
habitable
habitant
habitants
habitat
habitats
habited
habiting
habits
habitual
habituate
habitude
habitudes
habitué
habitués
habitus
haboob
haboobs
háček
háčeks
hacendado
hachured
hachures
hacienda
haciendas
hack
hackamore
hackberry
hacked
hacker

hackeries
hackers
hackery
hackette
hackettes
hacking
hackle
hackled
hackles
hackling
hackney
hackneyed
hackneys
hacks
hacksaw
hacksawed
hacksawn
hacksaws
had
hadada
hadadas
hadal
hadda
haddock
hade
haded
hadeda
hadedas
hades
hading
hadron
hadronic
hadrons
hadrosaur
hadst
haecceity
haed
haem
haemal
haematic
haematin
haematite

haematoma
haemocoel
haemostat
hafiz
hafizes
hafnium
haft
hafted
hafting
hafts
hag
hagfish
hagfishes
haggard
haggardly
haggis
haggises
haggish
haggle
haggled
haggler
hagglers
haggles
haggling
hagiology
hags
hah
haham
hahams
hahed
hahing
hahnium
hahs
haick
haicks
haik
haiks
haiku
haikus
hail
hailed
hailer

hailers
hailing
hails
hailstone
haing
hair
hairband
hairbands
hairbrush
haircloth
haircut
haircuts
hairdo
hairdos
hairdrier
hairdryer
haired
hairgrip
hairgrips
hairier
hairiest
hairily
hairiness
hairless
hairline
hairlines
hairnet
hairnets
hairpiece
hairpin
hairpins
hairs
hairslide
hairspray
hairstyle
hairy
haj
haji
hajis
hajj
hajji
hajjis

hajjs
hajs
hajs
haka
hakama
hakas
hake
hakes
hakim
hakims
halal
halala
halalas
halation
halberd
halberds
halbert
halberts
halcyon
haldi
hale
haled
haler
haleru
hales
halesome
half
halfback
halfbacks
halfbeak
halfbeaks
halfpence
halfpenny
halfway
halfwit
halfwits
halibut
halide
halides
haling
halite
halitosis

hall	halve	hamster	handlebar	hangings
hallmark	halved	hamsters	handled	hangis
hallmarks	halvers	hamstring	handler	hangman
hallo	halves	hamstrung	handlers	hangmen
halloed	halving	hamuli	handles	hangnail
halloes	halwa	hamulus	handless	hangnails
halloing	halwah	hamza	handling	hangover
halloo	halyard	hamzas	handlist	hangovers
hallooed	halyards	hand	handlists	hangs
hallooing	ham	handbag	handmade	hank
halloos	hamadryad	handbags	handmaid	hanker
hallos	hamadryas	handball	handmaids	hankered
hallow	hamamelis	handballs	handoff	hankerer
hallowed	hamartia	handbasin	handoffs	hankerers
hallowing	hamartias	handbell	handout	hankering
hallows	hamate	handbells	handouts	hankers
halls	hamates	handbill	handover	hankie
hallstand	hamba	handbills	handovers	hankies
halluces	hambaed	handbook	handprint	hanks
hallux	hambaing	handbooks	handpump	hanky
hallway	hambas	handbrake	handpumps	hansel
hallways	hambone	handcar	handrail	hanseled
halma	hambones	handcars	handrails	hanseling
halo	hamburger	handcart	hands	hanselled
haloed	hamel	handcarts	handsaw	hansels
haloes	hamels	handclap	handsaws	hansom
haloform	hamerkop	handclaps	handsel	hansoms
halogen	hamerkops	handcraft	handsels	hanuman
halogenic	hames	handcuff	handset	hanumans
halogens	hamlet	handcuffs	handsets	hap
haloing	hamlets	handed	handshake	haphazard
halon	hammed	handful	handsome	hapless
halons	hammer	handfuls	handsomer	haplessly
halophile	hammered	handgrip	handspike	haploid
halophyte	hammering	handgrips	handstand	haploids
halos	hammerkop	handgun	handwork	haploidy
halothane	hammers	handguns	handy	haplology
halt	hammier	handhold	handyman	haplont
halted	hammiest	handholds	handymen	haplontic
halter	hammily	handicap	hanepoot	haplonts
haltere	hamminess	handicaps	hang	happed
haltered	hamming	handier	hangar	happen
halteres	hammock	handiest	hangarage	happened
haltering	hammocks	handily	hangars	happening
halters	hammy	handiness	hangdog	happens
halting	hamper	handing	hanged	happi
haltingly	hampered	handiwork	hanger	happier
halts	hampering	handjob	hangers	happiest
halva	hampers	handjobs	hangi	happily
halvah	hams	handle	hanging	happiness

happing	hardish	harmonics	harshness	hatbox
happis	hardliner	harmonies	harslet	hatboxes
happy	hardly	harmonise	hart	hatch
haps	hardness	harmonist	hartal	hatchback
hapten	hardpan	harmonium	hartals	hatched
haptens	hards	harmonize	harts	hatchel
haptic	hardship	harmony	hartshorn	hatchels
hapu	hardships	harms	haruspex	hatchery
hapus	hardstone	harness	haruspicy	hatches
haram	hardtop	harnessed	harvest	hatchet
harangue	hardtops	harnesser	harvested	hatchets
harangued	hardware	harnesses	harvester	hatching
haranguer	hardwood	harp	harvests	hatchings
harangues	hardwoods	harped	has	hatchling
harass	hardy	harper	hash	hatchment
harassed	hare	harpers	hashed	hatchway
harasser	harebell	harpies	hashes	hatchways
harassers	harebells	harping	hashing	hate
harasses	hared	harpist	hashish	hateable
harassing	harelip	harpists	haslet	hated
harbinger	harelips	harpoon	hasp	hateful
harbor	harem	harpooned	hasped	hatefully
harborage	harems	harpooner	hasping	hater
harbored	hares	harpoons	hasps	haters
harboring	harewood	harps	hassium	hates
harbors	haricot	harpy	hassle	hatful
harbour	haricots	harquebus	hassled	hatfuls
harboured	haring	harridan	hassles	hath
harbours	harissa	harridans	hassling	hating
hard	hark	harried	hassock	hatless
hardback	harked	harrier	hassocks	hatpin
hardbacks	harken	harriers	hast	hatpins
hardball	harkened	harries	hastate	hatred
hardboard	harkening	harrow	haste	hats
hardcover	harkens	harrowed	hasted	hatstand
harden	harking	harrower	hasten	hatstands
hardened	harks	harrowers	hastened	hatted
hardener	harlequin	harrowing	hastening	hatter
hardeners	harlot	harrows	hastens	hatters
hardening	harlotry	harrumph	hastes	hauberk
hardens	harlots	harrumphs	hastier	hauberks
harder	harm	harry	hastiest	haugh
hardest	harmattan	harrying	hastily	haughtier
hardhead	harmed	harsh	hastiness	haughtily
hardheads	harmful	harshen	hasting	haughty
hardier	harmfully	harshened	hasty	haul
hardiest	harming	harshens	hat	haulage
hardihood	harmless	harsher	hatable	hauled
hardily	harmonic	harshest	hatband	hauler
hardiness	harmonica	harshly	hatbands	haulers

haulier
hauliers
hauling
haulm
haulms
hauls
haunch
haunches
haunt
haunted
haunter
haunters
haunting
haunts
haurient
hausfrau
hausfraus
haustella
haustoria
hautboy
hautboys
hauteur
havala
have
haveli
havelis
haven
havens
haver
havered
havering
havers
haversack
haversin
haversine
haversins
haves
havildar
havildars
having
havoc
havocked
havocking
haw
hawed
hawfinch
hawing
hawk
hawkbit
hawkbits

hawked
hawker
hawkers
hawkfish
hawking
hawkish
hawkishly
hawklike
hawkmoth
hawkmoths
hawks
hawksbill
hawkshaw
hawkshaws
hawkweed
haws
hawse
hawsepipe
hawser
hawsers
hawses
hawthorn
hawthorns
hay
haybox
hayboxes
haycock
haycocks
haying
haylage
hayloft
haylofts
haymaker
haymakers
haymaking
haymow
haymows
hayrick
hayricks
hayride
hayrides
hayseed
hayseeds
haystack
haystacks
haywire
hazard
hazarded
hazarding
hazardous

hazards
haze
hazed
hazel
hazelnut
hazelnuts
hazels
hazes
hazier
haziest
hazily
haziness
hazing
hazy
hazzan
hazzanim

H E

he
head
headache
headaches
headachy
headage
headband
headbands
headboard
headbutt
headbutts
headcount
headdress
headed
headend
headends
header
headers
headgear
headhunt
headhunts
headier
headiest
headily
headiness
heading
headings
headlamp
headlamps
headland
headlands

headless
headlight
headline
headlined
headliner
headlines
headlock
headlocks
headlong
headman
headmen
headmost
headnote
headnotes
headpiece
headrail
headrails
headrest
headrests
headroom
heads
headsail
headsails
headscarf
headset
headsets
headship
headships
headsman
headsmen
headstall
headstay
headstays
headstock
headstone
headward
headwards
headwater
headway
headwind
headwinds
headword
headwords
headwork
headworks
heady
heal
healable
heald
healds

healed
healer
healers
healing
heals
health
healthful
healthier
healthily
healthy
heap
heaped
heaping
heaps
hear
hearable
heard
hearer
hearers
hearing
hearings
hearken
hearkened
hearkens
hears
hearsay
hearse
hearses
heart
heartache
heartbeat
heartburn
hearted
hearten
heartened
heartens
heartfelt
hearth
hearthrug
hearths
heartier
hearties
heartiest
heartily
heartland
heartless
hearts
heartsick
heartsore
heartwood

hearty	hectic	hegemony	helium	helplines
heat	hectogram	hegira	helix	helpmate
heated	hector	heiau	hell	helpmates
heatedly	hectored	heiaus	hellcat	helpmeet
heater	hectoring	heifer	hellcats	helpmeets
heaters	hectors	heifers	hellebore	helps
heath	hedarim	heigh	heller	helve
heathen	heddle	height	hellers	helves
heathens	heddles	heighten	hellfire	hem
heather	heder	heightens	hellhole	hemal
heathery	heders	heights	hellholes	hematic
heathland	hedge	heinie	hellhound	hematin
heaths	hedged	heinies	hellion	hematite
heathy	hedgehog	heinous	hellions	hematites
heating	hedgehogs	heinously	hellish	hematoma
heatproof	hedger	heir	hellishly	hematuria
heats	hedgerow	heirdom	hello	heme
heatwave	hedgerows	heirdoms	helloed	hemicycle
heatwaves	hedgers	heiress	helloes	hemiola
heave	hedges	heiresses	helloing	hemiolas
heaved	hedging	heirless	hellos	hemipenes
heaven	hedonic	heirloom	hells	hemipenis
heavenly	hedonism	heirlooms	helluva	hemipode
heavens	hedonist	heirs	hellward	hemipodes
heaver	hedonists	heirship	helm	hemiptera
heavers	heed	heirships	helmed	hemistich
heaves	heeded	heist	helmet	hemline
heavier	heedful	heisted	helmeted	hemlines
heavies	heedfully	heisting	helmets	hemlock
heaviest	heeding	heists	helming	hemlocks
heavily	heedless	held	helminth	hemmed
heaviness	heeds	helenium	helminths	hemming
heaving	heel	heleniums	helms	hemocoel
heavy	heelball	helical	helmsman	hemocoels
heavyish	heeled	helically	helmsmen	hemolymph
hebe	heeling	helices	helot	hemolysis
hebes	heelless	helicity	helotage	hemolytic
hebetude	heels	helicoid	helotism	hemostat
hecatomb	heeltap	helicoids	helotry	hemostats
hecatombs	heeltaps	helicon	helots	hemp
heck	heft	heliconia	help	hempen
heckle	hefted	helicons	helped	hempseed
heckled	heftier	helictite	helper	hems
heckler	heftiest	heliogram	helpers	hemstitch
hecklers	heftily	heliostat	helpful	hen
heckles	heftiness	heliozoan	helpfully	henbane
heckling	hefting	helipad	helping	henbanes
hectarage	hefts	helipads	helpings	henbit
hectare	hefty	heliport	helpless	henbits
hectares	hegemonic	heliports	helpline	hence

henchman
henchmen
hendiadys
henequen
henge
henges
henna
hennaed
hennaing
hennas
henpeck
henpecked
henpecks
henries
henry
henrys
hens
hep
heparin
hepatic
hepatica
hepatitis
hepatoma
hepatomas
hepcat
hepcats
heptad
heptads
heptagon
heptagons
heptane
heptanes
heptarchy
heptyl
her
herald
heralded
heraldic
heralding
heraldist
heraldry
heralds
herb
herbage
herbal
herbalism
herbalist
herbals
herbaria
herbaries

herbarium
herbary
herbed
herbicide
herbier
herbiest
herbivore
herbs
herby
herd
herdboy
herdboys
herded
herder
herders
herding
herds
herdsman
herdsmen
here
hereabout
hereafter
hereat
hereby
heredity
herein
hereof
heresies
heresy
heretic
heretical
heretics
hereto
hereunder
hereunto
hereupon
herewith
heriot
heriots
heritable
heritably
heritage
heritor
heritors
herl
herls
herm
hermetic
hermit
hermitage

hermitic
hermits
herms
hernia
herniae
hernial
hernias
herniate
herniated
herniates
hero
heroes
heroic
heroics
heroin
heroine
heroines
heroise
heroised
heroises
heroising
heroism
heroize
heroized
heroizes
heroizing
heron
heronries
heronry
herons
herp
herpes
herpetic
herptile
herptiles
herring
herrings
hers
herself
herstory
hertz
hesitance
hesitancy
hesitant
hesitate
hesitated
hesitater
hesitates
hessian
hest

het
hetaera
hetaerae
hetaeras
hetaira
hetairai
hetairas
hetero
heterodox
heteronym
heteros
heterosis
heterotic
hetman
hetmen
heuchera
heucheras
heurige
heurigen
heuriger
heuristic
hevea
heveas
hew
hewed
hewer
hewers
hewing
hewn
hews
hex
hexachord
hexad
hexads
hexagon
hexagonal
hexagons
hexagram
hexagrams
hexahedra
hexameter
hexane
hexapla
hexaplas
hexaploid
hexapod
hexapods
hexastyle
hexed
hexes

hexing
hexose
hexoses
hexyl
hey
heyday

H I

hi
hiatal
hiatus
hiatuses
hiba
hibachi
hibachis
hibakusha
hibernate
hibiscus
hic
hiccough
hiccoughs
hiccup
hiccuped
hiccuping
hiccups
hiccupy
hick
hickey
hickeys
hickories
hickory
hicks
hid
hidalgo
hidalgos
hidden
hiddenite
hide
hideaway
hideaways
hidebound
hided
hideous
hideously
hideout
hideouts
hider
hiders
hides

hiding
hidings
hidrosis
hidrotic
hie
hied
hieing
hielaman
hielamans
hierarch
hierarchy
hieratic
hierogram
hierology
hies
higgle
higgled
higgler
higglers
higgles
higgling
high
highball
highballs
highboy
highboys
highbrow
highbrows
higher
highest
highland
highlands
highlife
highlight
highly
highness
highs
hight
hightail
hightails
highway
highways
hijack
hijacked
hijacker
hijackers
hijacking
hijacks
hijra

hike
hiked
hiker
hikers
hikes
hiking
hila
hilar
hilarious
hilarity
hili
hill
hillbilly
hilled
hillier
hilliest
hilliness
hilling
hillman
hillmen
hillock
hillocks
hillocky
hills
hillside
hillsides
hillstar
hillstars
hilltop
hilltops
hilly
hilt
hilted
hilts
hilum
hilus
him
himation
himself
hin
hind
hindbrain
hinder
hindered
hindering
hinders
hindmost
hindrance
hinds
hindsight

hindwing
hindwings
hinge
hinged
hingeing
hingeless
hinges
hinging
hinkier
hinkiest
hinky
hinnie
hinnies
hinny
hinoki
hint
hinted
hinting
hints
hip
hipness
hipped
hipper
hippest
hippie
hippiedom
hippies
hippiness
hippo
hippocras
hippos
hippurate
hippus
hippy
hippyish
hips
hipshot
hipster
hipsters
hirable
hiragana
hircine
hire
hireable
hired
hireling
hirelings
hirer
hirers
hires

hiring
hirola
hirolas
hirple
hirpled
hirples
hirpling
hirsute
hirsutism
hirundine
his
hispid
hiss
hissed
hisself
hisses
hissing
hist
histamine
histidine
histogeny
histogram
histology
histone
histones
historian
historic
histories
history
histosol
histosols
hit
hitch
hitched
hitcher
hitchers
hitches
hitching
hither
hitherto
hits
hitter
hitters
hitting
hive
hived
hives
hiving

hiya

hmm

ho
hoagie
hoagies
hoar
hoard
hoarded
hoarder
hoarders
hoarding
hoardings
hoards
hoarhound
hoarier
hoariest
hoarily
hoariness
hoarse
hoarsely
hoarsen
hoarsened
hoarsens
hoarser
hoarsest
hoarstone
hoary
hoatzin
hoatzins
hoax
hoaxed
hoaxer
hoaxers
hoaxes
hoaxing
hob
hobbies
hobbit
hobbits
hobble
hobbled
hobbler
hobblers
hobbles

hobbling	hoer	hokiness	hollowest	homemaker
hobby	hoers	hoking	hollowing	homeobox
hobbyist	hoes	hokkie	hollowly	homeopath
hobbyists	hog	hokkies	hollows	homeoses
hobday	hogan	hokku	holly	homeosis
hobdayed	hogans	hokonui	hollyhock	homeotic
hobdaying	hogback	hoks	holm	homeowner
hobdays	hogbacks	hokum	holme	homer
hobgoblin	hogfish	hold	holmes	homers
hobnail	hogfishes	holdable	holmium	homes
hobnailed	hogg	holdall	holms	homesick
hobnails	hogged	holdalls	holo	homesite
hobnob	hogger	holdback	holocaust	homesites
hobnobbed	hoggeries	holdbacks	hologram	homespun
hobnobs	hoggers	holder	holograms	homestead
hobo	hoggery	holders	holograph	homestyle
hoboes	hogget	holdfast	holos	homeward
hobos	hoggets	holdfasts	holotype	homewards
hobs	hoggin	holding	holotypes	homework
hock	hogging	holdings	hols	homey
hocked	hoggish	holdout	holster	homeyness
hocket	hoggishly	holdouts	holstered	homicidal
hocketing	hoggs	holdover	holsters	homicide
hockets	hognut	holdovers	holt	homicides
hockey	hognuts	holds	holts	homie
hockeys	hogs	hole	holy	homier
hocking	hogshead	holed	holystone	homies
hocks	hogsheads	holes	hom	homiest
hocus	hogwash	holey	homa	homiletic
hocused	hogweed	holiday	homage	homiliary
hocuses	hoick	holidayed	homas	homilies
hocusing	hoicked	holidays	hombre	homilist
hocussed	hoicking	holier	hombres	homilists
hocusses	hoicks	holiest	homburg	homily
hocussing	hoisin	holiness	homburgs	hominess
hod	hoist	holing	home	homing
hodden	hoisted	holism	homebody	hominid
hodiernal	hoister	holist	homeboy	hominids
hodman	hoisters	holistic	homeboys	hominoid
hodmen	hoisting	holla	homebuyer	hominoids
hodograph	hoists	holland	homed	hominy
hodoscope	hok	hollands	homegirl	homo
hods	hoke	holler	homegirls	homoeobox
hoe	hoked	hollered	homeland	homoeoses
hoecake	hokes	hollering	homelands	homoeosis
hoecakes	hokey	hollers	homeless	homogamy
hoed	hokeyness	hollies	homelier	homograft
hoedown	hoki	hollow	homeliest	homograph
hoedowns	hokier	hollowed	homelike	homolog
hoeing	hokiest	hollower	homely	homologs

homologue	honked	hookers	hooves	hornbills
homology	honker	hookey	hop	hornbook
homonym	honkers	hooking	hopak	hornbooks
homonymic	honkies	hookless	hopaks	horned
homonyms	honking	hooklet	hope	hornero
homonymy	honks	hooklets	hoped	horneros
homophobe	honky	hooks	hopeful	hornet
homophone	honor	hooktip	hopefully	hornets
homophony	honorable	hooktips	hopefuls	hornfels
homopolar	honorand	hookworm	hopeless	hornier
homoptera	honorands	hookworms	hoper	horniest
homos	honoraria	hooky	hopers	horniness
homousian	honorary	hooley	hopes	horning
homs	honored	hooleys	hophead	hornist
homuncule	honorific	hooligan	hopheads	hornists
homunculi	honoring	hooligans	hoping	hornless
homy	honors	hoolock	hoplite	hornpipe
hon	honour	hoolocks	hoplites	hornpipes
honcho	honoured	hoon	hopped	horns
honchoed	honouring	hooned	hopper	horntail
honchoes	honours	hooning	hoppers	horntails
honchoing	hooch	hoons	hopping	hornworm
honchos	hood	hoop	hopple	hornworms
hone	hooded	hooped	hoppled	hornwort
honed	hoodie	hooper	hopples	hornworts
hones	hoodies	hoopers	hoppling	horny
honest	hooding	hooping	hoppy	horologe
honestly	hoodless	hoopla	hops	horologer
honesty	hoodlum	hooplas	hopsack	horologes
honewort	hoodlums	hoopoe	hopsacks	horologic
honeworts	hoodoo	hoopoes	hopscotch	horology
honey	hoodooed	hoops	hora	horopter
honeybee	hoodooing	hooray	horah	horopters
honeybees	hoodoos	hoorayed	horahs	horoscope
honeybird	hoods	hooraying	horal	horoscopy
honeybun	hoodwink	hoorays	horary	horrent
honeybuns	hoodwinks	hooroo	horas	horrible
honeycomb	hooey	hoosegow	horchata	horribly
honeydew	hoof	hoosegows	horde	horrid
honeydews	hoofed	hoot	hordes	horridly
honeyed	hoofer	hootch	horehound	horrific
honeymoon	hoofers	hooted	horizon	horrified
honeypot	hoofing	hooter	horizons	horrifies
honeypots	hoofs	hooters	hormonal	horrify
honeys	hook	hooting	hormone	horror
honeywort	hookah	hoots	hormones	horrors
hongi	hookahs	hoover	horn	horse
honied	hookbait	hoovered	hornbeam	horseback
honing	hooked	hoovering	hornbeams	horsebean
honk	hooker	hoovers	hornbill	horsebox

horsed	hosta	hotshot	houseroom	hoyas
horsefly	hostage	hotshots	houses	hoyden
horsehair	hostages	hotspur	housetop	hoydenish
horseless	hostas	hotspurs	housetops	hoydens
horseman	hosted	hotted	housewife	hoyed
horsemen	hostel	hotter	housework	hoying
horsemint	hosteling	hotters	housey	hoys
horseplay	hosteller	hottest	housing	
horses	hostelry	hottie	houting	
horseshit	hostels	hotties	houtings	H U
horseshoe	hostess	hotting	hove	huarache
horsetail	hostesses	hottish	hovel	huaraches
horsewhip	hostie	hotty	hovels	hub
horsey	hosties	houbara	hover	hubbies
horsier	hostile	houbaras	hovered	hubbub
horsiest	hostilely	hough	hoverer	hubby
horsily	hostility	houghed	hoverers	hubcap
horsiness	hosting	houghing	hoverfly	hubcaps
horsing	hostler	houghs	hovering	hubris
horst	hostlers	hoummos	hoverport	hubristic
horsts	hosts	hound	hovers	hubs
horsy	hot	hounded	how	huchen
hortation	hotbed	houndfish	howbeit	huckaback
hortative	hotbeds	hounding	howdah	huckster
hortatory	hotchpot	hounds	howdahs	hucksters
hortensia	hotdog	houngan	howdy	huddle
hos	hotdogged	houngans	howe	huddled
hosanna	hotdogger	hour	howes	huddles
hosannah	hotdogs	hourglass	however	huddling
hosannahs	hotel	houri	howff	hue
hosannas	hotelier	houris	howffs	hued
hose	hoteliers	hourly	howitzer	hueless
hosed	hotels	hours	howitzers	hues
hosel	hotfoot	house	howk	huff
hosels	hotfooted	houseboat	howked	huffed
hosepipe	hotfoots	houseboy	howking	huffier
hosepipes	hothead	houseboys	howks	huffiest
hoses	hotheads	housecarl	howl	huffily
hosier	hothouse	housecoat	howled	huffiness
hosiers	hothoused	housed	howler	huffing
hosiery	hothouses	housefly	howlers	huffish
hosing	hotline	houseful	howlet	huffs
hospice	hotlines	housefuls	howling	huffy
hospices	hotly	household	howls	hug
hospital	hotness	housekeep	howsoever	huge
hospitals	hotplate	houseleek	howtowdie	hugely
hospodar	hotplates	houseless	howzat	hugeness
hospodars	hotpot	housemaid	howzit	huger
hoss	hotpots	houseman	hoy	hugest
host	hots	housemen	hoya	huggable

hugged	humbly	humpbacks	hunyaks	hushed
hugging	humbug	humped	hurdle	hushes
hugs	humbugged	humph	hurdled	hushing
huh	humbugs	humpier	hurdler	husk
hui	humdinger	humpiest	hurdlers	husked
huia	humdrum	humping	hurdles	huskier
huies	humectant	humpless	hurdling	huskies
huis	humeral	humps	hurl	huskiest
hula	humeri	humpy	hurled	huskily
hulas	humerus	hums	hurler	huskiness
hulk	humic	humungous	hurlers	husking
hulking	humid	humus	hurley	husks
hulks	humidify	hunch	hurleys	husky
hull	humidity	hunchback	hurling	huss
hulled	humidly	hunched	hurls	hussar
hulling	humidor	hunches	hurrah	hussars
hullo	humidors	hunching	hurrahed	husses
hulloed	humified	hundred	hurrahing	hussies
hulloes	humifies	hundreds	hurrahs	hussy
hulloing	humify	hundredth	hurray	hustings
hullos	humifying	hung	hurrayed	hustle
hulls	humiliate	hunger	hurraying	hustled
hum	humility	hungered	hurrays	hustler
human	hummable	hungering	hurricane	hustlers
humane	hummed	hungers	hurried	hustles
humanely	hummel	hungrier	hurriedly	hustling
humaner	hummels	hungriest	hurries	hut
humanest	hummer	hungrily	hurroo	hutch
humanise	hummers	hungry	hurry	hutches
humanised	humming	hunk	hurrying	hutia
humanises	hummock	hunker	hurst	hutias
humanism	hummocks	hunkered	hursts	hutment
humanist	hummocky	hunkering	hurt	hutments
humanists	hummus	hunkers	hurtful	huts
humanity	humongous	hunkier	hurtfully	hutted
humanize	humor	hunkiest	hurting	hutting
humanized	humoral	hunks	hurtle	huzza
humanizes	humored	hunky	hurtled	huzzaed
humankind	humoring	hunt	hurtles	huzzah
humanly	humorist	huntaway	hurtling	huzzahs
humanness	humorists	huntaways	hurts	huzzaing
humanoid	humorous	hunted	husband	huzzas
humanoids	humors	hunter	husbanded	
humans	humour	hunters	husbander	
humble	humoured	hunting	husbandly	
humbled	humouring	huntress	husbandry	H W
humbler	humours	hunts	husbands	
humbles	humous	huntsman	hush	
humblest	hump	huntsmen	hushaby	
humbling	humpback	hunyak	hushabye	hwyl

H Y

hyacinth
hyacinths
hyaena
hyaenas
hyalin
hyaline
hyalite
hyaloid
hybrid
hybridise
hybridism
hybridity
hybridize
hybrids
hydantoin
hydathode
hydatid
hydatids
hydra
hydrae
hydrangea
hydrant
hydrants
hydras
hydrate
hydrated
hydrates
hydrating
hydration
hydrator
hydrators
hydraulic
hydrazine

hydria
hydriae
hydriai
hydric
hydride
hydrides
hydro
hydrocele
hydrofoil
hydrogel
hydrogels
hydrogen
hydroid
hydroids
hydrolase
hydrology
hydrolyse
hydrolyze
hydromel
hydronic
hydros
hydrous
hydroxide
hydroxyl
hydroxyls
hydrozoan
hyena
hyenas
hygiene
hygienic
hygienist
hying
hyla
hylas
hylozoism

hymen
hymenal
hymeneal
hymenia
hymenial
hymenium
hymens
hymn
hymnal
hymnals
hymnaries
hymnary
hymned
hymnic
hymning
hymnodies
hymnodist
hymnody
hymnology
hymns
hyoid
hyoids
hyoscine
hypallage
hypalon
hypanthia
hype
hyped
hyper
hyperbola
hyperbole
hypercube
hyperemia
hypergamy
hypericum

hyperlink
hypernym
hypernyms
hyperon
hyperons
hyperopia
hyperopic
hyperreal
hypertext
hypes
hypethral
hypha
hyphae
hyphal
hyphen
hyphenate
hyphened
hyphens
hyping
hypnosis
hypnotic
hypnotics
hypnotise
hypnotism
hypnotist
hypnotize
hypo
hypoblast
hypocaust
hypocotyl
hypocrisy
hypocrite
hypogea
hypogeal
hypogean

hypogene
hypogenic
hypogeum
hypogyny
hypoid
hypoids
hypomania
hypomanic
hyponym
hyponyms
hyponymy
hypos
hypospray
hypostyle
hypotaxis
hypothec
hypothecs
hypotonia
hypotonic
hypoxemia
hypoxia
hypoxic
hyracoid
hyracoids
hyrax
hyraxes
hyson
hyssop
hyssops
hysteria
hysteric
hysterics

I

I A

iamb
iambi
iambic
iambics
iambs
iambus
iambuses

I B

iberis
ibex
ibexes
ibis
ibisbill
ibisbills
ibises
ibogaine
ibuprofen

I C

ice
iceberg
icebergs
iceblink
iceblinks
iceblock
iceblocks
iceboat
iceboats
icebox
iceboxes
iced
icefall
icefalls
icefish
icefished
icefishes
iceman

icemen
ices
ichneumon
ichor
ichorous
ichthyic
icicle
icicles
icier
iciest
icily
iciness
icing
ick
ickier
ickiest
ickiness
icky
icon
iconic
iconicity
iconified
iconifies
iconify
iconodule
iconology
icons
ictal
icteric
icterus
ictus
ictuses
icy

I D

id
ide
idea
ideal
idealise
idealised

idealises
idealism
idealist
idealists
ideality
idealize
idealized
idealizer
idealizes
ideally
ideals
ideas
ideate
ideated
ideates
ideating
ideation
idem
ident
identical
identify
identikit
identity
ideogram
ideograms
ideograph
ideologue
ideology
ides
idigbo
idiocies
idiocy
idiolect
idiolects
idiom
idiomatic
idioms
idiopathy
idiophone
idiot
idiotic

idiots
idiotype
idiotypes
idle
idled
idleness
idler
idlers
idles
idlest
idli
idling
idlis
idly
idocrase
idol
idolater
idolaters
idolatry
idolise
idolised
idolises
idolising
idolize
idolized
idolizer
idolizers
idolizes
idolizing
idols
idyl
idyll
idyllic
idylls
idyls

I F

if
iff
iffier
iffiest

iffy
ifs

I G

igloo
igloos
igneous
ignitable
ignite
ignited
igniter
igniters
ignites
igniting
ignition
ignitron
ignitrons
ignoble
ignobler
ignoblest
ignobly
ignominy
ignorable
ignoramus
ignorance
ignorant
ignore
ignored
ignorer
ignorers
ignores
ignoring
iguana
iguanas
iguanid
iguanids
iguanodon

I I

iimbongi
iiwi
iiwis

I K

ikat
ikebana
ikky
ikon
ikons

I L

ilea
ileac
ileal
ileitis
ileostomy
ileum
ileus
ileuses
ilex
ilexes
ilia
iliac
iliacus
ilium
ilk
ill
illation
illations
illative
illegal
illegally
illegals
illegible
illegibly
iller
illest
illiberal
illicit
illicitly
illiquid
illite
illness
illnesses
illogic
illogical
ills
illude
illuded
illudes
illuding

illume
illumed
illumes
illumine
illumined
illumines
illuming
illusion
illusions
illusive
illusory
illuvial
ilmenite
ilmenites
ilvaite

I M

image
imaged
imageless
imager
imagers
imagery
images
imaginal
imaginary
imagine
imagined
imagineer
imaginer
imaginers
imagines
imaging
imagining
imagism
imagist
imagistic
imagists
imago
imagos
imam
imamate
imamates
imams
imbalance
imbecile
imbeciles
imbecilic
imbed

imbedded
imbedding
imbeds
imbibe
imbibed
imbiber
imbibers
imbibes
imbibing
imbizo
imbizos
imbongi
imbongis
imbricate
imbroglio
imbrue
imbrued
imbrues
imbruing
imbue
imbued
imbues
imbuing
imidazole
imide
imides
imine
imines
imitable
imitate
imitated
imitates
imitating
imitation
imitative
imitator
imitators
imli
imlis
immanence
immanency
immanent
immature
immediacy
immediate
immense
immensely
immensity
immerse
immersed

immerses
immersing
immersion
immersive
immigrant
immigrate
imminence
imminent
immixture
immobile
immodest
immodesty
immolate
immolated
immolates
immolator
immoral
immorally
immortal
immortals
immotile
immovable
immovably
immune
immunise
immunised
immunises
immunity
immunize
immunized
immunizer
immunizes
immure
immured
immures
immuring
immutable
immutably
imp
impact
impacted
impacting
impaction
impactive
impactor
impactors
impacts
impair
impaired
impairing

impairs
impala
impalas
impale
impaled
impaler
impalers
impales
impaling
impanate
impanel
impaneled
impanels
impark
imparked
imparking
imparks
impart
imparted
impartial
imparting
imparts
impasse
impasses
impassion
impassive
impasto
impastos
impatiens
impatient
impeach
impeached
impeaches
imped
impedance
impede
impeded
impedes
impeding
impel
impelled
impeller
impellers
impelling
impellor
impellors
impels
impend
impended
impending

impends	implying	improved	inarched	inch
imperator	impolder	improver	inarches	inched
imperfect	impolders	improvers	inarching	inches
imperial	impolite	improves	inasmuch	inching
imperials	impolitic	improving	inaudible	inchmeal
imperil	import	improvise	inaudibly	inchoate
imperiled	important	improvs	inaugural	inchworm
imperils	imported	imprudent	inboard	inchworms
imperious	importer	imps	inborn	incidence
imperium	importers	impudence	inbound	incident
impetigo	importing	impudent	inbounded	incidents
impetrate	imports	impugn	inbounds	incipient
impetuous	importune	impugned	inbreathe	incipit
impetus	impose	impugning	inbred	incipits
impi	imposed	impugns	inbreed	incircle
impieties	imposes	impulse	inbreeds	incircles
impiety	imposing	impulses	inbuilt	incise
imping	impost	impulsion	inca	incised
impinge	imposter	impulsive	incant	incises
impinged	imposters	impunity	incanted	incising
impinger	impostor	impure	incanting	incision
impingers	impostors	impurely	incants	incisions
impinges	imposts	impurity	incapable	incisive
impinging	imposture	imputable	incapably	incisor
impious	impotence	impute	incarnate	incisors
impiously	impotency	imputed	incas	incisura
impis	impotent	imputes	incase	incisurae
impish	impound	imputing	incased	incisure
impishly	impounded	imshi	incases	incisures
implant	impounder		incasing	incite
implanted	impounds	**I N**	incaution	incited
implants	imprecate		incense	inciteful
implement	imprecise	in	incensed	inciter
implicate	impress	inability	incenses	inciters
implicit	impressed	inaction	incensing	incites
implied	impresses	inactive	incensory	inciting
impliedly	imprest	inamorata	incenter	inclement
implies	imprests	inamorato	incenters	incline
implode	imprint	inane	incentive	inclined
imploded	imprinted	inanely	incentre	incliner
implodes	imprints	inaneness	incept	incliners
imploding	imprison	inanga	incepted	inclines
implore	imprisons	inangas	incepting	inclining
implored	impro	inanimate	inception	inclose
implores	improbity	inanities	inceptive	inclosed
imploring	impromptu	inanition	inceptor	incloses
implosion	improper	inanity	inceptors	inclosing
implosive	impros	inapt	incepts	inclosure
impluvium	improv	inaptly	incessant	include
imply	improve	inarch	incest	included

includes	incurves	indicted	inducers	inept
including	incurving	indictee	induces	ineptly
inclusion	incus	indictees	inducible	ineptness
inclusive	incuse	indicter	inducing	inequity
incog	incused	indicters	induct	inerrancy
incognito	incuses	indicting	inducted	inerrant
income	incusing	indiction	inductee	inert
incomer	indaba	indicts	inductees	inertia
incomers	indabas	indie	inducting	inertial
incomes	indebted	indies	induction	inertly
incoming	indecency	indigence	inductive	inertness
incomings	indecent	indigene	inductor	inexact
incommode	indecorum	indigenes	inductors	inexactly
inconnu	indeed	indigent	inducts	inexpert
inconnus	indeedy	indigents	indue	infall
incorrect	indelible	indignant	indued	infamies
incorrupt	indelibly	indignity	indues	infamous
increase	indemnify	indigo	induing	infamy
increased	indemnity	indigoes	indulge	infancy
increases	indene	indigoid	indulged	infant
increate	indenes	indigos	indulgent	infanta
increment	indent	indigotin	indulger	infantas
incrust	indented	indirect	indulgers	infante
incrusted	indenter	indispose	indulges	infanteer
incrusts	indenters	indite	indulging	infantes
incubate	indenting	indited	induline	infantile
incubated	indention	indites	indulines	infantine
incubates	indentor	inditing	indult	infantry
incubator	indentors	indium	indults	infants
incubi	indents	indocile	indumenta	infarct
incubous	indenture	indole	induna	infarcts
incubus	index	indolence	indunas	infatuate
incudes	indexable	indolent	indurate	infauna
inculcate	indexed	indoles	indurated	infaunal
inculpate	indexer	indoor	indurates	infect
incumbent	indexers	indoors	indusia	infected
incunable	indexes	indorse	indusium	infecting
incur	indexible	indorsed	industry	infection
incurable	indexical	indorses	indwell	infective
incurably	indexing	indorsing	indweller	infector
incurious	indican	indoxyl	indwells	infectors
incurred	indicant	indraft	indwelt	infects
incurrent	indicants	indrafts	inebriate	infecund
incurring	indicate	indraught	inebriety	infeed
incurs	indicated	indrawn	inedible	infer
incursion	indicates	indri	inedited	inferable
incursive	indicator	indris	ineffable	inference
incurvate	indices	induce	ineffably	inferior
incurve	indicia	induced	inelastic	inferiors
incurved	indict	inducer	inelegant	infernal

inferno	inflexed	ingather	inhaling	injure
infernos	inflexion	ingathers	inhaul	injured
inferred	inflict	ingenious	inhere	injurer
inferring	inflicted	ingénue	inhered	injurers
infers	inflicter	ingénues	inherence	injures
infertile	inflicts	ingenuity	inherent	injuries
infest	inflow	ingenuous	inheres	injuring
infested	inflowing	ingest	inhering	injurious
infesting	inflows	ingesta	inherit	injury
infests	influence	ingested	inherited	injustice
infidel	influent	ingesting	inheritor	ink
infidels	influents	ingestion	inherits	inkberry
infield	influenza	ingestive	inhesion	inked
infielder	influx	ingests	inhibin	inker
infields	influxes	ingle	inhibit	inkers
infighter	info	inglenook	inhibited	inkhorn
infill	infobahn	ingles	inhibitor	inkhorns
infilled	infobahns	ingoing	inhibits	inkier
infilling	infolded	ingot	inhuman	inkiest
infills	infolding	ingots	inhumane	inkiness
infimum	inform	ingraft	inhumanly	inking
infimums	informal	ingrafted	inhume	inkle
infinite	informant	ingrafts	inhumed	inkling
infinity	informed	ingrain	inhumes	inklings
infirm	informer	ingrained	inhuming	inks
infirmary	informers	ingrains	inimical	inkstand
infirmity	informing	ingrate	inion	inkstands
infirmly	informs	ingrates	inions	inkwell
infix	infotech	ingress	iniquity	inkwells
infixed	infra	ingresses	initial	inky
infixes	infractor	ingrowing	initialed	inlaid
infixing	infradian	ingrown	initially	inland
inflame	infrared	ingrowth	initials	inlander
inflamed	infringe	ingrowths	initiand	inlanders
inflamer	infringed	inguinal	initiate	inlay
inflamers	infringer	ingulf	initiated	inlayer
inflames	infringes	ingulfed	initiates	inlayers
inflaming	infula	ingulfing	initiator	inlaying
inflate	infulae	ingulfs	inject	inlays
inflated	infuriate	inhabit	injected	inlet
inflater	infuse	inhabited	injecting	inlets
inflaters	infused	inhabits	injection	inlier
inflates	infuser	inhalant	injective	inliers
inflating	infusers	inhalants	injector	inly
inflation	infuses	inhalator	injectors	inlying
inflator	infusible	inhale	injects	inmate
inflators	infusing	inhaled	injera	inmates
inflect	infusion	inhaler	injunct	inmost
inflected	infusions	inhalers	injuncted	inn
inflects	infusoria	inhales	injuncts	innards

innate	inquires	insidious	instant	inswing
innately	inquiries	insight	instanter	inswinger
inner	inquiring	insights	instantly	intact
innerly	inquiry	insignia	instants	intaglio
innermost	inquorate	insignias	instar	intaglios
innerness	inro	insincere	instars	intake
innervate	inroad	insinuate	instate	intakes
inning	inroads	insipid	instated	intarsia
innings	inros	insipidly	instates	integer
inningses	inrush	insist	instating	integers
innit	inrushes	insisted	instead	integral
innkeeper	inrushing	insistent	instep	integrals
innocence	insane	insisting	insteps	integrand
innocency	insanely	insists	instigate	integrant
innocent	insanity	insofar	instil	integrate
innocents	insatiate	insole	instill	integrity
innocuous	inscape	insolence	instilled	intellect
innovate	inscribe	insolent	instills	intend
innovated	inscribed	insoles	instils	intendant
innovates	inscriber	insoluble	instinct	intended
innovator	inscribes	insolubly	instincts	intendeds
inns	inseam	insolvent	institute	intender
innuendo	inseams	insomnia	instruct	intenders
innuendos	insect	insomniac	instructs	intending
inocula	insectan	insomuch	insula	intends
inoculant	insectary	inspan	insulae	intense
inoculate	insectile	inspanned	insulant	intensely
inoculum	insects	inspans	insular	intenser
inodorous	insecure	inspect	insularly	intensest
inorganic	inselberg	inspected	insulate	intensify
inosine	insensate	inspector	insulated	intension
inosines	insert	inspects	insulates	intensity
inositol	inserted	inspire	insulator	intensive
inositols	inserter	inspired	insulin	intent
inotropic	inserters	inspirer	insulitis	intention
inpatient	inserting	inspirers	insult	intently
inpouring	insertion	inspires	insulted	intents
input	inserts	inspiring	insulter	inter
inputs	inset	inspirit	insulters	interact
inputted	insets	inspirits	insulting	interacts
inputter	insetted	instal	insults	interbed
inputters	insetter	install	insurable	interbeds
inputting	insetters	installed	insurance	interbred
inquest	insetting	installer	insure	intercede
inquests	inshallah	installs	insured	intercept
inquiline	inshore	instals	insurer	intercity
inquire	inside	instance	insurers	intercom
inquired	insider	instanced	insures	intercoms
inquirer	insiders	instances	insurgent	intercool
inquirers	insides	instancy	insuring	intercrop

intercut	interred	intrigues	inurned	investing
intercuts	interring	intrinsic	inurning	investor
interdict	interrupt	intro	inurns	investors
interest	inters	introduce	inutile	invests
interests	intersect	introit	inutility	inviable
interface	intersex	introits	invade	invidious
interfere	interval	introject	invaded	inviolacy
interfile	intervals	intron	invader	inviolate
interflow	intervene	intronic	invaders	inviscid
interfuse	interview	introns	invades	invisible
intergrew	interwar	introrse	invading	invisibly
intergrow	interwind	intros	invalid	invite
interim	interwork	introvert	invalided	invited
interims	interwove	intrude	invalidly	invitee
interior	intestacy	intruded	invalids	invitees
interiors	intestate	intruder	invariant	inviter
interject	intestine	intruders	invasion	inviters
interlace	inthrall	intrudes	invasions	invites
interlaid	intifada	intruding	invasive	inviting
interlard	intifadas	intrusion	invected	invoice
interlay	intima	intrusive	invective	invoiced
interlays	intimacy	intrust	inveigh	invoices
interleaf	intimae	intrusted	inveighed	invoicing
interline	intimal	intrusts	inveighs	invoke
interlink	intimate	intubate	inveigle	invoked
interlock	intimated	intubated	inveigled	invoker
interlope	intimates	intubates	inveigles	invokers
interlude	intimism	intuit	invent	invokes
interment	intimist	intuited	invented	invoking
intermesh	intimists	intuiting	inventing	involucre
intermit	intitule	intuition	invention	involute
intermits	intituled	intuitive	inventive	involuted
intermix	intitules	intuits	inventor	involutes
intern	into	intumesce	inventors	involve
internal	intone	intwine	inventory	involved
internals	intoned	intwined	invents	involves
internaut	intoner	intwines	inverse	involving
interne	intoners	intwining	inversely	inwale
interned	intones	inulin	inverses	inwales
internee	intoning	inulins	inversion	inward
internees	intraday	inunction	inversive	inwardly
internes	intrados	inundate	invert	inwards
interning	intrench	inundated	invertase	inwrap
internist	intrepid	inundates	inverted	inwrapped
internode	intricacy	inure	inverter	inwraps
interns	intricate	inured	inverters	inwreathe
interplay	intrigant	inurement	inverting	inwrought
interpole	intrigue	inures	inverts	inyanga
interpose	intrigued	inuring	invest	inyangas
interpret	intriguer	inurn	invested	

☐I☐ ☐O☐

iodate
iodates
iodide
iodides
iodinate
iodinated
iodinates
iodine
iodines
iodism
iodoform
iodometry
iodophor
iodophors
ion
ionic
ionically
ionise
ionised
ionises
ionising
ionizable
ionize
ionized
ionizer
ionizers
ionizes
ionizing
ionomer
ionopause
ionophore
ions
iora
ioras
iota
iotas

☐I☐ ☐P☐

ipecac
ipecacs
ipomoea
ippon

☐I☐ ☐R☐

irade
irascible
irascibly

irate
irately
irateness
ire
ireful
irenic
irenical
irenicon
irenicons
irenics
iridium
iridology
irie
iris
irised
irises
irising
iritis
irk
irked
irking
irks
irksome
irksomely
iroko
irokos
iron
ironbark
ironbarks
ironclad
ironclads
ironed
ironer
ironers
ironic
ironical
ironies
ironing
ironise
ironised
ironises
ironising
ironist
ironists
ironize
ironized
ironizes
ironizing
irons
ironstone

ironware
ironwood
ironwoods
ironwork
ironworks
irony
irradiant
irradiate
irregular
irrigable
irrigate
irrigated
irrigates
irrigator
irritable
irritably
irritancy
irritant
irritants
irritate
irritated
irritates
irritator
irrupt
irrupted
irrupting
irruption
irruptive
irrupts

☐I☐ ☐S☐

is
isagogic
isagogics
isallobar
isangoma
isangomas
isatin
ischaemia
ischaemic
ischemia
ischia
ischial
ischium
isinglass
island
islander
islanders
islands

isle
isles
islesman
islesmen
islet
islets
ism
isms
isobar
isobaric
isobars
isobutane
isobutyl
isocheim
isocheims
isochron
isochrons
isoclinal
isocline
isoclines
isoclinic
isocratic
isoenzyme
isogamete
isogamies
isogamous
isogamy
isogenic
isogloss
isogonic
isohel
isohels
isohyet
isohyets
isolable
isolate
isolated
isolates
isolating
isolation
isolator
isolators
isoline
isomer
isomerase
isomeric
isomerise
isomerism
isomerize

isomerous
isomers
isometric
isometry
isoniazid
isooctane
isopach
isopachs
isophote
isophotes
isopleth
isopleths
isopod
isopods
isoprene
isopropyl
isopteran
isopycnal
isopycnic
isosceles
isosmotic
isospin
isospins
isostasy
isostatic
isotactic
isothere
isotheres
isotherm
isotherms
isotonic
isotope
isotopes
isotopic
isotopies
isotopy
isotropic
isotropy
isozyme
isozymes
ispaghul
ispaghula
issei
issuable
issuance
issuant
issue
issued
issueless
issuer

issuers
issues
issuing
ist
isthmi
isthmian
isthmus
isthmuses
istle
ists

I T

it
ital
italic
italicise

italicize
italics
itch
itched
itches
itchier
itchiest
itchiness
itching
itchy
item
itemise
itemised
itemises
itemising
itemize

itemized
itemizer
itemizers
itemizes
itemizing
items
iterate
iterated
iterates
iterating
iteration
iterative
itineracy
itinerant
itinerary
itinerate

its
itself

I V

ivied
ivies
ivoried
ivories
ivorine
ivory
ivy

I W

iwi
iwis

I X

ixia
ixias
ixtle

I Z

izard
izards
izimbongi
izinyanga
izzat

J

J A

ja
jab
jabbed
jabber
jabbered
jabbering
jabbers
jabbing
jabiru
jabirus
jaborandi
jabot
jabots
jabs
jacal
jacales
jacamar
jacamars
jacana
jacanas

jacaranda
jacinth
jacinths
jack
jackal
jackals
jackaroo
jackaroos
jackass
jackasses
jackboot
jackboots
jackdaw
jackdaws
jacked
jackeen
jackeens
jackeroo
jackeroos
jacket
jacketed

jacketing
jackets
jackfish
jackfruit
jacking
jackknife
jackleg
jacklegs
jackpot
jackpots
jacks
jackshit
jacksie
jacksies
jackstaff
jackstay
jackstays
jackstone
jackstraw
jacksy
jacobin

jacobins
jaconet
jaconets
jacquard
jacquards
jacquerie
jacuzzi
jacuzzis
jade
jaded
jadedly
jadedness
jadeite
jades
jaeger
jaegers
jag
jagged
jaggedly
jagger
jaggers

jaggery
jaggie
jaggier
jaggiest
jagging
jaggy
jagir
jagirs
jags
jaguar
jaguars
jail
jailbait
jailbird
jailbirds
jailbreak
jailed
jailer
jailers
jailhouse
jailing

jails	janizary	jaunty	jeep	jerker
jake	jankers	java	jeepers	jerkers
jakes	japan	javelin	jeeps	jerkier
jalap	japanned	javelina	jeer	jerkiest
jalebi	japanning	javelinas	jeera	jerkily
jalebis	japans	javelins	jeered	jerkin
jaleo	jape	jaw	jeering	jerkiness
jaleos	japed	jawan	jeeringly	jerking
jalapeño	japeries	jawans	jeers	jerkins
jalapeños	japery	jawbone	jehad	jerks
jalopies	japes	jawbones	jehads	jerkwater
jalopy	japing	jawed	jejunal	jerky
jalousie	japonica	jawfish	jejune	jeroboam
jalousies	japonicas	jawfishes	jejunely	jeroboams
jam	jar	jawing	jejunum	jerrican
jamadar	jarful	jawless	jell	jerricans
jamadars	jargon	jawline	jellaba	jerries
jamb	jargonise	jawlines	jellabas	jerry
jambalaya	jargonize	jaws	jelled	jerrycan
jambeau	jargoon	jay	jellied	jerrycans
jambeaus	jarl	jays	jellies	jersey
jambeaux	jarls	jaywalk	jellified	jerseys
jamboree	jarool	jaywalked	jellifies	jess
jamborees	jarools	jaywalker	jellify	jessamine
jambs	jarrah	jaywalks	jelling	jessed
jammed	jarrahs	jazz	jello	jesses
jammer	jarred	jazzbo	jells	jessie
jammers	jarring	jazzbos	jelly	jessies
jammier	jars	jazzed	jellyfish	jessing
jammies	jarul	jazzer	jellying	jessy
jammiest	jaruls	jazzers	jelutong	jest
jamming	jasmine	jazzes	jelutongs	jested
jammy	jasmines	jazzier	jemadar	jester
jamrool	jaspé	jazziest	jemadars	jesters
jamrools	jasper	jazzily	jemmied	jesting
jams	jatha	jazziness	jemmies	jests
jamun	jathas	jazzing	jemmy	jet
jamuns	jati	jazzman	jemmying	jeté
jane	jatis	jazzmen	jennet	jetés
janes	jato	jazzy	jennies	jetfoil
jangle	jatos		jenny	jetfoils
jangled	jaundice	**J E**	jeon	jetliner
jangles	jaundiced		jeopardy	jetliners
janglier	jaunt	jealous	jerboa	jets
jangliest	jaunted	jealously	jerboas	jetsam
jangling	jauntier	jealousy	jeremiad	jetted
jangly	jauntiest	jean	jeremiads	jetties
janissary	jauntily	jeans	jerepigo	jetting
janitor	jaunting	jebel	jerk	jettison
janitors	jaunts	jebels	jerked	jettisons

jetton
jettons
jetty
jetway
jetways
jewel
jeweled
jeweler
jewelers
jewelfish
jewelled
jeweller
jewellers
jewellery
jewelry
jewels
jewfish
jewfishes

J H

jhuggi
jhuggis

J I

jiao
jib
jibba
jibbah
jibbahs
jibbas
jibbed
jibber
jibbers
jibbing
jibe
jibed
jibes
jibing
jibs
jicama
jiff
jiffies
jiffs
jiffy
jig
jigaboo
jigaboos
jigged

jigger
jiggered
jiggering
jiggers
jigging
jiggle
jiggled
jiggles
jiggling
jiggly
jigs
jigsaw
jigsaws
jihad
jihads
jill
jillaroo
jillion
jills
jilt
jilted
jilting
jilts
jimmied
jimmies
jimmy
jimmying
jing
jingbang
jingle
jingled
jingler
jinglers
jingles
jinglier
jingliest
jingling
jingly
jingo
jingoes
jingoism
jingoist
jingoists
jings
jink
jinked
jinker
jinkered
jinkering
jinkers

jinking
jinks
jinn
jinns
jinx
jinxed
jinxes
jinxing
jird
jirds
jism
jissom
jit
jitney
jitneys
jitter
jitterbug
jittered
jittering
jitters
jittery
jive
jived
jiver
jivers
jives
jivey
jiving
jizz
jizzes

J O

jo
joanna
joannas
job
jobbed
jobber
jobbers
jobbery
jobbie
jobbies
jobbing
jobcentre
jobless
jobs
jobsworth
jock
jockey

jockeyed
jockeying
jockeys
jockish
jocks
jockstrap
jocose
jocosely
jocosity
jocular
jocularly
jocund
jocundity
jocundly
jodhpurs
joe
joes
joey
joeys
jog
jogged
jogger
joggers
jogging
joggle
joggled
joggles
joggling
jogs
jogtrot
jogtrots
john
johnboat
johnboats
johnnies
johnny
johns
join
joinable
joinder
joined
joiner
joiners
joinery
joining
joins
joint
jointed
jointer
jointers

jointing
jointless
jointly
jointress
joints
jointure
jointures
joist
joisted
joists
jojoba
joke
joked
joker
jokers
jokes
jokey
jokily
jokiness
joking
jokingly
joky
jol
joliotium
jolled
joller
jollied
jollier
jollies
jolliest
jollily
jolliness
jolling
jollities
jollity
jollo
jollos
jolly
jollying
jollytail
jols
jolt
jolted
joltier
joltiest
jolting
jolts
jolty
jones
jonesed

joneses
jonesing
jong
jongleur
jongleurs
jongs
jonquil
jonquils
jorum
jorums
josh
joshed
josher
joshers
joshes
joshing
joss
josser
jossers
jostle
jostled
jostles
jostling
jot
jota
jotas
jots
jotted
jotter
jotters
jotting
jottings
joual
jougs
jouk
jouked
jouking
jouks
joule
joules
jounce
jounced
jounces
jouncing
journal
journals
journey
journeyed
journeyer
journeys

journo
journos
joust
jousted
jouster
jousters
jousting
jousts
jovial
joviality
jovially
jowar
jowl
jowled
jowlier
jowliest
jowls
jowly
joy
joyed
joyful
joyfully
joying
joyless
joylessly
joyous
joyously
joypad
joypads
joyride
joyrider
joyriders
joyrides
joyriding
joys
joystick
joysticks

J U

juba
jube
jubes
jubilance
jubilant
jubilate
jubilated
jubilates
jubilee
jubilees

judas
judases
judder
juddered
juddering
judders
juddery
judenrein
judge
judged
judgement
judges
judgeship
judging
judgment
judgments
judicial
judiciary
judicious
judo
judoist
judoists
judoka
judokas
jug
juga
jugal
jugful
jugfuls
jugged
jugging
juggins
jugginses
juggle
juggled
juggler
jugglers
jugglery
juggles
juggling
jugs
jugular
jugulars
jugulate
jugulated
jugulates
jugum
juice
juiced

juiceless
juicer
juicers
juices
juicier
juiciest
juicily
juiciness
juicing
juicy
juju
jujube
jujubes
jujus
jukebox
jukeboxes
jukskei
juku
julep
juleps
julia
julias
julienne
julienned
juliennes
jumar
jumared
jumaring
jumars
jumbie
jumbies
jumble
jumbled
jumbles
jumbling
jumbo
jumbos
jumbuck
jumbucks
jump
jumpable
jumpcut
jumpcuts
jumped
jumper
jumpers
jumpier
jumpiest
jumpily

jumpiness
jumping
jumps
jumpsuit
jumpsuits
jumpy
jun
junco
juncoes
juncos
junction
junctions
juncture
junctures
juneberry
jungle
jungled
jungles
jungli
junglier
jungliest
junglist
junglists
jungly
junior
juniority
juniors
juniper
junipers
junk
junked
junkerdom
junkerism
junket
junketed
junketing
junkets
junkie
junkies
junking
junks
junky
junkyard
junkyards
junta
juntas
junto
juntos
jural

jurat
jurats
juridical
juried
juries
jurist
juristic

jurists
juror
jurors
jury
jurying
jus
jussive

just
justice
justices
justiciar
justified
justifier
justifies

justify
justly
justness
jut
jute
juts
jutted

jutting
juvenile
juveniles
juvenilia
juvie
juvies
juxtapose

K A

ka
kaapenaar
kabaddi
kabaka
kabakas
kabeljauw
kabeljou
kabloona
kabloonas
kabloonat
kabob
kabobs
kaboodle
kaboom
kabuki
kachha
kachina
kachinas
kadai
kadaitcha
kadi
kadis
kaffiyeh
kaffiyehs
kafir
kafirs
kaftan
kaftans
kagoul

kagoule
kagoules
kagouls
kagu
kagus
kahawai
kahikatea
kahuna
kahunas
kai
kaikai
kainga
kaingas
kainite
kairomone
kairos
kaiser
kaisers
kaizen
kajal
kaka
kakapo
kakapos
kakas
kakemono
kakemonos
kaki
kalamkari
kalanchoe
kale
kalends

kali
kalimba
kalmia
kalmias
kalong
kalongs
kalpa
kalpas
kalsomine
kamacite
kamahi
kame
kameez
kameezes
kames
kami
kamikaze
kamikazes
kampong
kampongs
kana
kanaka
kanakas
kanamycin
kanat
kanats
kanban
kanbans
kanga
kangaroo
kangaroos

kangas
kangha
kanghas
kangri
kangris
kanji
kanuka
kanukas
kanzu
kanzus
kaoliang
kaolin
kaolinise
kaolinite
kaolinize
kaon
kaons
kapok
kappa
kapu
kapur
kapurs
kaput
kara
karabiner
karahi
karahis
karai
karaka
karakul
karakuls

karanga
karaoke
karat
karate
karateka
karatekas
karats
karee
karees
karez
karezza
karma
karmic
karo
karoshi
kaross
karree
karren
karri
karris
karst
karstic
karstify
kart
karting
karts
karyotype
karzies
karzy
kasbah
kasbahs

kasha	keck	keepnets	kennings	kerria
kashrut	kecked	keeps	keno	kersey
kashruth	kecking	keepsake	kenosis	keruing
kata	kecks	keepsakes	kenotic	kes
katabatic	ked	keeshond	kens	kesh
katakana	keddah	keeshonds	kent	keskidee
katana	keddahs	keester	kente	keskidees
katas	kedge	keesters	kentia	kestrel
kathaks	kedged	kef	kentias	kestrels
kathode	kedgeree	keffiyeh	kep	ketamine
kathodes	kedges	keffiyehs	kepi	ketch
katipo	kedging	keftedes	kepis	ketches
katipos	keds	keg	kepped	ketchup
katsina	keek	kegger	kepping	ketchups
katsinam	keeked	kegs	keps	ketene
katsura	keeking	keiretsu	kept	ketone
katydid	keeks	keister	keratin	ketonemia
katydids	keel	keisters	keratitis	ketones
kaumatua	keelage	kelim	keratoses	ketonic
kaumatuas	keelback	kelims	keratosis	ketonuria
kaupapa	keelbacks	keloid	kerb	ketosis
kaupapas	keelboat	keloids	kerbing	ketotic
kauri	keelboats	kelp	kerbs	kettie
kauris	keeled	kelpfish	kerbside	ketties
kava	keeler	kelpie	kerbsides	kettle
kayak	keelhaul	kelpies	kerbstone	kettleful
kayaked	keelhauls	kelson	kerchief	kettles
kayakeet	keelie	kelsons	kerchiefs	keurboom
kayakeets	keelies	kelt	kereru	keurbooms
kayaking	keeling	kelts	kererus	kevel
kayaks	keelless	kelvin	kerf	kevels
kayo	keels	kelvins	kerfed	kewpie
kayoed	keelson	kemp	kerfs	kewpies
kayoes	keelsons	kemps	kerfuffle	key
kayoing	keema	kempt	kermes	keyboard
kayos	keen	kempy	kermis	keyboards
kazachoc	keened	ken	kermises	keyed
kazachocs	keener	kenaf	kern	keyer
kazillion	keeners	kendo	kerne	keyers
kazoo	keenest	kendoist	kerned	keyholder
kazoos	keening	kendoists	kernel	keyhole
	keenly	kenned	kernels	keyholes
	keenness	kennel	kernes	keying
K E	keens	kenneled	kerning	keyless
kea	keep	kenneling	kernite	keynote
keaki	keepable	kennelled	kerns	keynoter
keakis	keeper	kennelman	kero	keynoters
keas	keepers	kennelmen	kerogen	keynotes
kebab	keeping	kennels	kerosene	keypad
kebabs	keepnet	kenning	kerosine	keypads

keypunch
keys
keystone
keystones
keystroke
keyway
keyways
keyword
keywords

K H

khaddar
khadi
khaki
khakis
khalasi
khalasis
khamsin
khamsins
khan
khana
khanate
khanates
khanga
khans
khansama
kharif
khat
khayal
khayals
khazi
khazies
kheda
khedas
kheddah
kheddahs
khichri
khir
khoum
khoums
khyal
khyals

K I

ki
kiaat
kiang
kiangs

kibble
kibbled
kibbles
kibbling
kibbutz
kibbutzim
kibe
kibes
kibitka
kibitkas
kibitz
kibitzed
kibitzer
kibitzers
kibitzes
kibitzing
kiblah
kibosh
kick
kickable
kickback
kickbacks
kickball
kicked
kicker
kickers
kicking
kicks
kickshaw
kickshaws
kickstand
kicky
kid
kidded
kidder
kidders
kiddie
kiddies
kidding
kiddingly
kiddle
kiddles
kiddo
kiddoes
kiddos
kiddush
kiddy
kideo
kideos
kidnap

kidnaped
kidnaping
kidnapped
kidnapper
kidnaps
kidney
kidneys
kidology
kids
kidskin
kidstakes
kidult
kidults
kidvid
kidvids
kiekie
kiekies
kielbasa
kier
kierie
kieries
kiers
kieserite
kif
kike
kikes
kikoi
kikois
kikuyu
kikuyus
kilderkin
kilim
kilims
kill
killas
killdeer
killdeers
killed
killer
killers
killick
killicks
killifish
killing
killingly
killings
killjoy
killjoys
kills
kiln

kilns
kilo
kilobase
kilobit
kilobits
kilobyte
kilobytes
kilocycle
kilogram
kilograms
kilohertz
kilojoule
kiloliter
kilolitre
kilometer
kilometre
kilos
kiloton
kilotonne
kilotons
kilovolt
kilovolts
kilowatt
kilowatts
kilt
kilted
kilter
kiltie
kilties
kilting
kilts
kilty
kimchi
kimono
kimonoed
kimonos
kin
kina
kinas
kinase
kinases
kincob
kind
kinda
kinder
kindest
kindie
kindies
kindle
kindled

kindler
kindlers
kindles
kindlier
kindliest
kindling
kindly
kindness
kindred
kinds
kindy
kine
kinematic
kinescope
kineses
kinesics
kinesis
kinetic
kinetics
kinetin
kinfolk
king
kingbird
kingbirds
kingbolt
kingbolts
kingcraft
kingcup
kingcups
kingdom
kingdoms
kinged
kingfish
kinghood
kinging
kingklip
kingklips
kingless
kinglet
kinglets
kinglier
kingliest
kinglike
kingly
kingmaker
kingpin
kingpins
kings
kingship
kingships

kingside
kingsides
kingsnake
kinin
kinins
kink
kinkajou
kinkajous
kinked
kinkier
kinkiest
kinkily
kinkiness
kinking
kinks
kinky
kinless
kino
kinos
kinsfolk
kinship
kinsman
kinsmen
kinswoman
kinswomen
kiosk
kiosks
kip
kipa
kipah
kipahs
kipas
kippa
kippah
kippahs
kippas
kipped
kipper
kippered
kippering
kippers
kipping
kips
kipsie
kipsies
kipsy
kirk
kirkman
kirkmen
kirks

kirkyard
kirkyards
kirpan
kirpans
kirsch
kirtan
kirtans
kirtle
kirtles
kish
kishke
kishkes
kiskadee
kiskadees
kismet
kiss
kissable
kissed
kissel
kisser
kissers
kisses
kissing
kissogram
kissy
kist
kists
kit
kitbag
kitbags
kitchen
kitchener
kitchens
kite
kited
kitenge
kites
kith
kiting
kitke
kitkes
kits
kitsch
kitschier
kitschy
kitted
kitten
kittened
kittening
kittenish

kittens
kitties
kitting
kittiwake
kittle
kitty
kiva
kivas
kiwi
kiwis

K L

klatch
klatches
klaxon
klaxons
klepht
klephts
klezmer
klezmorim
klick
klicks
klieg
kliegs
klik
kliks
klipfish
klong
klongs
kloof
kloofs
kludge
kludged
kludges
kludging
klutz
klutzes
klutzier
klutziest
klutzy
klystron
klystrons

K N

knack
knacker
knackered
knackers

knacks
knag
knags
knaidel
knaidels
knaidlach
knap
knapped
knapper
knappers
knapping
knaps
knapsack
knapsacks
knapweed
knar
knars
knave
knaveries
knavery
knaves
knavish
knavishly
knawel
knawels
knead
kneadable
kneaded
kneader
kneaders
kneading
kneads
knee
kneeboard
kneecap
kneecaps
kneed
kneehole
kneeholes
kneeing
kneel
kneeled
kneeler
kneelers
kneeling
kneels
knees
kneidel
kneidels
kneidlach

knell
knelled
knelling
knells
knelt
knew
knickered
knickers
knicks
knife
knifed
knifefish
knifeman
knifemen
knifer
knifers
knifes
knifing
knight
knightage
knighted
knighting
knightly
knights
kniphofia
knish
knishes
knit
knitbone
knitbones
knits
knitted
knitter
knitters
knitting
knitwear
knives
knob
knobbed
knobbier
knobbiest
knobbing
knobble
knobbles
knobblier
knobbly
knobby
knobs
knobstick
knock

knocked
knocker
knockers
knocking
knockout
knockouts
knocks
knoll
knolled
knolling
knolls
knop
knops
knot
knotgrass
knothole
knotholes
knotless
knots
knotted
knotter
knotters
knottier
knottiest
knottily
knotting
knotty
knotweed
knotwork
knout
knouted
knouting
knouts
know
knowable
knowbot
knowbots
knower
knowers
knowing
knowingly
knowledge
known
knows
knuckle
knuckled
knuckles
knuckling
knuckly
knur

knurl
knurled
knurls
knurs

K O

koa
koala
koalas
koan
koans
koas
kob
kobo
kobold
kobolds
kochia
kochias
koel
koels
koesister
kofta
koftas
koftgari
kohanim
kohen
kohl
kohlrabi
koi
koine
koinonia
kokako
kokakos
kokanee
kokanees
kokowai
kola
kolas
kolinsky
kolkhoz
kolkhozes
kolkhozy
kolo
kolos
komatiite
komatik
komatiks
kombi
kombis

kombu
koneke
konekes
kongoni
konimeter
kook
kookier
kookiest
kookily
kookiness
kooks
kooky
koori
koories
kop
kopeck
kopecks
kopek
kopeks
kopje
kopjes
koppie
koppies
kops
kora
koradji
koradjis
korai
koras
kore
korero
koreros
korfball
korhaan
korhaans
kori
korma
kormas
koru
koruna
korunas
kosher
koshered
koshering
koshers
koto
kotos
kotwal
kotwali
koulibiac

koumiss
kouprey
koupreys
kourbash
kouroi
kouros
kowari
kowaris
kowhai
kowhais
kowtow
kowtowed
kowtower
kowtowers
kowtowing
kowtows

K R

kraal
kraaled
kraaling
kraals
kraft
krai
krais
krait
kraits
kraken
krakens
krans
krantz
kray
kreef
kreefs
kremlin
kremlins
kreplach
krill
krimmer
kris
kromesky
krona
krone
kroner
kronor
kronur
kroon
krooni
kroons

krummholz
krummhorn
krypton
krytron
krytrons

K U

kuccha
kuchen
kudos
kudu
kudus
kudzu
kugel
kukri
kukris
kuku
kula
kulak
kulaks
kulan
kulans
kulcha
kulfi
kultarr
kumara
kumaras
kumis
kumiss
kumite
kumkum
kümmel
kumquat
kumquats
kuna
kundalini
kune
kunzite
kurbash
kurbashes
kurgan
kurgans
kuri
kuris
kurrajong
kursaal
kursaals
kurta
kurtas

kurtha
kurthas
kurtosis
kuru
kurus
kusimanse
kusti
kustis

K V
kvass
kvell
kvelled

kvelling
kvells
kvetch
kvetched
kvetches
kvetching

K W
kwacha
kwachas
kwanza
kwanzas
kwela

K Y
kyanise
kyanised
kyanises
kyanising
kyanite
kyanitic
kyanize
kyanized
kyanizes
kyanizing
kyat

kyats
kybosh
kyle
kyles
kylie
kylies
kylikes
kylin
kylins
kylix
kylixes
kyloe
kyloes

kymograph
kype
kypes
kyphosis
kyphotic
kyte
kytes
kyu
kyus

L A
la
laager
laagered
laagering
laagers
laaitie
laaities
lab
labarum
labarums
labdanum
labdanums
label
labeled
labeling
labella
labelled
labeller
labellers
labelling
labellum
labels
labia

labial
labialise
labialize
labially
labials
labiate
labiates
labile
lability
labium
lablab
labor
labored
laborer
laborers
laboring
laborious
laborism
labors
labour
laboured
labourer
labourers
labouring

labourism
labourist
labours
labra
labral
labret
labrets
labrish
labrum
labs
laburnum
laburnums
labyrinth
lac
laccase
laccolith
lace
lacebark
lacebarks
lacecap
lacecaps
laced
lacemaker
lacerate

lacerated
lacerates
lacertid
lacertids
laces
lacewing
lacewings
lacewood
lacework
laches
lachrymal
lacier
laciest
lacily
laciness
lacing
lacings
laciniate
lack
lackaday
lacked
lackey
lackeyed
lackeying

lackeys
lacking
lacks
laconic
laconica
laconicum
laconism
lacquer
lacquered
lacquerer
lacquers
lacquey
lacqueys
lacrimal
lacrimals
lacrosse
lacrymal
lacrymals
lacs
lactam
lactams
lactaria
lactarium
lactase

lactases	ladlefuls	laically	lambastes	laming
lactate	ladler	laicise	lambasts	lamington
lactated	ladlers	laicised	lambda	laminin
lactates	ladles	laicises	lambdas	laminitis
lactating	ladling ·	laicising	lambdoid	laminose
lactation	ladoo	laicism	lambed	lamium
lacteal	ladoos	laicisms	lambency	lamiums
lacteals	lads	laicity	lambent	lammed
lactic	lady	laicize	lambently	lamming
lactone	ladybird	laicized	lamber	lamp
lactones	ladybirds	laicizes	lambers	lampas
lactose	ladybug	laicizing	lambert	lampases
lactulose	ladybugs	laics	lamberts	lampblack
lacuna	ladyfied	laid	lambing	lamped
lacunae	ladyfies	lain	lambkin	lamper
lacunal	ladyfish	lair	lambkins	lampern
lacunar	ladyfy	lairage	lamblike	lamperns
lacunars	ladyfying	lairages	lambs	lampers
lacunary	ladyhood	laird	lambskin	lamping
lacunas	ladylike	lairds	lambswool	lampless
lacunate	ladyship	lairdship	lame	lamplight
lacunose	ladyships	laired	lamé	lamplit
lacy	laevulose	lairing	lamebrain	lampoon
lad	lag	lairs	lamed	lampooned
ladanum	lagan	lairy	lamella	lampooner
ladder	lagar	laity	lamellae	lampoons
laddered	lagares	lake	lamellar	lamprey
laddering	lagena	lakelet	lamellate	lampreys
ladders	lagenae	lakelets	lamellose	lamps
laddie	lager	laker	lamely	lampshade
laddies	lagers	lakes	lameness	lams
laddish	laggard	lakeside	lament	lanai
laddoo	laggardly	lakesides	lamented	lanais
laddoos	laggards	lakh	lamenter	lance
laddu	lagged	lakhs	lamenters	lanced
laddus	lagger	laksa	lamenting	lancejack
lade	laggers	laldy	laments	lancelet
laden	lagging	lallation	lames	lancelets
lades	laggings	lallygag	lamia	lancer
ladies	lagniappe	lallygags	lamiae	lancers
ladified	lagomorph	lam	lamias	lances
ladifies	lagoon	lama	lamina	lancet
ladify	lagoonal	lamas	laminable	lanceted
ladifying	lagoons	lamasery	laminae	lancets
lading	lags	lamb	laminal	lancewood
ladino	lah	lambada	laminar	lancing
ladinos	lahar	lambadas	laminate	land
ladle	lahars	lambast	laminated	landau
ladled	laic	lambaste	laminates	landaulet
ladleful	laical	lambasted	laminator	landaus

landed	language	lappet	largos	lashless
lander	languages	lappeted	lari	lasing
landfall	langue	lappets	lariat	lasque
landfalls	langued	lapping	lariats	lasques
landfill	langues	laps	laris	lass
landfills	languid	lapse	lark	lasses
landform	languidly	lapsed	larked	lassi
landforms	languish	lapses	larkiness	lassie
landgrave	languor	lapsing	larking	lassies
landing	langur	lapstone	larks	lassitude
landings	langurs	lapstones	larkspur	lasso
landlady	lani	lapstrake	larkspurs	lassoed
ländler	lanies	laptop	larky	lassoer
ländlers	lank	laptops	larn	lassoers
landless	lankier	lapwing	larned	lassoes
landline	lankiest	lapwings	larney	lassoing
landlines	lankily	lar	larneys	lassos
landlord	lankiness	larboard	larnie	last
landlords	lankly	larcener	larnies	lasted
landmark	lankness	larceners	larning	lasting
landmarks	lanky	larcenies	larns	lastingly
landmine	lanner	larcenist	larrikin	lastly
landmines	lanneret	larcenous	larrikins	lasts
landowner	lannerets	larceny	larrup	lat
landplane	lanners	larch	larruped	latch
landrace	lanolin	larches	larruping	latched
landraces	lantana	lard	larrups	latches
landrail	lantanas	lardass	larva	latchet
landrails	lantern	lardasses	larvacean	latchets
lands	lanterns	larded	larvae	latching
landscape	lanthanum	larder	larval	latchkey
landside	lanugo	larders	larvicide	latchkeys
landslide	lanyard	larding	laryngeal	late
landslip	lanyards	lardon	larynges	latecomer
landslips	laogai	lardons	larynx	lateen
landsman	lap	lardoon	las	lateens
landsmen	lapa	lardoons	lasagne	lately
landtie	lapdog	lards	lase	latencies
landties	lapdogs	lardy	lased	latency
landward	lapel	lares	laser	lateness
landwards	lapelled	large	laserdisc	latent
lane	lapels	largely	lasers	latently
lanes	lapful	largeness	lases	later
langlauf	lapfuls	larger	lash	lateral
langlaufs	lapidary	largess	lashed	laterally
langosta	lapilli	largesse	lasher	laterals
langostas	lapis	largest	lashers	laterite
langouste	lappa	larghetto	lashes	lateritic
langra	lappas	largish	lashing	laters
langras	lapped	largo	lashings	lates

latest	laughably	lavs	layouts	leafages
latex	laughed	law	layover	leafbird
latexes	laugher	lawful	layovers	leafbirds
lath	laughers	lawfully	layperson	leafed
lathe	laughing	lawgiver	lays	leafier
lathed	laughs	lawgivers	layshaft	leafiest
lather	laughter	lawks	layshafts	leafiness
lathered	launce	lawless	laywoman	leafing
lathering	launch	lawlessly	laywomen	leafless
lathers	launched	lawmaker	lazar	leaflet
lathery	launcher	lawmakers	lazaret	leafleted
lathes	launchers	lawman	lazarets	leaflets
lathi	launches	lawmen	lazarette	leaflove
lathing	launching	lawn	lazaretto	leafloves
lathis	launder	lawned	lazars	leafs
laths	laundered	lawnmower	laze	leafy
lathyrism	launderer	lawns	lazed	league
lati	launders	lawny	lazes	leagued
latices	laundress	laws	lazier	leaguer
laticifer	laundries	lawsuit	laziest	leaguers
latissimi	laundry	lawsuits	lazily	leagues
latitude	laureate	lawyer	laziness	leaguing
latitudes	laureates	lawyerly	lazing	leak
latke	laurel	lawyers	lazuli	leakage
latkes	laureled	lax	lazurite	leakages
latria	laureling	laxative	lazy	leaked
latrine	laurelled	laxatives	lazybones	leaker
latrines	laurels	laxer		leakers
lats	lav	laxest		leakier
latte	lava	laxities	**L E**	leakiest
latten	lavabo	laxity		leakiness
lattens	lavabos	laxly	lea	leaking
latter	lavage	laxness	leach	leaks
latterly	lavatera	laxnesses	leachate	leaky
lattes	lavation	lay	leached	leal
lattice	lavations	layabout	leaches	lean
latticed	lavatory	layabouts	leaching	leaned
lattices	lave	layaway	lead	leaner
latticino	laved	layaways	leaded	leanest
laud	lavender	layback	leaden	leaning
laudable	lavenders	layer	leadenly	leanings
laudably	laver	layered	leader	leanly
laudanum	lavers	layering	leaderene	leanness
laudation	laves	layers	leaders	leans
laudatory	laving	layette	leading	leant
lauded	lavish	layettes	leadings	leap
lauding	lavished	laying	leads	leaped
lauds	lavishes	layman	leadwort	leaper
laugh	lavishing	laymen	leadworts	leapers
laughable	lavishly	layout	leaf	leapfrog
			leafage	

leapfrogs	lecheries	leeriness	legator	lek
leaping	lecherous	leering	legators	leke
leaps	lechers	leeringly	legatos	lekked
leapt	lechery	leers	legend	lekker
learn	leches	leervis	legendary	lekking
learnable	leching	leery	legends	leks
learned	lechwe	lees	legged	leman
learnedly	lecithin	leet	legger	lemans
learner	lecker	leets	leggier	lemma
learners	lectern	leeward	leggiest	lemmas
learning	lecterns	leeway	legginess	lemmata
learns	lectin	left	legging	lemmatise
learnt	lectins	leftie	leggings	lemmatize
leas	lection	lefties	leggy	lemme
leasable	lections	leftish	leghorn	lemming
lease	lector	leftism	leghorns	lemmings
leaseback	lectors	leftist	legible	lemon
leased	lectrice	leftists	legibly	lemonade
leasehold	lectrices	leftmost	legion	lemonades
leases	lecture	leftover	legionary	lemons
leash	lectured	leftovers	legioned	lemonwood
leashed	lecturer	lefts	legions	lemony
leashes	lecturers	leftward	legislate	lempira
leashing	lectures	leftwards	legit	lempiras
leasing	lecturing	lefty	legless	lemur
least	lecythi	leg	legman	lemurs
leastways	lecythus	legacies	legmen	lend
leastwise	led	legacy	legroom	lendable
leat	ledge	legal	legs	lender
leather	ledged	legalese	leguaan	lenders
leathered	ledger	legalise	leguaans	lending
leathern	ledgered	legalised	leguan	lends
leathers	ledgering	legalises	leguans	length
leathery	ledgers	legalism	legume	lengthen
leats	ledges	legalisms	legumes	lengthens
leave	ledgier	legalist	legwork	lengthier
leaved	ledgiest	legalists	lehr	lengthily
leaven	ledgy	legality	lehrs	lengthman
leavened	lee	legalize	lei	lengthmen
leavening	leeboard	legalized	leiothrix	lengths
leavens	leech	legalizes	leis	lengthy
leaver	leeched	legally	leister	lenience
leavers	leeches	legate	leistered	leniences
leaves	leeching	legatee	leisters	leniency
leaving	leek	legatees	leisure	lenient
leavings	leeks	legates	leisured	leniently
leccy	leer	legatine	leisurely	lenis
lech	leered	legation	leisures	lenite
leched	leerier	legations	leitmotif	lenited
lecher	leeriest	legato	leitmotiv	lenites

leniting
lenition
lenitions
lenitive
lenitives
lenity
leno
lenos
lens
lensed
lenses
lensless
lensman
lensmen
lent
lentic
lenticel
lenticels
lentigo
lentil
lentils
lentisc
lentiscs
lento
lentoid
lentos
leone
leones
leonine
leopard
leopards
leotard
leotards
leper
lepers
leporine
leprosy
leprous
lepta
leptin
lepton
leptonic
leptons
leptotene
les
lesbian
lesbians
lesbo
lesbos
lesion

lesions
less
lessee
lessees
lessen
lessened
lessening
lessens
lesser
lessest
lesson
lessoned
lessoning
lessons
lessor
lessors
lest
let
lethal
lethality
lethally
lethargic
lethargy
lets
letted
letter
letterbox
lettered
lettering
letters
letterset
letting
lettings
lettuce
lettuces
leu
leucine
leucines
leucistic
leucocyte
leucoma
leucomas
leucon
leuconoid
leucosis
leucotic
leucotomy
leukaemia
leukaemic
leukemia

leukocyte
leukosis
lev
leva
levade
levant
levanted
levanter
levanters
levanting
levants
levas
levator
levators
levee
levees
level
leveled
leveler
levelers
leveling
levelled
leveller
levellers
levelling
levelly
levelness
levels
lever
leverage
leveraged
leverages
levered
leveret
leverets
levering
levers
leviable
leviathan
levied
levies
levigate
levigated
levigates
levin
levins
levirate
levirates
levitate
levitated

levitates
levitator
levity
levodopa
levs
levulose
levy
levying
lewd
lewder
lewdest
lewdly
lewdness
lewis
lewises
lewisite
lexeme
lexemes
lexical
lexically
lexicon
lexicons
lexigram
lexigrams
lexis
ley
leylandii
leys
lez
lezes
lezzies
lezzy

L I

li
liability
liable
liaise
liaised
liaises
liaising
liaison
liaisons
liana
lianas
liane
lianes
liar
liard

liars
lias
liassic
liatris
lib
libation
libations
libber
libbers
libeccio
libel
libeled
libeling
libelled
libeller
libellers
libelling
libellous
libelous
libels
liberal
liberally
liberals
liberate
liberated
liberates
liberator
libero
liberos
liberties
libertine
liberty
libidinal
libido
libidos
libra
librae
librarian
libraries
library
librate
librated
librates
librating
libration
libretti
libretto
librettos
lice
licence

licenced	lieges	ligatured	likelier	limerick
licences	lien	ligatures	likeliest	limericks
licencing	liens	liger	likely	limes
license	lierne	ligers	liken	limestone
licensed	liernes	ligged	likened	limewash
licensee	lies	ligger	likeness	limier
licensees	lieu	liggers	likening	limiest
licenser	life	ligging	likens	limina
licensers	lifebelt	light	likes	liminal
licenses	lifebelts	lighted	likewise	liming
licensing	lifeblood	lighten	liking	limit
licensor	lifeboat	lightened	likings	limitary
licensors	lifeboats	lightens	likkewaan	limited
lichee	lifebuoy	lighter	likuta	limiter
lichees	lifebuoys	lighters	lilac	limiters
lichen	lifeguard	lightest	lilacs	limiting
lichened	lifeless	lightfast	lilangeni	limitless
lichenous	lifelike	lighties	lilied	limits
lichens	lifeline	lighting	lilies	limn
lichgate	lifelines	lightish	lilo	limned
lichgates	lifelong	lightless	lilos	limner
licht	lifer	lightly	lilt	limners
licit	lifers	lightness	lilted	limning
licitly	lifesaver	lightning	lilting	limnology
lick	lifespan	lights	lilts	limns
licked	lifespans	lightship	lily	limo
licker	lifestyle	lightsome	limb	limonene
lickerish	lifetime	lightwood	limba	limonite
licking	lifetimes	lighty	limbed	limonitic
lickings	lifeworld	ligneous	limber	limos
licks	lift	lignified	limbered	limousine
licorice	liftable	lignifies	limbering	limp
licorices	lifted	lignify	limbers	limped
lictor	lifter	lignin	limbi	limper
lictors	lifters	lignite	limbless	limpest
lid	lifting	lignitic	limbo	limpet
lidar	lifts	ligroin	limboed	limpets
lidded	lig	ligs	limboing	limpid
lidless	ligament	ligula	limbos	limpidity
lido	ligaments	ligulae	limbs	limpidly
lidocaine	ligand	ligular	limbus	limping
lidos	ligands	ligulate	lime	limpkin
lids	ligase	ligule	limeade	limpkins
lie	ligases	ligules	limed	limply
lied	ligate	ligustrum	limekiln	limpness
lieder	ligated	likable	limekilns	limps
lief	ligates	like	limelight	limuli
liege	ligating	likeable	limen	limulus
liegeman	ligation	likeably	limepit	limy
liegemen	ligature	liked	limepits	linac

linacs	lings	lintelled	lippier	lissom
linage	lingual	lintels	lippiest	lissome
linchpin	lingually	linter	lipping	list
linchpins	linguine	linters	lippy	listable
linctus	linguist	lintie	lips	listed
linctuses	linguists	linties	lipsalve	listel
lindane	lingulate	linty	lipstick	listen
linden	linhay	liny	lipsticks	listened
lindens	linier	lion	liquate	listener
line	liniest	lioness	liquated	listeners
lineage	liniment	lionesses	liquates	listening
lineages	lining	lionhead	liquating	listens
lineal	linings	lionheads	liquation	lister
lineally	linish	lionise	liquefied	listeria
lineament	linished	lionised	liquefier	listers
linear	linisher	lionises	liquefies	listing
linearise	linishes	lionising	liquefy	listings
linearity	linishing	lionize	liqueur	listless
linearize	link	lionized	liqueurs	lists
linearly	linkage	lionizer	liquid	listserv
lineation	linkages	lionizers	liquidate	listservs
lined	linked	lionizes	liquidise	lit
linefeed	linker	lionizing	liquidity	litanies
linefish	linkers	lions	liquidize	litany
lineman	linking	lip	liquidly	litas
linemen	linkman	lipa	liquids	litchi
linen	linkmen	lipaemia	liquified	litchis
linenfold	links	lipas	liquifies	lite
liner	linksland	lipase	liquify	liter
liners	linkspan	lipemia	liquor	literacy
lines	linkspans	lipgloss	liquored	literal
lineside	linkwork	lipid	liquorice	literally
linesman	linn	lipidoses	liquoring	literals
linesmen	linnet	lipidosis	liquorish	literary
ling	linnets	lipids	liquors	literate
linga	linns	lipless	lira	literates
lingam	lino	lipline	lire	literati
lingams	linocut	lipliner	liripipe	literatim
lingas	linocuts	lipogenic	liripipes	liters
lingcod	linoleate	lipogram	lis	lith
linger	linoleum	lipograms	lisente	litharge
lingered	linos	lipolysis	lisle	litharges
lingerer	linsang	lipolytic	lisp	lithe
lingerers	linsangs	lipoma	lisped	lithely
lingerie	linseed	lipomas	lisper	litheness
lingering	linstock	lipomata	lispers	lither
lingers	linstocks	liposome	lisping	lithesome
lingo	lint	liposomes	lispingly	lithest
lingoes	lintel	lipped	lisps	lithia
lingos	linteled	lippie	lisses	lithiasis

lithic
lithified
lithifies
lithify
lithium
litho
lithoed
lithoes
lithoing
lithology
lithopone
lithos
lithosol
lithotomy
litie
lities
litigant
litigants
litigate
litigated
litigates
litigator
litigious
litmus
litoptern
litotes
litre
litreage
litres
litter
litterbug
littered
littering
litters
little
littler
littlest
littoral
littorals
liturgics
liturgies
liturgist
liturgy
livable
live
liveable
lived
livelier
liveliest
livelily

livelong
lively
liven
livened
livening
livens
liver
liveried
liveries
liverish
livers
liverwort
livery
liveryman
liverymen
lives
livestock
liveware
livid
lividity
lividly
lividness
living
livings
lixiviate
lizard
lizards

L L

llama
llamas
llanero
llaneros
llano
llanos

L O

lo
loa
loach
loaches
load
loaded
loader
loaders
loading
loadings
loads

loadsa
loadspace
loadstone
loaf
loafed
loafer
loafers
loafing
loafs
loam
loaminess
loamy
loan
loanable
loaned
loanee
loanees
loaner
loaners
loaning
loanings
loans
loanword
loanwords
loas
loath
loathe
loathed
loather
loathers
loathes
loathing
loathsome
loaves
lob
lobar
lobate
lobation
lobbed
lobbied
lobbies
lobbing
lobby
lobbying
lobbyist
lobbyists
lobe
lobectomy
lobed
lobefin

lobefins
lobeless
lobelia
lobelias
lobes
loblolly
lobo
lobola
lobolo
lobolos
lobopod
lobopodia
lobopods
lobos
lobotomy
lobs
lobscouse
lobster
lobstered
lobsters
lobular
lobulate
lobulated
lobule
lobules
lobworm
lobworms
local
locale
locales
localise
localised
localises
localism
localisms
localist
localists
locality
localize
localized
localizes
locally
localness
locals
locatable
locate
located
locates
locating
location

locations
locative
locator
locators
loch
lochan
lochans
lochia
lochial
lochias
lochs
loci
locie
locies
lock
lockable
lockage
lockdown
lockdowns
locked
locker
lockers
locket
lockets
lockfast
locking
lockjaw
lockless
locknut
locknuts
lockout
lockouts
locks
locksmith
lockstep
loco
locomotor
locos
locoweed
locular
locule
locules
loculi
loculus
locum
locums
locus
locust
locusts
locution

locutions
lode
loden
lodes
lodestar
lodestars
lodestone
lodge
lodged
lodgement
lodger
lodgers
lodges
lodging
lodgings
lodicule
lodicules
loerie
loeries
loess
loessial
loessic
loft
lofted
lofter
loftier
loftiest
loftily
loftiness
lofting
lofts
loftsman
loftsmen
lofty
log
logan
logarithm
logbook
logbooks
loge
loges
logged
logger
loggers
loggia
loggias
logging
logia
logic
logical

logically
logician
logicians
logicism
logicist
logics
logier
logiest
login
logins
logion
logistic
logistics
logjam
logjams
logo
logoff
logoffs
logogram
logograms
logograph
logomachy
logon
logons
logophile
logorrhea
logos
logotype
logotypes
logout
logouts
logroller
logrunner
logs
logwood
logwoods
logy
loiasis
loin
loincloth
loins
loiter
loitered
loiterer
loiterers
loitering
loiters
lokey
lokeys
lokies

loll
lolled
lollies
lolling
lollipop
lollipops
lollop
lolloped
lolloping
lollops
lolls
lolly
lollygag
lollygags
loment
loments
lomentum
lomentums
lone
lonelier
loneliest
lonely
loner
loners
lonesome
long
longan
longbill
longbills
longboard
longboat
longboats
longbow
longbows
longclaw
longclaws
longdog
longdogs
longe
longed
longer
longeron
longerons
longes
longest
longevity
longhair
longhairs
longhand
longhorn

longhorns
longhouse
longicorn
longing
longingly
longings
longish
longitude
longlist
longlists
longneck
longnecks
longs
longship
longships
longshore
longspur
longspurs
longstop
longstops
longtail
longtails
longueur
longueurs
longwall
longways
longwise
longwool
longwools
lonicera
loniceras
lonning
lonnings
loo
looey
looeys
loofah
loofahs
looie
looies
look
lookalike
looked
looker
lookers
looking
lookit
lookout
lookouts
looks

looky
loom
loomed
looming
looms
loon
looned
loonie
loonier
loonies
looniest
looniness
looning
loons
loony
loop
looped
looper
loopers
loophole
loopholed
loopholes
loopier
loopiest
loopiness
looping
loops
loopy
loos
loose
loosed
loosely
loosen
loosened
loosener
looseners
looseness
loosening
loosens
looser
looses
loosest
loosing
loot
looted
looter
looters
looting
loots
lop

lope
loped
lopes
lophodont
loping
lopolith
lopoliths
lopped
loppers
loppies
lopping
loppy
lops
lopsided
loquacity
loquat
loquats
loquitur
lor
loranthus
lorazepam
lord
lorded
lording
lordless
lordlier
lordliest
lordling
lordlings
lordly
lordosis
lordotic
lords
lordship
lordships
lore
lorgnette
lorica
loricae
loricas
loricate
lories
lorikeet
lorikeets
lorilet
lorilets
lorimer
lorimers
loriner
loriners

loris
lorises
lorn
lornies
lorny
lorries
lorry
lory
lose
losel
losels
loser
losers
loses
losing
loss
losses
lossless
lossy
lost
lot
lota
loth
loti
lotic
lotion
lotions
lots
lotsa
lotta
lotted
lotteries
lottery
lotting
lotto
lotus
lotusbird
lotuses
louche
loucher
louchest
loud
louden
loudened
loudening
loudens
louder
loudest
loudly
loudmouth

loudness
lough
loughs
louis
lounge
lounged
lounger
loungers
lounges
lounging
loup
loupe
louped
loupes
louping
loups
lour
lourdan
lourdans
loured
lourie
louries
louring
louringly
lours
loury
louse
loused
louser
louses
lousewort
lousier
lousiest
lousily
lousiness
lousing
lousy
lout
loutish
loutishly
louts
louvar
louver
louvers
louvre
louvred
louvres
lovable
lovably
lovage

lovat
love
loveable
lovebird
lovebirds
loved
loveless
lovelier
lovelies
loveliest
lovelily
lovelock
lovelocks
lovelorn
lovely
lover
loverless
lovers
loves
lovesick
lovesome
lovey
loveys
loving
lovingly
low
lowan
lowans
lowball
lowballs
lowboy
lowboys
lowbrow
lowbrows
lowed
lower
lowered
lowering
lowermost
lowers
lowest
lowing
lowish
lowland
lowlander
lowlands
lowlier
lowliest
lowlife
lowlight

lowlights
lowlily
lowliness
lowly
lowness
lows
lox
loxodrome
loyal
loyalism
loyalist
loyalists
loyally
loyalties
loyalty
lozenge
lozenges

L U

luau
luaus
lubber
lubberly
lubbers
lube
lubed
lubes
lubing
lubra
lubricant
lubricate
lubricity
lubricous
luce
lucencies
lucency
lucent
lucerne
lucid
lucider
lucidest
lucidity
lucidly
lucifer
lucine
lucines
lucite
luck
lucked

luckier
luckiest
luckily
luckiness
lucking
luckless
lucks
lucky
lucrative
lucre
lucubrate
luculent
lud
luderick
ludic
ludicrous
ludo
lues
luetic
luff
luffed
luffing
luffs
lug
luge
luged
luges
luggable
luggage
lugged
lugger
luggers
lugging
lughole
lugholes
luging
lugs
lugsail
lugsails
lugworm
lugworms
lukewarm
lull
lullabied
lullabies
lullaby
lulled
lulling
lulls

lulu
lulus
lum
luma
lumas
lumbago
lumbar
lumber
lumbered
lumberer
lumberers
lumbering
lumberman
lumbermen
lumbers
lumen
lumens
lumina
luminaire
luminal
luminance
luminary
luminesce
luminous
lumme
lummox
lummoxes
lump
lumped
lumpen
lumper
lumpers
lumpfish
lumpier
lumpiest
lumpily
lumpiness
lumping
lumpish
lumpishly
lumps
lumpy
lums
lunacies
lunacy
lunar
lunate
lunates
lunatic

lunatics
lunation
lunations
lunch
lunched
luncheon
luncheons
luncher
lunchers
lunches
lunching
lunchroom
lunchtime
lune
lunes
lunette
lunettes
lung
lunge
lunged
lungeing
lunges
lungfish
lungful
lungfuls
lungi
lunging
lungis
lungless
lungs
lungworm
lungworms
lungwort
lungworts
lunisolar
lunitidal
lunk
lunker
lunkers
lunkhead
lunkheads
lunks
lunula
lunulae
lunular
lunulate
lunule
lunules
lupara

lupin
lupine
lupines
lupins
lupoid
lupous
lupulin
lupus
lur
lurch
lurched
lurcher
lurchers
lurches
lurching
lurdan
lurdane
lurdanes
lurdans
lure
lured
lures
lurex
lurgies
lurgy
lurid
lurider
luridest
luridly
luridness
luring
lurk
lurked
lurker
lurkers
lurking
lurks
lurs
lurve
luscious
lush
lushed
lusher
lushes
lushest
lushing
lushly
lushness
lusophone
lust

lusted
luster
lusters
lustful
lustfully
lustier
lustiest
lustily
lustiness
lusting
lustra
lustral
lustrate
lustrated
lustrates
lustre
lustred
lustres
lustrine
lustring
lustrous
lustrum
lustrums
lusts
lusty
lutanist
lutanists
lutchet
lutchets
lute
luteal
luted
lutein
luteins
lutenist
lutenists
luteous
lutes
lutetium
luthern
luthier
luting
lutings
lutino
lutinos
lutist
lutz
lutzes
luv
luvvie

luvviedom
luvvies
luvvy
lux
luxate
luxated
luxates
luxating
luxation
luxations
luxe
luxuriant
luxuriate
luxuries
luxurious
luxury

L Y

lyase
lyases
lycaenid
lycée
lycées
lychee
lychees
lychgate
lychgates
lychnis
lycopene
lycopenes
lycopod
lycopods
lycopsid
lycopsids
lyddite

L W

lwei

lye
lying
lyingly
lymph
lymphatic
lymphoid
lymphoma
lymphomas
lymphous
lymphs
lynch
lynched
lyncher
lynchers
lynches
lynchet
lynchets
lynching
lynchpin

lynchpins
lynx
lynxes
lyonnaise
lyophilic
lyophobic
lyrate
lyre
lyrebird
lyrebirds
lyres
lyretail
lyric
lyrical
lyrically
lyricism
lyricist
lyricists
lyrics

lyrist
lyrists
lysate
lysates
lyse
lysed
lyses
lysin
lysine
lysing
lysis
lysosomal
lysosome
lysosomes
lysozyme
lysozymes
lytic
lytically

M A

ma
maar
maars
maas
mabela
mabele
mac
macabre
macadam
macadamed
macadamia
macajuel
macajuels
macaque
macaques
macaroni
macaronic

macaroon
macaroons
macaw
macaws
mace
maced
macédoine
macer
macerate
macerated
macerates
macerator
macers
maces
machair
machan
machans
mache

macher
machete
machetes
machinate
machine
machined
machinery
machines
machining
machinist
machismo
macho
machos
macing
macintosh
mack
mackerel
mackerels

mackinaw
mackinaws
mackle
mackles
macks
macle
macles
macramé
macro
macrocosm
macron
macrons
macropod
macropods
macros
macruran
macrurous
macs

macula
maculae
macular
maculate
maculated
maculates
macule
macules
macumba
macushla
mad
madam
madams
madarosis
madcap
madcaps
madded
madden

maddened	maestros	magnetite	mahua	mainplane
maddening	mafia	magnetize	mahwa	mains
maddens	mafic	magneto	mahwas	mainsail
madder	mag	magneton	maid	mainsails
madders	maga	magnetons	maidan	mainsheet
maddest	magalogue	magnetos	maidans	mainstay
madding	magazine	magnetron	maiden	mainstays
made	magazines	magnets	maidenish	maintain
madeleine	magdalen	magnifico	maidenly	maintains
maderized	magdalens	magnified	maidens	maintop
madhouse	mage	magnifier	maids	maintops
madhouses	magenta	magnifies	maieutic	maiolica
madison	mages	magnify	maieutics	maistries
madisons	maggie	magnitude	maigre	maistry
madly	maggies	magnolia	mail	maize
madman	magging	magnolias	mailable	maizena
madmen	maggot	magnox	mailbag	majestic
madness	maggots	magnum	mailbags	majesties
madnesses	maggoty	magnums	mailboat	majesty
mado	magi	magpie	mailboats	majlis
madonna	magic	magpies	mailbox	majolica
madonnas	magical	mags	mailboxes	major
mados	magically	magsman	mailed	majored
madras	magician	magsmen	mailer	majoring
madrasa	magicians	maguey	mailers	majority
madrasah	magick	magueys	mailing	majorly
madrasahs	magickal	magus	mailings	majors
madrasas	magicked	mahajan	maillot	majuscule
madrepore	magicking	mahajans	maillots	makable
madrigal	magics	mahant	mailman	make
madrigals	magilp	mahants	mailmen	makeable
madrilene	magister	maharaja	mails	makeover
madroña	magisters	maharajah	mailshot	makeovers
madroñas	magistral	maharajas	mailshots	maker
madroño	maglev	maharanee	maim	makeready
madroños	maglevs	maharani	maimed	makers
mads	magma	maharanis	maiming	makes
madtom	magmatic	mahatma	maims	makeshift
madtoms	magmatism	mahatmas	main	making
madwoman	magnate	mahimahi	maincrop	makings
madwomen	magnates	mahlstick	mainframe	mako
maedi	magnesia	mahoe	mainland	makos
maelstrom	magnesian	mahoes	mainline	makuta
maenad	magnesite	mahogany	mainlined	makutu
maenadic	magnesium	mahonia	mainliner	mala
maenads	magnet	mahonias	mainlines	malacca
maestoso	magnetic	mahout	mainly	malaccas
maestosos	magnetise	mahouts	mainmast	malachite
maestri	magnetism	mahseer	mainmasts	maladies
maestro		mahseers		maladroit

malady	malimbis	malty	manage	mane
malagueña	malinger	malvoisie	managed	maneater
malagueta	malingers	mam	manager	maneaters
malaise	malis	mama	managers	maneb
malaises	malison	mamaguy	manages	maned
malamute	malkoha	mamaguyed	managing	manège
malamutes	malkohas	mamaguys	manaia	manèges
malanga	mall	mamas	manakin	maneless
malapert	mallam	mamba	manakins	manes
malaperts	mallams	mambas	mañana	maneuver
malaprop	mallard	mambo	manas	maneuvers
malaprops	mallards	mamboed	manat	manful
malar	malleable	mamboes	manatee	manfully
malaria	malleably	mamboing	manatees	manga
malarial	mallee	mambos	manchet	mangabey
malarian	mallees	mamee	manciple	mangabeys
malarious	mallei	mamees	manciples	manganate
malarkey	malleoli	mamelon	mandala	manganese
malars	malleolus	mamelons	mandalas	manganic
malate	mallet	mamey	mandalic	manganite
malates	mallets	mameys	mandamus	manganous
malathion	malleus	mamilla	mandap	mange
malcoha	malling	mamillae	mandapam	mangel
male	mallow	mamillary	mandaps	mangels
maleate	mallows	mamillate	mandarin	manger
maleates	malls	mamma	mandarine	mangers
malefic	malm	mammae	mandarins	mangetout
malemute	malms	mammal	mandatary	mangey
malemutes	malmsey	mammalian	mandate	mangier
maleness	maloca	mammalogy	mandated	mangiest
maleo	malodour	mammals	mandates	manginess
maleos	malonate	mammaries	mandating	mangle
males	malope	mammary	mandatory	mangled
malformed	malopes	mammas	mandible	mangler
mali	maloti	mammee	mandibles	manglers
malice	malt	mammees	mandir	mangles
malicious	maltase	mammies	mandola	mangling
malign	malted	mammiform	mandolas	mango
malignant	malthouse	mammilla	mandolin	mangoes
maligned	maltier	mammogram	mandoline	mangold
maligner	maltiest	mammoth	mandolins	mangolds
maligners	maltiness	mammoths	mandorla	mangonel
maligning	malting	mammy	mandorlas	mangonels
malignity	maltings	mams	mandrake	mangos
malignly	maltose	man	mandrakes	mangrove
maligns	maltreat	mana	mandrel	mangroves
malik	maltreats	manacle	mandrels	mangy
maliks	malts	manacled	mandrill	manhandle
malimbe	maltster	manacles	mandrills	manhattan
malimbi	maltsters	manacling	manducate	manhole

manholes	manners	mantlet	maquila	marchesa
manhood	mannie	mantling	maquilas	marchese
manhunt	mannies	mantlings	maquis	marchesi
manhunts	mannikin	mantra	maquisard	marching
mania	mannikins	mantrap	mar	marchpane
maniac	manning	mantraps	mara	mardier
maniacal	mannish	mantras	marabou	mardiest
maniacs	mannishly	mantric	marabous	mardy
manias	mannitol	mantua	marabout	mare
manic	mannose	mantuas	marabouts	maremma
manically	manny	manual	marabunta	maremme
manicotti	manoeuvre	manually	maraca	mares
manicou	manoir	manuals	maracas	marg
manicous	manoirs	manubria	marae	marga
manicure	manometer	manubrial	maranta	margarine
manicured	manor	manubrium	marantas	margarita
manicures	manorial	manucode	marari	margate
manifest	manors	manucodes	mararis	margates
manifesto	manpower	manuka	marasmic	margay
manifests	manqué	manukas	marasmus	margays
manifold	manrope	manul	marathon	marge
manifolds	manropes	manuls	marathons	margin
manikin	mans	manumit	maraud	marginal
manikins	mansard	manumits	marauded	marginals
manilla	mansards	manure	marauder	marginate
manille	manse	manured	marauders	margined
manioc	manses	manures	marauding	margining
maniple	mansion	manuring	marauds	margins
maniples	mansions	manus	maravedi	margrave
manipular	manta	many	maravedis	margraves
manitou	mantas	manyatta	marble	margs
manitous	manteau	manyattas	marbled	maria
mankier	manteaus	manyfold	marbleise	mariachi
mankiest	mantel	manyplies	marbleize	mariachis
mankind	mantelet	manzanita	marbler	marigold
manky	mantelets	map	marblers	marigolds
manless	mantels	mapepire	marbles	marihuana
manlier	mantic	mapepires	marbling	marijuana
manliest	manticore	maple	marbly	marimba
manlike	mantid	maples	marc	marimbas
manliness	mantids	mapless	marcasite	marina
manly	mantilla	mappable	marcato	marinade
manna	mantillas	mapped	marcel	marinaded
manned	mantis	mapper	marcelled	marinades
mannequin	mantises	mappers	marcels	marinara
manner	mantissa	mapping	march	marinas
mannered	mantissas	mappings	marched	marinate
mannerism	mantle	maps	marcher	marinated
mannerist	mantled	maquette	marchers	marinates
mannerly	mantles	maquettes	marches	marine

mariner	marmalade	marshland	masculist	masseur
mariners	marmite	marshwort	maser	masseurs
marines	marmites	marshy	masers	masseuse
marinise	marmoreal	marsupia	mash	masseuses
marinised	marmoset	marsupial	mashed	massicot
marinises	marmosets	marsupium	masher	massif
marinize	marmot	mart	mashers	massifs
marinized	marmots	marten	mashes	massing
marinizes	marocain	martenot	mashie	massive
marital	maroon	martens	mashies	massively
maritally	marooned	martial	mashing	massless
maritime	marooning	martially	masjid	massy
marjoram	maroons	martin	masjids	mast
mark	marque	martinet	mask	mastaba
markdown	marquee	martinets	masked	mastabas
markdowns	marquees	martins	masker	masted
marked	marques	martlet	maskers	master
markedly	marquesa	martlets	masking	masterdom
marker	marquess	marts	masks	mastered
markers	marquetry	martyr	masochism	masterful
market	marquis	martyrdom	masochist	mastering
marketed	marquise	martyred	mason	masterly
marketeer	marquises	martyries	masoned	masters
marketer	marram	martyring	masoning	mastery
marketers	marrams	martyrise	masonry	masthead
marketing	marred	martyrize	masons	mastheads
marketise	marri	martyrs	masoor	mastic
marketize	marriage	martyry	masoors	masticate
markets	marriages	marvel	masque	mastiff
markhor	married	marveled	masquer	mastiffs
markhors	marrieds	marveling	masquers	mastitis
marking	marries	marvelled	masques	mastodon
markings	marring	marveller	mass	mastodons
markka	marris	marvelous	massa	mastoid
markkas	marron	marvels	massacre	mastoids
marks	marrons	marvy	massacred	masts
marksman	marrow	marzipan	massacres	mat
marksmen	marrows	marzipans	massage	matador
marl	marrowy	mas	massaged	matadors
marled	marry	masa	massager	matai
marlier	marrying	masala	massagers	matais
marliest	mars	mascara	massages	matamata
marlin	marsh	mascaraed	massaging	matamatas
marline	marshal	mascle	masse	match
marlines	marshaled	mascles	massé	matchable
marling	marshals	mascon	massed	matchbook
marlins	marshbird	mascons	masses	matchbox
marls	marshes	mascot	massés	matched
marly	marshier	mascots	masseter	matches
marm	marshiest	masculine	masseters	matching

matchless
matchlock
matchwood
mate
maté
mated
matelassé
mateless
matelot
matelote
matelots
mater
material
materials
materiel
maternal
maternity
mates
mateship
matey
mateyness
math
maths
matier
maties
matiest
matily
matin
matinal
matinee
matinees
matiness
mating
matins
matriarch
matric
matrices
matricide
matrimony
matrix
matrixes
matron
matronly
matrons
mats
matsuri
matsuris
matt
mattar
mattars

matte
matted
matter
mattered
mattering
matters
mattes
matting
mattins
mattock
mattocks
mattress
matts
maturate
maturated
maturates
mature
matured
maturely
maturer
matures
maturest
maturing
maturity
matutinal
maty
matzah
matzo
matzoh
matzohs
matzos
matzoth
mauby
maud
maudlin
mauds
maul
maulana
mauled
mauler
maulers
mauling
mauls
maulstick
maulvi
maulvis
maund
maunder
maundered
maunders

mausolea
mausoleum
mauve
mauveine
mauvish
maven
mavens
maverick
mavericks
mavis
mavises
maw
mawkish
mawkishly
maws
max
maxed
maxes
maxi
maxilla
maxillae
maxillary
maxim
maxima
maximal
maximally
maximand
maximin
maximise
maximised
maximises
maximize
maximized
maximizer
maximizes
maxims
maximum
maximums
maxing
maxis
maxixe
maxixes
maxwell
maxwells
may
maya
mayapple
mayapples
mayas
maybe

mayest
mayflies
mayflower
mayfly
mayhap
mayhem
maying
mayo
mayor
mayoral
mayoralty
mayoress
mayors
mayorship
maypole
maypoles
maypop
maypops
mayst
mayweed
mazdoor
mazdoors
maze
mazed
mazer
mazers
mazes
mazier
maziest
mazing
mazuma
mazurka
mazurkas
mazy
mazzard
mazzards

M B

mbaqanga
mbira
mbiras

M E

me
mead
meadow
meadows
meadowy

meager
meagre
meagrely
meal
mealie
mealiepap
mealier
mealies
mealiest
mealiness
meals
mealtime
mealtimes
mealworm
mealworms
mealy
mean
meander
meandered
meanders
meaner
meanest
meanie
meanies
meaning
meaningly
meanings
meanly
meanness
means
meant
meantime
meanwhile
meany
measles
measlier
measliest
measly
measure
measured
measures
measuring
meat
meatball
meatballs
meathead
meatheads
meatier
meatiest
meatily

meatiness	mediates	meed	megohms	mellowing
meatless	mediating	meeja	megrim	mellowly
meats	mediation	meejah	megrims	mellows
meatus	mediator	meek	megs	melodeon
meatuses	mediators	meeker	meibomian	melodeons
meaty	mediatory	meekest	meiofauna	melodic
mebos	medic	meekly	meioses	melodica
mech	medicable	meekness	meiosis	melodies
mechanic	medical	meerkat	meiotic	melodion
mechanics	medically	meerkats	mela	melodions
mechanise	medicate	meet	melaena	melodious
mechanism	medicated	meeting	melaleuca	melodise
mechanist	medicates	meetings	melamine	melodised
mechanize	medicinal	meetly	melange	melodises
mechs	medicine	meetness	melanges	melodist
meconium	medicines	meets	melanic	melodists
médaillon	medick	meg	melanin	melodize
medaka	medicks	mega	melanism	melodized
medal	medico	megabit	melanite	melodizes
medalist	medicos	megabits	melanoid	melodrama
medalists	medics	megabuck	melanoma	melody
medalled	medieval	megabucks	melanomas	melon
medallic	medina	megabyte	melanosis	melons
medallion	medinas	megabytes	melanotic	melt
medallist	mediocre	megadeath	melas	meltable
medals	meditate	megafauna	melatonin	meltdown
meddle	meditated	megaflop	meld	meltdowns
meddled	meditates	megaflops	melded	melted
meddler	meditator	megahertz	melding	meltemi
meddlers	medium	megalith	melds	meltemis
meddles	mediumism	megaliths	melee	melter
meddling	mediums	megamouth	melees	melters
medevac	medivac	megaphone	melena	melting
medevacks	medivacks	megapode	melic	meltingly
medflies	medlar	megapodes	melics	melton
medfly	medlars	megaron	melick	meltons
media	medley	megarons	melicks	melts
mediacy	medleyed	megaspore	melilot	meltwater
mediae	medleying	megastar	melilots	member
mediaeval	medleys	megastars	meliorate	membered
medial	medlied	megastore	meliorism	members
medially	medrese	megaton	meliorist	membrane
median	medreses	megatonne	melisma	membranes
medianly	medulla	megatons	melismas	meme
medians	medullary	megavolt	melismata	memento
mediant	medullas	megavolts	mellotron	mementoes
mediants	medusa	megawatt	mellow	mementos
mediate	medusae	megawatts	mellowed	memes
mediated	medusas	megilp	mellower	memetic
mediately	medusoid	megohm	mellowest	memo

memoir
memoirist
memoirs
memorable
memorably
memoranda
memorial
memorials
memories
memorise
memorised
memorises
memorize
memorized
memorizer
memorizes
memory
memos
memsahib
memsahibs
men
menace
menaced
menacer
menacers
menaces
menacing
menadione
ménage
menagerie
ménages
menarche
mend
mendable
mendacity
mended
mender
menders
mendicant
mendicity
mending
mends
menfolk
menfolks
menhaden
menhadens
menhir
menhirs
menial
menially

menials
meningeal
meninges
meninx
menisci
meniscus
meno
menology
menopause
menorah
menorahs
mensch
mensches
menses
mensh
menshes
menstrua
menstrual
menstruum
mensural
menswear
mental
mentalism
mentalist
mentality
mentally
mentation
menthol
mention
mentioned
mentions
mento
mentor
mentored
mentoring
mentors
mentos
mentum
menu
menudo
menudos
menus
meow
meowed
meowing
meows
mepacrine
mephitic
meranti
merantis

merbau
merbaus
merbromin
merc
mercado
mercados
mercaptan
mercenary
mercer
merceries
mercerise
mercerize
mercers
mercery
merchant
merchants
mercies
merciful
merciless
mercurial
mercuric
mercurous
mercury
mercy
merde
mere
merely
merengue
mereology
merganser
merge
merged
merger
mergers
merges
merging
meridian
meridians
meringue
meringues
merino
merinos
meristem
meristems
merit
merited
meriting
merits
merkin
merkins

merle
merles
merlin
merlins
merlon
merlons
mermaid
mermaids
merman
mermen
meronym
meronyms
meronymy
merrier
merriest
merrily
merriment
merriness
merry
mesa
mesas
mescal
mescalin
mescaline
mesclun
meself
mesentery
mesh
meshed
meshes
meshing
meshuga
meshugaas
meshugga
mesia
mesial
mesially
mesias
mesic
mesite
mesmeric
mesmerise
mesmerism
mesmerist
mesmerize
mesne
mesoblast
mesocarp
mesocarps
mesoderm

mesofauna
mesomeric
mesomorph
meson
mesonic
mesons
mesopause
mesophyll
mesophyte
mesosaur
mesosaurs
mesoscale
mesozoan
mesozoans
mespilus
mesquite
mesquites
mess
message
messages
messaging
messed
messenger
messes
messiah
messiahs
messianic
messier
messiest
messily
messiness
messing
messmate
messmates
messuage
messuages
messy
mestiza
mestizas
mestizo
mestizos
met
metabolic
metacarpi
metafile
metafiles
metage
metal
metaled
metaling

metalize
metalized
metalizes
metalled
metallic
metallics
metalline
metalling
metallise
metallize
metalloid
metalmark
metals
metalware
metalwork
metamere
metamere
metameres
metameric
metanoia
metaphase
metaphor
metaphors
metatarsi
metate
metazoa
metazoan
metazoans
mete
meted
meteor
meteoric
meteorite
meteoroid
meteors
meter
metered
metering
meters
metes
meth
methadone
methanal
methane
methanol
metheglin
methinks
metho
method
methodic

methodise
methodize
methods
methos
methought
meths
methyl
methylate
methylene
metic
meticais
metical
metics
métier
métiers
meting
metol
metonym
metonymic
metonyms
metonymy
metope
metopes
metre
metreage
metres
metric
metrical
metricate
metrics
metritis
metro
metrology
metronome
metroplex
metropole
metros
mettle
meunière
mew
mewed
mewing
mewl
mewled
mewling
mewls
mews
meze
mezereon
mezereons

mezes
mezuzah
mezuzahs
mezuzoth
mezuzoths
mezzanine
mezzo
mezzos
mezzotint

mho
mhos

mi
miaow
miaowed
miaowing
miaows
miasm
miasma
miasmal
miasmas
miasmatic
miasmic
miaul
miauled
miauling
miauls
mic
mica
micaceous
mice
micellar
micelle
micelles
mick
mickerie
mickeries
mickery
mickey
mickeys
mickle
micks
micrite
micritic
micro

microbe
microbes
microbial
microbic
microbrew
microcar
microcars
microchip
microcode
microcopy
microcosm
microcyte
microdot
microdots
microfilm
microform
microglia
microgram
microlith
micromesh
micron
micronise
micronize
microns
micropore
micropsia
micropyle
micros
microsome
microtome
microtone
microwave
micrurgy
mics
micturate
mid
midbrain
midbrains
midday
midden
middens
middies
middle
middled
middleman
middlemen
middles
middling
middlings
middy

midfield
midge
midges
midget
midgets
midgut
midguts
midheaven
midi
midibus
midibuses
midinette
midiron
midirons
midis
midland
midlander
midlands
midlife
midline
midlines
midmost
midnight
midrib
midribs
midriff
midriffs
midship
midships
midsole
midsoles
midst
midstream
midsummer
midterm
midterms
midtown
midway
midweek
midweeks
midwicket
midwife
midwifed
midwifery
midwifes
midwifing
midwinter
midwives
mielie
mielies

mien	mildness	milkwort	mime	mineable
miens	milds	milkworts	mimed	mined
miff	mile	milky	mimeo	minefield
miffed	mileage	mill	mimer	minelayer
miffing	mileages	millable	mimers	miner
miffs	milepost	millboard	mimes	mineral
miffy	mileposts	milled	mimesis	minerals
might	miler	millenary	mimetic	miners
mightier	milers	millennia	mimetite	mines
mightiest	miles	millepede	mimic	mineshaft
mightily	milestone	millepore	mimicked	minge
mighty	milfoil	miller	mimicker	mingier
migmatite	milfoils	millerite	mimickers	mingiest
migraine	milia	millers	mimicking	mingily
migraines	miliaria	millet	mimicries	mingle
migrant	miliary	millhand	mimicry	mingled
migrants	milieu	millhands	mimics	mingles
migrate	milieus	milliamp	miming	mingling
migrated	milieux	milliamps	mimosa	mingy
migrates	miling	milliard	mimosas	mini
migrating	militancy	milliards	mimsy	miniature
migration	militant	millibar	mimulus	minibar
migrator	militants	millibars	minable	minibars
migrators	militaria	millieme	minacious	minibeast
migratory	military	milliemes	minaret	minibus
mihrab	militate	milligram	minareted	minibuses
mihrabs	militated	milliner	minarets	minicab
mikado	militates	milliners	minatory	minicabs
mikados	militia	millinery	minbar	minicam
mike	militias	milling	minbars	minicams
miked	milium	million	mince	minidisc
mikes	milk	millions	minced	minidiscs
miking	milked	millionth	mincemeat	minidress
mikva	milker	millipede	mincer	minigolf
mil	milkers	millivolt	mincers	minikin
miladies	milkfish	millpond	minces	minim
milady	milkier	millponds	mincing	minima
milage	milkiest	mills	mincingly	minimal
milages	milkiness	millstone	mind	minimally
milch	milking	milo	minded	minimart
mild	milkmaid	milometer	minder	minimarts
milder	milkmaids	milord	minders	minimax
mildest	milkman	milords	mindful	minimaxes
mildew	milkmen	milreis	mindfully	minimise
mildewed	milks	mils	minding	minimised
mildewing	milkshake	milt	mindless	minimises
mildews	milksop	milts	minds	minimize
mildewy	milksops	mim	mindset	minimized
mildish	milkweed	mimbar	mindsets	minimizer
mildly	milkweeds	mimbars	mine	minimizes

minims	minuets	mirror	miserably	miskick
minimum	minus	mirrored	misère	miskicked
minimums	minuscule	mirroring	misères	miskicks
mining	minuses	mirrors	miserere	mislaid
minion	minute	mirth	misereres	mislay
minions	minuted	mirthful	miseries	mislaying
minis	minutely	mirthless	miserly	mislays
miniskirt	minuteman	miry	misers	mislead
minister	minutemen	mis	misery	misleader
ministers	minutes	misandry	misfeed	misleads
ministry	minutest	misapply	misfeeds	misled
minitower	minutia	misbehave	misfield	mislike
minivan	minutiae	misbelief	misfields	misliked
minivans	minuting	miscall	misfile	mislikes
miniver	minx	miscalled	misfiled	misliking
minivet	minxes	miscalls	misfiles	mismanage
minivets	minxish	miscarry	misfiling	mismatch
mink	minyan	miscast	misfire	mismated
minke	minyanim	miscasts	misfired	misname
minkes	miosis	mischance	misfires	misnamed
minks	miotic	mischief	misfiring	misnames
minneola	mirabelle	miscible	misfit	misnaming
minneolas	miracidia	miscount	misfits	misnomer
minnow	miracle	miscounts	misgave	misnomers
minnows	miracles	miscreant	misgive	miso
minor	mirador	miscue	misgiven	misogamy
minored	miradors	miscued	misgives	misogyny
minoring	mirage	miscueing	misgiving	mispickel
minority	mirages	miscues	misgovern	misplace
minors	mirch	miscuing	misguide	misplaced
minoxidil	mire	misdate	misguided	misplaces
minster	mired	misdated	misguides	misplay
minsters	mirepoix	misdates	mishandle	misplayed
minstrel	mires	misdating	mishap	misplays
minstrels	mirex	misdeal	mishaps	misprint
mint	mirid	misdeals	mishear	misprints
mintage	mirids	misdealt	misheard	misprize
mintages	mirin	misdeed	mishears	misprized
minted	miring	misdeeds	mishit	misprizes
minter	mirk	misdial	mishits	misquote
mintier	mirkier	misdialed	mishmash	misquoted
mintiest	mirkiest	misdials	mishugas	misquotes
minting	mirky	misdirect	misinform	misread
mints	mirliton	misdoing	misjudge	misreads
minty	mirlitons	misdoings	misjudged	misreport
minuend	mirnyong	misdoubt	misjudges	misroute
minuends	mirnyongs	misdoubts	miskey	misrouted
minuet	miro	misemploy	miskeyed	misroutes
minueted	miros	miser	miskeying	misrule
minueting	mirrnyong	miserable	miskeys	misruled

misrules	misters	mitigable	**M O**	mocks
misruling	mistier	mitigate		mocky
miss	mistiest	mitigated	mo	mocock
missable	mistily	mitigates	moa	mococks
missal	mistime	mitigator	moan	mod
missals	mistimed	mitogen	moaned	modal
missed	mistimes	mitogenic	moaner	modalism
misses	mistiming	mitogens	moaners	modalist
misshape	mistiness	mitoses	moanful	modality
misshaped	misting	mitosis	moaning	modally
misshapen	mistitle	mitotic	moans	modals
misshapes	mistitled	mitral	moas	mode
missies	mistitles	mitre	moat	model
missile	mistletoe	mitred	moated	modeled
missilery	mistook	mitres	moating	modeling
missiles	mistral	mitring	moats	modelled
missing	mistrals	mitt	mob	modeller
mission	mistreat	mitten	mobbed	modellers
missioner	mistreats	mittened	mobber	modelling
missions	mistress	mittens	mobbers	models
missis	mistrial	mitts	mobbing	modem
missish	mistrials	mitzvah	mobile	modemed
missive	mistrust	mitzvoth	mobiles	modeming
missives	mistrusts	mix	mobilise	modems
misspeak	mists	mixable	mobilised	moderate
misspeaks	misty	mixed	mobilises	moderated
misspell	mistype	mixer	mobility	moderates
misspells	mistyped	mixers	mobilize	moderato
misspelt	mistypes	mixes	mobilized	moderator
misspend	mistyping	mixing	mobilizer	moderatos
misspends	misusage	mixmaster	mobilizes	modern
misspent	misusages	mixology	mobocracy	moderne
misspoke	misuse	mixture	mobs	modernise
misspoken	misused	mixtures	mobster	modernism
misstate	misuser	mizen	mobsters	modernist
misstated	misusers	mizens	moc	modernity
misstates	misuses	mizuna	moccasin	modernize
misstep	misusing	mizzen	moccasins	modernly
missteps	mite	mizzens	mocha	moderns
missus	miter	mizzle	mock	modes
missy	mitered	mizzled	mockable	modest
mist	mitering	mizzles	mocked	modestly
mistake	miters	mizzling	mocker	modesty
mistaken	mites	mizzly	mockeries	modicum
mistakes	mithai		mockers	modicums
mistaking	mithan	**M N**	mockery	modified
mistaught	mither		mockies	modifier
misteach	mithered	mnemonic	mocking	modifiers
misted	mithering	mnemonics	mockingly	modifies
mister	mithers	mnemonist	mockney	modify

modifying	moister	moline	monamine	monikers
modillion	moistest	moll	monamines	monilia
modioli	moistly	mollie	monarch	monism
modiolus	moistness	mollies	monarchal	monist
modish	moisture	mollified	monarchic	monistic
modishly	moisty	mollifier	monarchy	monists
modiste	mojarra	mollifies	monastery	monition
modistes	mojarras	mollify	monastic	monitions
mods	mojo	mollisol	monatomic	monitor
modular	mojos	mollisols	monaural	monitored
modulate	moke	molls	monazite	monitors
modulated	mokes	mollusc	monazites	monitory
modulates	moko	molluscan	mondaine	monk
modulator	mokos	molluscs	mondaines	monkery
module	moksha	mollusk	mondial	monkey
modules	mola	mollusks	mondo	monkeyed
moduli	molal	molly	monetary	monkeying
modulo	molality	mollymawk	monetise	monkeyish
modulus	molar	moloch	monetised	monkeys
mofette	molarity	molochs	monetises	monkfish
mofettes	molars	molt	monetize	monkish
moffie	molas	molted	monetized	monkishly
moffies	molasses	molten	monetizes	monks
mofo	mold	molting	money	monkshood
mog	molded	molto	moneybags	mono
moggie	molder	molts	moneyed	monoamine
moggies	moldered	moly	moneyer	monobasic
moggy	moldering	molybdate	moneyers	monobloc
mogs	molders	mom	moneyless	monochord
mogul	moldier	moment	moneys	monocle
moguls	moldiest	momenta	moneywort	monocled
mohair	molding	momentary	mong	monocles
mohalla	moldings	momently	mongo	monocline
mohallas	molds	momentous	mongol	monocoque
mohel	moldy	moments	mongolism	monocot
mohels	mole	momentum	mongoloid	monocots
moi	molecular	momism	mongols	monocracy
moidore	molecule	momma	mongoose	monocrat
moidores	molecules	mommas	mongooses	monocrats
moieties	molehill	mommies	mongos	monocular
moiety	molehills	mommy	mongrel	monocycle
moil	moles	mompara	mongrels	monocyte
moiled	moleskin	momparas	monial	monocytes
moiling	molest	moms	monials	monodic
moils	molested	monad	monic	monodies
moire	molester	monadic	monicker	monodist
moist	molesters	monadisms	monickers	monodists
moisten	molesting	monadnock	monies	monodrama
moistened	molests	monads	moniker	monody
moistens	molies	monal	monikered	monoecies

monoecy	monosomy	moodiness	moorage	mopping
monofil	monotint	moods	moorages	moppy
monofils	monotints	moody	moorburn	mops
monogamy	monotone	mooed	moorcock	mopy
monogenic	monotones	mooi	moorcocks	moquette
monogeny	monotonic	mooing	moored	mor
monoglot	monotony	moolah	moorfowl	morainal
monoglots	monotreme	mooli	moorhen	moraine
monogram	monotrope	moolis	moorhens	moraines
monograms	monotropy	moomba	mooring	morainic
monograph	monotype	moombas	moorings	moral
monogyne	monotypes	moon	moorish	morale
monohull	monotypic	moonbeam	moorland	moralise
monohulls	monoxide	moonbeams	moorlands	moralised
monokini	monoxides	mooncalf	moors	moralises
monokinis	mons	mooned	moory	moralism
monolater	monsoon	moonfish	moos	moralist
monolatry	monsoonal	moong	moose	moralists
monolayer	monsoons	moongs	moosewood	morality
monolith	monster	moonier	moot	moralize
monoliths	monstera	mooniest	mooted	moralized
monologic	monsteras	mooning	mooting	moralizer
monologue	monstered	moonless	moots	moralizes
monomania	monsters	moonlet	mop	morally
monomer	monstrous	moonlets	mopane	morals
monomeric	montage	moonlight	mopani	moran
monomers	montages	moonlike	mopanis	morans
monometer	montane	moonlit	mopboard	morass
monomial	monte	moonquake	mopboards	morasses
monomials	month	moonraker	mope	moratoria
monophony	monthlies	moonrat	moped	moray
monoplane	monthly	moonrats	mopeds	morays
monoploid	months	moonrise	moper	morbid
monopod	montuno	moonrises	mopers	morbidity
monopodia	montunos	moons	mopery	morbidly
monopods	monty	moonscape	mopes	morbific
monopole	monument	moonseed	mopey	morbilli
monopoles	monuments	moonset	mopier	morceau
monopoly	monzonite	moonsets	mopiest	morceaux
monopsony	moo	moonshee	mopily	morcha
monorail	mooch	moonshees	mopiness	morchas
monorails	mooched	moonshine	moping	mordancy
monorchid	moocher	moonstomp	mopish	mordant
monos	moochers	moonstone	mopoke	mordanted
monosemy	mooches	moonwalk	mopokes	mordantly
monoski	mooching	moonwalks	mopped	mordants
monoskier	mood	moonwort	moppet	mordent
monosome	moodier	moonworts	moppets	mordents
monosomes	moodiest	moony	moppier	more
monosomic	moodily	moor	moppiest	moreen

moreish	mortally	moshed	motions	moufflon
morel	mortals	moshes	motivate	moufflons
morello	mortar	moshing	motivated	mouflon
morellos	mortared	moskonfyt	motivates	mouflons
moreover	mortaring	mosque	motivator	mouillé
morepork	mortarium	mosques	motive	mould
moreporks	mortars	mosquito	motives	mouldable
mores	mortary	moss	motivic	moulded
morganite	mortgage	mossback	motley	moulder
morgen	mortgaged	mossbacks	motlier	mouldered
morgens	mortgagee	mossed	motliest	moulders
morgue	mortgages	mosses	motmot	mouldier
morgues	mortgagor	mossie	motmots	mouldiest
moribund	mortice	mossier	motocross	moulding
morine	morticed	mossies	motor	mouldings
morion	mortices	mossiest	motorable	moulds
morions	mortician	mossiness	motorbike	mouldwarp
morn	morticing	mossing	motorcade	mouldy
mornay	mortified	mossy	motored	moulin
morning	mortifies	most	motorhome	moulins
mornings	mortify	mostest	motoring	moult
morns	mortise	mostly	motorise	moulted
morocco	mortised	mot	motorised	moulting
moroccos	mortiser	mote	motorises	moults
morocoy	mortisers	motel	motorist	moulvi
morocoys	mortises	motels	motorists	moulvis
moron	mortising	motes	motorize	mound
moronic	mortmain	motet	motorized	mounded
morons	morts	motets	motorizes	mounding
morose	mortuary	moth	motorman	mounds
morosely	morula	mothball	motormen	mount
morph	morulae	mothballs	motors	mountable
morphed	morwong	mother	motorway	mountain
morpheme	morwongs	mothered	motorways	mountains
morphemes	mosaic	mothering	mots	mountainy
morphemic	mosaicism	motherly	motser	mountant
morphia	mosaicist	mothers	motsers	mountants
morphine	mosaicked	mothier	motte	mounted
morphing	mosaics	mothiest	mottes	mounter
morpho	mosasaur	mothproof	mottle	mounters
morphogen	mosasaurs	moths	mottled	mounting
morphos	moscato	mothy	mottles	mountings
morphs	moschatel	motif	mottling	mounts
morrow	mosey	motifs	motto	mourn
morrows	moseyed	motile	mottoes	mourned
morsel	moseying	motility	mottos	mourner
morsels	moseys	motion	motza	mourners
mort	mosh	motional	motzas	mournful
mortal	moshav	motioned	moue	mourning
mortality	moshavim	motioning	moues	mourns

mouse
mousebird
moused
mouser
mousers
mouses
mousetrap
mousey
mousier
mousiest
mousiness
mousing
moussaka
mousse
moussed
mousseron
mousses
mousseux
moussing
moustache
mousy
mouth
mouthed
mouther
mouthers
mouthful
mouthfuls
mouthier
mouthiest
mouthing
mouthless
mouthpart
mouths
mouthwash
mouthy
mouton
movable
movables
movably
movant
movants
move
moveable
moveables
moved
moveless
movement
movements
mover
movers

moves
movie
movies
moving
movingly
moviola
moviolas
mow
mowed
mower
mowers
mowing
mowings
mown
mows
moxa
moxie
mozetta
mozo
mozos
mozz
mozzed
mozzes
mozzetta
mozzetta
mozzette
mozzie
mozzies
mozzing
mozzle

M R
mridangam

M S
msasa
msasas

M U
mu
much
muchacha
muchachas
muchacho
muchachos
muchly
muchness
mucho
mucilage

mucin
mucinous
mucins
muck
muckamuck
mucked
mucker
muckers
muckier
muckiest
muckiness
mucking
muckle
muckles
muckrake
muckraked
muckraker
muckrakes
mucks
mucky
mucoid
mucosa
mucosae
mucosal
mucosity
mucous
mucro
mucronate
mucros
mucus
mud
mudbank
mudbanks
mudbath
mudbaths
mudbug
mudbugs
muddied
muddier
muddies
muddiest
muddily
muddiness
muddle
muddled
muddler
muddlers
muddles
muddling
muddly

muddy
muddying
mudfish
mudfishes
mudflap
mudflaps
mudflat
mudflats
mudflow
mudflows
mudguard
mudguards
mudlark
mudlarker
mudlarks
mudminnow
mudra
mudras
mudslide
mudslides
mudstone
mudstones
mudwort
muesli
muezzin
muezzins
muff
muffed
muffin
muffing
muffins
muffle
muffled
muffler
mufflers
muffles
muffling
muffs
mufti
mug
mugful
mugfuls
mugged
mugger
muggers
muggier
muggiest
mugginess
mugging
muggings

muggins
mugginses
muggy
mugs
mugshot
mugshots
mugwort
mugworts
mugwump
mugwumps
muishond
muishonde
muishonds
mujahedin
mujahidin
mujtahid
mujtahids
mukhtar
mukhtars
mukluk
mukluks
mukti
muktuk
mulatto
mulattoes
mulattos
mulberry
mulch
mulched
mulches
mulching
mulct
mulcted
mulcting
mulcts
mule
mules
mulesing
muleta
muletas
muleteer
muleteers
muley
muleys
mulga
mulgara
mulgas
mulie
mulies
mulish

mulishly	mumbles	muntjac	murmurs	musher
mull	mumbling	muntjacs	murphies	mushes
mullah	mumchance	munts	murphy	mushier
mullahs	mummed	munyeroo	murrain	mushiest
mulled	mummer	munyeroos	murrains	mushily
mullein	mummeries	munyeru	murram	mushiness
mulleins	mummers	munyerus	murre	mushing
muller	mummery	muon	murrelet	mushrat
mullers	mummichog	muonic	murrelets	mushrats
mullet	mummies	muons	murres	mushroom
mullets	mummified	murage	murrey	mushrooms
mulligan	mummifies	murages	murreys	mushroomy
mulligans	mummify	mural	murther	mushy
mulling	mumming	muralist	murthers	music
mullion	mummy	muralists	mus	musical
mullioned	mumpish	murals	musambi	musicale
mullions	mumps	murder	muscadel	musicales
mullock	mumpsimus	murdered	muscadels	musically
mulloway	mums	murderer	muscadine	musicals
mulloways	mumsy	murderers	muscarine	musician
mulls	mun	murderess	muscat	musicians
multibuy	munch	murdering	muscatel	musing
multibuys	munched	murderous	muscatels	musingly
multicast	muncher	murders	muscats	musk
multifid	munchers	mure	muscid	muskeg
multifoil	munches	mured	muscids	muskegs
multifold	munchie	mures	muscimol	musket
multiform	munchies	murex	muscle	musketeer
multigym	munching	murexes	muscled	musketry
multigyms	munchkin	muriate	muscleman	muskets
multihull	mundane	muriates	musclemen	muskiness
multimode	mundanely	muricate	muscles	muskrat
multipack	mundanity	murices	muscling	muskrats
multipara	mung	murid	muscly	musks
multiplay	mungo	murine	muscovado	muskwood
multiple	muni	muring	muscovite	musky
multiples	munia	muriqui	muscular	muslin
multiplet	municipal	muriquis	muse	muslined
multiplex	muniment	murk	mused	muslins
multiply	muniments	murkier	museology	muso
multipole	munis	murkiest	muses	musos
multitask	munition	murkily	musette	musquash
multitude	munitions	murkiness	musettes	muss
multiway	munshi	murky	museum	mussed
multure	munshis	murmur	museums	mussel
mum	munsif	murmured	mush	mussels
mumble	munsifs	murmurer	mushaira	musses
mumbled	munt	murmurers	mushairas	mussing
mumbler	muntin	murmuring	mushed	mussy
mumblers	muntined	murmurous		

must
mustache
mustaches
mustang
mustangs
mustard
mustardy
mustelid
mustelids
muster
mustered
musterer
musterers
mustering
musters
musth
mustier
mustiest
mustily
mustiness
musty
mutable
mutagen
mutagenic
mutagens
mutant
mutants
mutate
mutated
mutates
mutating
mutation
mutations
mutative
mutator
mutators
mutch
mutches
mutchkin
mutchkins
mute
muted

mutely
muteness
mutes
mutha
muti
mutilate
mutilated
mutilates
mutilator
mutineer
mutineers
muting
mutinied
mutinies
mutinous
mutiny
mutinying
mutism
muton
mutons
mutt
mutter
muttered
mutterer
mutterers
muttering
mutters
mutton
muttony
mutts
mutual
mutualise
mutualism
mutualist
mutuality
mutualize
mutually
mutuel
mutuels
mutule
mutules
muumuu

muumuus
mux
muxed
muxes
muxing
muzak
muzhik
muzhiks
muzz
muzzier
muzziest
muzzily
muzziness
muzzle
muzzled
muzzles
muzzling
muzzy

MY

my
myalgia
myalgic
myalism
myall
myalls
mycelia
mycelial
mycelium
mycetoma
mycology
mycoses
mycosis
mycotic
mycotoxin
mydriasis
myelin
myelitis
myeloid
myeloma
myelomas

myelomata
myenteric
mylodon
mylodons
mylonite
myna
mynah
mynahs
mynas
myoclonic
myoclonus
myofibril
myogenic
myoglobin
myologist
myology
myomere
myomeres
myomorph
myomorphs
myopathic
myopathy
myope
myopes
myopia
myopic
myosin
myosins
myosis
myositis
myosotis
myotis
myotome
myotomes
myotonia
myotonic
myriad
myriads
myriapod
myriapods
myristate
myrmidon

myrmidons
myrobalan
myrrh
myrrhy
myrtle
myrtles
myself
mysid
mysids
mystagogy
mysteries
mystery
mystic
mystical
mysticete
mysticism
mystics
mystified
mystifier
mystifies
mystify
mystique
myth
mythi
mythic
mythical
mythicise
mythicism
mythicist
mythicize
mythoi
mythology
mythos
myths
mythus
myxedema
myxoedema
myxoma
myxomas
myxomata
myxovirus

N A

na
naan
naans
naartjie
naartjies
nab
nabbed
nabbing
nabe
nabob
nabobs
nabs
nacarat
nacelle
nacelles
nachas
naches
nacho
nachos
nacre
nacreous
nada
nadir
nae
naevi
naevus
naff
naffed
naffer
naffest
naffing
naffness
naffs
nag
naga
nagana
nagas
nagged
nagger
naggers
nagging

naggingly
naggy
nags
nagware
nah
naiad
naiades
naiads
naiant
naif
nail
nailed
nailer
naileries
nailers
nailery
nailing
naillless
nails
nainsook
naira
nairas
naissant
naive
naively
naiveness
naiver
naivest
naivety
naked
nakedly
nakedness
naker
nakers
naloxone
namaskar
namaste
name
nameable
namecheck
named
nameless

namely
nameplate
names
namesake
namesakes
naming
namkin
namma
nammas
nan
nana
nanas
nance
nances
nancies
nancy
nandina
nankeen
nankeens
nanna
nannas
nannied
nannies
nanny
nannygai
nannygais
nannying
nano
nanometer
nanometre
nanotube
nanotubes
nans
naoi
naos
nap
napa
napalm
napalmed
napalming
napalms
napas

nape
napery
napes
naphtha
naphthene
naphthol
napkin
napkins
napless
napoleon
napoleons
nappa
nappas
nappe
napped
napper
nappers
nappes
nappies
napping
nappy
naproxen
naps
narc
narcissi
narcissus
narco
narcos
narcosis
narcotic
narcotics
narcotise
narcotism
narcotize
narcs
nard
nardoo
nardoos
nards
nares
narghile
narghiles

narial
naris
nariyal
nark
narked
narkier
narkiest
narking
narks
narky
narrate
narrated
narrates
narrating
narration
narrative
narrator
narrators
narrow
narrowed
narrower
narrowest
narrowing
narrowish
narrowly
narrows
narthex
narthexes
narwhal
narwhals
nary
nasal
nasalise
nasalised
nasalises
nasality
nasalize
nasalized
nasalizes
nasally
nascency
nascent

naseberry
nashi
nastic
nastier
nasties
nastiest
nastily
nastiness
nasty
natal
natality
natant
natation
natatory
natch
nates
natheless
nathless
nation
national
nationals
nations
native
natively
natives
nativism
nativist
nativists
nativity
natron
natter
nattered
natterer
natterers
nattering
natters
nattier
nattiest
nattily
nattiness
natty
natural
naturally
naturals
nature
natured
natures
naturism
naturist
naturists

naught
naughtier
naughtily
naughts
naughty
nauplii
nauplius
nausea
nauseate
nauseated
nauseates
nauseous
nautch
nautches
nautical
nautili
nautiloid
nautilus
nav
navaid
naval
navarin
navarins
nave
navel
navels
navelwort
naves
navicular
navies
navigable
navigate
navigated
navigates
navigator
navvies
navvy
navy
naw
nawab
nawabs
nay
nays
naysaid
naysay
naysayer
naysayers
naysaying
naysays

N E

né
neap
neaped
neaping
neaps
near
nearby
neared
nearer
nearest
nearing
nearish
nearly
nearness
nears
nearshore
nearside
neat
neaten
neatened
neatening
neatens
neater
neatest
neath
neatly
neatness
neats
neb
nebbish
nebbishes
nebbishy
nebs
nebula
nebulae
nebular
nebulas
nebulise
nebulised
nebuliser
nebulises
nebulize
nebulized
nebulizer
nebulizes
nebulous
nebuly
necessary

necessity
neck
neckband
neckbands
neckcloth
necked
necker
neckers
necking
necklace
necklaced
necklaces
neckless
necklet
necklets
neckline
necklines
necks
necktie
neckties
neckwear
necrology
necropsy
necrosis
necrotic
nectar
nectarean
nectaries
nectarine
nectarous
nectary
neddies
neddy
née
need
needed
needful
needfully
needier
neediest
neediness
needing
needle
needled
needler
needles
needless
needling
needs
needy

neem
neems
neep
neeps
nef
nefarious
nefs
neg
negate
negated
negates
negating
negation
negative
negatived
negatives
negator
negators
negatory
neglect
neglected
neglects
negligee
negligees
negligent
negotiant
negotiate
negroni
negronis
negs
negus
neguses
neigh
neighbor
neighbors
neighbour
neighed
neighing
neighs
neither
nek
neks
nekton
nektonic
nellies
nelly
nelson
nelsons
nematic
nematode

nematodes
nemertean
nemertine
nemeses
nemesia
nemesis
nene
nenes
neocon
neocortex
neodymium
neologise
neologism
neologist
neologize
neomycin
neon
neonatal
neonate
neonates
neopagan
neophobia
neophobic
neophyte
neophytes
neoplasia
neoplasm
neoplasms
neoprene
neotenic
neotenous
neoteny
neoteric
nepenthe
nepenthes
neper
nepers
nepeta
nepheline
nephew
nephews
nephology
nephridia
nephrite
nephritic
nephritis
nephron
nephrons
nephrosis
nephrotic

nepotism
nepotist
nepotists
neptunium
nerd
nerdier
nerdiest
nerdish
nerds
nerdy
nereid
nereids
nerine
nerines
nerite
nerites
neritic
nerk
nerks
neroli
nervation
nerve
nerved
nerveless
nerves
nervier
nerviest
nervily
nervine
nervines
nerviness
nerving
nervous
nervously
nervure
nervures
nervy
nescience
nescient
nesh
neshness
ness
nesses
nest
nested
nester
nestful
nestfuls
nesting
nestle

nestled
nestles
nestling
nestlings
nests
net
neta
netball
netful
netfuls
nether
netizen
nets
netsuke
netsukes
nett
netted
netter
netters
netties
netting
nettle
nettled
nettles
nettling
netts
netty
network
networked
networker
networks
neum
neume
neumes
neums
neural
neuralgia
neuralgic
neurally
neuritic
neuritis
neuroglia
neurology
neuroma
neuromas
neuromast
neuromata
neuron
neuronal
neurone

neurones
neuronic
neurons
neuropath
neuropil
neuropile
neuroses
neurosis
neurotic
neurotics
neurotomy
neuston
neustonic
neustons
neuter
neutered
neutering
neuters
neutral
neutrally
neutrals
neutrino
neutrinos
neutron
neutrons
névé
never
nevermore
nevus
new
newbie
newbies
newborn
newborns
newbuild
newbuilds
newcomer
newcomers
newel
newels
newer
newest
newie
newies
newish
newly
newness
news
newsagent
newsboy

newsboys
newscast
newscasts
newsflash
newsgroup
newsie
newsier
newsies
newsiest
newsman
newsmen
newspaper
newspeak
newsprint
newsreel
newsreels
newsroom
newsrooms
newsy
newt
newton
newtons
newts
next
nexus
nexuses

N G

ngaio
ngaios
ngoma
ngomas
ngultrum
ngwee

N I

niacin
nib
nibbed
nibble
nibbled
nibbler
nibblers
nibbles
nibbling
niblet
niblets
niblick

niblicks
nibs
nice
nicely
niceness
nicer
nicest
niceties
nicety
niche
niched
niches
niching
nichrome
nick
nicked
nickel
nickeled
nickeling
nickelled
nickels
nicker
nickered
nickering
nickers
nicking
nickname
nicknamed
nicknames
nicks
nicotiana
nicotine
nictation
nidation
nide
nides
nidi
nidus
niduses
niece
nieces
niello
nielloed
niellos
niente
niff
niffed
niffier
niffiest
niffing

niffs
niffy
niftier
niftiest
niftily
niftiness
nifty
nigella
nigellas
niggard
niggardly
niggards
nigger
niggers
niggle
niggled
niggles
niggling
nigh
night
nightbird
nightcap
nightcaps
nightclub
nightfall
nightgown
nighthawk
nightie
nighties
nightjar
nightjars
nightless
nightlife
nightly
nightmare
nights
nightside
nightspot
nightwear
nigritude
nihilism
nihilist
nihilists
nihility
nikah
nikahs
nil
nilgai
nilgais
nilpotent

nim
nimbi
nimble
nimbler
nimblest
nimbly
nimbus
nimbuses
nimrod
nimrods
nine
ninefold
ninepins
nineteen
nineties
ninetieth
ninety
ninhydrin
ninja
ninjas
ninjutsu
ninnies
ninny
ninon
ninth
ninthly
niobium
nip
nipa
nipas
nipped
nipper
nippers
nippier
nippies
nippiest
nippily
nipping
nipple
nippled
nipples
nippling
nippy
nips
nirvana
nisei
niseis
nisi
nisin
nit

nite
niter
niterie
niteries
nitinol
nitrate
nitrated
nitrates
nitrating
nitration
nitre
nitride
nitrided
nitrides
nitriding
nitrified
nitrifies
nitrify
nitrile
nitriles
nitrite
nitrites
nitro
nitrogen
nitrous
nits
nitty
nitwit
nitwits
nitwitted
nival
nivation
niveous
nix
nixed
nixes
nixie
nixing

N O

no
noah
nob
nobble
nobbled
nobbler
nobblers
nobbles
nobbling

nobbut
nobby
nobelium
nobiliary
nobility
noble
nobleman
noblemen
nobleness
nobler
nobles
noblesse
noblest
nobly
nobodies
nobody
nobs
nock
nocked
nocking
nocks
noctiluca
noctuid
noctule
noctules
nocturn
nocturnal
nocturne
nocturnes
nocturns
nocuous
nod
nodal
nodded
noddies
nodding
noddle
noddled
noddles
noddling
noddy
node
nodes
nodi
nodical
nodose
nodosity
nods
nodular
nodulated

nodule	nomogram	noontides	nosegay	notarize
nodules	nomograms	noontime	nosegays	notarized
nodulose	nomograph	noontimes	noseless	notarizes
nodulous	nonage	noose	nosema	notary
nodus	nonagon	noosed	nosemas	notate
noes	nonagonal	nooses	nosepiece	notated
noetic	nonagons	noosing	noses	notates
nog	nonane	noosphere	nosey	notating
nogal	nonanes	nootropic	noseyed	notation
noggin	nonary	nopal	noseying	notations
nogging	nonce	nopales	nosh	notator
noggings	nonces	nopals	noshed	notators
noggins	nonda	nope	nosheries	notch
nogs	nondas	nor	noshery	notchback
nohow	none	nori	noshes	notched
noil	nonentity	noria	noshing	notcher
noils	nones	norite	nosied	notchers
noise	nonesuch	nork	nosier	notches
noised	nonet	norks	nosies	notchier
noiseless	nonets	norm	nosiest	notchiest
noises	nong	normal	nosily	notching
noisette	nongs	normalcy	nosiness	notchy
noisettes	nonpareil	normalise	nosing	note
noisier	nonplus	normality	nosode	notebook
noisiest	nonpluses	normalize	nosodes	notebooks
noisily	nonsense	normally	nosology	notecard
noisiness	nonsenses	normative	nostalgia	notecards
noising	nonsuch	norms	nostalgic	notecase
noisome	nonsuches	norteña	nostoc	notecases
noisy	nonsuit	norteño	nostocs	noted
nomad	nonsuited	norteños	nostril	notelet
nomadic	nonsuits	north	nostrils	notelets
nomadism	nonyl	norther	nostrum	notepad
nomadisms	noodle	northerly	nostrums	notepads
nomads	noodled	northern	nosy	notepaper
nomarch	noodles	northers	nosying	notes
nomarchy	noodling	northing	not	nothing
nombril	nook	northings	nota	nothosaur
nombrils	nookie	northland	notable	notice
nome	nooks	northward	notables	noticed
nomen	nooky	nose	notably	notices
nomes	noon	nosebag	notal	noticing
nominal	noonday	nosebags	notam	notified
nominally	nooner	noseband	notams	notifies
nominate	nooning	nosebands	notaphily	notify
nominated	noonings	nosebleed	notarial	notifying
nominates	noonoo	nosed	notaries	noting
nominator	noonoos	nosedive	notarise	notion
nominee	noons	nosedived	notarised	notional
nominees	noontide	nosedives	notarises	notions

notitia
notochord
notoriety
notorious
notornis
nots
notum
nougat
nougatine
nought
noughts
noumena
noumenal
noumenon
noun
nounal
nouns
nourish
nourished
nourisher
nourishes
nous
nouveau
nouvelle
nova
novae
novas
novate
novated
novates
novating
novation
novel
novelese
novelette
novelise
novelised
novelises
novelist
novelists
novelize
novelized
novelizes
novella
novellas
novelly
novels
novelties
novelty
novena

novenas
novice
novices
noviciate
novitiate
novocaine
now
nowadays
noway
noways
nowed
nowhere
nowise
nowness
nowt
noxious
noxiously
noyade
noyades
noyau
noyaux
nozzle
nozzles

N T

nth

N U

nu
nuance
nuanced
nuances
nuancing
nub
nubbin
nubbins
nubbly
nubby
nubile
nubility
nubs
nucellar
nucelli
nucellus
nuchal
nuclear
nuclease
nucleases

nucleate
nucleated
nucleates
nuclei
nucleolar
nucleoli
nucleolus
nucleon
nucleonic
nucleons
nucleus
nuclide
nuclides
nuclidic
nuddy
nude
nudes
nudge
nudged
nudger
nudgers
nudges
nudging
nudie
nudies
nudism
nudist
nudists
nudity
nudnick
nudnicks
nudnik
nudniks
nuff
nuffin
nuffink
nugacity
nugatory
nugget
nuggets
nuggetty
nuggety
nuisance
nuisances
nuke
nuked
nukes
nuking
null
nulla

nullah
nullahs
nullas
nulled
nullified
nullifier
nullifies
nullify
nulling
nullipara
nullities
nullity
nulls
numb
numbat
numbats
numbed
number
numbered
numbering
numbers
numbest
numbfish
numbing
numbles
numbly
numbness
numbs
numbskull
numdah
numdahs
numen
numerable
numeracy
numeraire
numeral
numerals
numerate
numerator
numerical
numerous
numina
numinous
nummular
nummulite
nummy
numnah
numnahs
numskull
numskulls

nun
nunatak
nunataks
nunbird
nunchaku
nunchakus
nuncio
nuncios
nuncle
nuncles
nunlike
nunneries
nunnery
nunnish
nuns
nunu
nunus
nuptial
nuptials
nuragh
nuraghe
nuraghi
nuraghic
nurd
nurds
nurse
nursed
nurseling
nursemaid
nurseries
nursery
nurses
nursey
nursie
nursies
nursing
nursling
nurslings
nurturant
nurture
nurtured
nurturer
nurturers
nurtures
nurturing
nus
nut
nutation
nutations
nutcase

nutcases
nutgall
nutgalls
nuthatch
nuthin
nuthouse
nuthouses
nutlet
nutlets
nutmeg
nutmegged
nutmegs
nutria

nutrient
nutrients
nutriment
nutrition
nutritive
nuts
nutshell
nutshells
nutsier
nutsiest
nutso
nutsos
nutsy

nutted
nutter
nutters
nuttier
nuttiest
nuttiness
nutting
nutty
nuzzle
nuzzled
nuzzles
nuzzling

N Y

nyaff
nyaffs
nyala
nyalas
nylon
nylons
nymph
nymphaea
nymphaeum
nymphal
nymphalid

nymphean
nymphet
nymphets
nymphette
nympho
nymphos
nymphs
nystagmic
nystagmus
nystatin

O

O A

oaf
oafish
oafishly
oafs
oak
oaken
oaks
oaktag
oakum
oaky
oar
oared
oarfish
oarfishes
oarless
oarlock
oarlocks
oars
oarsman
oarsmen
oarswoman
oarswomen
oarweed

oases
oasis
oast
oasts
oat
oatcake
oatcakes
oaten
oater
oath
oaths
oatmeal
oats
oaty

O B

oba
obbligati
obbligato
obconical
obcordate
obduct
obducted
obducting

obduction
obducts
obduracy
obdurate
obeah
obeche
obeches
obedience
obedient
obeisance
obeisant
obeli
obelia
obelias
obelise
obelised
obelises
obelising
obelisk
obelisks
obelize
obelized
obelizes
obelizing
obelus

obese
obesities
obesity
obey
obeyed
obeyer
obeyers
obeying
obeys
obfuscate
obi
obis
obit
obiter
obits
obituary
object
objected
objectify
objecting
objection
objective
objector
objectors
objects

objet
objets
objurgate
oblast
oblate
oblates
oblation
oblations
oblatory
oblietjie
obligate
obligated
obligates
obligato
obligator
oblige
obliged
obligee
obligees
obliger
obligers
obliges
obliging
obligor
obligors

oblique
obliquely
obliquity
oblivion
oblivious
oblong
oblongs
obloquy
obnoxious
oboe
oboes
oboist
oboists
obol
obols
obovate
obscene
obscenely
obscener
obscenest
obscenity
obscurant
obscure
obscured
obscurely
obscurer
obscures
obscurest
obscuring
obscurity
obsequies
observant
observe
observed
observer
observers
observes
observing
obsess
obsessed
obsesses
obsessing
obsession
obsessive
obsidian
obsolesce
obsolete
obsoleted
obsoletes
obstacle

obstacles
obstetric
obstinacy
obstinate
obstruct
obstructs
obstruent
obtain
obtained
obtainer
obtainers
obtaining
obtains
obtect
obtected
obtention
obtrude
obtruded
obtruder
obtruders
obtrudes
obtruding
obtrusion
obtrusive
obtund
obtunded
obtunding
obtunds
obturate
obturated
obturates
obturator
obtuse
obtusely
obtusity
obverse
obversely
obverses
obversion
obvert
obverted
obverting
obverts
obviate
obviated
obviates
obviating
obviation
obvious
obviously

O C

oca
ocarina
ocarinas
ocas
occasion
occasions
occipital
occiput
occiputs
occlude
occluded
occludes
occluding
occlusal
occlusion
occlusive
occult
occulted
occulting
occultism
occultist
occultly
occults
occupance
occupancy
occupant
occupants
occupied
occupier
occupiers
occupies
occupy
occupying
occur
occurred
occurrent
occurring
occurs
ocean
oceanaria
oceanic
oceans
oceanward
ocellar
ocellated
ocelli
ocellus

ocelot
ocelots
och
oche
ocher
oches
ochlocrat
ochone
ochre
ochrea
ochreae
ochreas
ochreish
ochreous
ochroid
ochrous
ochry
ocker
ockers
ocnophil
ocnophils
ocotillo
ocotillos
octad
octads
octagon
octagonal
octagons
octahedra
octal
octals
octameter
octane
octant
octants
octastyle
octave
octaves
octavo
octavos
octennial
octet
octets
octofoil
octofoils
octonary
octopod
octopods
octopoid

octopus
octopuses
octoroon
octoroons
octothorp
octroi
octrois
octuple
octupled
octuples
octuplet
octuplets
octupling
octyl
octyls
ocular
ocularist
ocularly
oculi
oculist
oculists
oculus

O D

od
odalisque
odd
oddball
oddballs
odder
oddest
oddish
oddities
oddity
oddly
oddment
oddments
oddness
odds
ode
odea
odeon
odeons
odes
odeum
odeums
odiferous
odious
odiously

odium
odometer
odometers
odonata
odonate
odonates
odontoid
odor
odorant
odorants
odorise
odorised
odoriser
odorisers
odorises
odorising
odorize
odorized
odorizer
odorizers
odorizes
odorizing
odorous
odors
odour
odourless
odours
odyssean
odyssey
odysseys

O E

oecology
oedema
oedemas
oenology
oenophile
oersted
oersteds
oesophagi
oestriol
oestriols
oestrogen
oestrone
oestrones
oestrous
oestrus
oeuvre

O F

of
ofay
ofays
off
offa
offal
offbeat
offbeats
offcomer
offcut
offcuts
offed
offence
offences
offend
offended
offender
offenders
offending
offends
offense
offenses
offensive
offer
offered
offerer
offerers
offering
offerings
offeror
offerors
offers
offertory
offhand
offhanded
office
officer
officered
officers
offices
official
officials
officiant
officiate
officinal
officious
offie
offies

offing
offish
offishly
offload
offloaded
offloads
offprint
offprints
offs
offsaddle
offset
offsets
offshoot
offshoots
offshore
offside
offsider
offsides
offspring
offstage
offtake
offy
oft
often
oftener
oftenest

O G

ogam
ogams
ogdoad
ogdoads
ogee
ogeed
ogees
ogham
oghams
ogival
ogive
ogives
ogle
ogled
ogler
oglers
ogles
ogling
ogre
ogreish
ogres

ogress
ogresses
ogrish

O H

oh
ohm
ohmic
ohmically
ohmmeter
ohmmeters
ohms
oho
ohone
ohs
ohu
ohus

O I

oi
oick
oicks
oidia
oidium
oik
oiks
oil
oilbird
oilbirds
oilcake
oilcakes
oilcan
oilcans
oilcloth
oilcloths
oiled
oiler
oilers
oilfield
oilfields
oilfish
oilfishes
oilier
oiliest
oilily
oiliness
oiling
oilman

oilmen
oils
oilseed
oilskin
oilskins
oilstone
oilstones
oily
oink
oinked
oinking
oinks
ointment
ointments

O K

oka
okapi
okapis
okas
okay
okays
oke
okes
okie
okies
okra
okrug
okrugs
okta
oktas

O L

old
olde
olden
older
oldest
oldie
oldies
oldish
oldness
oldspeak
oldsquaw
oldsquaws
oldster
oldsters
ole

olé
oleaceous
oleander
oleanders
oleaster
oleasters
oleate
oleates
olecranon
olefin
olefine
olefines
olefinic
olefins
oleograph
oleoresin
oleum
olfaction
olfactive
olfactory
olibanum
olibanums
oligaemia
oligaemic
oligarch
oligarchy
oligemia
oligo
oligomer
oligomers
oligopoly
oligos
oliguria
oliguric
olingo
olingos
olio
olios
olivary
olive
olives
olivette
olivettes
olivine
olivines
ollie
ollied
ollieing
ollies
ollycrock

olm
olms
ologies
ologist
ologists
ology
oloroso
olorosos

O M

om
omadawn
omadawns
omadhaun
omadhauns
omadhawn
omadhawns
omasa
omasum
ombre
ombré
ombudsman
ombudsmen
omega
omegas
omelet
omelets
omelette
omelettes
omen
omens
omenta
omental
omentum
omer
omers
omertà
omicron
omicrons
ominous
ominously
omissible
omission
omissions
omissive
omit
omits
omitted
omitting

ommatidia
omnibus
omnibuses
omnirange
omnivore
omnivores
omophagia
omophagic
omophagy
omphaloi
omphalos

O N

on
onager
onagers
onanism
onanist
onanistic
onanists
once
oncer
oncers
oncogene
oncogenes
oncogenic
oncology
oncoming
oncost
oncosts
one
onefold
oneiric
oneness
oner
onerous
onerously
oners
oneself
onflow
onglaze
ongoing
onion
onions
oniony
onkus
onliest
online
onlooker

onlookers
onlooking
only
onomast
onomastic
onrush
onrushed
onrushes
onrushing
onset
onsets
onshore
onside
onslaught
onstage
ontic
onto
ontogenic
ontogeny
ontology
onus
onward
onwards
onymous
onyx
onyxes

O O

oo
oocyst
oocysts
oocyte
oocytes
oodles
oof
oofier
oofiest
oofiness
oofy
oogamies
oogamous
oogamy
oogenesis
oogonia
oogonium
ooh
oohed
oohing
oohs

oojah
oojahs
oolite
oolites
oolith
ooliths
oolitic
oological
oologist
oologists
oology
oolong
oom
oompah
oompahed
oompahing
oomph
oops
oos
oosphere
oospheres
oospore
oospores
ootheca
oothecae
ootid
ootids
ooze
oozed
oozes
oozier
ooziest
oozing
oozy

O P

op
opacified
opacifier
opacifies
opacify
opacity
opah
opahs
opal
opaline
opalines
opals
opanci

opanka
opankas
opaque
opaquely
opaquer
opaquest
opcode
opcodes
ope
open
openable
openbill
openbills
opencast
opened
opener
openers
opening
openings
openly
openness
opens
openwork
opepe
opepes
opera
operable
operand
operands
operant
operants
operas
operate
operated
operates
operatic
operatics
operating
operation
operative
operator
operators
opercula
opercular
operculum
operetta
operettas
operon
operons
operose

ophidian
ophidians
ophiolite
ophitic
ophiuroid
opiate
opiated
opiates
opiating
opine
opined
opines
opining
opinion
opinions
opioid
opioids
opium
opopanax
opoponax
opossum
opossums
oppida
oppidum
oppo
opponens
opponent
opponents
opportune
oppos
opposable
oppose
opposed
opposer
opposers
opposes
opposing
opposite
opposites
oppress
oppressed
oppresses
oppressor
oppugn
oppugnant
oppugned
oppugner
oppugners
oppugning
oppugns

ops
opsimath
opsimaths
opsin
opsonic
opsonin
opsonins
opsonise
opsonised
opsonises
opsonize
opsonized
opsonizes
opt
optant
optative
opted
optic
optical
optically
optician
opticians
optics
optima
optimal
optimally
optimific
optimise
optimised
optimiser
optimises
optimism
optimist
optimists
optimize
optimized
optimizer
optimizes
optimum
optimums
opting
option
optional
optioned
optioning
options
optometer
optometry
optronic
optronics

opts
opulence
opulent
opulently
opuntia
opuntias
opus
opuscula
opuscule
opuscules
opusculum
opuses

| O | R |

or
ora
orach
orache
oraches
orachs
oracle
oracles
oracular
oracy
oral
oralism
oralist
oralists
orality
orally
orals
orang
orange
orangeade
orangery
oranges
orangey
orangish
orangy
orate
orated
orates
orating
oration
orations
orator
oratorial
oratories
oratorio

oratorios
orators
oratory
orb
orbat
orbed
orbicular
orbing
orbit
orbital
orbited
orbiter
orbiters
orbiting
orbits
orbs
orc
orca
orcas
orcein
orchard
orchards
orchestra
orchid
orchidist
orchids
orchil
orchils
orchis
orchises
orchitis
orcinol
orcs
ordain
ordained
ordainer
ordainers
ordaining
ordains
ordeal
ordeals
order
ordered
ordering
orderlies
orderly
orders
ordinal
ordinals
ordinance

ordinand
ordinands
ordinary
ordinate
ordinates
ordnance
ordure
ore
øre
öre
oread
oreads
orebodies
orebody
orectic
oregano
orenda
ores
orf
orfe
orfes
orfs
organ
organa
organdie
organdies
organdy
organelle
organic
organise
organised
organises
organism
organisms
organist
organists
organize
organized
organizer
organizes
organon
organons
organs
organum
organza
organzine
orgasm
orgasmed
orgasmic
orgasming

orgasms
orgastic
orgeat
orgiastic
orgies
orgone
orgulous
orgy
oribi
oribis
orichalc
oriel
oriels
orient
oriental
orientate
oriented
orienteer
orienting
orients
orifice
orifices
oriflamme
origami
origanum
origanums
origin
original
originals
originate
origins
oriole
orioles
orison
orisons
orle
orles
orlop
orlops
ormer
ormers
ormolu
ornament
ornaments
ornate
ornately
ornery
ornithine
orogen
orogenic

orogens
orogeny
orotund
orphan
orphanage
orphaned
orphaning
orphans
orpharion
orphrey
orphreys
orpiment
orpiments
orpin
orpine
orpines
orpins
orra
orreries
orrery
orris
orrises
ortanique
orthocone
orthodox
orthodoxy
orthoepic
orthoepy
orthopter
orthoptic
orthosis
orthostat
orthotic
orthotics
orthotist
ortolan
ortolans
orts
oryx
oryxes
orzo
orzos

os
oscar
oscars
oscillate
oscine

oscula
osculant
oscular
osculate
osculated
osculates
osculum
oshi
osier
osiers
osmic
osmically
osmium
osmometer
osmometry
osmose
osmosed
osmoses
osmosing
osmosis
osmotic
osmunda
osmundas
osnaburg
osprey
ospreys
ossa
osseous
ossicle
ossicles
ossified
ossifies
ossify
ossifying
ossuaries
ossuary
osteitis
ostensive
ostensory
osteocyte
osteoid
osteology
osteopath
osteotome
osteotomy
ostia
ostinati
ostinato
ostinatos
ostiole

ostium
ostler
ostlers
ostraca
ostracise
ostracism
ostracize
ostracod
ostracods
ostracon
ostraka
ostrakon
ostrich
ostriches

otaku
otalgia
otalgias
other
otherness
otherwise
otic
otiose
otiosely
otitis
otocyst
otolith
otolithic
otoliths
otologist
otology
otoplasty
otoscope
otoscopes
otoscopic
ototoxic
otter
otters
otto
ottocento
ottoman
ottomans

ou
ouabain
oubaas

oubliette
ouboet
ouch
oud
ouds
ouens
ought
ougiya
ougiyas
ouguiya
ouguiyas
ouklip
ouma
ounce
ounces
oupa
our
ouroboros
ours
ourself
ourselves
ous
ousel
ousels
oust
ousted
ouster
ousters
ousting
ousts
out
outa
outact
outacted
outacting
outacts
outage
outages
outasight
outback
outbacker
outbid
outbids
outboard
outboards
outbound
outbox
outboxed
outboxes
outboxing

outbrave
outbraved
outbraves
outbreak
outbreaks
outbred
outbreed
outbreeds
outburst
outbursts
outcall
outcalls
outcast
outcaste
outcasted
outcastes
outcasts
outclass
outcome
outcomes
outcries
outcrop
outcrops
outcross
outcry
outcurve
outdated
outdid
outdo
outdoes
outdoing
outdone
outdoor
outdoors
outdoorsy
outdrive
outdriven
outdrives
outdrove
outed
outer
outermost
outerwear
outface
outfaced
outfaces
outfacing
outfall
outfalls
outfield

outfields
outfight
outfights
outfit
outfits
outfitted
outfitter
outflank
outflanks
outflow
outflows
outfought
outfox
outfoxed
outfoxes
outfoxing
outgas
outgases
outgassed
outgo
outgoes
outgoing
outgoings
outgone
outgrew
outgross
outgrow
outgrown
outgrows
outgrowth
outguess
outgun
outgunned
outguns
outhaul
outhouse
outhoused
outhouses
outie
outies
outing
outings
outjie
outjies
outjockey
outlander
outlast
outlasted
outlasts
outlaw

outlawed
outlawing
outlawry
outlaws
outlay
outlays
outlet
outlets
outlier
outliers
outline
outlined
outliner
outliners
outlines
outlining
outlive
outlived
outlives
outliving
outlook
outlooks
outlying
outman
outmanned
outmans
outmatch
outmoded
outmost
outnumber
outpace
outpaced
outpaces
outpacing
outplay
outplayed
outplays
outpoint
outpoints
outport
outports
outpost
outposts
output
outputs
outputted
outrace
outraced
outraces
outracing

outrage
outraged
outrages
outraging
outran
outrank
outranked
outranks
outré
outreach
outridden
outride
outrider
outriders
outrides
outriding
outrigged
outrigger
outright
outrival
outrivals
outro
outrode
outros
outrun
outruns
outrush
outrushed
outrushes
outs
outsail
outsailed
outsails
outsang
outsat
outscore
outscored
outscores
outsell
outsells
outsert
outset
outshine
outshines
outshone
outshoot
outshoots
outshop
outshops
outshot

outshout
outshouts
outside
outsider
outsiders
outsides
outsing
outsings
outsize
outsized
outsizes
outskirts
outsmart
outsmarts
outsold
outsole
outsoles
outsource
outspan
outspans
outsped
outspeed
outspeeds
outspend
outspends
outspent
outspoken
outspread
outstare
outstared
outstares
outstay
outstayed
outstays
outstep
outsteps
outstrip
outstrips
outsung
outswing
outswings
outta
outvalue
outvalued
outvalues
outvote
outvoted
outvotes
outvoting
outwait

outwaited
outwaits
outwalk
outwalked
outwalks
outward
outwardly
outwards
outwash
outwashes
outwatch
outwear
outwears
outweigh
outweighs
outwent
outwit
outwith
outwits
outwitted
outwore
outwork
outworker
outworks
outworld
outworn
outyield
outyields
ouzel
ouzels
ouzo

O V

ova
oval
ovalbumin
ovalities
ovality
ovalness
ovals
ovarian
ovaries
ovaritis
ovary
ovate
ovates
ovation
ovations
oven

ovenbird
ovenbirds
ovenproof
ovens
ovenware
over
overact
overacted
overacts
overage
overages
overall
overalled
overalls
overarch
overarm
overate
overawe
overawed
overawes
overawing
overbear
overbears
overbid
overbids
overbite
overbites
overblown
overboard
overbold
overbook
overbooks
overboot
overboots
overbore
overborne
overbrim
overbrims
overbuild
overbuilt
overbusy
overbuy
overbuys
overcall
overcalls
overcame
overcast
overcasts
overcheck
overclass

overcloud
overcoat
overcoats
overcome
overcomes
overcook
overcooks
overcrop
overcrops
overcrowd
overdamp
overdamps
overdate
overdates
overdid
overdo
overdoes
overdoing
overdone
overdose
overdosed
overdoses
overdraft
overdrank
overdraw
overdrawn
overdraws
overdress
overdrew
overdrink
overdrive
overdrunk
overdub
overdubs
overdue
overeager
overeat
overeaten
overeater
overeats
overexert
overfall
overfalls
overfed
overfeed
overfeeds
overfill
overfills
overfine
overfish

overflew
overflies
overflow
overflown
overflows
overfly
overfold
overfolds
overfond
overfull
overglaze
overgraze
overgrew
overgrow
overgrown
overgrows
overhand
overhang
overhangs
overhasty
overhaul
overhauls
overhead
overheads
overhear
overheard
overhears
overheat
overheats
overhung
overissue
overjoyed
overkill
overladen
overlaid
overlain
overland
overlands
overlap
overlaps
overlarge
overlay
overlays
overleaf
overleap
overleaps
overleapt
overlie
overlies

overload
overloads
overlock
overlocks
overlong
overlook
overlooks
overlord
overlords
overly
overlying
overman
overmans
overmatch
overmen
overmuch
overnice
overnight
overpaid
overpaint
overpass
overpay
overpays
overpitch
overplay
overplays
overplus
overpower
overprice
overprint
overproof
overran
overrate
overrated
overrates
overreach
overreact
override
overrider
overrides
overripe
overrode
overruff
overruffs
overrule
overruled
overrules
overrun
overruns

overs
oversail
oversails
oversaw
overscan
oversea
overseas
oversee
overseen
overseer
overseers
oversees
oversell
oversells
overset
oversets
oversew
oversewed
oversewn
oversews
oversexed
overshoe
overshoes
overshoot
overshot
overside
oversight
oversite
oversize
oversized
overskirt
oversleep
overslept
oversold
oversoul
overspend
overspent
overspill
overspray
overstaff
overstate
overstay
overstays
oversteer
overstep
oversteps
overstock
overstuff
overt

overtake
overtaken
overtakes
overtask
overtasks
overtax
overtaxed
overtaxes
overthrew
overthrow
overtime
overtire
overtired
overtires
overtly
overtness
overtone
overtones
overtook
overtop
overtops
overtrade
overtrain
overtrick
overtrump
overture
overtures
overturn
overturns
overtype
overtyped
overtypes
overuse
overused
overuses
overusing
overvalue
overview
overviews
overwater
overwhelm
overwind
overwinds
overwork
overworks
overwound
overwrap
overwraps
overwrite
overwrote

oviducal
oviduct
oviductal
oviducts
oviform
ovine
oviparity
oviparous
oviposit
oviposits
ovoid
ovoids
ovoli
ovolo
ovotestes
ovotestis
ovular
ovulate
ovulated
ovulates
ovulating
ovulation
ovulatory
ovule
ovules
ovum

`O W`

ow
owe
owed
owes
owing
owl
owlet
owlets
owlish
owlishly
owls
own
owned
owner
ownerless
owners
ownership
owning
owns
owt

`O X`

ox
oxacillin
oxalate
oxalates
oxalis
oxazole
oxbow
oxbows
oxen
oxer
oxers
oxford
oxfords
oxherd
oxherds
oxhide
oxic
oxidant
oxidants
oxidase
oxidases
oxidation
oxidative
oxide
oxides
oxidise
oxidised
oxidises
oxidising
oxidize
oxidized
oxidizer
oxidizers
oxidizes
oxidizing
oximeter
oximeters
oximetry
oxisol
oxisols
oxlip
oxlips
oxpecker
oxpeckers
oxtail
oxtails
oxter

oxters
oxyacid
oxyacids
oxyanion
oxyanions
oxygen
oxygenate
oxygenise
oxygenize

oxygenous
oxymoron
oxymorons
oxyntic
oxytocin
oxytocins
oxytone
oxytones

O Y

oy
oyes
oyez
oyster
oysters

O Z

ozokerite
ozone
ozonic
ozonide
ozonides
ozonise
ozonised

ozonises
ozonising
ozonize
ozonized
ozonizer
ozonizers
ozonizes
ozonizing

P

P A

pa
paan
pablum
pabulum
paca
pacamac
pacamacs
pacarana
pacas
pace
paced
pacemaker
paceman
pacemen
pacer
pacers
paces
pacey
pacha
pachas
pachinko
pachisi
pachuco
pachucos
pachyderm
pachytene
pacier

paciest
pacific
pacified
pacifier
pacifiers
pacifies
pacifism
pacifist
pacifists
pacify
pacifying
pacing
pack
packable
package
packaged
packager
packagers
packages
packaging
packcloth
packed
packer
packers
packet
packeted
packeting
packetize
packets

packframe
packhorse
packing
packman
packmen
packs
packsack
packsacks
pact
pacts
pacu
pacy
pad
padauk
padauks
padded
paddies
padding
paddle
paddled
paddler
paddlers
paddles
paddling
paddock
paddocked
paddocks
paddy
pademelon

padkos
padlock
padlocked
padlocks
padloper
padlopers
padouk
padouks
padre
padres
padri
padrino
padrinos
padrona
padronas
padrone
padrones
pads
padsaw
padsaws
paduasoy
paean
paeans
paederast
paella
paeon
paeonic
paeonies
paeons

paeony
pagan
paganise
paganised
paganises
paganish
paganism
paganisms
paganize
paganized
paganizes
pagans
page
pageant
pageantry
pageants
pageboy
pageboys
paged
pager
pagers
pages
paginal
paginate
paginated
paginates
paging
pagoda
pagodas

pagri
pagris
pah
pahoehoe
paid
paideia
pail
pailful
pailfuls
paillasse
paillette
pails
pain
pained
painful
painfully
paining
painless
pains
paint
paintable
paintball
paintbox
painted
painter
painterly
painters
painting
paintings
paints
paintwork
painty
pair
paired
pairing
pairings
pairs
pairwise
paisa
paisan
paisano
paisanos
paise
paisley
pajamas
pakamac
pakamacs
pakapoo
pakapu
pakeha

pakehas
pakora
pal
palace
palaces
paladin
paladins
palaeosol
palaestra
palagi
palais
palankeen
palanquin
palapa
palatable
palatably
palatal
palatally
palatals
palate
palates
palatial
palatine
palatines
palaver
palavered
palavers
palazzi
palazzo
palazzos
pale
palea
paleae
paled
paleface
palefaces
palely
paleness
paleopole
paleosol
paleosols
paler
pales
palest
palestra
palestras
palette
palettes
palfrey
palfreys

pali
palilalia
palimony
paling
palings
palinode
palinodes
palis
palisade
palisaded
palisades
palish
pall
palladia
palladium
pallasite
palled
pallet
palletise
palletize
pallets
pallia
pallial
palliasse
palliate
palliated
palliates
palliator
pallid
pallidly
pallier
palliest
palling
pallium
palliums
pallor
palls
pally
palm
palmar
palmate
palmated
palmed
palmer
palmers
palmette
palmettes
palmetto
palmettos
palmful

palmfuls
palmier
palmiest
palming
palmist
palmistry
palmists
palmitate
palms
palmtop
palmtops
palmy
palmyra
palmyras
palomino
palominos
palooka
palookas
paloverde
palp
palpable
palpably
palpal
palpate
palpated
palpates
palpating
palpation
palpebral
palpi
palpitant
palpitate
palps
palpus
pals
palsgrave
palsied
palsies
palstave
palstaves
palsy
palsying
palter
paltered
palterer
palterers
paltering
palters
paltrier
paltriest

paltry
paludal
paly
pama
pamas
pampas
pamper
pampered
pampering
pampero
pamperos
pampers
pamphlet
pamphlets
pan
panacea
panacean
panaceas
panache
panada
panadas
panama
panamas
panatella
pancake
pancaked
pancakes
pancaking
pancetta
panchayat
pancreas
panda
pandal
pandan
pandans
pandanus
pandas
pandect
pandects
pandemic
pandemics
pander
pandered
pandering
panders
pandit
pandits
pandora
pandowdy
pane

paneer	panoplies	panzer	pappose	paragon
panegyric	panoply	panzers	pappus	paragons
panel	panoptic	pap	pappy	paragraph
paneled	panorama	papa	pappyshow	parakeet
paneling	panoramas	papabile	paprika	parakeets
panelist	panoramic	papacies	paps	paralegal
panelists	pans	papacy	papula	parallax
panelled	pansexual	papain	papulae	parallel
panelling	pansies	papal	papular	parallels
panellist	pansified	papalagi	papule	paralogy
panels	panstick	papalagis	papules	paralyse
panes	pansy	papalist	papulose	paralysed
panettone	pant	papalists	papulous	paralyses
panettoni	pantalets	papally	papyri	paralysis
panfish	pantaloon	paparazzi	papyrus	paralytic
panfished	pantec	paparazzo	papyruses	paralyze
panfishes	pantech	papas	par	paralyzed
panforte	pantechs	papaw	para	paralyzes
panful	pantecs	papaws	parabases	paramatta
panfuls	panted	papaya	parabasis	paramedic
pang	pantheism	papayas	parable	parameter
panga	pantheist	paper	parables	paramo
pangas	pantheon	paperback	parabola	paramos
pangolin	pantheons	paperbark	parabolae	paramount
pangolins	panther	papered	parabolas	paramour
pangs	panthers	paperer	parabolic	paramours
panhandle	panties	paperers	parachute	parang
pani	pantihose	papering	paracrine	parangs
panic	pantile	paperless	parade	paranoia
panicked	pantiled	papers	paraded	paranoiac
panicking	pantiles	paperwork	parader	paranoic
panicky	panting	papery	paraders	paranoid
panicle	pantingly	papilla	parades	parapente
panicled	panto	papillae	paradigm	parapet
panicles	pantomime	papillary	paradigms	parapeted
panics	pantos	papillate	parading	parapets
panir	pantoum	papilloma	paradisal	paraph
panmictic	pantoums	papillon	paradise	paraphs
panmixia	pantries	papillons	paradises	parapodia
pannage	pantry	papillose	parador	paraquat
panne	pantryman	papism	paradores	pararhyme
panned	pantrymen	papist	paradors	paras
pannier	pants	papistry	parados	parasail
panniers	pantsuit	papists	paradoses	parasails
pannikin	pantsuits	papoose	paradox	parascend
pannikins	pantsula	papooses	paradoxes	parasite
panning	pantsulas	pappi	paradrop	parasites
pannist	pantun	pappier	paradrops	parasitic
pannus	pantuns	pappies	paraffin	parasol
panoplied	pantyhose	pappiest	paraglide	parasols

parataxis	pares	parlance	parred	partisans
paratha	pareses	parlando	parricide	partita
parathion	paresis	parlay	parried	partitas
paratroop	paretic	parlayed	parries	partite
paravane	pareu	parlaying	parring	partition
paravanes	pareus	parlays	parrot	partitive
parawing	parfait	parley	parroted	partizan
paraxial	parfaits	parleyed	parroting	partizans
parboil	parfleche	parleying	parrotlet	partly
parboiled	pargana	parleys	parrots	partner
parboils	parge	parlor	parry	partnered
parbuckle	parges	parlors	parrying	partners
parcel	parget	parlour	pars	partook
parceled	pargeted	parlours	parse	partridge
parceling	pargeting	parlous	parsec	parts
parcelled	pargets	parlously	parsecs	party
parcels	parging	parochial	parsed	partying
parch	parhelia	parodic	parser	parure
parched	parhelion	parodied	parsers	parures
parcheesi	pariah	parodies	parses	parvenu
parches	pariahs	parodist	parsimony	parvenus
parching	parietal	parodists	parsing	parvis
parchment	parietals	parody	parsley	parvise
parclose	paring	parodying	parsnip	parvises
parcloses	parings	parol	parsnips	pas
pard	parish	parole	parson	pascal
pardalote	parishad	paroled	parsonage	pascals
pardner	parishes	parolee	parsonic	paschal
pardners	parison	parolees	parsons	paseo
pardon	parisons	paroles	part	paseos
pardoned	parities	paroling	partake	pash
pardoner	parity	paronym	partaken	pasha
pardoners	park	paronymic	partaker	pashas
pardoning	parka	paronyms	partakers	pashes
pardons	parkade	paronymy	partakes	pashka
pards	parkas	parotid	partaking	pashm
pare	parked	parotitis	parted	pashmina
pared	parkie	paroxysm	parter	pashminas
paregoric	parkier	paroxysms	parterre	paskha
paren	parkies	parp	parterres	paspalum
parent	parkiest	parped	partial	pass
parentage	parkin	parpen	partially	passable
parental	parking	parpens	partible	passably
parented	parkins	parping	particle	passade
parenting	parkland	parps	particles	passage
parents	parklands	parquet	partied	passaged
parer	parks	parquetry	parties	passages
parerga	parkway	parquets	parting	passaging
parergon	parkways	parr	partings	passant
parers	parky	parrakeet	partisan	passata

passband	pastier	patchy	patois	patties
passbands	pasties	pate	patonce	patting
passbook	pastiest	pâte	patootie	patty
passbooks	pastille	pâté	patooties	pattypan
passé	pastilles	patée	patria	pattypans
passed	pastime	patella	patrial	patulous
passel	pastimes	patellae	patrials	patwari
passels	pastiness	patellar	patriarch	patwaris
passenger	pasting	patellate	patriate	patzer
passepied	pastis	paten	patriated	patzers
passer	pastness	patency	patriates	paua
passerine	pastor	patens	patrician	pauas
passers	pastoral	patent	patricide	paucity
passes	pastorale	patented	patrimony	paulownia
passible	pastorali	patentee	patriot	paunch
passim	pastorals	patentees	patriotic	paunched
passing	pastorate	patenting	patriots	paunches
passingly	pastored	patently	patristic	paunchier
passings	pastorela	patents	patrol	paunching
passion	pastorie	pater	patrolled	paunchy
passional	pastoring	patera	patroller	pauper
passions	pastors	paterae	patrolman	pauperdom
passivate	pastrami	paternal	patrolmen	pauperise
passive	pastries	paternity	patrology	pauperism
passively	pastry	paters	patrols	pauperize
passives	pasts	pates	patron	paupers
passivise	pasturage	pâtés	patronage	paupiette
passivity	pasture	path	patronal	pauraque
passivize	pastured	pathetic	patroness	pauraques
passport	pastures	pathless	patronise	pauropod
passports	pasturing	pathname	patronize	pauropods
passus	pasty	pathnames	patronne	pause
password	pat	pathogen	patrons	paused
passwords	pataca	pathogens	patroon	pauses
past	patacas	pathology	patroons	pausing
pasta	patagia	pathos	pats	pavage
pastas	patagium	paths	patsies	pavan
paste	patas	pathway	patsy	pavane
pasted	patball	pathways	patta	pavanes
pastel	patch	patience	patted	pavans
pastelist	patched	patient	pattée	pave
pastels	patcher	patiently	patten	pavé
pastern	patchers	patients	pattens	paved
pasterns	patches	patina	patter	pavement
pastes	patchier	patinas	pattered	pavements
pasticcio	patchiest	patinated	pattering	paver
pastiche	patchily	patio	pattern	pavers
pastiched	patching	patios	patterned	paves
pastiches	patchouli	patly	patterns	pavés
pastie	patchwork	patness	patters	pavilion

pavilions	payouts	peals	peccable	pedants
paving	payphone	pean	peccancy	peddle
pavior	payphones	peanut	peccant	peddled
paviors	payroll	peanuts	peccaries	peddler
paviour	payrolls	pear	peccary	peddlers
paviours	pays	pearl	peccavi	peddles
pavlova	paysage	pearled	peck	peddling
pavlovas	paysages	pearler	pecked	pederast
pavonine	paysagist	pearlers	pecker	pederasts
paw	paysan	pearleye	peckers	pederasty
pawed	paysans	pearleyes	pecking	pedes
pawing	payslip	pearlfish	peckish	pedestal
pawkier	payslips	pearlier	pecks	pedestals
pawkiest		pearlies	pecorino	pedicab
pawkily	**P E**	pearliest	pecorinos	pedicabs
pawkiness		pearling	pecs	pedicel
pawky	pea	pearlised	pecten	pedicels
pawl	peaberry	pearlite	pectens	pedicle
pawls	peace	pearlized	pectic	pedicles
pawn	peaceable	pearls	pectin	pedicure
pawned	peaceably	pearlware	pectinate	pedicured
pawning	peaceful	pearlwort	pectines	pedicures
pawns	peacenik	pearly	pectins	pedigree
pawnshop	peaceniks	pears	pectoral	pedigreed
pawnshops	peacetime	peart	pectorals	pedigrees
pawpaw	peach	peas	peculate	pediment
pawpaws	peached	peasant	peculated	pediments
paws	peaches	peasantry	peculates	pedipalp
pax	peachick	peasants	peculator	pedipalps
pay	peachicks	peasanty	peculiar	pediplain
payable	peachier	pease	pecuniary	pedlar
payables	peachiest	peat	pedagogic	pedlaries
payback	peaching	peatier	pedagogue	pedlars
paybacks	peachy	peatiest	pedagogy	pedlary
payed	peacock	peatland	pedal	pedogenic
payee	peacocks	peatlands	pedaled	pedology
payees	peafowl	peats	pedaler	pedometer
payer	peafowls	peaty	pedalers	pedophile
payers	peahen	peavey	pedaling	peduncle
payess	peahens	peaveys	pedalled	peduncles
paying	peak	peavies	pedaller	pedway
payload	peaked	peavine	pedallers	pedways
payloads	peakier	peavy	pedalling	pee
paymaster	peakiest	pebble	pedalo	peed
payment	peaking	pebbled	pedaloes	peeing
payments	peaks	pebbles	pedalos	peek
paynim	peaky	pebbly	pedals	peekaboo
paynims	peal	pec	pedant	peeked
payola	pealed	pecan	pedantic	peeking
payout	pealing	pecans	pedantry	peeks

peel	pegboxes	pellitory	pendants	penology
peeled	pegged	pellucid	pendency	pens
peeler	peggies	pelmet	pendent	pensée
peelers	pegging	pelmets	pending	pensées
peeling	peggy	pelorus	pendular	pensile
peelings	pegmatite	peloruses	pendulous	pension
peels	pego	pelota	pendulum	pensione
peen	pegos	peloton	pendulums	pensioned
peened	pegs	pelotons	penectomy	pensioner
peening	pegtop	pelt	peneplain	pensioni
peens	pegtops	pelta	penes	pensions
peep	peignoir	peltae	penetrant	pensive
peeped	peignoirs	peltate	penetrate	pensively
peeper	pein	pelted	penfriend	penstemon
peepers	peined	pelting	penghulu	penstock
peephole	peining	peltries	penghulus	penstocks
peepholes	peins	peltry	pengö	pent
peeping	pekan	pelts	pengös	pentacle
peeps	pekans	pelves	penguin	pentacles
peepul	peke	pelvic	penguins	pentad
peepuls	pekes	pelvis	penile	pentads
peer	pekoe	pelvises	penillion	pentagon
peerage	pelage	pemmican	peninsula	pentagons
peerages	pelagic	pemphigus	penis	pentagram
peered	pelau	pen	penises	pentamer
peeress	pele	penal	penistone	pentamers
peeresses	pelecypod	penalise	penitence	pentamery
peerie	pelerine	penalised	penitent	pentane
peeries	pelerines	penalises	penitents	pentangle
peering	peles	penalize	penknife	pentathol
peerless	pelf	penalized	penknives	penthouse
peers	pelham	penalizes	penlight	pentode
peery	pelhams	penally	penlights	pentodes
pees	pelican	penalties	penman	pentose
peeve	pelicans	penalty	penmen	pentoses
peeved	pelikai	penance	pennant	pentoxide
peever	pelike	penanced	pennants	pentyl
peevers	pelisse	penances	pennate	penult
peeves	pelisses	penancing	penne	penults
peeving	pelite	penates	penned	penumbra
peevish	pelites	pence	penni	penumbrae
peevishly	pellagra	penchant	penniä	penumbral
peewee	pellet	penchants	pennies	penumbras
peewees	pelleted	pencil	penniless	penurious
peewit	pelleting	penciled	penning	penury
peewits	pelletise	penciling	pennon	peon
peg	pelletize	pencilled	pennoned	peonage
pegboard	pellets	penciller	pennons	peonages
pegboards	pellicle	pencils	penny	peones
pegbox	pellicles	pendant	pennywort	peonies

peons	perch	perfumer	perilymph	perlé
peony	perchance	perfumers	perimeter	perlemoen
people	perched	perfumery	perimetry	perlite
peopled	percheron	perfumes	perinatal	perlites
peoples	perches	perfuming	perinea	perm
peopling	perching	perfumy	perineal	permalloy
pep	percid	perfusate	perineum	permanent
peperomia	perciform	perfuse	period	permeable
peperoni	percoid	perfused	periodate	permeance
pepino	percoids	perfuses	periodic	permeate
pepinos	percolate	perfusing	periodise	permeated
peplos	percuss	perfusion	periodize	permeates
peploses	percussed	pergana	periods	permeator
peplum	percusses	perganas	periostea	permed
peplums	perdition	pergola	peripatus	perming
pepo	perdure	pergolas	periphery	permit
pepos	perdured	pergunnah	perique	permits
pepped	perdures	perhaps	peris	permitted
pepper	perduring	peri	periscope	permittee
pepperbox	père	perianal	perish	permitter
peppered	peregrine	perianth	perished	perms
peppering	pereiopod	perianths	perisher	permutate
pepperoni	perennate	periapses	perishers	permute
peppers	perennial	periapsis	perishes	permuted
peppery	perentie	periapt	perishing	permutes
peppier	perenties	periapts	perisperm	permuting
peppiest	perenty	pericarp	peristome	peroba
peppily	pères	pericarps	peristyle	perogi
peppiness	perfect	periclase	periti	peroneal
pepping	perfecta	pericope	peritonea	perorate
peppy	perfected	pericopes	peritus	perorated
peps	perfecter	pericycle	periwig	perorates
pepsin	perfectly	periderm	periwigs	peroxide
pepsins	perfecto	periderms	perjure	peroxided
peptic	perfectos	peridia	perjured	peroxides
peptidase	perfects	peridium	perjurer	perp
peptide	perfervid	peridot	perjurers	perpend
peptides	perfidies	perigee	perjures	perpends
peptone	perfidy	perigees	perjuries	perpetual
peptones	perfin	perigyny	perjuring	perplex
per	perfins	perihelia	perjury	perplexed
peracute	perforate	perikarya	perk	perplexes
perborate	perforce	peril	perked	perps
percale	perforin	periled	perkier	perries
perceive	perform	periling	perkiest	perron
perceived	performed	perilled	perkily	perrons
perceiver	performer	perilling	perkiness	perry
perceives	performs	perilous	perking	persecute
percept	perfume	perils	perks	persevere
percepts	perfumed	perilune	perky	persimmon

persist
persisted
persists
person
persona
personae
personage
personal
personals
personas
personate
personify
personnel
persons
perspex
perspire
perspired
perspires
persuade
persuaded
persuader
persuades
pert
pertain
pertained
pertains
pertinent
pertly
pertness
perturb
perturbed
perturbs
pertussis
peruke
perukes
perusal
peruse
perused
peruser
perusers
peruses
perusing
perv
pervade
pervaded
pervader
pervaders
pervades
pervading
pervasion

pervasive
perve
perved
perverse
pervert
perverted
perverter
perverts
perves
perving
pervious
pervs
pervy
pes
peseta
pesetas
pesewa
pesewas
peshmerga
peskier
peskiest
peskily
peskiness
pesky
peso
pesos
pessaries
pessary
pessimism
pessimist
pest
pester
pestered
pesterer
pesterers
pestering
pesters
pesticide
pestilent
pestle
pestled
pestles
pestling
pesto
pests
pet
petal
petaline
petalled
petaloid

petals
pétanque
petard
petards
petasus
petasuses
petcock
petcocks
petechia
petechiae
petechial
peter
petered
petering
peterman
petermen
peters
petersham
pethidine
pétillant
petiolar
petiolate
petiole
petioles
petit
petite
petition
petitions
petrel
petrels
petrified
petrifies
petrify
petrol
petroleum
petrology
petrosal
petrosals
petrous
pets
petted
petter
petters
petticoat
pettier
pettiest
pettifog
pettifogs
pettily
pettiness

petting
pettish
pettishly
petty
petulance
petulant
petunia
petunias
petuntse
pew
pewee
pewees
pewit
pewits
pews
pewter
pewterer
pewterers
peyote
peyotes

P F

pfennig
pfennigs
pfft
pfui

P H

phacelia
phaeton
phaetons
phage
phages
phagocyte
phagosome
phalange
phalanger
phalanges
phalanx
phalanxes
phalarope
phalera
phalerae
phalli
phallic
phallism
phallus
phalluses

phantasm
phantasms
phantast
phantasts
phantasy
phantom
phantoms
pharaoh
pharaohs
pharaonic
pharmacy
pharos
pharoses
pharynges
pharynx
phase
phased
phaser
phasers
phases
phasic
phasing
phasmid
phasmids
phasor
phasors
phat
phatic
pheasant
pheasants
phenocopy
phenol
phenolic
phenology
phenom
phenomena
phenotype
phenyl
phenytoin
pheromone
phew
phi
phial
phials
philander
philately
philibeg
philibegs
philippic
philobat

philogyny	phonies	photons	physios	piccies
philology	phoniest	photopic	physique	piccolo
philter	phonily	photos	physiques	piccolos
philters	phoniness	photoset	phytolith	piccy
philtre	phoning	photosets		pice
philtres	phono	photostat	**P I**	pichi
phimosis	phonolite	phototube		pick
phimotic	phonology	phots	pi	pickaback
phis	phonon	phrasal	pia	pickable
phiz	phonons	phrasally	piacular	pickax
phizes	phons	phrase	piaffe	pickaxe
phizog	phony	phrased	piaffed	pickaxed
phizogs	phooey	phrases	piaffer	pickaxes
phlebitic	phorbol	phrasing	piaffes	pickaxing
phlebitis	phoresy	phratries	piaffing	picked
phlegm	phoretic	phratry	pial	picker
phlegmy	phormium	phreak	piani	pickerel
phloem	phormiums	phreaker	pianism	pickerels
phlox	phoronid	phreakers	pianist	pickers
phloxes	phoronids	phreaking	pianistic	picket
phobia	phosgene	phreaks	pianists	picketed
phobias	phosphate	phreatic	piano	picketer
phobic	phosphene	phrenic	pianola	picketers
phocine	phosphide	phthalate	pianolas	picketing
phoebe	phosphine	phthisic	pianos	pickets
phoebes	phosphite	phthisis	piapiac	pickier
phoenix	phosphor	phulkari	piapiacs	pickiest
phoenixes	phosphors	phulkaris	pias	pickiness
phon	phot	phut	piassava	picking
phonate	photic	phwoah	piassavas	pickings
phonated	photino	phwoor	piaster	pickle
phonates	photinos	phycology	piasters	pickled
phonating	photo	phyla	piastre	pickler
phonation	photocall	phyletic	piastres	picklers
phonatory	photocell	phyllite	piazza	pickles
phone	photocopy	phyllo	piazzas	pickling
phonecard	photoed	phyllode	pibroch	picklock
phoned	photoes	phyllodes	pibrochs	picklocks
phoneme	photofit	phyllopod	pic	pickney
phonemes	photofits	phylogeny	pica	pickneys
phonemic	photog	phylum	picador	pickoff
phonemics	photogram	physalis	picadors	pickoffs
phones	photograms	physic	picante	picks
phonetic	photoing	physical	picaro	pickup
phonetics	photolyse	physicals	picaroon	pickups
phoney	photomap	physician	picaroons	picky
phoneys	photomaps	physicist	picaros	picnic
phonic	photomask	physicked	picas	picnicked
phonics	photon	physics	picayune	picnicker
phonier	photonics	physio	picayunes	picnics

picong	pierced	pigmented	piles	pilotfish
picot	piercer	pigments	pileus	piloting
picotee	piercers	pigmies	pilewort	pilotless
picotees	pierces	pigmy	pileworts	pilots
picots	piercing	pignut	pilfer	pilous
picquet	pierid	pignuts	pilferage	pilular
picquets	pierids	pigpen	pilfered	pimento
picrate	pieris	pigpens	pilferer	pimentos
picrates	pierogi	pigs	pilferers	pimiento
picrite	piers	pigskin	pilfering	pimientos
picritic	pies	pigskins	pilfers	pimp
pics	pietà	pigsties	pilgrim	pimped
pictogram	pietas	pigsty	pilgrims	pimpernel
pictorial	pietàs	pigswill	piling	pimping
picture	pieties	pigtail	pill	pimple
pictured	pietism	pigtailed	pillage	pimpled
pictures	pietist	pigtails	pillaged	pimples
picturing	pietistic	pigweed	pillager	pimply
piculet	pietists	pika	pillagers	pimps
piculets	piety	pikas	pillages	pin
piddle	piezo	pike	pillaging	pinafore
piddled	piffle	piked	pillar	pinafores
piddler	piffling	pikelet	pillared	pinball
piddlers	pig	pikelets	pillaret	pinboard
piddles	pigeon	pikeman	pillarets	pinboards
piddling	pigeonite	pikemen	pillars	pincer
piddock	pigeons	pikeperch	pillbox	pincers
piddocks	pigface	piker	pillboxes	pincette
pidgin	pigfaces	pikers	pilled	pincettes
pidgins	pigfish	pikes	pilling	pinch
pie	pigfishes	pikestaff	pillion	pinchbeck
piebald	pigged	piki	pillions	pinched
piebalds	piggeries	piking	pillock	pinches
piece	piggery	pikkie	pillocks	pinching
pieced	piggies	pikkies	pilloried	pine
piecemeal	pigging	pilaf	pillories	pineal
piecer	piggish	pilaff	pillory	pineapple
piecers	piggishly	pilaffs	pillow	pined
pieces	piggy	pilafs	pillowed	pinene
piecework	piggyback	pilaster	pillowing	pineries
piecing	pightle	pilasters	pillows	pinery
piecrust	pightles	pilau	pillowy	pines
piecrusts	piglet	pilaus	pills	pinesap
pied	piglets	pilchard	pillwort	pinesaps
piedmont	piglike	pilchards	pillworts	pineta
piedmonts	pigling	pile	pilose	pinetum
pieman	piglings	pilea	pilosity	piney
piemen	pigman	pileas	pilot	pinfold
pier	pigmen	piled	pilotage	pinfolded
pierce	pigment	pilei	piloted	pinfolds

ping	pinnies	pipa	piquing	pissabeds
pinged	pinning	pipal	pir	pissant
pinger	pinniped	pipals	piracies	pissants
pingers	pinnipeds	pipas	piracy	pissed
pinging	pinnule	pipe	piranha	pisser
pingo	pinnules	pipeclay	piranhas	pisses
pingos	pinny	pipeclays	pirate	pisshead
pings	pinochle	piped	pirated	pissheads
pinguid	pinole	pipefish	pirates	pissing
pinguin	piñon	pipeful	piratic	pissoir
pinguins	piñons	pipefuls	piratical	pissoirs
pingwing	pinotage	pipeless	pirating	pisspot
pingwings	pinout	pipeline	piriform	pisspots
pinhead	pinouts	pipelined	piripiri	pissy
pinheaded	pinpoint	pipelines	piripiris	pistachio
pinheads	pinpoints	piper	pirk	pistacite
pinhole	pinprick	pipers	pirog	piste
pinholes	pinpricks	pipes	pirogen	pistes
pining	pins	pipette	pirogi	pisteur
pinion	pinspot	pipetted	pirogies	pisteurs
pinioned	pinspots	pipettes	pirogue	pistil
pinioning	pinstripe	pipetting	pirogues	pistils
pinions	pint	pipework	piroshki	pistol
pink	pinta	pipewort	pirouette	pistole
pinked	pintail	pipeworts	pirozhki	pistoled
pinker	pintails	pipi	pirs	pistoleer
pinkest	pintle	piping	pis	pistolero
pinkie	pintles	pipings	piscaries	pistoles
pinkies	pinto	pipis	piscary	pistoling
pinking	pintos	pipit	piscatory	pistolled
pinkish	pints	pipits	piscina	pistols
pinkly	pinwheel	pipkin	piscinae	piston
pinkness	pinwheels	pipkins	piscinas	pistons
pinko	pinworm	pipless	piscine	pistou
pinkoes	pinworms	pipped	piscivore	pit
pinkos	piny	pippin	pisco	pita
pinks	pinyon	pipping	pisé	pitahaya
pinky	pinyons	pippins	pish	pitapat
pinna	piolet	pips	pishogue	pitapats
pinnace	piolets	pipsqueak	pishogues	pitas
pinnaces	pion	pipy	pishrogue	pitch
pinnacle	pioneer	piquancy	pisiform	pitched
pinnacled	pioneered	piquant	pismire	pitcher
pinnacles	pioneers	piquantly	pismires	pitchers
pinnae	pionic	pique	pisolite	pitches
pinnate	pions	piqué	pisolith	pitchfork
pinnated	pious	piqued	pisoliths	pitchier
pinnately	piously	piques	pisolitic	pitchiest
pinnation	piousness	piquet	piss	pitching
pinned	pip	piquets	pissabed	pitchman

pitchmen
pitchout
pitchouts
pitchpole
pitchy
piteous
piteously
pitfall
pitfalls
pith
pithead
pitheads
pithed
pithier
pithiest
pithily
pithiness
pithing
pithivier
pithless
pithoi
pithos
piths
pithy
pitiable
pitiably
pitied
pities
pitiful
pitifully
pitiless
pitman
pitmans
pitmen
piton
pitons
pitot
pitots
pitpan
pitpans
pits
pitta
pittance
pittances
pittas
pitted
pitting
pituitary
pity
pitying

pityingly
pivot
pivotable
pivotal
pivoted
pivoting
pivotman
pivotmen
pivots
pix
pixel
pixelate
pixelated
pixelates
pixellate
pixels
pixie
pixieish
pixies
pixilate
pixilated
pixilates
pixy
pizazz
pizza
pizzas
pizzazz
pizzeria
pizzerias
pizzicati
pizzicato
pizzle
pizzles

P L

placable
placably
placard
placarded
placards
placate
placated
placates
placating
placation
placatory
place
placebo
placebos

placed
placeless
placeman
placemen
placement
placenta
placentae
placental
placentas
placer
placers
places
placet
placets
placid
placidity
placidly
placing
placings
placket
plackets
placoderm
placodont
placoid
plafond
plafonds
plagal
plage
plages
plague
plagued
plagues
plaguey
plaguing
plaguy
plaice
plaid
plaided
plaids
plain
plained
plainer
plainest
plaining
plainly
plainness
plains
plainsman
plainsmen
plainsong

plaint
plaintiff
plaintive
plaints
plait
plaited
plaiting
plaits
plan
planar
planarian
planation
planche
planches
planchet
planchets
plane
planed
planer
planers
planes
planesman
planesmen
planet
planetary
planetoid
planets
planform
planforms
plangency
plangent
planigale
planing
planish
planished
planisher
planishes
plank
planked
planking
planks
planktic
plankton
planned
planner
planners
planning
plans
plant
plantable

plantain
plantains
plantar
planted
planter
planters
planting
plantlet
plantlets
plants
plantsman
plantsmen
planula
planulae
plaque
plaques
plaquette
plash
plashed
plashes
plashing
plashy
plasm
plasma
plasmatic
plasmic
plasmid
plasmids
plasmin
plasmins
plasmodia
plasmon
plasmons
plasteel
plaster
plastered
plasterer
plasters
plastery
plastic
plasticky
plastics
plastid
plastids
plastique
plastisol
plastral
plastron
plastrons
plat

platan	playbills	pleasure	pleural	plocked
platanna	playboy	pleasured	pleurisy	plocking
plate	playboys	pleasures	pleuritic	plocks
plateau	playdown	pleat	pleuron	plod
plateaued	playdowns	pleated	plew	plodded
plateaus	played	pleating	plews	plodder
plateaux	player	pleats	plexiform	plodders
plated	players	pleb	plexiglas	plodding
plateful	playful	plebby	plexor	plods
platefuls	playfully	plebe	plexors	ploidy
plateless	playgroup	plebeian	plexus	plongeur
platelet	playhouse	plebeians	plexuses	plongeurs
platelets	playing	plebes	pliable	plonk
platen	playlet	plebs	pliably	plonked
platens	playlets	plectra	pliancies	plonker
plater	playlist	plectrum	pliancy	plonkers
platers	playlists	plectrums	pliant	plonking
plates	playmaker	pled	pliantly	plonks
platform	playmate	pledge	plica	plook
platforms	playmates	pledged	plicae	plooks
platies	playpen	pledgee	plicas	plop
plating	playpens	pledgees	plicate	plopped
platings	playroom	pledger	plicated	plopping
platinise	playrooms	pledgers	plication	plops
platinize	plays	pledges	plié	plosion
platinoid	playsuit	pledget	plied	plosions
platinum	playsuits	pledgets	pliéd	plosive
platitude	plaything	pledging	plieing	plosives
platonic	plaza	pledgor	pliers	plot
platoon	plazas	pledgors	plies	plotless
platooned	plea	pleiad	pliés	plots
platoons	pleach	plenaries	plight	plotted
plats	pleached	plenary	plighted	plotter
platted	pleaches	plenitude	plighting	plotters
platter	pleaching	plenteous	plights	plotting
platters	plead	plentiful	plimsole	plotty
platting	pleadable	plenty	plimsoles	plotz
platy	pleaded	plenum	plimsoll	plotzed
platypus	pleader	plenums	plimsolls	plotzes
platysma	pleaders	pleonasm	plink	plotzing
platysmas	pleading	pleonasms	plinked	plough
plaudits	pleadings	pleopod	plinking	ploughed
plausible	pleads	pleopods	plinks	plougher
plausibly	pleas	pleroma	plinky	ploughers
play	pleasance	plessor	plinth	ploughing
playa	pleasant	plessors	plinths	ploughman
playable	please	plethora	pliosaur	ploughmen
playas	pleased	plethoric	pliosaurs	ploughs
playback	pleases	pleura	plissé	plover
playbill	pleasing	pleurae	plock	plovers

plow
plowed
plowing
plowland
plowman
plowmen
plows
plowshare
ploy
ploys
pluck
plucked
plucker
pluckier
pluckiest
pluckily
plucking
plucks
plucky
plug
plugboard
plugged
plugger
pluggers
plugging
plughole
plugholes
plugs
plum
plumage
plumaged
plumages
plumb
plumbago
plumbagos
plumbate
plumbates
plumbed
plumbeous
plumber
plumbers
plumbic
plumbing
plumbism
plumbless
plumbous
plumbs
plume
plumed
plumeless

plumeria
plumeries
plumery
plumes
plumier
plumiest
pluming
plummet
plummeted
plummets
plummier
plummiest
plummy
plumose
plump
plumped
plumper
plumpest
plumping
plumpish
plumply
plumpness
plumps
plumpy
plums
plumule
plumules
plumy
plunder
plundered
plunderer
plunders
plunge
plunged
plunger
plungers
plunges
plunging
plunk
plunked
plunking
plunks
plural
pluralise
pluralism
pluralist
plurality
pluralize
plurally
plurals

plus
pluses
plush
plusher
plushest
plushier
plushiest
plushly
plushness
plushy
plutei
pluteus
plutocrat
pluton
plutonic
plutonism
plutonium
plutons
pluvial
ply
plying
plywood

P N

pneuma
pneumatic
pneumonia
pneumonic

P O

po
poach
poached
poacher
poachers
poaches
poaching
poblano
poblanos
pochard
pochards
pochette
pochettes
pocho
pochos
pock
pocked
pocket

pocketed
pocketful
pocketing
pockets
pockmark
pockmarks
pocks
pocky
poco
pod
podagra
podagral
podagric
podagrous
podded
podding
podge
podger
podgier
podgiest
podginess
podgy
podia
podiatry
podium
podiums
podocarp
pods
podsol
podsols
podzol
podzolic
podzolise
podzolize
podzols
poem
poems
poenskop
poesy
poet
poetaster
poetess
poetesses
poetic
poetical
poeticise
poeticism
poeticize
poetics
poetise

poetised
poetises
poetising
poetize
poetized
poetizes
poetizing
poetries
poetry
poets
pogey
pogeys
pogo
pogoed
pogoes
pogoing
pogos
pogrom
pogroms
poi
poignance
poignancy
poignant
poilu
poilus
poinciana
poind
poinded
poinding
poinds
point
pointe
pointed
pointedly
pointelle
pointer
pointers
pointier
pointiest
pointing
pointless
points
pointy
pois
poise
poised
poises
poisha
poising
poison

poisoned	poleward	polled	polygenic	polyuria
poisoner	polewards	pollee	polygeny	polyurias
poisoners	police	pollees	polyglot	polyuric
poisoning	policed	pollen	polyglots	polyvinyl
poisonous	policeman	pollex	polygon	polyzoan
poisons	policemen	pollices	polygonal	polyzoans
poke	polices	pollie	polygons	poma
poked	policier	pollies	polygonum	pomace
poker	policiers	pollinate	polygraph	pomaces
pokers	policies	polling	polygyne	pomade
pokerwork	policing	pollinia	polygyny	pomaded
pokes	policy	pollinium	polyhedra	pomades
pokeweed	poling	polliwog	polyimide	pomading
pokey	polio	polliwogs	polymath	pomander
pokier	polis	pollo	polymaths	pomanders
pokiest	polish	pollock	polymathy	pomatum
pokily	polished	pollocks	polymer	pomatums
pokiness	polisher	polls	polymeric	pombe
poking	polishers	pollster	polymers	pome
poky	polishes	pollsters	polymict	pomelo
pol	polishing	pollutant	polymorph	pomelos
polack	politburo	pollute	polymyxin	pomes
polacks	polite	polluted	polynya	pomfret
polar	politely	polluter	polynyas	pomfrets
polarise	politer	polluters	polyp	pommel
polarised	politesse	pollutes	polypary	pommeled
polarises	politest	polluting	polyphase	pommeling
polarity	politic	pollution	polyphony	pommelled
polarize	political	polly	polypi	pommels
polarized	politick	pollywog	polyploid	pomology
polarizer	politicly	pollywogs	polypod	pomp
polarizes	politico	polo	polypody	pompadour
polars	politicos	poloidal	polypoid	pompano
polder	politics	polonaise	polypore	pompanos
polders	polities	polonies	polypores	pompier
pole	polity	polonium	polyposis	pompiers
poleax	polje	polony	polypous	pompom
poleaxe	poljes	pols	polyps	pompoms
poleaxed	polka	poltroon	polyptych	pompon
poleaxes	polkaed	poltroons	polypus	pompons
poleaxing	polkaing	poly	polys	pomposity
polecat	polkas	polyadic	polysemic	pompous
polecats	poll	polyamide	polysemy	pompously
poled	pollack	polyandry	polysome	pomps
poleis	pollacks	polyene	polytene	ponce
polemic	pollan	polyenes	polythene	ponced
polemical	pollans	polyester	polytonal	ponces
polemics	pollard	polygamy	polytype	poncey
polenta	pollarded	polygene	polytypes	poncho
poles	pollards	polygenes	polytypic	ponchos

poncier	ponytail	poorly	poppet	porker
ponciest	ponytails	poorness	poppets	porkers
poncing	poo	poort	poppied	porkier
poncy	pooch	poorts	poppies	porkies
pond	pooched	poorwill	popping	porkiest
ponded	pooches	poorwills	popple	porking
ponder	pooching	poos	poppled	porkling
pondered	poodle	poot	popples	porklings
pondering	poodled	pooted	poppling	porky
ponderosa	poodles	pooter	popply	porn
ponderous	poodling	pooters	poppy	porno
ponders	pooed	pooting	poppycock	porosity
ponding	poof	pootle	pops	porous
pondok	poofier	pootled	popsie	porphyria
pondokkie	poofiest	pootles	popsies	porphyrin
pondoks	poofs	pootling	popsock	porphyry
ponds	poofter	poots	popsocks	porpoise
pondweed	poofters	pop	popster	porpoised
pone	poofy	popadom	popsy	porpoises
pong	pooh	popadoms	populace	porridge
ponga	poohed	popadum	popular	porridgy
pongal	poohing	popadums	popularly	porringer
ponged	poohs	popcorn	populate	port
pongee	pooing	pope	populated	portable
pongees	pooja	popedom	populates	portables
pongid	poojas	popery	populism	portably
pongids	pooka	popes	populist	portage
pongier	pookas	popgun	populists	portaged
pongiest	pool	popguns	populous	portages
ponging	pooled	popinjay	porangi	portaging
pongo	pooling	popinjays	porbeagle	portal
pongos	poolroom	popish	porcelain	portals
pongs	poolrooms	popishly	porch	ported
pongy	pools	poplar	porched	portend
poniard	poolside	poplars	porches	portended
poniards	poolsides	poplin	porchless	portends
ponies	poon	popliteal	porcine	portent
pons	pooned	popover	porcini	portents
pont	pooning	popovers	porcupine	porter
pontes	poons	poppa	pore	porterage
pontifex	poontang	poppadam	pored	porters
pontiff	poop	poppadams	pores	portfire
pontiffs	pooped	poppadom	porgies	portfires
pontil	pooping	poppadoms	porgy	portfolio
pontils	poops	poppadum	poriferan	porthole
pontine	poopy	poppadums	porin	portholes
pontoon	poor	poppas	poring	portico
pontoons	poorer	popped	porins	porticoes
ponts	poorest	popper	pork	porticos
pony	poorhouse	poppers	porked	portière

portières
porting
portion
portioned
portions
portlier
portliest
portly
portolan
portolano
portolans
portrait
portraits
portray
portrayal
portrayed
portrayer
portrays
ports
pos
posada
pose
posed
poser
posers
poses
poseur
poseurs
poseuse
posey
posh
poshed
posher
poshes
poshest
poshing
poshly
poshness
posho
posies
posing
posit
posited
positif
positing
position
positions
positive
positives
positron

positrons
posits
posology
posse
posses
possess
possessed
possesses
possessor
posset
possets
possetted
possible
possibles
possibly
possum
possums
post
postage
postages
postal
postally
postbag
postbags
postbox
postboxes
postcard
postcards
postcode
postcoded
postcodes
postdoc
postdocs
posted
poster
posterior
posterise
posterity
posterize
postern
posterns
posters
postface
postfaces
postfix
postfixed
postfixes
postgrad
postgrads
postie

posties
postil
postilion
postils
posting
postings
postlude
postludes
postman
postmark
postmarks
postmen
postpone
postponed
postponer
postpones
postpose
postposed
postposes
posts
postulant
postulate
postural
posture
postured
posturer
posturers
postures
posturing
postwoman
postwomen
posy
pot
potable
potage
potager
potagers
potash
potassic
potassium
potation
potations
potato
potboiler
potch
poteen
potence
potencies
potency
potent

potentate
potential
potentise
potentize
potently
potful
potfuls
pothead
potheads
potheen
pother
pothole
potholed
potholer
potholers
potholes
potholing
potion
potions
potjie
potjiekos
potjies
potlatch
potluck
potman
potmen
potoo
potoos
potoroo
potoroos
potrero
potreros
pots
potsherd
potsherds
potshot
potshots
pottage
potted
potter
pottered
potterer
potterers
potteries
pottering
potters
pottery
pottier
potties
pottiest

pottiness
potting
pottle
pottles
potto
pottos
potty
pouch
pouched
pouches
pouchier
pouchiest
pouching
pouchong
pouchy
pouf
pouffe
pouffes
poufs
poui
pouis
poult
poulterer
poultice
poulticed
poultices
poultry
poults
pounce
pounced
pouncer
pouncers
pounces
pouncing
pound
poundage
poundages
poundal
poundals
pounded
pounder
pounders
pounding
pounds
pour
pourable
pourboire
poured
pourer
pourers

pouring
pours
pousada
pousadas
poussin
poussins
pout
pouted
pouter
pouters
poutier
poutiest
pouting
poutingly
pouts
pouty
poverty
pow
powan
powans
powder
powdered
powdering
powders
powdery
power
powerboat
powered
powerful
powering
powerless
powers
powwow
powwowed
powwowing
powwows
pox
poxes
poxier
poxiest
poxvirus
poxy
pozzolana

PR

practical
practice
practiced
practices

practicum
practise
practised
practiser
practises
prad
prads
praecipe
praecipes
praenomen
praetor
praetors
pragmatic
prahu
prahus
prairie
prairies
praise
praised
praiseful
praiser
praises
praising
prajna
praline
pralines
pram
prams
prana
pranam
pranayama
prance
pranced
prancer
prancers
prances
prancing
prandial
prang
pranged
pranging
prangs
prank
prankish
pranks
prankster
prasad
prasads
prase
prat

prate
prated
prater
praters
prates
pratfall
pratfalls
pratie
praties
prating
pratique
prats
prattle
prattled
prattler
prattlers
prattles
prattling
prau
praus
prawn
prawner
prawners
prawning
prawns
praxis
pray
prayed
prayer
prayerful
prayers
praying
prays
preach
preached
preacher
preachers
preaches
preachify
preaching
preachy
preamble
preambles
preamp
preamps
prebend
prebendal
prebends
prebiotic
precast

precasts
precatory
precede
preceded
precedent
precedes
preceding
precent
precented
precentor
precents
precept
preceptor
precepts
precess
precessed
precesses
precinct
precincts
precious
precipice
precis
precise
precised
precisely
precises
precisian
precising
precision
preclude
precluded
precludes
precocial
precocity
precoital
preconise
preconize
precursor
predacity
predation
predator
predators
predatory
predella
predellas
predial
predials
predicant
predicate
predict

predicted
predictor
predicts
predigest
predikant
predoom
predoomed
preemie
preemies
preen
preened
preener
preeners
preening
preens
prefab
prefabs
preface
prefaced
prefaces
prefacing
prefatory
prefect
prefects
prefer
preferred
prefers
prefetch
prefigure
prefix
prefixed
prefixes
prefixing
preflight
prefocus
preform
preformed
preforms
preggers
pregnable
pregnancy
pregnant
preheat
preheated
preheats
prehuman
prejudge
prejudged
prejudges
prejudice

prelacies	prepare	presented	preterite	preyed
prelacy	prepared	presentee	preterits	preyer
prelate	preparer	presenter	preterm	preyers
prelates	preparers	presently	pretermit	preying
prelatic	prepares	presents	pretext	preys
prelature	preparing	preserve	pretexts	prez
prelim	prepay	preserved	pretor	prezzie
prelims	prepaying	preserver	pretorian	prezzies
preload	prepays	preserves	pretors	prial
preloaded	prepense	preset	pretreat	prials
preloads	prepone	presets	pretreats	priapic
prelude	preponed	preside	prettied	priapism
preluded	prepones	presided	prettier	priapulid
preludes	preponing	president	pretties	price
preludial	prepose	presides	prettiest	priced
preluding	preposed	presiding	prettify	priceless
premaster	preposes	presidio	prettily	prices
premature	preposing	presidios	pretty	pricey
premier	prepostor	presidium	prettying	pricier
premiere	prepotent	press	prettyish	priciest
premiered	prepped	pressed	pretzel	priciness
premieres	preppie	presses	pretzeled	pricing
premiers	preppies	pressie	pretzels	prick
premise	prepping	pressies	prevail	pricked
premised	preppy	pressing	prevailed	pricker
premises	prepreg	pressings	prevails	prickers
premising	prepregs	pressman	prevalent	pricket
premiss	preps	pressmark	prevent	prickets
premisses	prepuce	pressmen	prevented	pricking
premium	prepuces	pressor	preventer	prickle
premiums	preputial	pressure	prevents	prickled
premix	prequel	pressured	preverbal	prickles
premixed	prequels	pressures	preview	pricklier
premixes	presage	presswork	previewed	prickling
premixing	presaged	prestige	previews	prickly
premodify	presager	presto	previous	pricks
premolar	presagers	prestos	previse	pricy
premolars	presages	presume	prevised	pride
premorbid	presaging	presumed	previses	prided
premotor	presbyter	presumes	prevising	prideful
prenatal	prescient	presuming	prevision	prides
prentice	prescind	pretence	prewire	priding
prentices	prescinds	pretences	prewired	pried
prenup	prescribe	pretend	prewires	pries
prenups	prescript	pretended	prewiring	priest
preoccupy	preseason	pretender	prex	priested
preocular	presence	pretends	prexes	priestess
preordain	presences	pretense	prexies	priesting
prep	presenile	pretenses	prexy	priestly
prepaid	present	preterit	prey	priests

prig	primuses	prisoning	probation	prodigals
priggery	prince	prisons	probative	prodigies
priggish	princedom	prissier	probe	prodigy
prigs	princely	prissiest	probed	prodromal
prill	princes	prissily	prober	prodrome
prilled	princess	prissy	probers	prodromes
prills	principal	pristine	probes	prodromic
prim	principe	prithee	probing	prodrug
primacy	principi	privacies	probingly	prodrugs
primaeval	principle	privacy	probit	prods
primal	prink	private	probits	produce
primally	prinked	privateer	probity	produced
primaries	prinking	privately	problem	producer
primarily	prinks	privates	problems	producers
primary	print	privation	probosces	produces
primate	printable	privatise	proboscis	producing
primates	printed	privatism	probs	product
primatial	printer	privative	procaine	products
primavera	printers	privatize	procedure	proem
prime	printery	privet	proceed	proemial
primed	printhead	privets	proceeded	proems
primeness	printing	privies	proceeds	proenzyme
primer	printings	privilege	process	prof
primers	printout	privily	processed	profane
primes	printouts	privities	processes	profaned
primeur	prints	privity	processor	profanely
primeurs	prion	privy	proclaim	profaner
primeval	prions	prize	proclaims	profaners
priming	prior	prized	proclitic	profanes
primipara	priorate	prizeman	proconsul	profaning
primitive	priorates	prizemen	procreant	profanity
primly	prioress	prizes	procreate	proferens
primmed	priories	prizing	proctitis	proferred
primmer	priority	pro	proctor	profess
primmest	priors	proa	proctors	professed
primming	priorship	proaction	procuracy	professes
primness	priory	proactive	procure	professor
primo	prise	proas	procured	proffer
primordia	prised	prob	procurer	proffered
primos	prises	probable	procurers	proffers
primp	prising	probables	procures	profile
primped	prism	probably	procuress	profiled
primping	prismatic	proband	procuring	profiler
primps	prismoid	probands	procyonid	profilers
primrose	prismoids	probang	prod	profiles
primroses	prisms	probangs	prodded	profiling
prims	prison	probate	prodder	profit
primula	prisoned	probated	prodders	profited
primulas	prisoner	probates	prodding	profiteer
primus	prisoners	probating	prodigal	profiting

profits	prologues	pronation	propose	prosit
profound	prolong	pronator	proposed	prosocial
profs	prolonged	pronators	proposer	prosodic
profuse	prolonger	prone	proposers	prosodist
profusely	prolongs	proneness	proposes	prosody
profusion	prolusion	prong	proposing	prosoma
prog	prom	pronged	propound	prosomas
progenies	promenade	pronghorn	propounds	prospect
progeny	prominent	pronging	propped	prospects
progeria	promise	prongs	propping	prosper
progestin	promised	pronk	propriety	prospered
prognoses	promisee	pronked	props	prospers
prognosis	promisees	pronking	propshaft	prossed
prograde	promiser	pronks	proptosis	prossing
prograded	promisers	pronoun	propulsor	prostate
progrades	promises	pronounce	propyl	prostates
program	promising	pronouns	propyla	prostatic
programed	promisor	pronto	propylaea	prostrate
programme	promisors	pronuclei	propylene	prostyle
programs	prommer	proof	propylon	prostyles
progress	prommers	proofed	propylons	prosy
progs	promo	proofing	prorate	protamine
proguanil	promos	proofs	prorated	protandry
prohibit	promote	prop	prorates	protanope
prohibits	promoted	propagate	prorating	protases
project	promoter	propagule	proration	protasis
projected	promoters	propane	prorogue	protea
projector	promotes	propanol	prorogued	protean
projects	promoting	propanone	prorogues	proteas
prolactin	promotion	propel	pros	protease
prolapse	promotive	propelled	prosaic	proteases
prolapsed	promotor	propeller	prosaism	protect
prolapses	promotors	propels	prosaist	protected
prolapsus	prompt	propene	prosaists	protector
prolate	prompted	proper	proscenia	protects
prole	prompter	properdin	proscribe	protégé
proleg	prompters	properly	prose	protégée
prolegs	prompting	property	prosector	protégées
prolepses	promptly	prophage	prosecute	protégés
prolepsis	prompts	prophages	prosed	protein
proleptic	proms	prophase	proselyte	proteins
proles	promulge	prophecy	proser	protest
prolific	promulged	prophesy	prosers	protested
proline	promulges	prophet	proses	protester
prolix	pronaoi	prophetic	prosier	protestor
prolixity	pronaos	prophets	prosiest	protests
prolixly	pronate	propolis	prosily	proteus
prolog	pronated	proponent	prosimian	proteuses
prologs	pronates	proposal	prosiness	prothalli
prologue	pronating	proposals	prosing	protheses

prothesis
prothetic
prothorax
protist
protistan
protists
protium
protocol
protocols
protogyny
proton
protonate
protonic
protons
protopod
protopods
protostar
prototype
protozoa
protozoal
protozoan
protozoic
protozoon
protract
protracts
protrude
protruded
protrudes
proturan
proturans
proud
prouder
proudest
proudly
proudness
provable
provably
prove
proved
proven
provender
proverb
proverbs
proves
provide
provided
provident
provider
providers
provides

providing
province
provinces
proving
proviral
provirus
provision
proviso
provisor
provisors
provisory
provisos
provoke
provoked
provoker
provokers
provokes
provoking
provolone
provost
provosts
prow
prowess
prowfish
prowl
prowled
prowler
prowlers
prowling
prowls
prows
proxemics
proxies
proximal
proximate
proximity
proximo
proxy
prozone
prude
prudence
prudences
prudent
prudently
pruderies
prudery
prudes
prudish
prudishly
pruinose

prune
pruned
prunella
prunellas
pruner
pruners
prunes
pruning
prunus
prurience
pruriency
prurient
prurigo
pruritic
pruritus
prusik
prusiked
prusiking
prusiks
prussiate
pry
prying
pryingly
prytanies
prytany

P S

psalm
psalmic
psalmist
psalmists
psalmodic
psalmody
psalms
psalter
psalters
psaltery
pseud
pseudo
pseudonym
pseudopod
pseudos
pseuds
pshaw
pshawed
pshawing
pshaws
psi
psionic

psoas
psocid
psocids
psoralen
psoralens
psoriasis
psoriatic
psst
psych
psyche
psyched
psyches
psychic
psychical
psychics
psyching
psychism
psycho
psychos
psychoses
psychosis
psychotic
psyllid
psyllids
psyllium
psylliums

P T

ptarmigan
pteropod
pteropods
pterosaur
pterygote
ptomaine
ptomaines
ptosis
ptotic
ptyalin

P U

pub
pubbed
pubbing
pube
pubertal
puberty
pubes
pubescent

pubic
pubis
public
publican
publicans
publicise
publicist
publicity
publicize
publicly
publish
published
publisher
publishes
pubs
puccoon
puccoons
puce
puck
pucka
pucker
puckered
puckering
puckers
puckery
puckish
puckishly
pucks
pud
pudding
puddings
puddingy
puddle
puddled
puddler
puddlers
puddles
puddling
puddly
pudenda
pudendal
pudendum
pudeur
pudge
pudges
pudgier
pudgiest
pudgily
pudginess
pudgy

pudic	pujas	pulpiest	pumping	punishers
puds	puke	pulpiness	pumpkin	punishes
pudsticks	puked	pulping	pumpkins	punishing
pudu	pukeko	pulpit	pumps	punitive
pudus	pukekos	pulpits	pun	punjabi
pueblo	pukes	pulps	puna	punjabis
pueblos	pukey	pulpwood	punas	punk
puerile	puking	pulpy	punch	punkah
puerilely	pukka	pulque	punchbag	punkahs
puerility	pukkah	puls	punchbags	punker
puerperal	puku	pulsar	punchball	punkette
puff	pukus	pulsars	punchbowl	punkier
puffback	pul	pulsate	punchcard	punkiest
puffbacks	pula	pulsated	punched	punkish
puffball	pulao	pulsates	puncheon	punks
puffballs	pulaos	pulsatile	puncheons	punky
puffbird	pulas	pulsating	puncher	punned
puffbirds	pulaski	pulsation	punchers	punner
puffed	pulaskis	pulsator	punches	punners
puffer	pule	pulsators	punchier	punnet
puffers	puled	pulsatory	punchiest	punnets
puffery	pules	pulse	punchily	punning
puffier	puli	pulsed	punching	punningly
puffiest	pulik	pulseless	punchline	puns
puffily	puling	pulses	punchy	punster
puffin	pull	pulsing	puncta	punsters
puffiness	pullback	pultrude	punctae	punt
puffing	pullbacks	pultruded	punctate	punted
puffins	pulled	pultrudes	punctilio	punter
puffs	puller	pulverise	punctual	punters
puffy	pullers	pulverize	punctuate	punties
pug	pullet	pulvini	punctum	punting
puggaree	pullets	pulvinus	puncture	punts
puggarees	pulley	puma	punctured	punty
pugged	pulleyed	pumas	punctures	puny
pugging	pulleying	pumice	pundit	pup
puggish	pulleys	pumiced	punditry	pupa
puggy	pulling	pumiceous	pundits	pupae
pugilism	pullover	pumices	punga	pupal
pugilist	pullovers	pumicing	pungas	puparia
pugilists	pulls	pummel	pungency	puparium
pugnacity	pullulate	pummeled	pungent	pupate
pugs	pulmonary	pummeling	pungently	pupated
puha	pulmonate	pummelled	punier	pupates
puisne	pulmonic	pummelo	puniest	pupating
puissance	pulp	pummelos	punily	pupation
puissant	pulped	pummels	puniness	pupfish
puja	pulper	pump	punish	pupfishes
pujari	pulpers	pumped	punished	pupil
pujaris	pulpier	pumper	punisher	pupillage

pupillary
pupils
pupped
puppet
puppeteer
puppetry
puppets
puppies
pupping
puppy
puppyhood
puppyish
pups
purblind
purchase
purchased
purchaser
purchases
purdah
pure
purée
puréed
puréeing
purées
purely
pureness
purer
purest
purfle
purfled
purfles
purfling
purgation
purgative
purgatory
purge
purged
purger
purgers
purges
purging
puri
purified
purifier
purifiers
purifies
purify
purifying
purine
purines

puris
purism
purist
puristic
purists
puritan
puritans
purity
purl
purled
purler
purlers
purlieu
purlieus
purlieux
purlin
purling
purlins
purloin
purloined
purloiner
purloins
purls
puro
puromycin
puros
purple
purpled
purpler
purples
purplest
purpling
purplish
purply
purport
purported
purports
purpose
purposed
purposely
purposes
purposing
purposive
purpura
purpure
purpuric
purpurin
purr
purred
purring

purrs
purse
pursed
purser
pursers
purses
pursiness
pursing
purslane
purslanes
pursuable
pursuance
pursuant
pursue
pursued
pursuer
pursuers
pursues
pursuing
pursuit
pursuits
pursy
purulent
purvey
purveyed
purveying
purveyor
purveyors
purveys
purview
purviews
pus
push
pushbike
pushbikes
pushcart
pushcarts
pushchair
pushed
pusher
pushers
pushes
pushful
pushfully
pushier
pushiest
pushily
pushiness
pushing
pushover

pushovers
pushpin
pushpins
pushpit
pushpits
pushrod
pushrods
pushy
puss
pusses
pussies
pussy
pussyfoot
pustular
pustulate
pustule
pustules
put
puta
putamen
putamens
putamina
putaminal
putas
putative
putlock
putlocks
putlog
putlogs
putonghua
putrefied
putrefies
putrefy
putrid
putridity
putridly
puts
putsch
putsches
putt
putted
puttee
puttees
putter
puttered
puttering
putters
putti
puttied
putties

putting
putto
putts
putty
puttying
putz
putzed
putzes
putzing
puzzle
puzzled
puzzler
puzzlers
puzzles
puzzling

P Y

pya
pyaemia
pyaemic
pyas
pyelitis
pyelogram
pyemia
pygidia
pygidium
pygmean
pygmies
pygmy
pygostyle
pyinkado
pyinkados
pyjama
pyjamas
pyknic
pylon
pylons
pylori
pyloric
pylorus
pyoderma
pyogenic
pyorrhea
pyorrhoea
pyralid
pyralids
pyramid
pyramidal
pyramided

pyramids
pyre
pyrene
pyres
pyrethrin
pyrethrum
pyretic
pyrexia
pyrexial
pyrexic
pyridine
pyridoxal
pyriform
pyrite

pyrites
pyritic
pyritise
pyritised
pyritises
pyritize
pyritized
pyritizes
pyritous
pyro
pyroclast
pyrogen
pyrogenic
pyrogens

pyrolyse
pyrolysed
pyrolyses
pyrolysis
pyrolytic
pyrolyze
pyrolyzed
pyrolyzes
pyromania
pyromanic
pyrometer
pyrometry
pyrope
pyropes

pyros
pyrosis
pyroxene
pyroxenes
pyroxylin
pyrrhic
pyrrhics
pyrrole
pyrroles
pyruvate
pyruvates
python
pythoness
pythonic

pythons
pyuria
pyx
pyxes
pyxidia
pyxidium

pzazz

qanat
qanats
qawwali

quadplex
quadrant
quadrants
quadrat
quadrate
quadrated
quadrates
quadrati
quadratic
quadrats
quadratus
quadric
quadrille
quadroon
quadroons
quadruped
quadruple
quadruply
quads
quaestor
quaestors
quaff
quaffable
quaffed

quaffer
quaffers
quaffing
quaffs
quag
quagga
quaggas
quaggier
quaggiest
quaggy
quagmire
quagmires
quags
quahaug
quahaugs
quahog
quahogs
quaich
quaichs
quaigh
quaighs
quail
quailed
quailing

quails
quaint
quainter
quaintest
quaintly
quake
quaked
quakes
quakier
quakiest
quaking
quaky
quale
qualia
qualified
qualifier
qualifies
qualify
qualities
quality
qualm
qualmish
qualms
quamash

quamashes
quandary
quandong
quandongs
quango
quangos
quant
quanta
quantal
quantally
quantic
quantify
quantile
quantise
quantised
quantiser
quantises
quantity
quantize
quantized
quantizer
quantizes
quants
quantum

qi
qibla
qigong
qindarka
qintar
qintars

qua
quack
quacked
quackery
quacking
quackish
quacks
quad

quare	quatrains	quencher	quickies	quincunx
quark	quaver	quenchers	quicklime	quinella
quarks	quavered	quenches	quickly	quinellas
quarrel	quavering	quenching	quickness	quinidine
quarreled	quavers	quenelle	quicksand	quinine
quarrels	quavery	quenelles	quickset	quinoa
quarried	quay	quercetin	quickstep	quinoline
quarrien	quayage	querencia	quid	quinone
quarriens	quays	queried	quiddity	quinones
quarriens	quayside	queries	quidnunc	quins
quarries	quaysides	querist	quidnuncs	quinsy
quarrion	quean	querists	quids	quint
quarrions	queans	quern	quiescent	quinta
quarry	queasier	querns	quiet	quintain
quarrying	queasiest	querulous	quieted	quintains
quarryman	queasily	query	quieten	quintal
quarrymen	queasy	querying	quietened	quintals
quart	quebracho	quest	quietens	quintas
quartan	queen	quested	quieter	quinte
quarte	queendom	quester	quietest	quintet
quarter	queendoms	questers	quieting	quintets
quartered	queened	questing	quietism	quintile
quarterly	queenfish	question	quietist	quints
quartern	queenie	questions	quietists	quintuple
quarterns	queenies	questor	quietly	quintuply
quarters	queening	questors	quietness	quip
quartet	queenlier	quests	quiets	quipped
quartets	queenly	quetzal	quietude	quipping
quartette	queens	quetzals	quietus	quips
quartic	queenship	queue	quietuses	quipster
quartier	queenside	queued	quiff	quipsters
quartiers	queer	queueing	quiffs	quipu
quartile	queered	queues	quill	quipus
quartiles	queerer	queuing	quilled	quire
quarto	queerest	quibble	quilling	quires
quartos	queering	quibbled	quills	quirk
quarts	queerish	quibbler	quillwork	quirked
quartz	queerly	quibblers	quillwort	quirkier
quartzite	queerness	quibbles	quilt	quirkiest
quasar	queers	quibbling	quilted	quirkily
quasars	quelea	quiche	quilter	quirking
quash	queleas	quiches	quilters	quirkish
quashed	quell	quick	quilting	quirks
quashes	quelled	quickbeam	quilts	quirky
quashing	queller	quicken	quim	quirt
quassia	quellers	quickened	quims	quirted
quassias	quelling	quickens	quin	quirting
quatorze	quells	quicker	quinary	quirts
quatorzes	quench	quickest	quince	quisling
quatrain	quenched	quickie	quinces	quislings

quit
quitch
quitclaim
quite
quits
quittance
quitted
quitter
quitters
quitting
quiver
quivered
quiverful

quivering
quivers
quivery
quixotic
quixotism
quixotry
quiz
quizzed
quizzer
quizzers
quizzes
quizzical
quizzing

quod
quodlibet
quods
quoin
quoined
quoining
quoins
quoit
quoited
quoiting
quoits
quokka
quokkas

quoll
quolls
quondam
quorate
quorum
quorums
quota
quotable
quotas
quotation
quote
quoted
quotes

quoth
quotidian
quotient
quotients
quoting
qursh

qwerty

R

rabbet
rabbets
rabbi
rabbinate
rabbinic
rabbis
rabbit
rabbited
rabbiting
rabbits
rabbity
rabble
rabbles
rabi
rabid
rabidity
rabidly
rabidness
rabies
raccoon
raccoons
race
racecard

racecards
raced
racehorse
racemate
racemates
raceme
racemes
racemic
racemise
racemised
racemises
racemize
racemized
racemizes
racemose
racer
racers
races
racetrack
raceway
raceways
rachides
rachis
rachitic
rachitis

racial
racialise
racialism
racialist
racialize
racially
racier
raciest
racily
raciness
racing
racism
racist
racists
rack
racked
racket
racketed
racketeer
racketing
rackets
rackety
racking
racks
raclette

raclettes
racon
racons
raconteur
racoon
racoons
racquet
racquets
racy
rad
radar
radars
raddle
raddled
raddles
raddling
radial
radially
radials
radian
radiance
radiancy
radians
radiant
radiantly

radiate
radiated
radiates
radiating
radiation
radiative
radiator
radiators
radical
radically
radicals
radicchio
radices
radicle
radicles
radicular
radii
radio
radioed
radioes
radiogram
radioing
radiology
radionics
radios

radish	raggedy	railings	raising	ramify
radishes	raggier	raillery	raisins	ramifying
radium	raggiest	railless	raisiny	ramin
radius	ragging	railman	raita	ramins
radiused	raggy	railmen	raj	ramjet
radiuses	raghead	railroad	raja	ramjets
radiusing	ragheads	railroads	rajah	rammed
radix	ragi	rails	rajahs	rammer
radome	raging	railway	rajas	rammers
radomes	raglan	railways	rake	rammies
radon	raglans	raiment	raked	ramming
rads	ragman	raiments	raker	rammy
radula	ragmen	rain	rakers	ramp
radulae	ragout	rainbird	rakes	rampage
radular	ragouts	rainbirds	rakhi	rampaged
radwaste	ragpicker	rainbow	rakhis	rampager
raffia	rags	rainbows	raki	rampagers
raffinate	ragstone	raincoat	raking	rampages
raffinose	ragtag	raincoats	rakish	rampaging
raffish	ragtime	raindrop	rakishly	rampancy
raffishly	ragtop	raindrops	raku	rampant
raffle	ragtops	rained	rale	rampantly
raffled	raguly	rainfall	rales	rampart
raffles	ragweed	rainfast	rallied	ramparted
rafflesia	ragworm	rainflies	rallier	ramparts
raffling	ragworms	rainfly	ralliers	ramped
raft	ragwort	rainier	rallies	ramping
rafted	ragworts	rainiest	rally	rampion
rafter	rah	raininess	rallying	rampions
raftered	rai	raining	rallyist	ramps
rafters	raid	rainless	rallyists	ramrod
rafting	raided	rainmaker	ram	ramrodded
rafts	raider	rainout	ramada	ramrods
raftsman	raiders	rainouts	ramadas	rams
raftsmen	raiding	rainproof	ramble	ramsons
rag	raids	rains	rambled	ramus
raga	rail	rainstorm	rambler	ran
ragas	railage	rainswept	ramblers	ranch
ragbag	railbus	rainwash	rambles	ranched
ragbags	railbuses	rainwater	rambling	rancher
rage	railcar	rainworm	rambutan	rancheria
raged	railcard	rainworms	rambutans	ranchero
rager	railcards	rainy	ramekin	rancheros
ragers	railcars	raisable	ramekins	ranchers
rages	railed	raise	ramen	ranches
ragfish	railer	raised	rami	ranching
ragfishes	railers	raiser	ramie	rancid
ragga	railhead	raisers	ramies	rancidity
ragged	railheads	raises	ramified	rancor
raggedly	railing	raisin	ramifies	rancorous

rancour	ransom	raptly	rass	ratings
rancours	ransomed	raptness	rasses	ratio
rand	ransoming	raptor	rassle	ration
randier	ransoms	raptorial	rassled	rational
randiest	rant	raptors	rassler	rationale
randily	ranted	rapture	rassles	rationed
randiness	ranter	raptured	rassling	rationing
random	ranters	raptures	raster	rations
randomise	ranting	rapturing	rasterise	ratios
randomize	rantingly	rapturous	rasterize	ratite
randomly	rants	rare	rasters	ratites
rands	ranunculi	rarebit	rat	ratlines
randy	rap	rarefied	rata	ratoon
ranee	rapacious	rarely	ratable	ratooned
ranees	rapacity	rareness	ratafia	ratooning
rang	rape	rarer	ratafias	ratoons
rangatira	raped	rarest	ratamacue	rats
range	raper	raring	rataplan	ratsbane
rangé	rapers	rarities	rataplans	rattan
ranged	rapes	rarity	ratas	rattans
rangeland	rapeseed	rasa	ratatat	ratted
ranger	raphae	rasam	ratbag	ratter
rangers	raphe	rascal	ratbags	ratters
ranges	raphide	rascality	ratchet	rattier
rangier	raphides	rascally	ratcheted	rattiest
rangiest	rapid	rascals	ratchets	rattily
ranging	rapidity	rascasse	rate	rattiness
rangoli	rapidly	rascasses	rateable	ratting
rangy	rapidness	rase	rateably	rattle
rani	rapids	rased	rated	rattled
ranis	rapier	rases	ratel	rattler
rank	rapiers	rasgulla	ratels	rattlers
ranked	rapine	rasgullas	ratepayer	rattles
ranker	raping	rash	rates	rattlier
rankers	rapist	rasher	ratfish	rattliest
rankest	rapists	rashers	ratfishes	rattling
ranking	rapparee	rashes	rath	rattly
rankings	rapparees	rashest	rathe	ratty
rankle	rapped	rashly	rather	raucous
rankled	rappee	rashness	rathole	raucously
rankles	rappel	rasing	ratholed	rauli
rankling	rappelled	rasp	ratholes	raulis
rankly	rappen	raspberry	ratholing	raunch
rankness	rapper	rasped	ratified	raunchier
ranks	rappers	rasper	ratifier	raunchily
rankshift	rapping	raspers	ratifiers	raunchy
ransack	rapport	rasping	ratifies	rauvolfia
ransacked	rapports	raspingly	ratify	rauwolfia
ransacker	raps	rasps	ratifying	rav
ransacks	rapt	raspy	rating	ravage

ravaged	rayless	readdress	realizing	reasoned
ravager	rayon	reader	really	reasoner
ravagers	rayonnant	readerly	realm	reasoners
ravages	rays	readers	realms	reasoning
ravaging	raze	readied	realness	reasons
rave	razed	readier	realo	reassert
raved	razes	readies	realos	reasserts
ravel	razing	readiest	reals	reassess
raveled	razoo	readily	realtor	reassign
ravelin	razor	readiness	realtors	reassigns
raveling	razorback	reading	realty	reassume
ravelins	razorbill	readings	ream	reassumed
ravelled	razored	readjust	reamed	reassumes
ravelling	razorfish	readjusts	reamer	reassure
ravels	razoring	readmit	reamers	reassured
raven	razors	readmits	reaming	reassures
ravened	razz	readopt	reams	reattach
ravening	razzed	readopted	reanimate	reattain
ravenous	razzes	readopts	reap	reattains
ravens	razzia	reads	reaped	reattempt
raver	razzias	ready	reaper	reave
ravers	razzing	readying	reapers	reaver
raves	razzle	reaffirm	reaping	reavers
ravigote		reaffirms	reappear	reaves
ravigotte	R E	reagent	reappears	reaving
ravin		reagents	reapplied	reawaken
ravine	re	reagin	reapplies	reawakens
ravined	reabsorb	reaginic	reapply	rebab
ravines	reabsorbs	real	reappoint	rebabs
raving	reach	realgar	reaps	rebadge
ravings	reachable	realgars	rear	rebadged
ravioli	reached	realia	reared	rebadges
ravish	reacher	realign	rearer	rebadging
ravished	reaches	realigned	rearers	rebar
ravisher	reaching	realigns	rearguard	rebase
ravishers	react	realise	rearing	rebased
ravishes	reactance	realised	rearm	rebases
ravishing	reactant	realises	rearmed	rebasing
ravs	reactants	realising	rearming	rebatable
raw	reacted	realism	rearmost	rebate
rawer	reacting	realist	rearms	rebated
rawest	reaction	realistic	rearrange	rebates
rawhide	reactions	realists	rearrest	rebating
rawhides	reactive	realities	rearrests	rebbe
rawish	reactor	reality	rears	rebbes
rawly	reactors	realize	rearward	rebbetzin
rawness	reacts	realized	rearwards	rebbitzin
ray	read	realizer	reascend	rebec
rayed	readable	realizers	reascends	rebeck
raying	readably	realizes	reason	rebecks

rebecs	reburials	receives	reclaims	recorders
rebel	reburied	receiving	recline	recording
rebelled	reburies	recency	reclined	recordist
rebelling	rebury	recension	recliner	records
rebellion	reburying	recent	recliners	recount
rebels	rebus	recently	reclines	recounted
rebid	rebuses	reception	reclining	recounts
rebidding	rebut	receptive	reclothe	recoup
rebids	rebuts	receptor	reclothed	recouped
rebind	rebuttal	receptors	reclothes	recouping
rebinding	rebuttals	recess	recluse	recoups
rebinds	rebutted	recessed	recluses	recourse
rebirth	rebutter	recesses	reclusion	recover
rebirther	rebutters	recessing	reclusive	recovered
rebirths	rebutting	recession	recode	recoverer
reblochon	rec	recessive	recoded	recovers
reboot	recall	recharge	recodes	recovery
rebooted	recalled	recharged	recoding	recreancy
rebooting	recalling	recharger	recognise	recreant
reboots	recalls	recharges	recognize	recreants
rebore	recant	réchauffé	recoil	recreate
rebored	recanted	recheck	recoiled	recreated
rebores	recanter	rechecked	recoiling	recreates
reboring	recanters	rechecks	recoils	recross
reborn	recanting	recherché	recollect	recrossed
rebound	recants	recipe	recolor	recrosses
rebounded	recap	recipes	recolored	recruit
rebounder	recapped	recipient	recolors	recruited
rebounds	recapping	recital	recolour	recruiter
rebozo	recaps	recitals	recolours	recruits
rebozos	recaption	recite	recombine	recs
rebrand	recapture	recited	recommend	recta
rebranded	recast	reciter	recommit	rectal
rebrands	recasting	reciters	recommits	rectally
rebreathe	recasts	recites	recompose	rectangle
rebuff	recce	reciting	recon	recti
rebuffed	recced	reck	reconcile	rectified
rebuffing	recceing	recked	recondite	rectifier
rebuffs	recces	recking	reconfirm	rectifies
rebuild	recede	reckless	reconnect	rectify
rebuilder	receded	reckon	reconned	rectitude
rebuilds	recedes	reckoned	reconning	recto
rebuilt	receding	reckoner	reconquer	rectocele
rebuke	receipt	reckoners	recons	rector
rebuked	receipted	reckoning	reconsign	rectorate
rebuker	receipts	reckons	reconvene	rectorial
rebukers	receive	recks	reconvert	rectories
rebukes	received	reclaim	record	rectors
rebuking	receiver	reclaimed	recorded	rectory
reburial	receivers	reclaimer	recorder	rectos

rectrices	redcap	redivivus	reduced	reeler
rectrix	redcaps	redline	reducer	reelers
rectum	redcoat	redlined	reducers	reeling
rectums	redcoats	redlines	reduces	reels
rectus	redd	redlining	reducible	reeve
recumbent	redden	redly	reducing	reeved
recur	reddened	redneck	reductant	reeves
recurred	reddening	rednecked	reductase	reeving
recurrent	reddens	rednecks	reduction	ref
recurring	redder	redness	reductive	reface
recurs	reddest	redo	redundant	refaced
recursion	redding	redoes	redux	refaces
recursive	reddish	redoing	redwater	refacing
recurve	reddle	redolence	redwing	refashion
recurved	redds	redolent	redwings	refection
recurves	reddy	redone	redwood	refectory
recurving	rede	redouble	redwoods	refer
recusal	reded	redoubled	redworm	referable
recusals	redeem	redoubles	redworms	referee
recusance	redeemed	redoubt	reebok	refereed
recusancy	redeemer	redoubts	reeboks	referees
recusant	redeemers	redound	reed	reference
recusants	redeeming	redounded	reedbuck	referenda
recuse	redeems	redounds	reedbucks	referent
recused	redefine	redox	reeded	referents
recuses	redefined	redpoll	reedier	referral
recusing	redefines	redpolls	reediest	referrals
recycle	redeploy	redraft	reediness	referred
recycled	redeploys	redrafted	reeding	referrer
recycler	redes	redrafts	reedings	referrers
recyclers	redesign	redraw	reedling	referring
recycles	redesigns	redrawing	reedlings	refers
recycling	redevelop	redrawn	reeds	reffo
red	redfish	redraws	reedy	reffos
redact	redfishes	redress	reef	refill
redacted	redhead	redressal	reefed	refilled
redacting	redheads	redressed	reefer	refilling
redaction	redial	redresser	reefers	refills
redactor	redialed	redresses	reefing	refinance
redactors	redialing	redrew	reefpoint	refine
redacts	redialled	reds	reefs	refined
redan	redials	redshank	reek	refiner
redans	redid	redshanks	reeked	refiners
redback	reding	redshirt	reekier	refinery
redbacks	redingote	redshirts	reekiest	refines
redbone	redirect	redskin	reeking	refining
redbones	redirects	redskins	reeks	refinish
redbreast	redivide	redstart	reeky	refit
redbud	redivided	redstarts	reel	refits
redbuds	redivides	reduce	reeled	refitted

refitting	refract	refuters	regional	regulator
reflag	refracted	refutes	regionals	reguli
reflagged	refractor	refuting	regions	reguline
reflags	refracts	reg	regisseur	regulo
reflate	refrain	regain	register	regulos
reflated	refrained	regained	registers	regulus
reflates	refrains	regaining	registrar	reguluses
reflating	refreeze	regains	registry	rehab
reflation	refreezes	regal	reglaze	rehabbed
reflect	refresh	regale	reglazed	rehabbing
reflected	refreshed	regaled	reglazes	rehabs
reflector	refresher	regales	reglazing	rehang
reflects	refreshes	regalia	reglet	rehanging
reflet	refroze	regalian	reglets	rehangs
reflex	refrozen	regaling	regnal	rehash
reflexes	refs	regalism	regnant	rehashed
reflexion	reft	regalist	rego	rehashes
reflexive	refuel	regalists	regolith	rehashing
reflexly	refueled	regality	regorge	rehear
refloat	refueling	regally	regorged	reheard
refloated	refuelled	regard	regorges	rehearing
refloats	refuels	regardant	regorging	rehears
reflow	refuge	regarded	regrade	rehearsal
reflowed	refugee	regardful	regraded	rehearse
reflowing	refugees	regarding	regrades	rehearsed
refluence	refuges	regards	regrading	rehearser
refluent	refugia	regather	regress	rehearses
reflux	refugium	regathers	regressed	reheat
refluxed	refulgent	regatta	regresses	reheated
refluxes	refund	regattas	regret	reheater
refluxing	refunded	regelate	regretful	reheaters
refocus	refunding	regelated	regrets	reheating
refocused	refunds	regelates	regretted	reheats
refocuses	refurbish	regencies	regrew	reheel
reforest	refurnish	regency	regroup	reheeled
reforests	refusal	regent	regrouped	reheeling
reforge	refusals	regents	regroups	reheels
reforged	refuse	reggae	regrow	rehoboam
reforges	refused	reggo	regrowing	rehoboams
reforging	refusenik	reggos	regrown	rehome
reform	refuser	regicidal	regrows	rehomed
reformat	refusers	regicide	regrowth	rehomes
reformats	refuses	regicides	regrowths	rehoming
reformed	refusing	regime	regulable	rehouse
reformer	refutable	regimen	regular	rehoused
reformers	refutal	regimens	regularly	rehouses
reforming	refutals	regiment	regulars	rehousing
reformism	refute	regiments	regulate	rehung
reformist	refuted	regimes	regulated	rehydrate
reforms	refuter	region	regulates	reified

reifies
reify
reifying
reign
reigned
reigning
reignite
reignited
reignites
reigns
reiki
reimburse
reimport
reimports
reimpose
reimposed
reimposes
rein
reindeer
reindeers
reined
reinfect
reinfects
reinforce
reining
reins
reinsert
reinserts
reinstate
reinsure
reinsured
reinsurer
reinsures
reinter
reinters
reinvent
reinvents
reinvest
reinvests
reissue
reissued
reissues
reissuing
reiterate
reive
reived
reiver
reivers
reives
reiving

reject
rejected
rejecting
rejection
rejective
rejector
rejectors
rejects
rejig
rejigged
rejigger
rejiggers
rejigging
rejigs
rejoice
rejoiced
rejoicer
rejoicers
rejoices
rejoicing
rejoin
rejoinder
rejoined
rejoining
rejoins
rekey
rekeyed
rekeying
rekeys
rekindle
rekindled
rekindles
relabel
relabeled
relabels
relaid
relapse
relapsed
relapser
relapsers
relapses
relapsing
relatable
relate
related
relater
relaters
relates
relating
relation

relations
relatival
relative
relatives
relator
relators
relaunch
relax
relaxant
relaxants
relaxed
relaxedly
relaxer
relaxers
relaxes
relaxin
relaxing
relay
relayed
relaying
relays
relearn
relearned
relearns
relearnt
release
released
releasee
releasees
releaser
releasers
releases
releasing
releasor
releasors
relegate
relegated
relegates
relent
relented
relenting
relents
relet
relets
reletting
relevance
relevancy
relevant
relevé
relevés

reliable
reliables
reliably
reliance
reliant
relic
relics
relict
relicts
relied
relief
reliefs
relies
relieve
relieved
reliever
relievers
relieves
relieving
relievo
relievos
relight
relighted
relights
religion
religions
religiose
religious
reline
relined
relines
relining
reliquary
reliquiae
relish
relished
relishes
relishing
relit
relive
relived
relives
reliving
relleno
rellenos
rellie
rellies
relo
reload
reloaded

reloading
reloads
relocate
relocated
relocates
relos
reluctant
relume
relumed
relumes
reluming
rely
relying
rem
remade
remain
remainder
remained
remaining
remains
remake
remakes
remaking
reman
remand
remanded
remanding
remands
remanence
remanent
remanned
remanning
remans
remap
remapped
remapping
remaps
remark
remarked
remarking
remarks
remarried
remarries
remarry
remaster
remasters
rematch
rematches
remeasure
remedial

remediate	remontant	renegado	renvers	repat
remedied	remora	renege	renverse	repats
remedies	remoras	reneged	renverses	repay
remedy	remorse	reneger	renvoi	repayable
remedying	remote	renegers	reoccupy	repaying
remember	remotely	reneges	reoccur	repayment
remembers	remoter	reneging	reoccurs	repays
remex	remotes	renegue	reoffend	repeal
remiges	remotest	renegued	reoffends	repealed
remind	remoulade	renegues	reopen	repealing
reminded	remould	reneguing	reopened	repeals
reminder	remoulded	renew	reopening	repeat
reminders	remoulds	renewable	reopens	repeated
remindful	remount	renewal	reorder	repeater
reminding	remounted	renewals	reordered	repeaters
reminds	remounts	renewed	reorders	repeating
reminisce	removable	renewer	reorg	repeats
remise	removal	renewers	reorgs	repêchage
remised	removals	renewing	reorient	repel
remises	remove	renews	reorients	repellant
remising	removed	renga	reovirus	repelled
remiss	remover	rengas	rep	repellent
remission	removers	reniform	repack	repeller
remissly	removes	renin	repackage	repellers
remit	removing	renminbi	repacked	repelling
remits	remuage	rennet	repacking	repels
remittal	remuda	rennin	repacks	repent
remittals	remudas	renounce	repaid	repentant
remitted	renal	renounced	repaint	repented
remittent	rename	renouncer	repainted	repenter
remitter	renamed	renounces	repaints	repenters
remitters	renames	renovate	repair	repenting
remitting	renaming	renovated	repaired	repents
remix	renascent	renovates	repairer	repeople
remixed	rencontre	renovator	repairers	repeopled
remixer	rend	renown	repairing	repeoples
remixers	render	renowned	repairman	repertory
remixes	rendered	rent	repairmen	repetend
remixing	renderer	rentable	repairs	repetends
remnant	renderers	rental	repaper	rephrase
remnants	rendering	rentals	repapered	rephrased
remodel	renders	rented	repapers	rephrases
remodeled	rending	renter	reparable	repine
remodeler	rendition	renters	repartee	repined
remodels	rends	rentier	repass	repines
remodify	rendzina	rentiers	repassed	repining
remold	rendzinas	renting	repasses	repique
remolded	renegade	rents	repassing	repiqued
remolding	renegaded	renumber	repast	repiques
remolds	renegades	renumbers	repasts	repiquing

replace	reposal	reprovers	reredos	resemble
replaced	repose	reproves	rerun	resembled
replacer	reposed	reproving	rerunning	resembler
replacers	reposeful	reps	reruns	resembles
replaces	reposes	reptile	res	resent
replacing	reposing	reptiles	resalable	resented
replan	repossess	reptilian	resale	resentful
replanned	repot	republic	resales	resenting
replans	repots	republics	resat	resents
replant	repotted	republish	rescind	reserpine
replanted	repotting	repudiate	rescinded	reserve
replants	repoussé	repugnant	rescinds	reserved
replay	repp	repulse	rescript	reserver
replayed	repped	repulsed	rescripts	reservers
replaying	repping	repulses	rescuable	reserves
replays	repps	repulsing	rescue	reserving
replenish	reprehend	repulsion	rescued	reservist
replete	represent	repulsive	rescuer	reservoir
repletion	repress	reputable	rescuers	reset
replevied	repressed	reputably	rescues	resets
replevies	represser	repute	rescuing	resetting
replevin	represses	reputed	reseal	resettle
replevy	repressor	reputedly	resealed	resettled
replica	reprieve	reputes	resealing	resettles
replicas	reprieved	reputing	reseals	reshape
replicase	reprieves	request	research	reshaped
replicate	reprimand	requested	reseat	reshapes
replicon	reprint	requester	reseated	reshaping
replicons	reprinted	requests	reseating	reshuffle
replied	reprinter	requiem	reseats	reside
replier	reprints	requiems	réseau	resided
repliers	reprisal	requinto	réseaux	residence
replies	reprisals	requintos	resect	residency
reply	reprise	require	resected	resident
replying	reprised	required	resecting	residents
repmobile	reprises	requirer	resection	resides
repo	reprising	requirers	resects	residing
repoing	repro	requires	reseda	residua
repoint	reproach	requiring	resedas	residual
repointed	reprobate	requisite	reseed	residuals
repoints	reprocess	requital	reseeded	residuary
repolish	reproduce	requitals	reseeding	residue
report	reprogram	requite	reseeds	residues
reportage	reproof	requited	reselect	residuum
reported	reproofed	requites	reselects	resign
reporter	reproofs	requiting	resell	resignal
reporters	repros	reran	reseller	resignals
reporting	reprove	reread	resellers	resigned
reports	reproved	rereading	reselling	resigner
repos	reprover	rereads	resells	resigners

resigning	resolver	responsum	resubmit	retch
resigns	resolvers	respray	resubmits	retched
resile	resolves	resprayed	result	retches
resiled	resolving	resprays	resultant	retching
resiles	resonance	rest	resulted	rete
resilient	resonant	restage	resulting	retell
resilin	resonate	restaged	results	retelling
resiling	resonated	restages	resumable	retells
resin	resonates	restaging	resume	retention
resinate	resonator	restart	resumé	retentive
resinated	resorb	restarted	resumed	retexture
resinates	resorbed	restarts	resumes	rethink
resined	resorbing	restate	resumés	rethinks
resining	resorbs	restated	resuming	rethought
resinous	resort	restates	resupply	retia
resins	resorted	restating	resurface	retiarii
resist	resorter	rested	resurgent	retiarius
resistant	resorters	restful	resurrect	reticence
résistant	resorting	restfully	resurvey	reticent
resisted	resorts	resting	resurveys	reticle
resister	resound	restive	ret	reticles
resisters	resounded	restively	retable	reticula
resisting	resounds	restless	retables	reticular
resistive	resource	restock	retablo	reticule
resistor	resourced	restocked	retablos	reticules
resistors	resources	restocks	retail	reticulin
resists	respect	restore	retailed	reticulum
resit	respected	restored	retailer	retie
resite	respecter	restorer	retailers	retied
resited	respects	restorers	retailing	reties
resites	respell	restores	retails	retiform
resiting	respelled	restoring	retain	retina
resits	respells	restrain	retained	retinae
resitting	respelt	restrains	retainer	retinal
resize	respirate	restraint	retainers	retinas
resized	respire	restrict	retaining	retinitis
resizes	respired	restricts	retains	retinoid
resizing	respires	restring	retake	retinoids
reskill	respiring	restrings	retaken	retinol
reskilled	respite	restroom	retakes	retinue
reskills	respited	restrooms	retaking	retinues
reskin	respites	restrung	retaliate	retiral
reskinned	respiting	rests	retard	retirals
reskins	respond	restudied	retardant	retire
resold	responded	restudies	retardate	retiré
resoluble	responder	restudy	retarded	retired
resolute	responds	restyle	retarder	retirer
resolve	responsa	restyled	retarders	retirers
resolved	response	restyles	retarding	retires
resolvent	responses	restyling	retards	retirés

retiring	retrofit	rev	revering	revisited
retitle	retrofits	revalue	revers	revisits
retitled	retroflex	revalued	reversal	revisory
retitles	retroject	revalues	reversals	revivable
retitling	retrorse	revaluing	reverse	revival
retold	retros	revamp	reversed	revivals
retook	retroussé	revamped	reversely	revive
retool	retry	revamping	reverser	revived
retooled	retrying	revamps	reversers	reviver
retooling	rets	revanche	reverses	revivers
retools	retsina	revarnish	reversing	revives
retort	retted	reveal	reversion	revivify
retorted	retting	revealed	revert	reviving
retorting	retune	revealer	revertant	revocable
retorts	retuned	revealers	reverted	revoke
retouch	retunes	revealing	reverter	revoked
retouched	retuning	reveals	reverters	revoker
retoucher	returf	reveille	reverting	revokers
retouches	returfed	réveillon	reverts	revokes
retrace	returfing	revel	revet	revoking
retraced	returfs	reveled	revetment	revolt
retraces	return	reveling	revets	revolted
retracing	returned	revelled	revetted	revolting
retract	returnee	reveller	revetting	revolts
retracted	returnees	revellers	review	revolute
retractor	returner	revelling	reviewal	revolve
retracts	returners	revelries	reviewals	revolved
retrain	returning	revelry	reviewed	revolver
retrained	returns	revels	reviewer	revolvers
retrains	retying	revenant	reviewers	revolves
retread	retype	revenants	reviewing	revolving
retreaded	retyped	revenge	reviews	revs
retreads	retypes	revenged	revile	revue
retreat	retyping	revenger	reviled	revues
retreated	reunified	revengers	reviler	revulsion
retreats	reunifies	revenges	revilers	revved
retrench	reunify	revenging	reviles	revving
retrial	reunion	revenue	reviling	reward
retrials	reunions	revenues	revisable	rewarded
retried	reunite	reverb	revisal	rewarding
retries	reunited	reverbs	revisals	rewards
retrieval	reunites	revere	revise	rewarewa
retrieve	reuniting	revered	revised	rewarewas
retrieved	reusable	reverence	reviser	rewash
retriever	reuse	reverend	revisers	rewashed
retrieves	reused	reverends	revises	rewashes
retro	reuses	reverent	revising	rewashing
retrocede	reusing	reveres	revision	reweigh
retrod	reutilise	reverie	revisions	reweighed
retrodden	reutilize	reveries	revisit	reweighs

rewind
rewinder
rewinders
rewinding
rewinds
rewirable
rewire
rewired
rewires
rewiring
reword
reworded
rewording
rewords
rework
reworked
reworking
reworks
rewound
rewrap
rewrapped
rewraps
rewrite
rewrites
rewriting
rewritten
rewrote

R H

rhabdom
rhabdome
rhabdomes
rhabdoms
rhamnose
rhapsode
rhapsodes
rhapsodic
rhapsody
rhatanies
rhatany
rhea
rheas
rhebok
rheboks
rhebuck
rhebucks
rheme
rhemes
rhenium

rheology
rheostat
rheostats
rhetor
rhetoric
rhetors
rheum
rheumatic
rheumy
rhinal
rhinitis
rhino
rhinos
rhizobium
rhizoid
rhizoidal
rhizoids
rhizome
rhizomes
rhizopod
rhizopods
rho
rhodamine
rhodium
rhodonite
rhodopsin
rhodora
rhodoras
rhomb
rhombi
rhombic
rhomboid
rhomboids
rhombs
rhombus
rhombuses
rhos
rhotic
rhoticity
rhubarb
rhumb
rhumba
rhumbas
rhumbs
rhyme
rhymed
rhymer
rhymers
rhymes
rhymester

rhyming
rhymist
rhymists
rhyolite
rhyta
rhythm
rhythmic
rhythms
rhyton
rhytons

R I

ria
rial
rials
rias
rib
ribald
ribalder
ribaldest
ribaldry
riband
ribands
ribbed
ribber
ribbers
ribbie
ribbies
ribbing
ribbon
ribboned
ribboning
ribbons
ribby
ribcage
ribcages
ribitol
ribless
ribose
ribosomal
ribosome
ribosomes
ribozyme
ribozymes
ribs
ribulose
ribwort
ribworts
rice

riced
ricepaper
ricer
ricercar
ricercare
ricercari
ricercars
ricers
rices
rich
richen
richened
richening
richens
richer
riches
richest
richly
richness
ricin
ricing
rick
ricked
rickets
rickety
rickey
rickeys
ricking
rickle
rickles
rickrack
ricks
rickshaw
rickshaws
ricochet
ricochets
ricotta
rictal
rictus
rid
ridable
riddance
ridded
ridden
ridding
riddle
riddled
riddler
riddlers
riddles

riddling
ride
rideable
rider
riderless
riders
ridership
rides
ridge
ridgeback
ridged
ridges
ridgeway
ridgeways
ridgier
ridgiest
ridging
ridgy
ridicule
ridiculed
ridicules
riding
ridings
ridley
ridleys
rids
riel
riels
riem
riempie
riempies
riems
rietbok
rietboks
rifampin
rife
rifeness
riff
riffed
riffing
riffle
riffled
riffler
riffles
riffling
riffs
rifle
rifled
rifleman
riflemen

rifles	rigors	ringer	ripeness	risky
rifling	rigour	ringers	ripening	risotto
rift	rigours	ringette	ripens	risottos
rifted	rigs	ringgit	riper	risqué
rifting	rikishi	ringgits	ripest	rissole
rifts	rile	ringhals	ripieni	rissoles
rig	riled	ringing	ripieno	rite
rigadoon	riles	ringingly	ripienos	ritenuti
rigadoons	rilievo	ringless	riposte	ritenuto
rigatoni	rilievos	ringlet	riposted	ritenutos
rigged	riling	ringleted	ripostes	rites
rigger	rill	ringlets	riposting	ritual
riggers	rille	ringlety	ripped	ritualise
rigging	rilles	ringneck	ripper	ritualism
riggings	rillettes	ringnecks	rippers	ritualist
right	rills	rings	ripping	ritualize
rightable	rim	ringside	rippingly	ritually
righted	rime	ringsider	ripple	rituals
righten	rimed	ringster	rippled	ritz
rightened	rimes	ringsters	ripples	ritzier
rightens	rimfire	ringtail	ripplet	ritziest
righteous	rimier	ringtails	ripplets	ritzily
righter	rimiest	ringwork	rippling	ritziness
righters	riming	ringworks	ripply	ritzy
rightful	rimland	ringworm	riprap	rival
righties	rimlands	rink	riprapped	rivaled
righting	rimless	rinkhals	ripraps	rivaling
rightish	rimmed	rinks	rips	rivalled
rightism	rimming	rinse	ripsaw	rivalling
rightist	rimrock	rinsed	ripsaws	rivalries
rightists	rims	rinser	ripstop	rivalrous
rightly	rimu	rinsers	rise	rivalry
rightmost	rimus	rinses	risen	rivals
rightness	rimy	rinsing	riser	rive
righto	rind	riot	risers	rived
rights	rinded	rioted	rises	riven
rightsize	rinding	rioter	rishi	river
rightward	rindless	rioters	rishis	rivered
righty	rinds	rioting	risible	riverine
rigid	ring	riotous	risibly	riverless
rigidify	ringbark	riotously	rising	rivers
rigidity	ringbarks	riots	risings	riverside
rigidly	ringbolt	rip	risk	rives
rigidness	ringbolts	riparian	risked	rivet
rigmarole	ringbone	ripcord	riskier	riveted
rigor	ringbones	ripcords	riskiest	riveter
rigorism	ringcraft	ripe	riskily	riveters
rigorist	ringdove	ripely	riskiness	riveting
rigorists	ringdoves	ripen	risking	rivets
rigorous	ringed	ripened	risks	riviera

rivieras
rivière
rivières
riving
rivulet
rivulets
rivulus
riyal
riyals

| R | O |

roach
roached
roaches
road
roadbed
roadbeds
roadblock
roadhouse
roadie
roadied
roadies
roadless
roadman
roadmen
roads
roadshow
roadshows
roadside
roadstead
roadster
roadsters
roadway
roadways
roadwork
roadworks
roadying
roam
roamed
roamer
roamers
roaming
roams
roan
roans
roar
roared
roarer
roarers

roaring
roaringly
roars
roast
roasted
roaster
roasters
roasting
roasts
rob
robbed
robber
robberies
robbers
robbery
robbing
robe
robed
robes
robin
robing
robinia
robinias
robins
robot
robotic
robotics
robotise
robotised
robotises
robotize
robotized
robotizes
robots
robs
robust
robusta
robustas
robuster
robustest
robustly
roc
rocaille
rocailles
rocambole
rochet
rochets
rock
rockburst
rocked

rocker
rockeries
rockers
rockery
rocket
rocketed
rocketeer
rocketing
rocketry
rockets
rockfall
rockfalls
rockfish
rockfowl
rockfowls
rockhound
rockier
rockiest
rockily
rockiness
rocking
rockless
rockling
rocklings
rocks
rockslide
rocky
rococo
rocs
rod
rode
roded
rodent
rodents
rodeo
rodeoed
rodeoing
rodeos
rodes
rodgersia
rodham
rodhams
roding
rodless
rodlet
rodlets
rods
roe
roebuck
roebucks

roentgen
roentgens
roes
rogation
rogations
roger
rogered
rogering
rogers
rogue
rogued
rogueries
roguery
rogues
roguing
roguish
roguishly
roil
roiled
roiling
roils
roily
roister
roistered
roisterer
roisters
role
roles
roll
rollable
rollaway
rollaways
rollback
rollbacks
rolled
roller
rollers
rollick
rollicked
rollicks
rolling
rollmop
rollmops
rollover
rollovers
rolls
romaine
romaines
romaji
roman

romance
romanced
romancer
romancers
romances
romancing
romanise
romanised
romanises
romanize
romanized
romanizes
romans
romantic
romantics
romer
romers
romp
romped
romper
rompers
romping
romps
rondavel
rondavels
ronde
rondeau
rondeaux
rondel
rondels
rondes
rondo
rondos
rone
rones
ronin
ronins
ronquil
ronquils
röntgen
röntgens
roo
rood
roods
roof
roofed
roofer
roofers
roofing
roofless

roofline	rootier	rosalines	rostering	rottenly
roofs	rootiest	rosaria	rosters	rotter
roofscape	rooting	rosarian	rostra	rotters
rooftop	rootle	rosarians	rostral	rotting
rooftops	rootled	rosaries	rostrally	rotund
rooibos	rootles	rosarium	rostrate	rotunda
rooiboses	rootless	rosariums	rostrum	rotundas
rooigras	rootlet	rosary	rostrums	rotundity
rooikat	rootlets	roscoe	rosy	rotundly
rooikats	rootling	roscoes	rot	rouble
rooinek	roots	rose	rota	roubles
rooineks	rootsier	rosé	rotamer	roucou
rook	rootsiest	roseapple	rotamers	roucous
rooked	rootstock	roseate	rotaries	roué
rookeries	rootsy	rosebay	rotary	roués
rookery	rooty	rosebays	rotas	rouge
rookie	ropable	rosebud	rotatable	rouged
rookies	rope	rosebuds	rotate	rouges
rooking	ropeable	rosed	rotated	rouget
rookoo	roped	rosefinch	rotates	rougets
rookoos	ropes	rosefish	rotating	rough
rooks	ropesight	rosella	rotation	roughage
room	ropeway	rosellas	rotations	roughcast
roomed	ropeways	rosemaled	rotative	roughed
roomer	ropey	rosemary	rotator	roughen
roomers	ropier	roseola	rotators	roughened
roomette	ropiest	roseolas	rotatory	roughens
roomettes	ropily	roseroot	rotavate	rougher
roomful	ropiness	roseroots	rotavated	roughest
roomfuls	roping	roses	rotavates	roughie
roomie	ropy	rosés	rotavator	roughies
roomier	roque	rosette	rotavirus	roughing
roomies	roquet	rosetted	rote	roughish
roomiest	roqueted	rosettes	rotenone	roughly
roomily	roqueting	rosewood	rotgut	roughneck
roominess	roquets	rosewoods	roti	roughness
rooming	roquette	rosier	rotifer	roughs
rooms	rorqual	rosiest	rotifers	roughshod
roomy	rorquals	rosily	rotis	roughy
roos	rort	rosin	rotor	rouging
roost	rortier	rosined	rotors	rouille
roosted	rortiest	rosiness	rotoscope	roulade
rooster	rorts	rosing	rototill	roulades
roosters	rorty	rosining	rototills	rouleau
roosting	rosace	rosins	rotovator	rouleaus
roosts	rosacea	rosiny	rots	rouleaux
root	rosaceas	rosolio	rotted	roulement
rooted	rosaceous	rosolios	rotten	roulette
rooter	rosaces	roster	rottener	rouletted
rooters	rosaline	rostered	rottenest	roulettes

round	routing	rozzers	ruching	ruefully
roundball	routining		ruck	rueing
rounded	routinise	R U	rucked	rues
roundel	routinism		rucking	ruff
roundelay	routinist	rub	ruckle	ruffe
roundels	routinize	rubati	ruckled	ruffed
rounder	routs	rubato	ruckles	ruffian
rounders	roux	rubatos	ruckling	ruffianly
roundest	rove	rubbed	rucks	ruffians
roundheel	roved	rubber	rucksack	ruffing
rounding	rover	rubberise	rucksacks	ruffle
roundish	rovers	rubberize	ruckus	ruffled
roundly	roves	rubberoid	ruckuses	ruffles
roundness	roving	rubbers	rucola	ruffling
rounds	row	rubbery	ruction	ruffs
roundsman	rowan	rubbies	ructions	rufiyaa
roundsmen	rowans	rubbing	rudaceous	rufous
roundwood	rowboat	rubbings	rudbeckia	rug
roundworm	rowboats	rubbish	rudd	rugby
roup	rowdier	rubbished	rudder	rugged
rouped	rowdies	rubbishes	rudders	ruggedly
rouping	rowdiest	rubbishy	ruddied	rugger
roups	rowdily	rubble	ruddier	rugola
roupy	rowdiness	rubbled	ruddies	rugosa
rousable	rowdy	rubbly	ruddiest	rugosas
rouse	rowdyism	rubby	ruddily	rugose
roused	rowed	rube	ruddiness	rugosity
rouser	rowel	rubella	ruddle	rugs
rousers	roweled	rubellite	ruddles	ruin
rouses	roweling	rubeola	rudds	ruination
rousette	rowelled	rubes	ruddy	ruined
rousettes	rowelling	rubescent	ruddying	ruing
rousing	rowels	rubicon	rude	ruining
rousingly	rowen	rubiconed	rudely	ruinous
roust	rowens	rubicons	rudeness	ruinously
rousted	rower	rubicund	ruder	ruins
rousting	rowers	rubidium	ruderal	rukh
rousts	rowing	rubies	ruderals	rukhs
rout	rowlock	rubisco	ruderies	rule
route	rowlocks	ruble	rudery	ruled
routed	rows	rubles	rudest	ruleless
routeing	royal	rubric	rudiment	ruler
router	royalism	rubrical	rudiments	rulers
routers	royalist	rubricate	rudist	rulership
routes	royalists	rubrics	rudistid	rules
routier	royally	rubs	rudistids	ruling
routine	royals	ruby	rudists	rulings
routined	royalties	ruche	rue	rum
routinely	royalty	ruched	rued	rumba
routines	rozzer	ruches	rueful	rumbaed

rumbaing
rumbas
rumble
rumbled
rumbler
rumblers
rumbles
rumbling
rumblings
rumdum
rumdums
rumen
rumens
rumina
ruminant
ruminants
ruminate
ruminated
ruminates
ruminator
rumly
rummage
rummaged
rummager
rummagers
rummages
rummaging
rummer
rummers
rummest
rummier
rummies
rummiest
rummy
rumness
rumor
rumored

rumoring
rumors
rumour
rumoured
rumouring
rumours
rump
rumple
rumpled
rumples
rumpless
rumpling
rumply
rumpot
rumpots
rumps
rumpus
rumpuses
run
runabout
runabouts
runaround
runaway
runaways
rundown
rundowns
rune
runes
rung
runged
rungless
rungs
runic
runlet
runlets
runnable
runnel

runnels
runner
runners
runnier
runniest
running
runny
runs
runt
runts
runty
runway
runways
rupee
rupees
rupiah
rupiahs
rupture
ruptured
ruptures
rupturing
rural
ruralise
ruralised
ruralises
ruralism
ruralisms
ruralist
ruralists
rurality
ruralize
ruralized
ruralizes
rurally
rusa
rusas
rusbank

rusbanke
rusbanks
ruse
ruses
rush
rushed
rusher
rushers
rushes
rushier
rushiest
rushing
rushingly
rushlight
rushlike
rushy
rusk
rusks
russet
russets
russety
russula
russulas
rust
rusted
rustic
rusticate
rusticity
rustics
rustier
rustiest
rustily
rustiness
rusting
rustle
rustled
rustler

rustlers
rustles
rustless
rustling
rustproof
rusts
rusty
rut
rutabaga
rutabagas
ruth
ruthenium
ruther
ruthless
rutilant
rutile
rutin
ruts
rutted
rutting
ruttish
rutty

rye
ryegrass
ryokan
ryokans
ryot
ryots
ryu
ryus

S A

saag
sab
sabadilla
sabayon
sabbath
sabbaths
sabbed
sabbing
saber
sabered
sabering
sabers
sabicu
sabicus
sabji
sabjis
sabkha
sabkhas
sable
sablefish
sables
sabot
sabotage
sabotaged
sabotages
saboted
saboteur
saboteurs
sabots
sabra
sabras
sabre
sabred
sabres
sabreur
sabreurs
sabrewing
sabring
sabs
sabzi
sabzis

sac
saccade
saccades
saccadic
saccate
saccharin
saccular
saccule
saccules
sacculus
sachem
sachems
sachet
sachets
sack
sackable
sackbut
sackbuts
sackcloth
sacked
sackful
sackfuls
sacking
sackings
sacklike
sacks
sacra
sacral
sacralise
sacrality
sacralize
sacrament
sacraria
sacrarium
sacred
sacredly
sacrifice
sacrilege
sacring
sacrist
sacristan
sacrists

sacristy
sacrum
sacrums
sacs
sad
sadden
saddened
saddening
saddens
sadder
saddest
saddish
saddle
saddlebag
saddled
saddler
saddlers
saddlery
saddles
saddling
saddo
saddos
sadhana
sadhu
sadhus
sadism
sadist
sadistic
sadists
sadly
sadness
sadza
sae
safari
safaris
safe
safeguard
safelight
safely
safeness
safer
safes

safest
safeties
safety
safflower
saffron
saffrons
saffrony
safranin
safranine
safranins
sag
saga
sagacious
sagacity
sagamore
sagamores
saganaki
sagas
sagbag
sagbags
sage
sagebrush
sagely
sageness
sages
saggar
saggars
sagged
sagger
saggers
saggier
saggiest
sagging
saggy
sagitally
sagittal
sagittate
sago
sagos
sags
saguaro
saguaros

sahib
sahibs
sahitya
sai
said
saiga
saigas
sail
sailable
sailboard
sailboat
sailboats
sailcloth
sailed
sailer
sailers
sailfish
sailing
sailings
sailmaker
sailor
sailorly
sailors
sailplane
sails
sainfoin
saint
saintdom
sainted
sainthood
sainting
saintlier
saintlike
saintly
saints
saintship
saith
saithe
saithes
sakabula
sakabulas
sake

saker	saline	salterns	salvo	samphires
sakers	salinity	salters	salvoes	sample
sakes	saliva	saltier	salvor	sampled
saki	salivary	saltiest	salvors	sampler
sakis	salivate	saltine	salvos	samplers
sal	salivated	saltines	salwar	samples
salaam	salivates	saltiness	salwars	sampling
salaamed	sallee	salting	samaan	samplings
salaaming	sallees	saltings	samaans	samsara
salaams	sallet	saltire	samadhi	samsaric
salable	sallets	saltires	samadhis	samskara
salacious	sallied	saltish	saman	samskaras
salacity	sallies	saltless	samango	samurai
salad	sallow	saltness	samangos	san
salade	sallowed	saltpeter	samans	sanative
salades	sallowing	saltpetre	samara	sanatoria
salads	sallowish	salts	samaras	sancoche
salal	sallows	saltus	samarium	sancocho
salals	sallowy	saltuses	samariums	sanctify
salami	sally	saltwater	samba	sanction
salamis	sallying	saltwort	sambaed	sanctions
salariat	salmi	saltworts	sambaing	sanctity
salaried	salmis	salty	sambal	sanctuary
salaries	salmon	salubrity	sambar	sanctum
salary	salmonid	saluki	sambars	sanctums
salarying	salmonids	salukis	sambas	sand
salaryman	salmonoid	salut	sambhar	sandal
salarymen	salmons	salutary	sambo	sandaled
salat	salmony	salute	sambuca	sandalled
salchow	salon	saluted	same	sandals
salchows	salons	saluter	sameness	sandarac
sale	saloon	saluters	samey	sandaracs
saleable	saloons	salutes	sameyness	sandbag
salep	salotti	saluting	samfu	sandbags
saleratus	salotto	salvable	samfus	sandbank
saleroom	salp	salvage	samier	sandbanks
salerooms	salpicon	salvaged	samiest	sandbar
sales	salpicons	salvager	samisen	sandbars
salesgirl	salps	salvagers	samisens	sandblast
salesman	salsa	salvages	samite	sandbox
salesmen	salsify	salvaging	samites	sandboxes
salesroom	salt	salvation	samizdat	sandboy
salicin	saltation	salve	samosa	sandboys
salience	saltatory	salved	samosas	sanded
saliency	saltbox	salver	samovar	sander
salient	saltboxes	salvers	samovars	sanders
saliently	saltbush	salves	samp	sandesh
salients	salted	salvia	sampan	sandfish
salina	salter	salvias	sampans	sandflies
salinas	saltern	salving	samphire	sandfly

sandglass
sandhi
sandhog
sandhogs
sandier
sandiest
sandiness
sanding
sandiver
sandlot
sandlots
sandman
sandpaper
sandpiper
sandpit
sandpits
sands
sandshoe
sandshoes
sandstone
sandstorm
sandveld
sandwich
sandwort
sandworts
sandy
sandyish
sane
sanely
saneness
saner
sanest
sang
sanga
sangam
sangar
sangaree
sangars
sangas
sangfroid
sangha
sanghas
sangoma
sangomas
sangrail
sangrails
sangreal
sangreals
sangria
sanguine

sanicle
sanicles
sanidine
sanitaria
sanitary
sanitise
sanitised
sanitises
sanitize
sanitized
sanitizer
sanitizes
sanity
sanjak
sanjaks
sank
sannyasi
sannyasin
sanpro
sans
sansa
sansas
sansei
sanserif
sant
santeria
santero
santeros
santim
santims
santo
santolina
santon
santonica
santonin
santons
santoor
santoors
santos
sants
sanyasi
sap
sapele
sapeles
saphenous
sapid
sapidity
sapience
sapient
sapiently

sapients
sapless
sapling
saplings
sapodilla
saponify
saponin
saponins
sapped
sapper
sappers
sapphic
sapphics
sapphire
sapphires
sapphism
sappier
sappiest
sappily
sappiness
sapping
sappy
saps
sapsucker
sapwood
saraband
sarabande
sarabands
sarangi
sarangis
sarape
sarapes
sarcasm
sarcastic
sarcenet
sarcoid
sarcoma
sarcomas
sarcomata
sarcomere
sarcosine
sard
sardar
sardars
sardelle
sardelles
sardine
sardined
sardines
sardining

sardius
sardiuses
sardonic
sardonyx
sards
saree
sarees
sargasso
sargassum
sarge
sari
sarin
saris
sark
sarkar
sarkars
sarkier
sarkiest
sarkily
sarkiness
sarking
sarks
sarky
sarmie
sarmies
sarnie
sarnies
sarod
sarods
sarong
sarongs
saros
sarpanch
sarsen
sarsenet
sarsens
sartorial
sartorius
sarvodaya
sasanqua
sasanquas
sash
sashay
sashayed
sashaying
sashays
sashed
sashes
sashimi
sashless

sasin
sasine
sasines
sasins
sass
sassabies
sassaby
sassafras
sassed
sasses
sassier
sassiest
sassily
sassiness
sassing
sassy
sastra
sastras
sastrugi
sat
satai
satang
satangs
satanic
satanise
satanised
satanises
satanism
satanist
satanists
satanize
satanized
satanizes
satay
satchel
satchels
satcom
sate
saté
sated
sateen
sateless
satellite
sates
satés
sati
satiable
satiate
satiated
satiates

satiating
satiation
satiety
satin
satined
satinet
satinette
sating
satining
satinise
satinised
satinises
satinize
satinized
satinizes
satins
satinwood
satiny
satire
satires
satiric
satirical
satirise
satirised
satirises
satirist
satirists
satirize
satirized
satirizes
satis
satisfice
satisfied
satisfies
satisfy
satnav
satori
satrap
satrapies
satraps
satrapy
satsang
satsangs
satsuma
satsumas
saturable
saturate
saturated
saturates
saturnic

saturniid
saturnine
saturnism
satyr
satyric
satyrid
satyrs
sauce
sauced
sauceless
saucepan
saucepans
saucer
saucerful
saucers
sauces
saucier
sauciest
saucily
sauciness
saucing
saucisson
saucy
saudade
sauger
saugers
sauna
saunas
saunf
saunter
sauntered
saunterer
saunters
saurian
saurians
sauries
sauropod
sauropods
saury
sausage
sausages
sauté
sautéd
sautéed
sautéing
sautés
sautoir
sautoirs
savable
savage

savaged
savagely
savagery
savages
savaging
savanna
savannah
savannahs
savannas
savant
savante
savantes
savants
savarin
savarins
savate
save
saveable
saved
saveloy
saveloys
saver
savers
saves
savin
saving
savings
savins
savior
saviors
saviour
saviours
savor
savored
savories
savoring
savors
savory
savour
savoured
savouries
savourily
savouring
savours
savoury
savoy
savoys
savvied
savvier
savvies

savviest
savvy
savvying
saw
sawbench
sawbill
sawbills
sawbones
sawbuck
sawbucks
sawdust
sawed
sawfish
sawfishes
sawflies
sawfly
sawgrass
sawhorse
sawhorses
sawing
sawlike
sawlog
sawlogs
sawmill
sawmills
sawn
saws
sawtooth
sawyer
sawyers
sax
saxe
saxes
saxhorn
saxhorns
saxifrage
saxist
saxists
saxonies
saxony
saxophone
say
sayable
sayer
saying
sayings
sayonara
says
sayyid
sayyids

saz
sazes

S C

scab
scabbard
scabbards
scabbed
scabbing
scabby
scabies
scabious
scablands
scabrous
scabs
scad
scads
scaffold
scaffolds
scag
scagliola
scalable
scalar
scalars
scalawag
scalawags
scald
scalded
scaldfish
scalding
scalds
scale
scaled
scaleless
scalene
scalenes
scaleni
scalenus
scaler
scalers
scales
scalier
scaliest
scaliness
scaling
scallies
scallion
scallions
scallop

scalloped	scantly	scarps	scent	schlepp
scalloper	scantness	scarred	scented	schlepped
scallops	scants	scarring	scenting	schlepper
scally	scanty	scars	scentless	schlepps
scallywag	scape	scarved	scents	schleps
scalp	scapegoat	scarves	scepter	schlieren
scalped	scapes	scary	scepters	schlock
scalpel	scaphoid	scat	sceptic	schlocks
scalpels	scaphoids	scathe	sceptical	schlocky
scalper	scaphopod	scathed	sceptics	schloss
scalpers	scapula	scathes	sceptre	schlub
scalping	scapulae	scathing	sceptred	schlubs
scalps	scapular	scatology	sceptres	schlump
scaly	scapulary	scats	schappe	schmaltz
scalyfoot	scapulas	scatted	schedular	schmaltzy
scam	scar	scatter	schedule	schmatte
scammed	scarab	scattered	scheduled	schmattes
scammer	scarabs	scatterer	scheduler	schmear
scammers	scarce	scatters	schedules	schmeared
scamming	scarcely	scattier	scheelite	schmears
scammony	scarcer	scattiest	schellies	schmeer
scamp	scarcest	scattily	schelly	schmeered
scamped	scarcity	scatting	schema	schmeers
scamper	scare	scatty	schemas	schmo
scampered	scarecrow	scaup	schemata	schmoes
scampers	scared	scauper	schematic	schmooze
scampi	scarer	scaupers	scheme	schmoozed
scamping	scarers	scaups	schemed	schmoozer
scampish	scares	scaur	schemer	schmoozes
scamps	scarf	scaurs	schemers	schmoozy
scams	scarfed	scavenge	schemes	schmuck
scan	scarfing	scavenged	scheming	schmucks
scandal	scarfs	scavenger	scherzi	schnapps
scandals	scarier	scavenges	scherzo	schnauzer
scandent	scariest	scazon	scherzos	schnitzel
scandium	scarified	scazons	schilling	schnook
scannable	scarifier	scena	schism	schnooks
scanned	scarifies	scenario	schisms	schnorrer
scanner	scarify	scenarios	schist	schnozz
scanners	scarily	scenarist	schistose	schnozzes
scanning	scariness	scenas	schists	scholar
scans	scaring	scend	schizo	scholarly
scansion	scarless	scended	schizoid	scholars
scant	scarlet	scending	schizoids	scholia
scanted	scarp	scends	schizont	scholiast
scantier	scarped	scene	schizonts	scholium
scantiest	scarper	scenery	schizos	school
scantily	scarpered	scenes	schlemiel	schoolboy
scanting	scarpers	scenester	schlenter	schooled
scantling	scarping	scenic	schlep	schooler

schoolie	scissel	scoosh	scotch	scrags
schoolies	scissile	scooshed	scotched	scram
schooling	scission	scooshes	scotches	scramasax
schoolman	scissions	scooshing	scotching	scramble
schoolmen	scissor	scoot	scoter	scrambled
schools	scissored	scooted	scoters	scrambler
schooner	scissors	scooter	scotia	scrambles
schooners	sclera	scootered	scotias	scramjet
schorl	scleral	scooters	scotoma	scramjets
schtuck	sclerite	scooting	scotomas	scrammed
schtum	scleritis	scoots	scotomata	scramming
schtup	sclerosed	scope	scotopic	scrams
schtupped	sclerosis	scoped	scots	scran
schtups	sclerotia	scopes	scoundrel	scrap
schuss	sclerotic	scoping	scour	scrapbook
schussed	sclerotin	scorbutic	scoured	scrape
schusses	sclerous	scorch	scourer	scraped
schussing	scoff	scorched	scourers	scraper
schwa	scoffed	scorcher	scourge	scrapers
schwas	scoffer	scorchers	scourged	scrapes
sciaenid	scoffers	scorches	scourger	scrapie
sciaenids	scoffing	scorching	scourgers	scraping
sciagram	scofflaw	score	scourges	scrapings
sciagrams	scofflaws	scorebook	scourging	scrapped
sciagraph	scoffs	scorebox	scouring	scrapper
sciamachy	scold	scorecard	scours	scrappers
sciatic	scolded	scored	scout	scrappier
sciatica	scolder	scoreless	scouted	scrappily
science	scolders	scoreline	scouter	scrapping
sciences	scolding	scorer	scouters	scrapple
scienter	scolds	scorers	scouting	scrapples
sciential	scolex	scores	scouts	scrappy
scientism	scolices	scoria	scow	scraps
scientist	scoliosis	scoriae	scowl	scrapyard
scilicet	scoliotic	scoring	scowled	scratch
scilla	scollop	scorn	scowler	scratched
scillas	scollops	scorned	scowlers	scratcher
scimitar	scombroid	scorner	scowling	scratches
scimitars	sconce	scorners	scowls	scratchy
scintilla	sconces	scornful	scows	scrawl
sciolism	scone	scorning	scrabble	scrawled
sciolist	scones	scorns	scrabbled	scrawling
sciolists	scoop	scorp	scrabbles	scrawls
scion	scooped	scorper	scrag	scrawly
scions	scooper	scorpers	scragged	scrawnier
scirocco	scoopers	scorpioid	scraggier	scrawny
sciroccos	scoopful	scorpion	scraggily	scream
scirrhi	scoopfuls	scorpions	scragging	screamed
scirrhous	scooping	scorps	scraggly	screamer
scirrhus	scoops	scot	scraggy	screamers

screaming
screams
scree
screech
screeched
screecher
screeches
screechy
screed
screeding
screeds
screel
screeled
screeling
screels
screen
screened
screener
screeners
screenful
screening
screens
screes
screw
screwable
screwball
screwed
screwer
screwers
screwgate
screwier
screwiest
screwing
screws
screwy
scribal
scribble
scribbled
scribbler
scribbles
scribbly
scribe
scribed
scriber
scribers
scribes
scribing
scried
scries
scrim

scrimmage
scrimp
scrimped
scrimping
scrimps
scrims
scrimshaw
scrip
scrips
script
scripted
scripting
scripts
scripture
scrivener
scrod
scrods
scrofula
scroggin
scroll
scrolled
scroller
scrollers
scrolling
scrolls
scrooch
scrooched
scrooches
scrota
scrotal
scrotum
scrotums
scrounge
scrounged
scrounger
scrounges
scrub
scrubbed
scrubber
scrubbers
scrubbier
scrubbing
scrubby
scrubfowl
scrubland
scrubs
scruff
scruffed
scruffier
scruffily

scruffing
scruffs
scruffy
scrum
scrummage
scrummed
scrummier
scrumming
scrummy
scrump
scrumped
scrumping
scrumple
scrumpled
scrumples
scrumps
scrumpy
scrums
scrunch
scrunched
scrunches
scrunchie
scrunchy
scruple
scrupled
scruples
scrupling
scrutator
scrutiny
scry
scryer
scryers
scrying
scuba
scubas
scud
scudded
scudding
scudi
scudo
scuds
scuff
scuffed
scuffing
scuffle
scuffled
scuffles
scuffling
scuffs
scull

scullcap
scullcaps
sculled
sculler
scullers
scullery
sculling
scullion
scullions
sculls
sculp
sculped
sculpin
sculping
sculpins
sculps
sculpt
sculpted
sculpting
sculptor
sculptors
sculpts
sculpture
scum
scumbag
scumbags
scumble
scumbled
scumbles
scumbling
scummed
scumming
scummy
scums
scuncheon
scunge
scunges
scungier
scungiest
scungile
scungille
scungilli
scungy
scunner
scunnered
scunners
scup
scupper
scuppered
scuppers

scurf
scurfy
scurried
scurries
scurry
scurrying
scurvier
scurviest
scurvily
scurvy
scut
scuta
scutage
scutages
scutch
scutched
scutcheon
scutcher
scutchers
scutches
scutching
scute
scutella
scutellar
scutellum
scutes
scuts
scutter
scuttered
scutters
scuttle
scuttled
scuttles
scuttling
scutum
scutwork
scuzz
scuzzbag
scuzzbags
scuzzball
scuzzier
scuzziest
scuzzy
scythe
scythed
scythes
scything

S E

sea
seabag
seabags
seabed
seabeds
seabird
seabirds
seaboard
seaboards
seaborne
seacock
seacocks
seafarer
seafarers
seafaring
seafood
seafront
seafronts
seagoing
seagrass
seagull
seagulls
seakale
seal
sealable
sealant
sealants
sealed
sealer
sealers
sealift
sealifts
sealing
sealpoint
seals
sealskin
sealstone
seam
seaman
seamanly
seamark
seamarks
seamed
seamen
seamer
seamers
seamfree
seamier

seamiest
seaminess
seaming
seamless
seamount
seamounts
seams
seamy
seance
seances
seaplane
seaplanes
seaport
seaports
seaquake
seaquakes
sear
search
searched
searcher
searchers
searches
searching
seared
searing
sears
seas
seascape
seascapes
seashell
seashells
seashore
seashores
seasick
seaside
season
seasonal
seasoned
seasoning
seasons
seat
seated
seating
seatless
seats
seaward
seawards
seaway
seaways
seaweed

seaworthy
sebaceous
seborrhea
sebum
sec
secant
secants
secateurs
secco
seccos
secede
seceded
seceder
seceders
secedes
seceding
secession
seclude
secluded
secludes
secluding
seclusion
seclusive
second
secondary
seconde
seconded
secondee
secondees
seconder
seconders
secondes
secondi
seconding
secondly
secondo
seconds
secrecy
secret
secretary
secrete
secreted
secretes
secretin
secreting
secretion
secretive
secretly
secretor
secretors

secretory
secrets
secs
sect
sectarian
sectaries
sectary
section
sectional
sectioned
sections
sector
sectoral
sectorial
sectors
sects
secular
secularly
secund
secundly
securable
secure
secured
securely
securer
secures
securest
securing
security
sedan
sedans
sedate
sedated
sedately
sedates
sedating
sedation
sedative
sedatives
sedentary
sederunt
sederunts
sedge
sedges
sedgy
sedile
sedilia
sediment
sediments
sedition

seditious
seduce
seduced
seducer
seducers
seduces
seducible
seducing
seduction
seductive
sedulity
sedulous
sedum
sedums
see
seeable
seed
seedbed
seedbeds
seedcorn
seedeater
seeded
seeder
seeders
seedier
seediest
seedily
seediness
seeding
seedless
seedling
seedlings
seeds
seedsman
seedsmen
seedy
seeing
seek
seeker
seekers
seeking
seeks
seel
seeled
seeling
seels
seem
seemed
seeming
seemingly

seemlier	seisins	selfness	semiotics	sennas
seemliest	seismic	selfs	semis	sennet
seemly	seismical	selfsame	semitone	sennight
seems	seiza	selkie	semitones	sennights
seen	seizable	selkies	semivowel	sennit
seep	seize	selky	semmit	señor
seepage	seized	sell	semmits	señora
seeped	seizer	sella	semolina	señoras
seeping	seizers	sellable	semplice	señores
seeps	seizes	sellae	sempre	señorita
seer	seizin	seller	sen	señoritas
seers	seizing	sellers	senarii	sensa
sees	seizins	selling	senarius	sensate
seethe	seizure	sells	senary	sensation
seethed	seizures	seltzer	senate	sense
seethes	sejant	selva	senates	sensed
seething	selachian	selvage	senator	sensei
segment	seladang	selvages	senators	senseless
segmental	seladangs	selvedge	send	senses
segmented	selah	selvedges	sendable	sensible
segments	seldom	selves	sendal	sensibly
segregate	select	semanteme	sendals	sensilla
segue	selected	semantic	sended	sensillum
segued	selectee	semantics	sender	sensing
segues	selectees	semaphore	senders	sensitise
seguing	selecting	semblable	sending	sensitive
sei	selection	semblance	sends	sensitize
seicento	selective	seme	sene	sensor
seiche	selectman	semé	senecio	sensoria
seiches	selectmen	semée	senecios	sensorial
seidel	selector	sememe	senes	sensorily
seidels	selectors	sememes	senesce	sensorium
seif	selects	semen	senesced	sensors
seifs	selenate	semes	senescent	sensory
seigneur	selenide	semester	senesces	sensual
seigneurs	selenides	semesters	seneschal	sensually
seigneury	selenite	semi	senescing	sensum
seignior	selenium	semibold	senex	sensuous
seigniors	self	semibreve	senhor	sent
seigniory	selfed	semicolon	senhora	sente
seine	selfhood	semilunar	senhoras	sentence
seined	selfing	semimetal	senhorita	sentenced
seiner	selfish	seminal	senhors	sentences
seiners	selfishly	seminally	senile	sentience
seines	selfism	seminar	senility	sentient
seining	selfist	seminars	senior	sentiment
seise	selfists	seminary	seniority	sentinel
seised	selfless	semiology	seniors	sentinels
seises	selfmate	semiosis	seniti	sentries
seisin	selfmates	semiotic	senna	sentry

sepal	sequelae	sergeancy	serotypes	sesses
sepals	sequels	sergeant	serotypic	sessile
separable	sequence	sergeants	serous	session
separably	sequenced	serger	serow	sessional
separate	sequencer	serial	serows	sessions
separated	sequences	serialise	serpent	sesterce
separates	sequent	serialism	serpents	sesterces
separator	sequently	serialist	serpulid	sestertii
sephira	sequester	seriality	serpulids	sestet
sephiroth	sequestra	serialize	serranid	sestets
sepia	sequin	serially	serranids	sestina
sepias	sequined	serials	serrate	sestinas
sepoy	sequinned	seriate	serrated	set
sepoys	sequins	seriated	serration	seta
seppuku	sequoia	seriates	serried	setaceous
seps	sequoias	seriatim	sertão	setae
sepsis	sera	seriating	sertãos	setal
sept	serac	seriation	serum	setback
septa	seracs	sericite	serums	setbacks
septage	seraglio	seriema	serval	seth
septal	seraglios	seriemas	servals	seton
septaria	serai	series	servant	setons
septarian	serais	serif	servants	setose
septarium	serang	seriffed	serve	sets
septate	serangs	serifs	served	sett
septation	serape	serigraph	server	settee
septenary	serapes	serin	serveries	settees
septennia	seraph	serine	servers	setter
septet	seraphic	serins	servery	setters
septets	seraphim	serious	serves	setting
septette	seraphs	seriously	service	settings
septettes	seraskier	serjeant	serviced	settle
septic	sere	serjeants	services	settled
septicity	serenade	serjeanty	servicing	settler
septimal	serenaded	sermon	serviette	settlers
septime	serenader	sermonic	servile	settles
septimes	serenades	sermonise	servilely	settling
septoria	serenata	sermonize	servility	settlor
septs	serenatas	sermons	serving	settlors
septum	serene	serologic	servings	setts
septuple	serenely	serology	servitor	sev
septupled	serenity	serosa	servitors	seven
septuples	seres	serosal	servitude	sevenfold
septuplet	serf	serositis	servo	sevens
sepulcher	serfage	serosity	servos	seventeen
sepulchre	serfages	serotine	sesame	seventh
sepulture	serfdom	serotines	sesamoid	seventhly
sequacity	serfdoms	serotonin	sesamum	seventies
sequel	serfs	serotype	sesh	seventy
sequela	serge	serotyped	sess	sever

severable
several
severally
severalty
severance
severe
severed
severely
severer
severest
severies
severing
severity
severs
severy
seviche
sevruga
sevrugas
sew
sewage
sewed
sewellel
sewellels
sewen
sewens
sewer
sewerage
sewers
sewin
sewing
sewins
sewn
sews
sex
sexcapade
sexed
sexennia
sexennial
sexennium
sexer
sexers
sexes
sexfoil
sexfoils
sexier
sexiest
sexily
sexiness
sexing
sexism

sexist
sexless
sexlessly
sexology
sexpert
sexperts
sexpot
sexpots
sext
sextant
sextants
sextet
sextets
sextette
sextettes
sextile
sexton
sextons
sexts
sextuple
sextupled
sextuples
sextuplet
sextuply
sexual
sexualise
sexuality
sexualize
sexually
sexy
sez

| S | F |

sforzandi
sforzando
sforzato
sfumato

| S | G |

sgraffiti
sgraffito

| S | H |

sh
shabash
shabbier
shabbiest
shabbily

shabby
shabrack
shabracks
shabti
shabtis
shack
shacked
shacking
shackland
shackle
shackled
shackles
shackling
shacks
shacky
shad
shadblow
shadblows
shadbush
shadchan
shadchans
shaddock
shaddocks
shaddup
shade
shaded
shadeless
shader
shaders
shades
shadier
shadiest
shadily
shadiness
shading
shadings
shadkhan
shadkhans
shadoof
shadoofs
shadow
shadowed
shadower
shadowers
shadowier
shadowing
shadows
shadowy
shads
shady

shaft
shafted
shafting
shafts
shag
shagged
shagger
shaggers
shaggier
shaggiest
shaggily
shagging
shaggy
shagreen
shags
shah
shahada
shahadah
shahadahs
shahadas
shahdom
shahdoms
shaheed
shaheeds
shahid
shahids
shahs
shahtoosh
shaikh
shaikhs
shaitan
shaitans
shake
shakedown
shaken
shaker
shakers
shakes
shakier
shakiest
shakily
shakiness
shaking
shako
shakos
shakudo
shaky
shale
shaley
shalier

shaliest
shall
shallop
shallops
shallot
shallots
shallow
shallowed
shallower
shallowly
shallows
shalom
shalt
shalwar
shalwars
shaly
sham
shama
shamal
shaman
shamanic
shamanise
shamanism
shamanist
shamanize
shamans
shamas
shamateur
shamba
shambas
shamble
shambled
shambles
shambling
shambly
shambolic
shame
shamed
shameful
shameless
shames
shamiana
shaming
shamisen
shamisens
shammed
shammer
shammers
shammies
shamming

shammy	shareware	shaw	shedhand	shellacs
shampoo	sharia	shawl	shedhands	shellback
shampooed	shariah	shawled	sheds	shelled
shampoos	shariat	shawls	sheen	shellfire
shamrock	sharif	shawm	sheened	shellfish
shamrocks	sharifian	shawms	sheenier	shelling
shams	sharifs	shaws	sheeniest	shells
shamus	sharing	shay	sheening	shelly
shamuses	shark	shaykh	sheens	shelter
shandies	sharks	shaykhs	sheeny	sheltered
shandy	sharkskin	shays	sheep	shelterer
shanghai	sharp	shazam	sheepdog	shelters
shanghais	sharped	shchi	sheepdogs	sheltie
shank	sharpen	she	sheepfold	shelties
shanked	sharpened	shea	sheepish	shelty
shanking	sharpener	sheading	sheeplike	shelve
shanks	sharpens	sheadings	sheepskin	shelved
shannies	sharper	sheaf	sheer	shelver
shanny	sharpers	sheafed	sheered	shelvers
shanti	sharpest	sheafing	sheerer	shelves
shanties	sharpie	sheafs	sheerest	shelving
shantung	sharpies	shealing	sheering	shemozzle
shanty	sharping	shealings	sheerly	shen
shantyman	sharpish	shear	sheerness	sheng
shantymen	sharply	sheared	sheers	shepherd
shapable	sharpness	shearer	sheet	shepherds
shape	sharps	shearers	sheeted	sherbet
shapeable	shashlik	shearing	sheeting	sherd
shaped	shashliks	shearling	sheetlet	sherds
shapeless	shastra	shears	sheetlets	shereef
shapelier	shastras	sheas	sheets	shereefs
shapely	shat	sheatfish	sheik	sherif
shaper	shatter	sheath	sheikh	sheriff
shapers	shattered	sheathe	sheikhdom	sheriffs
shapes	shatterer	sheathed	sheikhs	sherifs
shaping	shatters	sheathes	sheiks	sherries
shapka	shauri	sheathing	sheila	sherry
shapkas	shauries	sheaths	sheilas	sherwani
sharable	shauris	sheave	sheitel	shew
sharara	shave	sheaved	sheitels	shewbread
shararas	shaved	sheaves	shekel	shewed
shard	shavehook	sheaving	shekels	shewing
shards	shaveling	shebang	shelduck	shews
share	shaven	shebeen	shelducks	shh
shareable	shaver	shebeens	shelf	shiatsu
sharecrop	shavers	shed	shelfed	shicer
shared	shaves	shedded	shelfing	shicers
sharer	shavetail	shedder	shelfs	shicker
sharers	shaving	shedders	shell	shickered
shares	shavings	shedding	shellac	shickers

shidduch	shimmied	shippable	shitface	shoaling
shied	shimmies	shipped	shitfaces	shoals
shield	shimming	shippen	shithole	shoaly
shielded	shimmy	shippens	shitholes	shoat
shielding	shimmying	shipper	shithouse	shoats
shields	shims	shippers	shitless	shochet
shieling	shin	shipping	shitlist	shochetim
shielings	shindies	shippon	shitlists	shochu
shies	shindig	shippons	shits	shock
shift	shindigs	ships	shitted	shockable
shiftable	shindy	shipshape	shittier	shocked
shifted	shine	shipway	shittiest	shocker
shifter	shined	shipways	shitting	shockers
shifters	shiner	shipworm	shitty	shocking
shiftier	shiners	shipworms	shitwork	shocks
shiftiest	shines	shipwreck	shiur	shod
shiftily	shingle	shipyard	shiurim	shoddier
shifting	shingled	shipyards	shiv	shoddiest
shiftless	shingles	shiralee	shiva	shoddily
shifts	shingling	shiralees	shivah	shoddy
shifty	shingly	shire	shivaree	shoe
shigella	shinier	shires	shivarees	shoebill
shigellae	shiniest	shirk	shive	shoebills
shigellas	shinily	shirked	shiver	shoeblack
shiitake	shininess	shirker	shivered	shoebox
shiitakes	shining	shirkers	shiverer	shoeboxes
shikar	shiningly	shirking	shiverers	shoehorn
shikara	shinned	shirks	shivering	shoehorns
shikari	shinnied	shirr	shivers	shoeing
shikaris	shinnies	shirred	shivery	shoelace
shikars	shinning	shirring	shivoo	shoelaces
shikker	shinny	shirrs	shivoos	shoeless
shikkered	shinnying	shirt	shivs	shoemaker
shikkers	shins	shirted	shlub	shoepack
shikra	shinties	shirtier	shlubs	shoepacks
shikras	shinty	shirtiest	shmatte	shoes
shiksa	shiny	shirtily	shmattes	shoeshine
shiksas	ship	shirting	shmear	shofar
shill	shipboard	shirtless	shmeared	shofars
shilled	shiplap	shirts	shmearing	shofroth
shilling	shiplaped	shirty	shmears	shogun
shillings	shiplaps	shisham	shmeer	shogunate
shills	shipless	shishams	shmeered	shoguns
shim	shipload	shit	shmeering	shoji
shimiyana	shiploads	shitake	shmeers	shojis
shimmed	shipmate	shitakes	shmo	shone
shimmer	shipmates	shitbag	shmoes	shonk
shimmered	shipment	shitbags	sho	shonkier
shimmers	shipments	shite	shoal	shonkies
shimmery	shipowner	shitepoke	shoaled	shonkiest

shonks	shortfall	showband	shrewd	shrub
shonky	shorthair	showbands	shrewder	shrubbery
shoo	shorthand	showbiz	shrewdest	shrubbier
shooed	shorthold	showbizzy	shrewdly	shrubby
shooing	shorthorn	showboat	shrewish	shrubs
shook	shortie	showboats	shrews	shrug
shoos	shorties	showcard	shriek	shrugged
shoot	shorting	showcards	shrieked	shrugging
shootable	shortish	showcase	shrieker	shrugs
shooter	shortlist	showcased	shriekers	shrunk
shooters	shortly	showcases	shrieking	shrunken
shooting	shortness	showdown	shrieks	shtetl
shootings	shorts	showdowns	shrieval	shtetlach
shoots	shortstop	showed	shrift	shtetls
shop	shortwing	shower	shrike	shtick
shopfront	shorty	showered	shrikes	shticks
shophouse	shot	showering	shrill	shtook
shoplift	shotcrete	showers	shrilled	shtum
shoplifts	shote	showery	shrilling	shtummed
shopman	shotes	showgirl	shrills	shtumming
shopmen	shotgun	showgirls	shrilly	shtums
shoppe	shotguns	showier	shrimp	shtup
shopped	shotmaker	showiest	shrimped	shtupped
shopper	shots	showily	shrimper	shtupping
shoppers	shotted	showiness	shrimpers	shtups
shopping	shottist	showing	shrimping	shubunkin
shops	should	showings	shrimps	shuck
shopworn	shoulder	showjump	shrine	shucked
shore	shoulders	showjumps	shrined	shucker
shorebird	shout	showman	shrines	shuckers
shored	shouted	showmen	shrining	shucking
shorelark	shouter	shown	shrink	shucks
shoreless	shouters	showpiece	shrinkage	shudder
shoreline	shouting	showplace	shrinker	shuddered
shores	shouts	showreel	shrinkers	shudders
shoreside	shouty	showreels	shrinkfit	shuddery
shoreward	shove	showroom	shrinking	shuffle
shoreweed	shoved	showrooms	shrinks	shuffled
shoring	shovel	shows	shrive	shuffler
shorn	shoveled	showy	shrivel	shufflers
short	shoveler	shoyu	shriveled	shuffles
shortage	shovelers	shrank	shrivels	shuffling
shortages	shovelful	shrapnel	shriven	shufti
shortcake	shoveling	shred	shrives	shuftis
shorted	shovelled	shredded	shriving	shul
shorten	shoveller	shredder	shroud	shuls
shortened	shovels	shredders	shrouded	shun
shortens	shoves	shredding	shrouding	shunned
shorter	shoving	shreds	shrouds	shunning
shortest	show	shrew	shrove	shuns

shunt	siblicide	siddhi	sideways	sigla
shunted	sibling	siddhis	sidewind	siglum
shunter	siblings	side	sidewinds	sigma
shunters	sibs	sidearm	sidewise	sigmas
shunting	sibship	sidearmed	siding	sigmate
shunts	sibships	sidearmer	sidings	sigmoid
shura	sibyl	sidearms	sidle	sigmoidal
shuriken	sibylline	sideband	sidled	sigmoids
shurikens	sibyls	sidebands	sidles	sign
shush	sic	sidebar	sidling	signage
shushed	siccative	sidebars	siege	signal
shushes	sice	sideboard	sieges	signaled
shushing	sices	sideburn	siemens	signaling
shut	siciliana	sideburns	sienna	signalise
shutdown	siciliano	sidecar	sierra	signalize
shutdowns	sick	sidecars	sierras	signalled
shutout	sickbay	sidecut	siesta	signaller
shutouts	sickbays	sidecuts	siestas	signally
shuts	sickbed	sided	sieve	signalman
shutter	sickbeds	sidedly	sieved	signalmen
shuttered	sicked	sidedness	sievert	signals
shutters	sicken	sidehill	sieverts	signatory
shutting	sickened	sidehills	sieves	signature
shuttle	sickener	sidekick	sieving	signboard
shuttled	sickeners	sidekicks	sifaka	signed
shuttles	sickening	sideless	sifakas	signee
shuttling	sickens	sidelight	sift	signees
shy	sicker	sideline	sifted	signer
shyer	sickest	sidelined	sifter	signers
shyers	sickie	sidelines	sifters	signet
shyest	sickies	sidelong	sifting	signets
shying	sicking	sideman	sifts	signifié
shyly	sickish	sidemeat	sig	signified
shyness	sickle	sidemen	sigh	signifier
shynesses	sickles	sidereal	sighed	signifies
shyster	sicklier	siderite	sighing	signify
shysters	sickliest	sideritic	sighs	signing
	sickly	sides	sight	signings
S I	sickness	sideshow	sighted	signor
	sicko	sideshows	sighter	signora
si	sickos	sidesman	sighters	signoras
sial	sickroom	sidesmen	sighting	signore
sialidase	sickrooms	sidestep	sightings	signori
siamang	sicks	sidesteps	sightless	signories
siamangs	sida	sideswipe	sightly	signorina
sib	sidalcea	sidetrack	sights	signory
sibia	sidalceas	sidewalk	sightsee	signpost
sibilance	sidas	sidewalks	sightseer	signposts
sibilant	siddha	sideward	sigil	signs
sibilants	siddhas	sidewards	sigils	sigri

sigris	silkily	simmered	sinciput	sinless
sika	silkiness	simmering	sinciputs	sinlessly
sikas	silks	simmers	sine	sinned
sike	silkworm	simoleon	sinecure	sinner
sikes	silkworms	simoleons	sinecures	sinners
silage	silky	simoniac	sines	sinnet
silaged	sill	simonize	sinew	sinnets
silages	sillabub	simonized	sinewed	sinning
silaging	sillabubs	simonizes	sinewing	sinology
silane	sillier	simony	sinewless	sins
silanes	sillies	simoom	sinews	sinter
silastic	silliest	simooms	sinewy	sintered
sild	sillily	simoon	sinfonia	sintering
silence	silliness	simoons	sinfonias	sinters
silenced	sills	simp	sinful	sinuate
silencer	silly	simpatico	sinfully	sinuosity
silencers	silo	simper	sing	sinuous
silences	silos	simpered	singable	sinuously
silencing	siloxane	simpering	singalong	sinus
sileni	siloxanes	simpers	singe	sinuses
silent	silt	simple	singed	sinusitis
silently	siltation	simpler	singeing	sinusoid
silenus	silted	simples	singer	sinusoids
silex	silting	simplest	singers	sip
silica	silts	simpleton	singes	sipe
silicate	siltstone	simplex	singing	sipes
silicates	silty	simplify	singingly	siphon
siliceous	siluroid	simplism	single	siphonage
silicic	siluroids	simply	singled	siphonal
silicide	silvan	simps	singles	siphoned
silicides	silver	sims	singlet	siphonic
silicify	silvered	simul	singleton	siphoning
silicious	silvereye	simulacra	singlets	siphons
silicon	silvering	simulant	singling	siphuncle
silicone	silvern	simulants	singly	sipped
siliconed	silvers	simulate	sings	sipper
silicones	silvery	simulated	singular	sippers
silicosis	sim	simulates	singulars	sippet
silicotic	sima	simulator	sinister	sippets
siliqua	simazine	simulcast	sinistral	sipping
siliquae	simcha	simuls	sink	sips
silique	simchas	simurg	sinkable	sir
siliques	simian	simurgs	sinkage	sirdar
siliquose	simians	sin	sinkages	sirdars
silk	similar	since	sinker	sire
silken	similarly	sincere	sinkers	sired
silkie	similars	sincerely	sinkhole	siree
silkier	simile	sincerer	sinkholes	siren
silkies	similes	sincerest	sinking	sirenian
silkiest	simmer	sincerity	sinks	sirenians

sirens
sires
siring
sirloin
sirocco
siroccos
sirrah
sirree
sirs
sirtaki
sirup
sirupy
sis
sisal
siskin
siskins
sissier
sissies
sissiest
sissified
sissiness
sissy
sissyish
sister
sisterly
sisters
sistra
sistrum
sit
sitar
sitarist
sitarists
sitars
sitatunga
sitcom
sitcoms
site
sited
sitella
sitellas
sites
siting
sitkamer
sitkamers
sitrep
sitreps
sits
sittella
sittellas
sitter

sitters
sitting
sittings
situate
situated
situates
situating
situation
situs
sitzkrieg
six
sixain
sixains
sixer
sixers
sixes
sixfold
sixpence
sixpences
sixpenny
sixte
sixteen
sixteenmo
sixteenth
sixtes
sixth
sixthly
sixties
sixtieth
sixty
sixtyfold
sizable
sizar
sizars
sizarship
size
sizeable
sizeably
sized
sizer
sizers
sizes
sizing
sizzle
sizzled
sizzler
sizzlers
sizzles
sizzling

S J

sjambok
sjamboked
sjamboks

S K

ska
skag
skald
skaldic
skalds
skank
skanked
skanking
skanks
skanky
skarn
skat
skate
skated
skatepark
skater
skaters
skates
skating
skean
skeans
skebenga
sked
skedaddle
skedded
skedding
skedonk
skeds
skeet
skeeter
skeetered
skeeters
skeets
skeg
skegs
skein
skeins
skeletal
skeleton
skeletons
skelf
skelfs

skellies
skelly
skelm
skelms
skelp
skelped
skelping
skelps
skene
skep
skeps
skeptic
skeptical
skeptics
skerm
skerms
skerrick
skerricks
skerries
skerry
sketch
sketched
sketcher
sketchers
sketches
sketchier
sketchily
sketching
sketchy
skew
skewback
skewbacks
skewbald
skewbalds
skewed
skewer
skewered
skewering
skewers
skewing
skewness
skews
ski
skiable
skid
skidded
skidding
skiddoo
skiddooed
skiddoos

skidoo
skidooed
skidooing
skidoos
skidpad
skidpads
skidpan
skidpans
skids
skied
skier
skiers
skies
skiff
skiffle
skiffs
skiing
skijorer
skijorers
skijoring
skilfish
skilful
skilfully
skill
skilled
skilless
skillet
skillets
skillful
skillies
skilling
skills
skilly
skim
skimboard
skimmed
skimmer
skimmers
skimmia
skimmias
skimming
skimobile
skimp
skimped
skimpier
skimpiest
skimpily
skimping
skimps
skimpy

skims
skin
skincare
skinder
skindered
skinders
skinflint
skinfold
skinfolds
skinful
skinfuls
skinhead
skinheads
skink
skinks
skinless
skinned
skinner
skinners
skinnier
skinniest
skinning
skinny
skins
skint
skintight
skip
skipjack
skipjacks
skipped
skipper
skippered
skippers
skippet
skippets
skipping
skips
skirl
skirled
skirling
skirls
skirmish
skirr
skirred
skirret
skirrets
skirring
skirrs
skirt

skirted
skirting
skirtings
skirts
skis
skit
skite
skited
skites
skiting
skits
skitter
skittered
skitters
skittery
skittish
skittle
skittled
skittles
skittling
skive
skived
skiver
skivers
skives
skiving
skivvied
skivvies
skivvy
skivvying
skoal
skokiaan
skol
skollies
skolly
skookum
skookums
skosh
skua
skuas
skulk
skulked
skulker
skulkers
skulking
skulks
skull
skullcap
skullcaps
skulled

skulling
skulls
skunk
skunked
skunking
skunks
skunkweed
sky
skybox
skyboxes
skycap
skycaps
skydive
skydived
skydiver
skydivers
skydives
skydiving
skyer
skyers
skyey
skyflower
skyglow
skyhook
skyhooks
skying
skyjack
skyjacked
skyjacker
skyjacks
skylark
skylarked
skylarks
skyless
skylight
skylights
skyline
skylines
skylit
skyr
skyrocket
skysail
skysails
skyscape
skyscapes
skywalk
skywalks
skyward
skywards
skywatch

skyway
skyways

S L

slab
slabbed
slabber
slabbered
slabbers
slabbing
slabby
slabs
slack
slacked
slacken
slackened
slackens
slacker
slackers
slackest
slacking
slackly
slackness
slacks
slag
slagged
slaggier
slaggiest
slagging
slaggy
slags
slain
slainte
slake
slaked
slakes
slaking
slalom
slalomed
slalomer
slalomers
slaloming
slaloms
slam
slammed
slammer
slammers
slamming
slams

slander
slandered
slanderer
slanders
slang
slanged
slangier
slangiest
slangily
slanging
slangs
slangy
slant
slanted
slanting
slants
slantwise
slap
slapdash
slaphead
slapheads
slapjack
slapjacks
slapped
slapper
slappers
slapping
slaps
slapstick
slash
slashed
slasher
slashers
slashes
slashing
slasto
slat
slate
slated
slater
slaters
slates
slather
slathered
slathers
slating
slats
slatted
slattern
slatterns

slaty	sleeper	slicked	slings	slobbered
slaughter	sleepers	slicker	slingshot	slobbers
slave	sleepier	slickers	slink	slobbery
slaved	sleepiest	slickest	slinkier	slobbing
slaver	sleepily	slicking	slinkiest	slobbish
slavered	sleeping	slickly	slinkily	slobby
slavering	sleepless	slickness	slinking	slobs
slavers	sleepover	slicks	slinks	sloe
slavery	sleeps	slid	slinky	sloes
slaves	sleepsuit	slidable	slip	slog
slavey	sleepwalk	slidably	slipover	slogan
slaveys	sleepy	slide	slipovers	sloganeer
slaving	sleet	slider	slippage	slogans
slavish	sleeted	sliders	slippages	slogged
slavishly	sleeting	slides	slipped	slogger
slaw	sleets	sliding	slipper	sloggers
slay	sleety	slight	slippered	slogging
slayer	sleeve	slighted	slippers	slogs
slayers	sleeved	slighter	slippery	sloka
slaying	sleeveen	slightest	slippier	slokas
slays	sleeveens	slighting	slippiest	sloop
sleaze	sleeves	slightish	slipping	sloops
sleazebag	sleeving	slightly	slippy	sloosh
sleazed	sleigh	slights	slips	slooshed
sleazes	sleighed	slily	slipshod	slooshes
sleazier	sleighing	slim	slipstone	slooshing
sleaziest	sleighs	slime	slipware	sloot
sleazily	sleight	slimeball	slipway	sloots
sleazing	slender	slimed	slipways	slop
sleazo	slenderer	slimes	slit	slope
sleazoid	slenderly	slimier	slither	sloped
sleazos	slept	slimiest	slithered	slopes
sleazy	sleuth	slimily	slithers	sloping
sled	sleuthed	sliminess	slithery	slopped
sledded	sleuthing	sliming	slits	sloppier
sledding	sleuths	slimline	slitted	sloppiest
sledge	slew	slimly	slitter	sloppily
sledged	slewed	slimmed	slitters	slopping
sledges	slewing	slimmer	slittier	sloppy
sledging	slews	slimmers	slittiest	slops
sleek	sley	slimmest	slitting	slosh
sleeked	sleys	slimming	slitty	sloshed
sleeker	slice	slimness	sliver	sloshes
sleekest	sliceable	slims	slivered	sloshier
sleeking	sliced	slimy	slivering	sloshiest
sleekly	slicer	sling	slivers	sloshing
sleekness	slicers	slingback	slivovitz	sloshy
sleeks	slices	slinger	slob	slot
sleeky	slicing	slingers	slobbed	slotback
sleep	slick	slinging	slobber	slotbacks

sloth
slothful
sloths
slots
slotted
slotting
slouch
slouched
slouches
slouchier
slouching
slouchy
slough
sloughed
sloughier
sloughing
sloughs
sloughy
sloven
slovenly
slovens
slow
slowcoach
slowdown
slowdowns
slowed
slower
slowest
slowing
slowish
slowly
slowness
slowpoke
slowpokes
slows
slub
slubbed
slubbing
slubs
sludge
sludges
sludgier
sludgiest
sludgy
slue
slued
slues
slug
slugabed
slugabeds

slugfest
slugfests
sluggard
sluggards
slugged
slugger
sluggers
slugging
sluggish
slugs
sluice
sluiced
sluices
sluiceway
sluicing
sluing
sluit
sluits
slum
slumber
slumbered
slumberer
slumbers
slumbrous
slumlord
slumlords
slummed
slummer
slummers
slummier
slummiest
slumming
slummock
slummocks
slummy
slump
slumped
slumping
slumps
slumpy
slums
slung
slunk
slur
slurp
slurped
slurping
slurps
slurpy
slurred

slurries
slurring
slurry
slurs
slush
slushed
slushes
slushier
slushiest
slushing
slushy
slut
sluts
sluttish
sly
slyboots
slyer
slyest
slyly
slyness
slype
slypes

smack
smacked
smacker
smackeroo
smackers
smacking
smacks
small
smaller
smallest
smallish
smallness
smallpox
smalls
smalt
smaltite
smarm
smarmed
smarmier
smarmiest
smarmily
smarming
smarms
smarmy
smart

smarted
smarten
smartened
smartens
smarter
smartest
smarties
smarting
smartish
smartly
smartness
smarts
smartweed
smarty
smash
smashed
smasher
smashers
smashes
smashing
smatter
smatterer
smatters
smaze
smear
smeared
smearer
smearers
smearing
smears
smeary
smectic
smectite
smegma
smell
smellable
smelled
smeller
smellers
smellier
smelliest
smelling
smells
smelly
smelt
smelted
smelter
smelters
smelting
smelts

smetana
smew
smews
smidge
smidgen
smidgens
smidgeon
smidgeons
smidges
smidgin
smidgins
smilax
smilaxes
smile
smiled
smiler
smilers
smiles
smiley
smileys
smilie
smilies
smiling
smilingly
smirch
smirched
smirches
smirching
smirk
smirked
smirker
smirkers
smirkily
smirking
smirks
smirky
smit
smite
smiter
smiters
smites
smith
smithed
smithers
smithery
smithies
smithing
smiths
smithy
smiting

smitten
smock
smocked
smocking
smocks
smog
smoggier
smoggiest
smoggy
smokable
smoke
smokeable
smokebox
smoked
smokeless
smoker
smokers
smokes
smokie
smokier
smokiest
smokily
smokiness
smoking
smoko
smokos
smoky
smolder
smoldered
smolders
smolt
smolts
smooch
smooched
smoocher
smoochers
smooches
smooching
smoochy
smoodge
smoodged
smoodger
smoodgers
smoodges
smoodging
smooge
smooged
smooger
smooges
smooging

smoor
smoored
smooring
smoors
smooth
smoothe
smoothed
smoother
smoothers
smoothes
smoothest
smoothie
smoothies
smoothing
smoothish
smoothly
smooths
smorzando
smote
smother
smothered
smothers
smoulder
smoulders
smriti
smritis
smudge
smudged
smudges
smudgier
smudgiest
smudgily
smudging
smudgy
smug
smugger
smuggest
smuggle
smuggled
smuggler
smugglers
smuggles
smuggling
smugly
smugness
smush
smushed
smushes
smushing
smut

smuts
smutted
smuttier
smuttiest
smuttily
smutting
smutty

| S | N |

snack
snacked
snackette
snacking
snacks
snaffle
snaffled
snaffles
snaffling
snafu
snafued
snafuing
snafus
snag
snagged
snagging
snaggle
snaggled
snaggles
snaggling
snaggy
snags
snail
snailfish
snails
snake
snakebird
snakebite
snaked
snakefish
snakehead
snakepit
snakepits
snakeroot
snakes
snakeskin
snakeweed
snakewood
snakier
snakiest

snakily
snakiness
snaking
snaky
snap
snapped
snapper
snappers
snappier
snappiest
snappily
snapping
snappish
snappy
snaps
snapshot
snapshots
snare
snared
snarer
snarers
snares
snarf
snarfed
snarfing
snarfs
snaring
snark
snarkier
snarkiest
snarks
snarky
snarl
snarled
snarler
snarlers
snarlier
snarliest
snarling
snarls
snarly
snash
snatch
snatched
snatcher
snatchers
snatches
snatching
snatchy
snavel

snaveled
snaveling
snavels
snavle
snavled
snavles
snavling
snavvle
snavvled
snavvles
snavvling
snazzier
snazziest
snazzily
snazzy
sneak
sneakbox
sneaked
sneaker
sneakers
sneakier
sneakiest
sneakily
sneaking
sneaks
sneaky
sneck
snecked
snecking
snecks
sneer
sneered
sneerer
sneerers
sneering
sneers
sneeze
sneezed
sneezer
sneezers
sneezes
sneezing
sneezy
snell
snelled
snelling
snells
snib
snibbed
snibbing

snibs	sniper	snooped	snowball	snubbed
snick	snipers	snooper	snowballs	snubber
snicked	snipes	snoopers	snowbell	snubbers
snicker	sniping	snooping	snowbells	snubbing
snickered	snipped	snoops	snowberry	snubs
snickers	snippet	snoopy	snowbird	snuck
snicket	snippets	snoot	snowbirds	snuff
snickets	snippety	snootful	snowblink	snuffed
snicking	snippier	snootier	snowboard	snuffer
snicks	snippiest	snootiest	snowbound	snuffers
snide	snippily	snootily	snowcap	snuffier
snidely	snipping	snoots	snowcaps	snuffiest
snideness	snippy	snooty	snowcat	snuffing
snidey	snips	snooze	snowcats	snuffle
sniff	snit	snoozed	snowcock	snuffled
sniffed	snitch	snoozer	snowcocks	snuffler
sniffer	snitched	snoozers	snowdrift	snufflers
sniffers	snitches	snoozes	snowdrop	snuffles
sniffier	snitching	snoozier	snowdrops	snuffling
sniffiest	snits	snooziest	snowed	snuffly
sniffily	snivel	snoozing	snowfall	snuffs
sniffing	sniveled	snoozy	snowfalls	snuffy
sniffle	sniveling	snore	snowfield	snug
sniffled	snivelled	snored	snowflake	snugged
sniffler	sniveller	snorer	snowier	snugger
snifflers	snivels	snorers	snowiest	snuggery
sniffles	snob	snores	snowily	snuggest
sniffling	snobbery	snoring	snowiness	snugging
sniffly	snobbier	snorkel	snowing	snuggle
sniffs	snobbiest	snorkeled	snowless	snuggled
sniffy	snobbish	snorkels	snowlike	snuggles
snifter	snobbism	snort	snowline	snuggling
snifters	snobby	snorted	snowlines	snugly
snig	snobs	snorter	snowman	snugness
snigged	snoek	snorters	snowmelt	snugs
snigger	snoeks	snorting	snowmen	
sniggered	snog	snorts	snowpack	
sniggerer	snogged	snot	snowpacks	
sniggers	snogger	snots	snowplow	so
sniggery	snoggers	snotter	snowplows	soak
snigging	snogging	snotters	snows	soakage
sniggle	snogs	snottier	snowscape	soakaway
sniggled	snood	snottiest	snowshoe	soakaways
sniggles	snoods	snottily	snowshoed	soaked
sniggling	snook	snotty	snowshoer	soaker
snigs	snooker	snout	snowshoes	soaking
snip	snookered	snouted	snowstorm	soaks
snipe	snookers	snouts	snowsure	soap
sniped	snooks	snouty	snowy	soapberry
snipefish	snoop	snow	snub	soapbox

soapboxes
soaped
soapfish
soapier
soapiest
soapily
soapiness
soaping
soapless
soaps
soapstone
soapsuds
soapwort
soapworts
soapy
soar
soaraway
soared
soarer
soarers
soaring
soaringly
soars
sob
soba
sobbed
sobbing
sobbingly
sober
sobered
soberer
soberest
sobering
soberly
sobers
sobriety
sobriquet
sobs
soc
soca
socage
soccage
soccer
sociable
sociably
social
socialise
socialism
socialist
socialite

sociality
socialize
socially
socials
societal
societies
society
sociolect
sociology
sociopath
sock
socked
socket
socketed
socketing
sockets
sockeye
sockeyes
socking
socko
socks
socle
socles
sod
soda
sodalite
sodality
sodas
sodbuster
sodded
sodden
soddened
soddening
soddenly
soddens
sodding
sodger
sodgers
sodic
sodium
sodomise
sodomised
sodomises
sodomite
sodomites
sodomitic
sodomize
sodomized
sodomizes
sodomy

sods
soever
sofa
sofas
soffit
soffits
soft
softa
softas
softback
softbacks
softball
softcover
soften
softened
softener
softeners
softening
softens
softer
softest
softie
softies
softish
softly
softness
softshell
software
softwood
softwoods
softy
soggier
soggiest
soggily
sogginess
soggy
soh
sohs
soigné
soignée
soigneur
soil
soiled
soiling
soils
soirée
soirées
sojourn
sojourned
sojourner

sojourns
sokaiya
soke
sokes
sol
sola
solace
solaced
solaces
solacing
solan
solander
solanders
solanine
solanines
solans
solanum
solar
solaria
solarise
solarised
solarises
solarium
solariums
solarize
solarized
solarizes
solatia
solatium
sold
solder
soldered
solderer
solderers
soldering
solders
soldi
soldier
soldiered
soldierly
soldiers
soldiery
soldo
sole
solebar
solebars
solecism
solecisms
soled
solely

solemn
solemner
solemnest
solemnise
solemnity
solemnize
solemnly
solenodon
solenoid
solenoids
soleplate
solera
soleras
soles
soleus
solfatara
solfège
solfèges
solfeggi
solfeggio
soli
solicit
solicited
solicitor
solicits
solid
solidago
solidagos
solidary
solider
solidest
solidi
solidify
solidity
solidly
solidness
solids
solidus
solifuge
solifugid
soliloquy
soling
solipsism
solipsist
solitaire
solitary
soliton
solitons
solitude
solmizate

solo	sometimes	sonometer	soppy	sorrowful
soloed	someway	sonorant	sopranino	sorrowing
soloes	someways	sonority	soprano	sorrows
soloing	somewhat	sonorous	sopranos	sorry
soloist	somewhen	sons	sops	sort
soloists	somewhere	sonship	sora	sortable
solos	somite	sonsie	soras	sortal
sols	somites	sonsier	sorb	sorted
solstice	sommelier	sonsiest	sorbent	sorter
solstices	sommer	sonsy	sorbet	sorters
soluble	somnolent	sook	sorbets	sortes
solunar	son	sooks	sorbitan	sortie
solus	sonar	sool	sorbitol	sortied
solute	sonars	sooled	sorbs	sortieing
solutes	sonata	sooler	sorbus	sorties
solution	sonatas	soolers	sorcerer	sortilege
solutions	sonatina	sooling	sorceress	sorting
solvable	sonatinas	sools	sorcerous	sortition
solvate	sonde	soon	sorcery	sorts
solvated	sondes	soonish	sordid	sorus
solvates	sone	soot	sordidly	sos
solvating	sones	sooted	sordini	sosatie
solvation	song	sooth	sordino	sosaties
solve	songbird	soothe	sordor	sostenuto
solved	songbirds	soothed	sordors	sot
solvency	songbook	soother	sore	sotol
solvent	songbooks	soothers	sorehead	sots
solvents	songololo	soothes	soreheads	sotted
solver	songs	soothing	sorel	sotting
solvers	songsmith	sootier	sorels	sottish
solves	songster	sootiest	sorely	sou
solving	songsters	sootily	soreness	soubise
som	sonic	sootiness	sorer	soubrette
soma	sonically	sooting	sores	souchong
soman	sonicate	soots	sorest	soufflé
somas	sonicated	sooty	sorghum	soufflés
somatic	sonicates	sop	sori	sough
somber	sonics	sophism	sororal	soughed
sombre	sonnet	sophist	sorority	soughing
sombrely	sonneted	sophistic	soroses	soughs
sombrero	sonneteer	sophistry	sorosis	sought
sombreros	sonneting	sophists	sorption	souk
some	sonnets	sophomore	sorrel	soukous
somebody	sonnies	soporific	sorrels	souks
someday	sonny	sopped	sorrier	soul
somehow	sonobuoy	soppier	sorriest	souled
someone	sonobuoys	soppiest	sorrily	soulful
someplace	sonogram	soppily	sorriness	soulfully
something	sonograms	soppiness	sorrow	soulless
sometime	sonograph	sopping	sorrowed	soulmate

soulmates
souls
soulster
soulsters
sound
soundbox
sounded
sounder
sounders
soundest
soundhole
sounding
soundings
soundless
soundly
soundness
sounds
soup
soupçon
soupçons
souped
soupier
soupiest
soupily
soupiness
souping
soups
soupy
sour
source
sourced
sources
sourcing
sourdough
soured
sourer
sourest
souring
sourish
sourly
sourness
sourpuss
sours
soursop
soursops
sourveld
sourwood
sourwoods
sous
souse

soused
souses
sousing
souslik
sousliks
soutache
soutaches
soutane
soutanes
soutar
soutars
souteneur
souter
souters
south
southed
southerly
southern
southing
southings
southpaw
southpaws
souths
southward
souvenir
souvenirs
souvlaki
souvlakia
souvlakis
sov
sovereign
soviet
soviets
sovkhoz
sovkhozes
sovkhozy
sovs
sow
sowback
sowbacks
sowbread
sowbreads
sowed
sowel
sowels
sower
sowers
sowing
sown
sows

sox
soy
soya
soybean
soybeans
sozzled

S P

spa
space
spaced
spaceman
spacemen
spaceport
spacer
spacers
spaces
spaceship
spacesuit
spacey
spacial
spacier
spaciest
spacing
spacings
spacious
spackle
spackled
spackles
spackling
spacy
spade
spaded
spadefish
spadefoot
spadeful
spadefuls
spades
spadework
spadices
spadille
spadilles
spading
spadix
spae
spaed
spaes
spaetzle
spaewife

spaghetti
spahi
spahis
spaing
spake
spall
spalled
spalling
spalls
spalpeen
spalpeens
spalted
spam
spammed
spammer
spammers
spamming
spams
span
spandex
spandrel
spandrels
spang
spangle
spangled
spangles
spanglier
spangling
spangly
spaniel
spaniels
spank
spanked
spanker
spankers
spanking
spankings
spanks
spanned
spanner
spanners
spanning
spans
spanspek
spanspeks
spansule
spansules
spar
sparable
sparables

sparagmos
sparaxis
spare
spared
sparely
spareness
sparer
spares
sparest
sparge
sparged
sparger
spargers
sparges
sparging
sparid
sparids
sparing
sparingly
spark
sparked
sparking
sparkish
sparkle
sparkled
sparkler
sparklers
sparkles
sparkless
sparkling
sparkly
sparks
sparky
sparling
sparlings
sparred
sparring
sparrow
sparrows
sparry
spars
sparse
sparsely
sparser
sparsest
sparsity
spartan
spartina
spartinas
spas

spasm	speaks	spected	spence	spices
spasmodic	spear	specter	spencer	spicey
spasms	speared	specters	spencers	spicier
spastic	spearfish	specting	spences	spiciest
spastics	speargun	spectra	spend	spicily
spat	spearguns	spectral	spendable	spiciness
spate	spearhead	spectre	spender	spicing
spates	spearing	spectres	spenders	spics
spathe	spearman	spectrum	spending	spicular
spathes	spearmen	spects	spends	spiculate
spatial	spearmint	specula	spent	spicule
spatially	spears	specular	sperm	spicules
spats	spearwort	speculate	spermatic	spicy
spatted	spec	speculum	spermatid	spider
spatter	speccy	sped	spermine	spidered
spattered	special	speech	spermines	spidering
spatters	specially	speeches	sperms	spiderish
spatting	specials	speechify	spew	spiderman
spatula	specialty	speed	spewed	spidermen
spatulas	speciate	speedball	spewer	spiders
spatulate	speciated	speedboat	spewers	spiderweb
spätzle	speciates	speeded	spewing	spidery
spavin	specie	speeder	spews	spied
spavined	species	speeders	sphagnum	spiel
spavins	specific	speedier	sphene	spieled
spawn	specifics	speediest	sphenoid	spieler
spawned	specified	speedily	sphenoids	spielers
spawner	specifier	speeding	spheral	spieling
spawners	specifies	speedo	sphere	spiels
spawning	specify	speedos	sphered	spies
spawns	specimen	speeds	spheres	spiff
spay	specimens	speedster	spheric	spiffed
spayed	specious	speedway	spherical	spiffier
spaying	speck	speedways	sphering	spiffiest
spays	specked	speedwell	spheroid	spiffily
spaz	specking	speedy	spheroids	spiffing
spaza	speckle	speiss	spherular	spiffs
spazed	speckled	spekboom	spherule	spiffy
spazes	speckles	spekbooms	spherules	spignel
spazing	speckless	spell	sphincter	spignels
spazz	speckling	spellbind	sphingid	spigot
spazzed	specks	spelled	sphinx	spigots
spazzes	specky	speller	sphinxes	spike
spazzing	specs	spellers	spic	spiked
speak	spect	spelling	spica	spikelet
speakable	spectacle	spellings	spicas	spikelets
speakeasy	spectate	spells	spiccato	spikemoss
speaker	spectated	spelt	spice	spikenard
speakers	spectates	spelter	spicebush	spikes
speaking	spectator	spelunker	spiced	spikier

spikiest	spinneret	spitball	splenetic	splurted
spikily	spinners	spitballs	splenial	splurting
spikiness	spinney	spite	splenic	splurts
spiking	spinneys	spited	splenii	splutter
spiky	spinning	spiteful	splenitis	splutters
spile	spinose	spites	splenium	spod
spiled	spinous	spitfire	splenius	spoddier
spiles	spins	spitfires	splice	spoddiest
spiling	spinster	spiting	spliced	spoddy
spilite	spinsters	spits	splicer	spodic
spilitic	spinto	spitted	splicers	spodosol
spill	spintos	spitter	splices	spodosols
spillage	spinulose	spitters	splicing	spods
spillages	spiny	spitting	spliff	spodumene
spilled	spiracle	spittle	spliffs	spoil
spiller	spiracles	spittly	spline	spoilage
spillers	spiraea	spittoon	splined	spoiled
spillikin	spiraeas	spittoons	splines	spoiler
spilling	spiral	spitty	splining	spoilers
spillover	spiraled	spitz	splint	spoiling
spills	spiraling	spitzes	splinted	spoils
spillway	spiralled	spiv	splinter	spoilsman
spillways	spirally	spivs	splinters	spoilsmen
spilt	spirals	spivvish	splintery	spoilt
spilth	spirant	spivvy	splinting	spoke
spin	spirants	splake	splints	spoked
spinach	spire	splakes	split	spoken
spinachy	spirea	splash	splits	spokes
spinal	spireas	splashed	splitter	spokesman
spinally	spired	splashes	splitters	spokesmen
spindle	spires	splashing	splitting	spoliator
spindles	spirilla	splashy	splittism	spondaic
spindlier	spirillum	splat	splittist	spondee
spindly	spirit	splats	splodge	spondees
spindrift	spirited	splatted	splodges	spondulix
spine	spiriting	splatter	splodgier	sponge
spined	spiritism	splatters	splodgy	sponged
spinel	spiritist	splatting	splosh	spongeing
spineless	spiritous	splay	sploshed	sponger
spinels	spirits	splayed	sploshes	spongers
spines	spiritual	splaying	sploshing	sponges
spinet	spiritus	splays	splotch	spongier
spinetail	spirogyra	spleen	splotched	spongiest
spinets	spirt	spleenful	splotches	spongily
spinier	spirted	spleens	splotchy	spongin
spiniest	spirting	splendent	splurge	sponging
spinifex	spirts	splendid	splurged	spongy
spininess	spirulina	splendor	splurges	sponson
spinnaker	spiry	splendors	splurging	sponsons
spinner	spit	splendour	splurt	sponsor

sponsored	sporrans	spraing	springers	sprues
sponsors	sport	spraining	springes	spruik
spoof	sported	sprains	springier	spruiked
spoofed	sporter	spraint	springily	spruiker
spoofer	sporters	spraints	springing	spruikers
spoofers	sportier	sprang	springlet	spruiking
spoofery	sportiest	sprat	springs	spruiks
spoofing	sportif	sprats	springy	spruit
spoofs	sportifs	spratted	sprinkle	spruits
spook	sportily	spratting	sprinkled	sprung
spooked	sporting	sprauncy	sprinkler	spry
spookier	sportive	sprawl	sprinkles	spryer
spookiest	sports	sprawled	sprint	spryest
spookily	sportsman	sprawling	sprinted	spryly
spooking	sportsmen	sprawls	sprinter	spryness
spooks	sportster	spray	sprinters	spud
spooky	sporty	sprayable	sprinting	spudded
spool	sporulate	spraydeck	sprints	spudding
spooled	spot	sprayed	sprit	spuds
spooling	spotlamp	sprayer	sprite	spue
spools	spotlamps	sprayers	spritely	spued
spoon	spotless	spraying	sprites	spues
spoonbill	spotlight	sprays	sprits	spuing
spooned	spotlit	spread	spritsail	spumante
spooner	spots	spreader	spritz	spume
spooners	spotted	spreaders	spritzed	spumed
spoonful	spotter	spreading	spritzer	spumes
spoonfuls	spotters	spreads	spritzers	spumier
spoonier	spottier	spree	spritzes	spumiest
spoonies	spottiest	spreed	spritzing	spuming
spooniest	spottily	spreeing	sprocket	spumone
spoonily	spotting	sprees	sprockets	spumoni
spooning	spotty	spreeu	sprog	spumous
spoons	spousal	spreeus	sprogged	spumy
spoonworm	spouse	spreite	sprogging	spun
spoony	spouses	spreiten	sprogs	spunk
spoor	spout	spreites	sprosser	spunkier
spoored	spouted	sprew	sprossers	spunkiest
spoorer	spouter	sprews	sprout	spunkily
spoorers	spouters	sprig	sprouted	spunks
spooring	spouting	sprigged	sprouting	spunky
spoors	spoutless	spriggier	sprouts	spur
sporadic	spouts	sprigging	spruce	spurfowl
sporangia	spraddle	spriggy	spruced	spurfowls
spore	spraddled	sprightly	sprucely	spurge
spores	spraddles	sprigs	sprucer	spurges
sporocyst	sprag	spring	sprucers	spurious
sporogony	sprags	springbok	spruces	spurless
sporozoan	sprain	springe	sprucing	spurn
sporran	sprained	springer	sprue	spurned

spurner
spurners
spurning
spurns
spurred
spurrey
spurreys
spurrier
spurriers
spurries
spurring
spurry
spurs
spurt
spurted
spurting
spurts
sputnik
sputniks
sputter
sputtered
sputterer
sputters
sputum
spy
spyglass
spyhole
spyholes
spying
spymaster

S Q

squab
squabble
squabbled
squabbler
squabbles
squabs
squad
squaddie
squaddies
squaddy
squadron
squadrons
squads
squalene
squalid
squalidly
squall

squalled
squalling
squalls
squally
squalor
squamate
squamates
squamosal
squamous
squamule
squamules
squander
squanders
square
squared
squarely
squarer
squarers
squares
squarest
squaring
squarish
squark
squarks
squash
squashed
squashes
squashier
squashily
squashing
squashy
squat
squatly
squatness
squats
squatt
squatted
squatter
squatters
squattest
squatting
squaw
squawfish
squawk
squawked
squawker
squawkers
squawking
squawks
squawroot

squaws
squeak
squeaked
squeaker
squeakers
squeakier
squeakily
squeaking
squeaks
squeaky
squeal
squealed
squealer
squealers
squealing
squeals
squeamish
squeegee
squeegeed
squeegees
squeeze
squeezed
squeezer
squeezers
squeezes
squeezing
squeezy
squelch
squelched
squelcher
squelches
squelchy
squib
squibbed
squibbing
squibs
squid
squidded
squidding
squidge
squidged
squidges
squidgier
squidging
squidgy
squids
squiffed
squiffier
squiffy
squiggle

squiggled
squiggles
squiggly
squill
squillion
squills
squinch
squinched
squinches
squint
squinted
squinter
squinters
squinting
squints
squinty
squire
squired
squiredom
squireen
squireens
squires
squiring
squirl
squirls
squirm
squirmed
squirmer
squirmers
squirming
squirms
squirmy
squirrel
squirrels
squirt
squirted
squirter
squirters
squirting
squirts
squish
squished
squishes
squishier
squishing
squishy
squit
squits
squitters
squiz

squized
squizes
squizing

S T

stab
stabbed
stabber
stabbers
stabbing
stabbings
stabile
stabiles
stabilise
stability
stabilize
stable
stabled
stableful
stableman
stablemen
stabler
stables
stablest
stabling
stablish
stably
stabs
staccato
staccatos
stack
stackable
stacked
stacker
stackers
stacking
stacks
stackyard
staddle
staddles
stadia
stadium
stadiums
staff
staffage
staffed
staffer
staffers
staffing

staffroom	stairwell	stampeder	star	started
staffs	staithe	stampedes	starboard	starter
stag	staithes	stamper	starburst	starters
stage	stake	stampers	starch	starting
stageable	staked	stamping	starched	startle
staged	staker	stamps	starcher	startled
stagehand	stakers	stance	starchers	startler
stager	stakes	stances	starches	startlers
stagers	staking	stanch	starchier	startles
stages	stale	stanched	starchily	startling
stagey	staled	stanches	starching	starts
stagged	stalely	stanching	starchy	starve
stagger	stalemate	stanchion	stardom	starved
staggered	staleness	stand	stardust	starves
staggerer	staler	standard	stare	starving
staggers	stales	standards	stared	starwort
stagging	stalest	standby	starer	starworts
staghorn	staling	standbys	starers	stash
staghorns	stalk	standee	stares	stashed
staghound	stalked	standees	starfish	stashes
stagier	stalker	stander	starfruit	stashing
stagiest	stalkers	standers	stargaze	stasis
stagily	stalkier	standing	stargazed	stat
staginess	stalkiest	standings	stargazer	statable
staging	stalking	standish	stargazes	statant
stagnancy	stalkless	standout	staring	state
stagnant	stalks	standouts	stark	stated
stagnate	stalky	standpipe	starker	statehood
stagnated	stall	stands	starkers	stateless
stagnates	stallage	stanhope	starkest	statelet
stags	stalled	stanhopes	starkly	statelets
stagy	stalling	stank	starkness	statelier
staid	stallion	stannary	starless	stately
staidly	stallions	stannic	starlet	statement
staidness	stalls	stannous	starlets	stater
stain	stalwart	stanza	starlight	stateroom
stainable	stalwarts	stanzaed	starlike	staters
stained	stamen	stanzaic	starling	states
stainer	stamens	stanzas	starlings	stateside
stainers	stamina	stapedial	starlit	statesman
staining	staminate	stapelia	starred	statesmen
stainless	staminode	stapes	starrier	statewide
stains	stammer	staph	starriest	static
stair	stammered	staphs	starrily	statice
staircase	stammerer	staple	starring	statices
stairhead	stammers	stapled	starry	statics
stairlift	stamp	stapler	stars	stating
stairs	stamped	staplers	starship	station
stairway	stampede	staples	starships	stationed
stairways	stampeded	stapling	start	stationer

stations	steady	steepen	stems	sterility
statism	steadying	steepened	stemware	sterilize
statist	steak	steepens	stench	sterlet
statistic	steaks	steeper	stenches	sterlets
statists	steal	steepest	stencil	sterling
stative	stealer	steeping	stenciled	stern
statocyst	stealers	steepish	stencils	sterna
statolith	stealing	steeple	steno	sternal
stator	steals	steepled	stenos	sterned
stators	stealth	steeples	stenosed	sterner
stats	stealthy	steeply	stenoses	sternest
statuary	steam	steepness	stenosing	sternite
statue	steamboat	steeps	stenosis	sternly
statued	steamed	steer	stenotic	sternmost
statues	steamer	steerable	stenotype	sternness
statuette	steamers	steerage	stent	sternpost
stature	steamie	steered	stented	sterns
statured	steamier	steerer	stenter	sternum
status	steamies	steerers	stenting	sternums
statuses	steamiest	steering	stentor	sternway
statute	steamily	steers	stentors	steroid
statutes	steaming	steersman	stents	steroidal
statutory	steamroll	steersmen	step	steroids
staunch	steams	steeve	stepchild	sterol
staunched	steamy	steeved	stepdad	sterols
stauncher	stearate	steeves	stepdads	stet
staunches	stearates	steeving	stepmum	stets
staunchly	stearin	stegosaur	stepmums	stetted
stave	steatite	stein	steppe	stetting
staved	steatitic	steinbock	stepped	steups
staves	steatosis	steinbok	stepper	steupsed
staving	steed	steinboks	steppes	steupses
stay	steeds	steins	stepping	steupsing
stayed	steel	stela	steps	stevedore
stayer	steeled	stelae	stepson	stew
stayers	steelhead	stelar	stepsons	steward
staying	steelier	stele	stepwise	stewarded
stays	steeliest	steles	steradian	stewardry
staysail	steeling	stellar	sterane	stewards
staysails	steels	stellate	steranes	stewartry
stead	steelwork	stellated	stere	stewbum
steadfast	steely	stellium	stereo	stewbums
steadied	steelyard	stem	stereos	stewed
steadier	steen	stemless	steres	stewing
steadiers	steenbok	stemma	steric	stewpot
steadies	steenboks	stemmata	sterigma	stewpots
steadiest	steenbras	stemmed	sterilant	stews
steadily	steenbuck	stemming	sterile	sthenic
steading	steep	stemple	sterilely	stibnite
steadings	steeped	stemples	sterilise	stick

stickball	stilb	stinko	stoat	stoics
sticker	stilbene	stinkpot	stoats	stoke
stickers	stilbs	stinkpots	stob	stoked
stickier	stile	stinks	stobs	stokehold
stickiest	stiles	stinkweed	stock	stokehole
stickily	stiletto	stinkwood	stockade	stoker
sticking	stilettos	stinky	stockaded	stokers
stickler	still	stint	stockades	stokes
sticklers	stillage	stinted	stocked	stoking
sticklike	stillages	stinting	stocker	stokvel
stickpin	stillborn	stints	stockers	stokvels
stickpins	stilled	stipe	stockfish	stole
sticks	stiller	stipend	stockier	stolen
stickseed	stillest	stipends	stockiest	stoles
stickum	stilling	stipes	stockily	stolid
stickums	stillness	stipitate	stockinet	stolidity
stickweed	stills	stipites	stocking	stolidly
sticky	stilly	stipple	stockings	stollen
stiction	stilt	stippled	stockist	stollens
stied	stilted	stippler	stockists	stolon
sties	stiltedly	stipplers	stockless	stolonate
stifado	stilts	stipples	stocklist	stolons
stiff	stimulant	stippling	stockman	stoma
stiffed	stimulate	stipular	stockmen	stomach
stiffen	stimuli	stipulate	stockpile	stomached
stiffened	stimulus	stipule	stockpot	stomacher
stiffener	sting	stipules	stockpots	stomaches
stiffens	stingaree	stir	stockroom	stomachic
stiffer	stinge	stirabout	stocks	stomal
stiffest	stinger	stirk	stocktake	stomas
stiffie	stingers	stirks	stocky	stomata
stiffies	stinges	stirred	stockyard	stomatal
stiffing	stingier	stirrer	stodge	stomatas
stiffish	stingiest	stirrers	stodgier	stomate
stiffly	stingily	stirring	stodgiest	stomates
stiffness	stinging	stirrings	stodgily	stomp
stiffs	stingless	stirrup	stodgy	stomped
stifftail	stingray	stirrups	stoep	stomper
stiffy	stingrays	stirs	stoeps	stompers
stifle	stings	stitch	stog	stompie
stifled	stingy	stitched	stogged	stompies
stifler	stink	stitcher	stogging	stomping
stiflers	stinkard	stitchers	stogie	stomps
stifles	stinkards	stitchery	stogies	stompy
stifling	stinker	stitches	stogs	stone
stigma	stinkers	stitching	stogy	stonechat
stigmaria	stinkhorn	stiver	stoic	stonecrop
stigmas	stinkier	stivers	stoical	stoned
stigmata	stinkiest	stoa	stoically	stonefish
stigmatic	stinking	stoas	stoicism	stonefly

stoneless	stoped	storming	strafing	strategic
stoner	stopes	storms	straggle	strategy
stones	stopgap	stormy	straggled	strath
stonewall	stopgaps	story	straggler	straths
stoneware	stoping	storybook	straggles	stratify
stonewash	stopover	storyline	straggly	stratum
stonework	stopovers	stot	straight	stratus
stonewort	stoppable	stotin	straights	stravage
stonier	stoppage	stotinka	strain	stravaged
stoniest	stoppages	stotinki	strained	stravages
stonily	stopped	stots	strainer	stravaig
stoniness	stopper	stotted	strainers	stravaigs
stoning	stoppered	stotties	straining	straw
stonk	stoppers	stotting	strains	straws
stonked	stopping	stotty	strait	strawy
stonker	stopple	stoup	straiten	stray
stonkered	stoppled	stoups	straitens	strayed
stonkers	stopples	stour	straitly	strayer
stonking	stoppling	stoury	straits	strayers
stonks	stops	stoush	strake	straying
stony	stopwatch	stoushed	strakes	strays
stood	storable	stoushes	stramash	streak
stooge	storage	stoushing	strand	streaked
stooged	storax	stout	stranded	streaker
stooges	storaxes	stouter	stranding	streakers
stooging	store	stoutest	strands	streakier
stook	stored	stoutish	strange	streakily
stooked	storeman	stoutly	strangely	streaking
stooking	storemen	stoutness	stranger	streaks
stooks	storer	stouts	strangers	streaky
stool	storeroom	stove	strangest	stream
stoolball	storers	stoved	strangle	streamed
stooled	stores	stovepipe	strangled	streamer
stoolie	storey	stoves	strangler	streamers
stoolies	storeyed	stovies	strangles	streaming
stooling	storeys	stoving	strangury	streamlet
stools	storiated	stow	strap	streams
stoop	storied	stowage	strapless	streel
stooped	stories	stowaway	strapline	streeled
stooping	storing	stowaways	strappado	streeling
stoops	stork	stowed	strapped	streelish
stoor	storks	stowing	strapper	streels
stop	storm	stows	strappers	street
stopband	stormcock	straddle	strapping	streetcar
stopbands	stormed	straddled	strappy	streeted
stopbank	stormer	straddler	straps	streets
stopbanks	stormers	straddles	strapwork	strength
stopcock	stormier	straddles	strata	strengths
stopcocks	stormiest	strafe	stratagem	strenuous
stope	stormily	strafed	stratal	strep
		strafes		

streps	striding	strobed	strudel	studied
stress	stridor	strobes	strudels	studiedly
stressed	stridors	strobili	struggle	studies
stresses	strife	strobilus	struggled	studio
stressful	strigil	strobing	struggler	studios
stressing	strigils	strode	struggles	studious
stressor	strigose	stroke	strum	studs
stressors	strike	stroked	struma	study
stretch	strikeout	strokes	strumae	studying
stretched	striker	stroking	strummed	stuff
stretcher	strikers	stroll	strummer	stuffed
stretches	strikes	strolled	strummers	stuffer
stretchy	striking	stroller	strumming	stuffier
stretti	strimmer	strollers	strumous	stuffiest
stretto	strimmers	strolling	strumpet	stuffily
streusel	strine	strolls	strumpets	stuffing
streusels	strines	stroma	strums	stuffings
strew	string	stromal	strung	stuffs
strewed	stringed	stromata	strut	stuffy
strewer	stringent	stromatic	struts	stultify
strewers	stringer	strong	struth	stum
strewing	stringers	strongbox	strutted	stumble
strewn	stringier	stronger	strutter	stumbled
strews	stringily	strongest	strutters	stumbler
strewth	stringing	strongish	strutting	stumblers
stria	strings	strongly	stub	stumbles
striae	stringy	strongman	stubbed	stumbling
striata	strip	strongmen	stubbier	stumer
striatal	stripe	strongyle	stubbies	stumers
striate	striped	strontia	stubbiest	stummed
striated	stripes	strontium	stubbily	stumming
striates	stripey	strop	stubbing	stump
striating	stripier	strophe	stubble	stumped
striation	stripiest	strophes	stubbled	stumper
striatum	striping	strophic	stubbles	stumpers
stricken	stripling	stropped	stubbly	stumpier
strickle	stripped	stroppier	stubborn	stumpiest
strickles	stripper	stroppily	stubby	stumpily
strict	strippers	stropping	stubs	stumping
stricter	stripping	stroppy	stucco	stumpnose
strictest	strips	strops	stuccoed	stumps
strictly	stripy	stroud	stuccoes	stumpy
stricture	strive	strove	stuccoing	stums
stridden	strived	strow	stuck	stun
stride	striven	strowed	stud	stung
stridency	striver	strowing	studded	stunk
strident	strivers	strown	studding	stunned
strider	strives	strows	student	stunner
striders	striving	struck	students	stunners
strides	strobe	structure	studenty	stunning

stuns	stylets	suavities	subgenus	submucosa
stunsail	styli	suavity	subgroup	subnet
stunsails	styling	sub	subgroups	subnets
stunt	stylise	subacid	subhuman	subnormal
stunted	stylised	subacute	subjacent	suborder
stunting	stylises	subadult	subject	suborders
stuntman	stylish	subadults	subjected	suborn
stuntmen	stylishly	subaerial	subjects	suborned
stunts	stylising	subagency	subjoin	suborner
stupa	stylist	subagent	subjoined	suborners
stupas	stylistic	subagents	subjoins	suborning
stupe	stylists	subalpine	subjugate	suborns
stuped	stylite	subaltern	subjunct	suboscine
stupefied	stylites	subarctic	subjuncts	suboxide
stupefier	stylize	subatomic	sublate	suboxides
stupefies	stylized	subbed	sublated	subphyla
stupefy	stylizes	subbing	sublates	subphylum
stupes	stylizing	subclass	sublating	subpoena
stupid	stylo	subcostal	sublation	subpoenas
stupider	stylobate	subdeacon	sublease	subregion
stupidest	styloid	subdivide	subleased	subrogate
stupidity	stylolite	subduable	subleases	subs
stupidly	stylopid	subduct	sublet	subsample
stuping	stylopids	subducted	sublethal	subscribe
stupor	stylops	subducts	sublets	subscript
stuporous	stylopses	subdue	sublimate	subsea
stupors	stylos	subdued	sublime	subsellia
sturdied	stylus	subdues	sublimed	subserve
sturdier	styluses	subduing	sublimely	subserved
sturdiest	stymie	subdural	sublimer	subserves
sturdily	stymied	subedit	sublimes	subset
sturdy	stymieing	subedited	sublimest	subsets
sturgeon	stymies	subeditor	subliming	subshrub
sturgeons	stymying	subedits	sublimity	subshrubs
stutter	styptic	suberin	sublunar	subside
stuttered	styptics	suberise	sublunary	subsided
stutterer	styrax	suberised	submarine	subsides
stutters	styraxes	suberises	submenu	subsidies
sty	styrene	suberize	submenus	subsiding
stye	styrofoam	suberized	submerge	subsidise
styes		suberizes	submerged	subsidize
stying		subfamily	submerges	subsidy
stylar		S U	subfloor	submerse	subsist
style	suasion	subfloors	submersed	subsisted
styled	suasive	subform	submerses	subsists
styleless	suave	subforms	submit	subsoil
styler	suavely	subframe	submits	subsoiled
stylers	suaveness	subframes	submitted	subsoiler
styles	suaver	subfusc	submitter	subsoils
stylet	suavest	subgenera	submodify	subsong

subsonic	subvented	suckers	suety	suiciding
subspace	subvents	suckhole	suffer	suing
subspaces	subvert	suckholed	suffered	suint
substage	subverted	suckholes	sufferer	suit
substages	subverter	sucking	sufferers	suitable
substance	subverts	suckle	suffering	suitably
substorm	subvocal	suckled	suffers	suitcase
substorms	subway	suckler	suffice	suitcases
substrata	subways	sucklers	sufficed	suite
substrate	subwoofer	suckles	suffices	suited
subsume	succah	suckling	sufficing	suites
subsumed	succahs	sucklings	suffix	suiting
subsumes	succeed	sucks	suffixed	suitor
subsuming	succeeded	sucky	suffixes	suitors
subsystem	succeeder	sucrase	suffixing	suits
subtenant	succeeds	sucrases	suffocate	suji
subtend	succentor	sucre	suffragan	suk
subtended	success	sucres	suffrage	sukh
subtends	successes	sucrier	suffrages	sukhs
subtense	successor	sucriers	suffragi	sukiyaki
subtenses	succinate	sucrose	suffragis	sukkah
subtext	succinct	suction	suffuse	sukkahs
subtexts	succor	suctioned	suffused	suks
subtilise	succored	suctions	suffuses	sulcate
subtilize	succories	suctorial	suffusing	sulci
subtitle	succoring	sudaria	suffusion	sulcus
subtitled	succors	sudarium	sug	sulfa
subtitles	succory	sudatoria	sugan	sulfate
subtle	succotash	sudd	sugans	sulfates
subtler	succour	sudden	sugar	sulfide
subtlest	succoured	suddenly	sugarbird	sulfides
subtlety	succours	sudds	sugared	sulfite
subtly	succubi	sudorific	sugaring	sulfites
subtonic	succubous	suds	sugarless	sulfonate
subtonics	succubus	sudsed	sugarloaf	sulfone
subtopia	succulent	sudser	sugarplum	sulfones
subtopian	succumb	sudsers	sugars	sulfonic
subtopias	succumbed	sudses	sugary	sulfonics
subtotal	succumbs	sudsing	sugged	sulfonyl
subtotals	succursal	sudsy	suggest	sulfur
subtract	succuss	sue	suggested	sulfured
subtracts	succussed	sued	suggester	sulfuric
subulate	succusses	suede	suggests	sulfuring
subunit	such	suedehead	sugging	sulfurous
subunits	suchlike	suer	sugs	sulfurs
suburb	suck	suers	suh	sulk
suburban	sucked	suerte	suicidal	sulked
suburbia	sucker	suertes	suicide	sulker
suburbs	suckered	sues	suicided	sulkers
subvent	suckering	suet	suicides	sulkier

sulkies	summa	sunbeds	sunlight	superacid
sulkiest	summae	sunbelt	sunlike	superadd
sulkily	summand	sunbelts	sunlit	superadds
sulkiness	summaries	sunbird	sunned	superb
sulking	summarily	sunbirds	sunnier	superbike
sulks	summarise	sunblind	sunnies	superbly
sulky	summarize	sunblinds	sunniest	superbug
sull	summary	sunblock	sunnily	superbugs
sullage	summat	sunblocks	sunniness	supercar
sulled	summation	sunburn	sunning	supercars
sullen	summative	sunburned	sunny	supercede
sullenly	summed	sunburns	sunray	supercoil
sullied	summer	sunburnt	sunrays	supercool
sullies	summered	sunburst	sunrise	superego
sulling	summering	sunbursts	sunrises	superegos
sulls	summers	suncream	sunroof	superette
sully	summery	suncreams	sunroofs	superfine
sullying	summing	sundae	sunroom	superfly
sulpha	summit	sundaes	sunrooms	supergene
sulphate	summiteer	sunder	suns	superglue
sulphates	summits	sundered	sunscreen	superheat
sulphide	summon	sundering	sunset	superhero
sulphides	summoned	sunders	sunsets	superhet
sulphite	summoner	sundew	sunshade	superior
sulphites	summoners	sundews	sunshades	superiors
sulphone	summoning	sundial	sunshine	superius
sulphones	summons	sundials	sunshiny	superman
sulphonyl	summonsed	sundown	sunspace	supermen
sulphur	summonses	sundowner	sunspaces	supermini
sulphured	sumo	sundress	sunspot	supernal
sulphuric	sumos	sundries	sunspots	supernova
sulphurs	sump	sundrops	sunstar	superpose
sulphury	sumph	sundry	sunstars	supersede
sultan	sumphs	sunfast	sunstone	superset
sultana	sumps	sunfish	sunstones	superstar
sultanas	sumpter	sunfishes	sunstroke	supertax
sultanate	sumpters	sunflower	sunsuit	supervene
sultans	sumptuary	sung	sunsuits	supervise
sultrier	sumptuous	sungazer	suntan	supinate
sultriest	sums	sungazers	suntaning	supinated
sultrily	sun	sungrebe	suntanned	supinates
sultry	sunbath	sungrebes	suntans	supinator
sulu	sunbathe	suni	suntrap	supine
sulus	sunbathed	sunis	suntraps	supinely
sum	sunbather	sunk	sunup	supped
sumac	sunbathes	sunken	sunward	supper
sumach	sunbaths	sunlamp	sunwards	suppers
sumaches	sunbeam	sunlamps	sunyata	supping
sumacs	sunbeams	sunless	sup	supplant
sumi	sunbed		super	supplants

supple
suppled
supplely
suppler
supples
supplest
suppliant
supplied
supplier
suppliers
supplies
suppling
supply
supplying
support
supported
supporter
supports
suppose
supposed
supposes
supposing
suppress
suppurate
supra
supremacy
supreme
supremely
supremes
supremo
supremos
supremum
supremums
sups
suq
suqs
sura
surah
surahi
surahis
surahs
sural
suramin
suras
surcease
surceased
surceases
surcharge
surcingle

surcoat
surcoats
surd
surds
sure
surely
sureness
surer
surest
sureties
surety
surf
surface
surfaced
surfacer
surfacers
surfaces
surfacing
surfbird
surfbirds
surfboard
surfed
surfeit
surfeited
surfeits
surfer
surfers
surficial
surfie
surfier
surfies
surfiest
surfing
surfperch
surfs
surfy
surge
surged
surgeon
surgeons
surgeries
surgery
surges
surgical
surging
suricate
suricates
surlier
surliest

surlily
surliness
surly
surmise
surmised
surmises
surmising
surmount
surmounts
surmullet
surname
surnamed
surnames
surnaming
surpass
surpassed
surpasses
surplice
surpliced
surplices
surplus
surpluses
surprise
surprised
surprises
surra
surreal
surreally
surrender
surrey
surreys
surrogacy
surrogate
surround
surrounds
surtax
surtitle
surtitled
surtitles
surtout
surtouts
survey
surveyed
surveying
surveyor
surveyors
surveys
survival
survivals
survive

survived
survives
surviving
survivor
survivors
sus
sushi
suslik
susliks
suspect
suspected
suspects
suspend
suspended
suspender
suspends
suspense
suspicion
suspire
suspired
suspires
suspiring
suss
sussed
susses
sussing
sustain
sustained
sustainer
sustains
susurrus
sutler
sutlers
sutra
sutras
suttee
suttees
sutural
suture
sutured
sutures
suturing
suzerain
suzerains

svelte
svelter
sveltest

swab
swabbed
swabbie
swabbies
swabbing
swabs
swacked
swaddle
swaddled
swaddles
swaddling
swadeshi
swag
swage
swaged
swages
swagged
swagger
swaggered
swaggerer
swaggers
swagging
swaging
swagman
swagmen
swags
swain
swains
swale
swales
swallow
swallowed
swallower
swallows
swam
swami
swamis
swamp
swamped
swamper
swamphen
swamphens
swampier
swampiest
swamping
swampland
swamps

swampy	swastika	sweepings	swiftlet	swinges
swan	swastikas	sweeps	swiftlets	swingier
swank	swat	sweet	swiftly	swingiest
swanked	swatch	sweetcorn	swiftness	swinging
swankier	swatches	sweeten	swifts	swingle
swankiest	swath	sweetened	swifty	swingled
swankily	swathe	sweetener	swig	swingles
swanking	swathed	sweetens	swigged	swingling
swankpot	swather	sweeter	swigger	swings
swankpots	swathes	sweetest	swiggers	swingy
swanks	swathing	sweetie	swigging	swinish
swanky	swaths	sweeties	swigs	swinishly
swanlike	swats	sweeting	swill	swipe
swanned	swatted	sweetings	swilled	swiped
swannery	swatting	sweetish	swiller	swiper
swanning	sway	sweetlip	swillers	swipers
swans	swayback	sweetlips	swilling	swipes
swansdown	swayed	sweetly	swills	swiping
swansong	swaying	sweetmeal	swim	swipple
swansongs	sways	sweetmeat	swimmable	swipples
swap	swear	sweetness	swimmer	swirl
swapfile	swearer	sweets	swimmeret	swirled
swapfiles	swearers	sweetsop	swimmers	swirlier
swappable	swearing	sweetsops	swimming	swirliest
swapped	swears	sweetveld	swims	swirling
swapper	sweat	swell	swimsuit	swirls
swappers	sweatband	swelled	swimsuits	swirly
swapping	sweated	swelling	swimwear	swish
swaps	sweater	swellings	swindle	swished
swaption	sweaters	swells	swindled	swisher
sward	sweatier	swelter	swindler	swishes
swarded	sweatiest	sweltered	swindlers	swishest
swards	sweatily	swelters	swindles	swishier
sware	sweating	swept	swindling	swishiest
swarf	sweats	swerve	swine	swishing
swarm	sweatshop	swerved	swineherd	swishy
swarmed	sweatsuit	swerver	swines	switch
swarmer	sweaty	swervers	swing	switched
swarmers	swede	swerves	swingback	switcher
swarming	swedes	swerving	swingbies	switchers
swarms	swedge	swidden	swingbin	switches
swart	swedged	swiddened	swingbins	switching
swarthier	swedges	swiddens	swingboat	swither
swarthily	swedging	swies	swingby	swithered
swarthy	sweep	swift	swinge	swithers
swash	sweepback	swifter	swinged	swive
swashed	sweeper	swiftest	swingeing	swived
swashes	sweepers	swiftie	swinger	swivel
swashing	sweeping	swifties	swingers	swiveled

swiveling
swivelled
swivels
swives
swivet
swiving
swiz
swizes
swizz
swizzes
swizzle
swizzled
swizzles
swizzling
swollen
swoon
swooned
swooning
swoons
swoop
swooped
swooping
swoops
swoosh
swooshed
swooshes
swooshing
swop
swoppable
swopped
swopper
swopping
swops
sword
swordbill
swordfish
swordplay
swords
swordsman
swordsmen
swordtail
swore
sworn
swot
swots
swotted
swotting
swotty
swum

swung
swy

S Y

sybarite
sybarites
sybaritic
sycamine
sycamines
sycamore
sycamores
syce
syces
sycomore
sycomores
sycon
syconia
syconium
syconoid
sycons
sycophant
sycosis
syenite
syenitic
syllabary
syllabi
syllabic
syllabify
syllabise
syllabize
syllable
syllabled
syllables
syllabub
syllabubs
syllabus
syllepses
syllepsis
sylleptic
syllogise
syllogism
syllogize
sylph
sylphlike
sylphs
sylvan
sylvatic
sylvine
sylvinite

sylvite
symbiont
symbionts
symbioses
symbiosis
symbiotic
symbol
symboled
symbolic
symboling
symbolise
symbolism
symbolist
symbolize
symbolled
symbology
symbols
symmetric
symmetry
sympathy
sympatric
sympatry
sympetaly
symphonic
symphony
symphylan
symphyses
symphysis
symplasm
symplasms
symplast
symplasts
sympodia
sympodial
sympodium
symposia
symposium
symptom
symptoms
synagogal
synagogue
synapse
synapses
synapsid
synapsids
synapsis
synaptic
synarchic
synarchy

synastry
sync
synced
synch
synched
synches
synching
synchro
synchrony
syncing
synclinal
syncline
synclines
syncopal
syncopate
syncope
syncretic
syncs
syncytia
syncytial
syncytium
syndactyl
syndetic
syndic
syndical
syndicate
syndics
syndrome
syndromes
syndromic
syne
synectics
synereses
syneresis
synergic
synergies
synergism
synergist
synergy
synfuel
syngamy
syngas
syngeneic
synod
synodal
synodic
synodical
synods
synonym
synonymic

synonyms
synonymy
synopses
synopsis
synopsise
synopsize
synoptic
synoptist
synovial
synovitis
synsacra
synsacrum
syntactic
syntagm
syntagma
syntagmas
syntagms
syntax
syntenic
synteny
synth
synthase
synthases
syntheses
synthesis
synthetic
synthon
synths
synthy
syntone
syntonic
syntype
syntypes
syphilis
syphon
syphoned
syphons
syrette
syrettes
syringa
syringas
syringe
syringed
syringes
syringing
syrinx
syrinxes
syrphid
syrphids
syrtaki

syrtakis   syrupy   system   systemize   systolic
syrup   sysop   systemic   systems   syzygies
syrups   sysops   systemise   systole   syzygy

T

T A	tabliers	tachi	tacos	tagatied
	tabling	tachis	tacrine	tagatiing
ta	tabloid	tachism	tact	tagatis
tab	tabloids	tachisme	tactful	tagetes
tabac	taboo	tacho	tactfully	tagged
tabacs	tabooed	tachos	tactic	tagging
tabanca	tabooing	tachs	tactical	tagma
tabard	taboos	tachyon	tactician	tagmata
tabards	tabor	tachyons	tacticity	tagmatize
tabaret	taboret	tachypnea	tactics	tagmeme
tabarets	taborets	tacit	tactile	tagmemes
tabbed	tabors	tacitly	tactility	tagmemic
tabbies	tabouret	taciturn	tactless	tagmemics
tabbing	tabourets	tack	tactual	tags
tabbouleh	tabs	tacked	tactus	tahina
tabby	tabu	tacker	tactuses	tahini
tabes	tabued	tackers	tad	tahr
tabescent	tabuing	tackie	tadger	tahrs
tabetic	tabular	tackier	tadgers	tahsil
tabi	tabularly	tackies	tadpole	tahsils
tabla	tabulate	tackiest	tadpoles	tai
tablas	tabulated	tackily	tael	taiga
tablature	tabulates	tackiness	taels	taiko
table	tabulator	tacking	taenia	taikos
tableau	tabun	tackle	taeniae	tail
tableaux	tabus	tackled	taenias	tailback
tabled	tacamahac	tackler	taenioid	tailbacks
tableful	tacan	tacklers	taffeta	tailboard
tablefuls	tacet	tackles	taffies	tailcoat
tableland	taceted	tackling	taffrail	tailcoats
tables	taceting	tacks	taffrails	tailed
tablet	tacets	tacky	taffy	tailgate
tablets	tach	taco	tafia	tailgated
tableware	tache	taconite	tag	tailgater
tablier	taches	taconites	tagati	tailgates

tailing	takers	talkers	tamarau	tampons
tailings	takes	talkfest	tamaraus	tamps
taille	takht	talkfests	tamari	tams
tailles	takhts	talkie	tamarillo	tan
tailless	takin	talkies	tamarin	tanager
tailleur	taking	talking	tamarind	tanagers
tailleurs	takingly	talks	tamarinds	tanbark
tailor	takings	talktime	tamarins	tanbarks
tailored	takins	tall	tamarisk	tandem
tailoring	tala	tallage	tamarisks	tandems
tailors	talapoin	tallages	tamasha	tandoor
tailpiece	talapoins	tallboy	tamashas	tandoori
tailpipe	talaq	tallboys	tambala	tandooris
tailpipes	talaria	taller	tambalas	tandoors
tailplane	talas	tallest	tambotie	tang
tails	talbot	tallied	tamboties	tanga
tailspin	talbots	tallier	tambour	tangas
tailspins	talc	talliers	tamboura	tangata
tailspun	talced	tallies	tambouras	tanged
tailstock	talcing	tallish	tamboured	tangelo
tailwater	talcose	tallith	tambourin	tangelos
tailwheel	talcs	talliths	tambours	tangency
tailwind	talcum	tallness	tambura	tangent
tailwinds	talcumed	tallow	tamburas	tangents
taimen	talcuming	tallowed	tame	tangerine
taint	talcums	tallowing	tameable	tangi
tainted	talcy	tallowy	tamed	tangible
tainting	tale	tally	tamely	tangibles
taintless	taleggio	tallying	tameness	tangibly
taints	talent	tallyman	tamer	tangier
taipan	talented	tallymen	tamers	tangiest
taipans	talents	talon	tames	tanginess
taj	tales	taloned	taming	tanging
tajes	talesman	talons	tamoxifen	tangis
taka	talesmen	taluk	tamp	tangle
takable	tali	taluka	tampax	tangled
takahe	talik	talukas	tamped	tangles
takahes	taliks	taluks	tamper	tanglier
take	talipes	taluq	tampered	tangliest
takeable	talipot	taluqs	tamperer	tangling
takeaway	talipots	talus	tamperers	tangly
takeaways	talisman	taluses	tampering	tango
takedown	talismans	tam	tampers	tangoed
takedowns	talk	tamable	tamping	tangoes
taken	talkathon	tamale	tampion	tangoing
takeout	talkative	tamales	tampions	tangos
takeouts	talkback	tamandua	tampon	tangram
takeover	talkbacks	tamanduas	tamponade	tangrams
takeovers	talked	tamarack	tamponed	tangs
taker	talker	tamaracks	tamponing	tangy

tania	tantalite	tappings	tarnished	tartuffe
tanias	tantalize	taproom	tarnishes	tartuffes
tanist	tantalum	taprooms	tarns	tartufo
tanistry	tantalus	taproot	taro	tartufos
tanists	tante	taproots	tarot	tarty
taniwha	tantes	taps	tarp	tarweed
taniwhas	tantivies	tapster	tarpan	tarwhine
tank	tantivy	tapsters	tarpans	tasca
tanka	tanto	tapu	tarpaulin	tascas
tankage	tantos	taqueria	tarpon	taser
tankard	tantra	taquerias	tarpons	tasers
tankards	tantras	tar	tarps	tash
tankas	tantric	tarakihi	tarragon	tashes
tanked	tantrism	tarakihis	tarras	task
tanker	tantrist	tarama	tarred	tasked
tankered	tantrists	tarantass	tarried	tasking
tankering	tantrum	tarantism	tarrier	tasks
tankers	tantrums	tarantula	tarriers	tass
tankful	tanzanite	tarata	tarries	tassel
tankfuls	taonga	taratas	tarriest	tasseled
tanking	tap	tarboosh	tarriness	tasseling
tankless	tapa	tarbrush	tarring	tasselled
tanks	tapas	tardier	tarry	tassels
tannable	tape	tardiest	tarrying	tasses
tannate	taped	tardily	tars	tassie
tannates	tapenade	tardiness	tarsal	tassies
tanned	taper	tardy	tarsals	taste
tanner	tapered	tare	tarsi	tasted
tanneries	taperer	tares	tarsier	tasteful
tanners	tapering	targa	tarsiers	tasteless
tannery	tapers	targe	tarsus	taster
tannia	tapes	targes	tart	tasters
tannic	tapestry	target	tartan	tastes
tannie	tapetum	targeted	tartans	tastevin
tannies	tapetums	targeting	tartar	tastevins
tannin	tapeworm	targets	tartare	tastier
tanning	tapeworms	tariff	tartars	tastiest
tannish	taphonomy	tariffed	tarted	tastily
tannoy	taping	tariffing	tartier	tastiness
tannoyed	tapioca	tariffs	tartiest	tasting
tannoying	tapir	tariqa	tartily	tastings
tannoys	tapirs	tariqat	tartiness	tasty
tanpura	tapis	tarlatan	tarting	tat
tanpuras	tappable	tarlatans	tartlet	tatami
tans	tapped	tarmac	tartlets	tatamis
tansies	tapper	tarmacked	tartly	tater
tansu	tappers	tarmacs	tartness	taters
tansy	tappet	tarn	tartrate	tathata
tantalic	tappets	tarnation	tartrates	tatie
tantalise	tapping	tarnish	tarts	taties

tats
tatted
tattered
tatters
tattie
tattier
tatties
tattiest
tattily
tattiness
tatting
tattle
tattled
tattler
tattlers
tattles
tattling
tattoo
tattooed
tattooer
tattooers
tattooing
tattooist
tattoos
tatty
tau
taught
taunt
taunted
taunter
taunters
taunting
taunts
taupe
taurine
taut
tauten
tautened
tautening
tautens
tauter
tautest
tautly
tautness
tautog
tautogs
tautology
tautomer
tautomers
tautonym

tautonyms
tautonymy
tavern
taverna
tavernas
taverns
taw
tawa
tawas
tawdrier
tawdriest
tawdrily
tawdry
tawed
tawer
tawers
tawing
tawnier
tawniest
tawniness
tawny
taws
tawse
tawses
tax
taxa
taxable
taxation
taxed
taxer
taxers
taxes
taxi
taxicab
taxicabs
taxidermy
taxied
taxies
taxiing
taximeter
taxing
taxis
taxiway
taxiways
taxman
taxmen
taxol
taxols
taxon
taxonomic

taxonomy
taxpayer
taxpayers
taxying
tayberry
tayra
tayras
tazza
tazzas

T C

tch
tchagra
tchagras
tchotchke

T E

te
tea
teacake
teacakes
teach
teachable
teacher
teacherly
teachers
teaches
teaching
teachings
teacup
teacupful
teacups
teaed
teahead
teaheads
teaing
teak
teaks
teal
teals
team
teamed
teaming
teammate
teammates
teams
teamster
teamsters

teamwork
teapot
teapots
teapoy
teapoys
tear
tearable
tearaway
tearaways
teardrop
teardrops
tearer
tearers
tearful
tearfully
tearing
tearless
tears
teas
tease
teased
teasel
teaseled
teaseling
teasels
teaser
teasers
teases
teasing
teasingly
teaspoon
teaspoons
teat
teatime
teats
teazel
teazeled
teazeling
teazels
teazle
teazled
teazles
teazling
tec
tech
techie
techier
techies
techiest
technic

technical
technics
technikon
technique
techno
techy
tecs
tectonic
tectonics
tectorial
tectrices
tectrix
tectum
ted
tedded
tedder
tedders
teddies
tedding
teddy
tedious
tediously
tedium
teds
tee
teed
teeing
teem
teemed
teeming
teems
teen
teenage
teenaged
teenager
teenagers
teenier
teeniest
teens
teensier
teensiest
teensy
teeny
teepee
teepees
tees
teeter
teetered
teetering
teeters

teeth	telefaxes	tellin	temples	tending
teethe	teleferic	telling	templet	tendinous
teethed	telefilm	tellingly	templets	tendon
teethes	telefilms	tellins	tempo	tendons
teething	telegenic	tells	temporal	tendre
teetotal	telegram	telltale	temporary	tendresse
teetotum	telegrams	telltales	temporise	tendril
teetotums	telegraph	tellurate	temporize	tendrils
teevee	telemark	tellurian	tempos	tends
teevees	telemarks	telluric	temps	tendu
teff	telematic	telluride	tempt	tenebrism
tefillin	telemeter	tellurite	temptable	tenebrist
teg	telemetry	tellurium	tempted	tenebrous
tegmen	teleology	telly	tempter	tenement
tegmenta	teleost	telnet	tempters	tenements
tegmental	teleosts	telnets	tempting	tenesmus
tegmentum	telepath	telnetted	temptress	tenet
tegmina	telepaths	telogen	tempts	tenets
tegs	telepathy	teloi	tempura	tenfold
tegu	telephone	telomere	ten	tenge
tegula	telephony	telomeres	tenable	tenges
tegulae	telephoto	telomeric	tenace	tenia
tegument	teleport	telophase	tenaces	tenné
teguments	teleports	telos	tenacious	tenner
tegus	teles	telson	tenacity	tenners
tehsil	telesales	telsons	tenacula	tennies
tehsils	telescope	temazepam	tenaculum	tennis
teichoate	teletex	temblor	tenancies	tenon
teichoic	teletext	temblors	tenancy	tenoned
tein	telethon	temenoi	tenant	tenoner
teins	telethons	temenos	tenanted	tenoners
tej	teletype	temerity	tenanting	tenoning
tekke	teletyped	temp	tenantry	tenons
tekkes	teletypes	temped	tenants	tenor
tektite	televise	tempeh	tench	tenorini
tektites	televised	temper	tenches	tenorino
telamon	televises	tempera	tend	tenorist
telamones	telework	temperate	tendance	tenorists
telco	teleworks	tempered	tended	tenors
telcos	telex	temperer	tendency	tenotomy
tele	telexed	temperers	tender	tenpin
telecast	telexes	tempering	tendered	tenpins
telecasts	telexing	tempers	tenderer	tenrec
telecine	telic	tempest	tenderers	tenrecs
telecomms	telicity	tempests	tenderest	tense
telecoms	tell	tempi	tendering	tensed
teledu	tellable	temping	tenderise	tenseless
teledus	teller	template	tenderize	tensely
telefax	tellers	templates	tenderly	tenseness
telefaxed	tellies	temple	tenders	tenser

tenses	tepals	termitary	terrorist	testiness
tensest	tepee	termite	terrorize	testing
tensile	tepees	termites	terrors	testis
tensility	tephra	termly	terry	tests
tensing	tephras	terms	terse	testudo
tension	tepid	tern	tersely	testudos
tensional	tepidaria	ternary	terseness	testy
tensioned	tepidity	terne	terser	tetanic
tensioner	tepidly	ternlet	tersest	tetanise
tensions	tepidness	ternlets	tertian	tetanised
tensity	tequila	terns	tertiary	tetanises
tensive	terabyte	terpene	tervalent	tetanize
tenson	terabytes	terpenes	terylene	tetanized
tensons	teraflop	terpenoid	terzetti	tetanizes
tensor	teraflops	terra	terzetto	tetanoid
tensorial	terai	terrace	terzettos	tetanus
tensors	terais	terraced	tes	tetany
tent	teraphim	terraces	tesla	tetchier
tentacle	teratogen	terracing	teslas	tetchiest
tentacled	teratoma	terraform	tessera	tetchily
tentacles	teratomas	terrain	tesserae	tetchy
tentage	terawatt	terramare	tesseral	tether
tentative	terawatts	terrane	tessitura	tethered
tented	terbium	terranes	test	tethering
tenter	terce	terrapin	testa	tethers
tenters	tercel	terrapins	testable	tetra
tenth	tercels	terraria	testae	tetrad
tenthly	terces	terrarium	testament	tetrads
tenting	tercet	terrasse	testate	tetragram
tentoria	tercets	terrasses	testates	tetralogy
tentorium	terebinth	terrazzo	testation	tetramer
tents	teredo	terrene	testator	tetramers
tenuity	teredos	terret	testators	tetrapack
tenuous	teres	terrets	testatrix	tetrapod
tenuously	terete	terrible	tested	tetrapods
tenure	terga	terribly	testee	tetrarch
tenured	tergal	terrier	testees	tetrarchy
tenures	tergite	terriers	tester	tetrazole
tenurial	tergum	terries	testers	tetrode
tenuring	teriyaki	terrific	testes	tetrodes
tenuti	term	terrified	testicle	tetrose
tenuto	termagant	terrifier	testicles	tetroxide
tenutos	termed	terrifies	testier	tetter
tenzon	terminal	terrify	testiest	tetters
tenzons	terminals	terrine	testified	text
teocalli	terminate	terrines	testifier	textbook
teocallis	terminer	territory	testifies	textbooks
teosinte	terming	terror	testify	textile
tepache	termini	terrorise	testily	textiles
tepal	terminus	terrorism	testimony	textless

texts	thatch	theocracy	therm	thicko
textual	thatched	theocrat	thermae	thickos
textually	thatcher	theocrats	thermal	thickset
textural	thatchers	theodicy	thermally	thief
texture	thatches	theogony	thermals	thieve
textured	thatching	theology	thermic	thieved
textures	thaumatin	theomachy	thermion	thievery
texturing	thaw	theophany	thermions	thieves
texturise	thawed	theorbo	thermit	thieving
texturize	thawing	theorbos	thermite	thievish
	thaws	theorem	thermites	thigh
T H	the	theorems	thermoset	thighed
	thearchy	theoretic	therms	thighs
thakur	theater	theories	theropod	thill
thakurs	theaters	theorise	theropods	thiller
thalami	theatre	theorised	thesauri	thillers
thalamic	theatres	theorises	thesaurus	thills
thalamus	theatric	theorist	these	thimble
thalassic	theatrics	theorists	theses	thimbles
thaler	thebe	theorize	thesis	thin
thalers	thebes	theorized	thespian	thine
thali	theca	theorizer	thespians	thing
thalis	thecae	theorizes	theta	thingamy
thalli	thecate	theory	thetas	thingies
thallium	thecodont	theosophy	theurgic	things
thalloid	thee	therapies	theurgies	thingummy
thallus	theft	therapist	theurgist	thingy
thalweg	thefts	therapsid	theurgy	think
thalwegs	thegn	therapy	thew	thinkable
thamin	thegns	there	thews	thinker
thamins	theine	thereat	thewy	thinkers
than	their	thereby	they	thinking
thana	theirs	therefor	thiamin	thinkings
thanage	theism	therefore	thiamine	thinks
thanas	theist	therefrom	thiazide	thinly
thane	theistic	therein	thiazides	thinned
thanedom	theists	thereinto	thiazole	thinner
thanedoms	them	theremin	thick	thinners
thanes	thematic	theremins	thicken	thinness
thang	thematics	thereof	thickened	thinnest
thank	thematise	thereon	thickener	thinning
thanked	thematize	thereout	thickens	thinnings
thankful	theme	thereto	thicker	thinnish
thanking	themed	thereunto	thickest	thins
thankless	themes	thereupon	thicket	thiol
thanks	theming	therewith	thickets	thiols
thar	themself	theriac	thickhead	thionyl
thars	then	theriacs	thickish	thiourea
that	thenar	therian	thickly	thiram
thataway	thence	therians	thickness	third

thirdly	those	thrifty	throwers	thumping
thirst	thou	thrill	throwing	thumps
thirsted	though	thrilled	thrown	thumri
thirstier	thought	thriller	throws	thumris
thirstily	thoughts	thrillers	throwster	thunder
thirsting	thous	thrilling	thru	thundered
thirsts	thousand	thrills	thrum	thunderer
thirsty	thousands	thrip	thrummed	thunders
thirteen	thraldom	thrips	thrummer	thundery
thirties	thrall	thrive	thrummers	thunk
thirtieth	thralldom	thrived	thrummier	thurible
thirty	thrash	thriven	thrumming	thuribles
this	thrashed	thrives	thrummy	thurifer
thistle	thrasher	thriving	thrums	thurifers
thistles	thrashers	throat	thrush	thus
thistly	thrashes	throated	thrushes	thusly
thither	thrashing	throatier	thrust	thuya
tho	thrawn	throatily	thruster	thuyas
thole	thread	throats	thrusters	thwack
tholed	threaded	throaty	thrusting	thwacked
tholeiite	threader	throb	thrusts	thwacking
tholes	threaders	throbbed	thrutch	thwacks
tholing	threadfin	throbbing	thrutched	thwaite
tholoi	threadier	throbs	thrutches	thwart
tholos	threading	throes	thruway	thwarted
thong	threads	thrombi	thruways	thwarting
thonged	thready	thrombin	thud	thwarts
thonging	threat	thrombose	thudded	thy
thongs	threaten	thrombus	thudding	thylacine
thongy	threatens	throne	thuds	thylakoid
thoraces	threats	throned	thug	thyme
thoracic	three	thrones	thuggee	thymi
thorax	threefold	throng	thuggery	thymic
thoraxes	threesome	thronged	thuggish	thymidine
thoria	threnodic	thronging	thuggism	thymine
thorium	threnody	throngs	thugs	thymocyte
thorn	threonine	throning	thuja	thymol
thornback	thresh	throstle	thujas	thymoma
thornbill	threshed	throstles	thulium	thymomas
thornier	thresher	throttle	thumb	thymomata
thorniest	threshers	throttled	thumbed	thymus
thornily	threshes	throttler	thumbing	thymy
thornless	threshing	throttles	thumbless	thyristor
thorns	threshold	through	thumbnail	thyroid
thorntail	threw	throve	thumbs	thyroids
thornveld	thrice	throw	thumbtack	thyroxine
thorny	thrift	throwable	thump	thyrsi
thorough	thriftier	throwaway	thumped	thyrsus
thorp	thriftily	throwback	thumper	thysanura
thorpe	thrifts	thrower	thumpers	thyself

ti
tian
tians
tiara
tiaras
tiare
tiarella
tiarellas
tibia
tibiae
tibial
tibialis
tic
tich
tiches
tick
ticked
ticker
tickers
ticket
ticketed
ticketing
tickets
tickey
tickeys
ticking
tickle
tickled
tickler
ticklers
tickles
tickling
ticklish
tickly
tickover
ticks
tickseed
tickseeds
tics
tidal
tidally
tidbit
tidbits
tiddler
tiddlers
tiddlier
tiddliest
tiddly

tide
tided
tideland
tidelands
tideless
tideline
tidelines
tidemark
tidemarks
tides
tidewater
tideway
tideways
tidied
tidier
tidies
tidiest
tidily
tidiness
tiding
tidings
tidy
tidying
tie
tiebreak
tiebreaks
tied
tief
tiefed
tiefing
tiefs
tieless
tienda
tiendas
tiento
tientos
tiepin
tiepins
tier
tierce
tiercé
tierced
tiercel
tiercels
tierces
tiered
tiers
ties
tiff
tiffany

tiffin
tiffs
tig
tiger
tigerish
tigers
tigerwood
tight
tighten
tightened
tightens
tighter
tightest
tightly
tightness
tightrope
tights
tightwad
tightwads
tiglon
tiglons
tignon
tignons
tigon
tigons
tigress
tigresses
tigs
tika
tikas
tike
tikes
tiki
tikia
tikis
tikka
tilak
tilaks
tilapia
tilapias
tilburies
tilbury
tilde
tildes
tile
tiled
tilefish
tiler
tilers
tiles

tiling
till
tillable
tillage
tilled
tiller
tillered
tillering
tillers
tilleul
tilleuls
tilling
tillite
tills
tilt
tilted
tilter
tilters
tilth
tilting
tilts
timbal
timbale
timbales
timbals
timber
timbered
timbering
timberman
timbermen
timbers
timbre
timbrel
timbrels
timbres
time
times
timed
timeless
timely
timeous
timeously
timeout
timeouts
timepiece
timer
timers
times
timescale
timesed

timeshare
timesing
timetable
timid
timider
timidest
timidity
timidly
timidness
timing
timings
timocracy
timolol
timorous
timothy
timpani
timpanist
tin
tinamou
tinamous
tincture
tinctured
tinctures
tinder
tinderbox
tindery
tine
tinea
tined
tines
tinfoil
ting
tinge
tinged
tingeing
tinges
tinging
tingle
tingled
tingles
tinglier
tingliest
tingling
tingly
tings
tinhorn
tinhorns
tinier
tinies
tiniest

tinily	tipcat	tissuey	titre	toadyish
tininess	tipi	tit	titres	toadyism
tinker	tipis	titan	tits	toast
tinkered	tipped	titanate	titter	toasted
tinkerer	tipper	titanates	tittered	toaster
tinkerers	tippers	titaness	titterer	toasters
tinkering	tippet	titanic	titterers	toastie
tinkers	tippets	titanite	tittering	toasties
tinkle	tippier	titanium	titters	toasting
tinkled	tippiest	titanous	tittie	toasts
tinkles	tipping	titans	titties	toasty
tinkling	tipple	titbit	tittivate	tobacco
tinkly	tippled	titbits	tittle	tobaccos
tinned	tippler	titch	tittles	tobies
tinner	tipplers	titches	tittup	toboggan
tinners	tipples	titchier	tittuped	toboggans
tinnier	tippling	titchiest	tittuping	toby
tinnies	tippy	titchy	tittupped	toccata
tinniest	tips	titer	tittups	toccatas
tinnily	tipsier	titers	titty	toco
tinniness	tipsiest	titfer	titular	tocos
tinning	tipsily	titfers	titularly	tocsin
tinnitus	tipsiness	tithable	tiyin	tocsins
tinny	tipstaff	tithe	tiyins	tod
tinplate	tipstaffs	tithed	tizz	today
tinplated	tipster	tithes	tizzes	toddies
tinplates	tipsters	tithing	tizzies	toddle
tinpot	tipsy	tithings	tizzy	toddled
tins	tiptoe	titi		toddler
tinsel	tiptoed	titihoya		toddlers
tinseled	tiptoeing	titihoyas	**T M**	toddles
tinselled	tiptoes	titillate		toddling
tinselly	tirade	titis	tmeses	toddy
tinsels	tirades	titivate	tmesis	todger
tinsmith	tiramisu	titivated		todies
tinsmiths	tire	titivates	**T O**	tody
tinsnips	tired	titlark		toe
tinstone	tiredly	titlarks	to	toea
tint	tiredness	title	toad	toecap
tinted	tireless	titled	toadfish	toecaps
tinter	tires	titles	toadflax	toed
tinters	tiresome	titling	toadied	toehold
tinting	tiring	titlings	toadies	toeholds
tinto	tiro	titmice	toadish	toeing
tints	tiros	titmouse	toadlet	toeless
tintype	tis	titrate	toadlets	toenail
tintypes	tisane	titrated	toads	toenailed
tinware	tisanes	titrates	toadstone	toenails
tiny	tissue	titrating	toadstool	toerag
tip	tissues	titration	toady	toerags

toes	tokers	tombs	tonged	toolmaker
toey	tokes	tombstone	tonging	tools
toff	toking	tomcat	tongs	toon
toffed	tokkin	tomcats	tongue	toons
toffee	tokkins	tomcod	tongued	toot
toffees	tokoloshe	tomcods	tongues	tooted
toffing	tokonoma	tome	tonguing	tooter
toffs	tolar	tomenta	tonic	tooters
toft	tolars	tomentose	tonically	tooth
tofts	tolbooth	tomentous	tonicity	toothache
tofu	tolbooths	tomentum	tonics	toothcarp
tog	told	tomes	tonier	toothcomb
toga	tole	tomfool	toniest	toothed
togas	tolerable	tomfools	tonified	toothier
together	tolerably	tomme	tonifies	toothiest
togged	tolerance	tommed	tonify	toothily
toggery	tolerant	tomming	tonifying	toothing
togging	tolerate	tommyrot	tonight	toothless
toggle	tolerated	tomogram	toning	toothpick
toggled	tolerates	tomograms	tonnage	toothsome
toggles	tolerator	tomorrow	tonne	toothwort
toggling	toleware	tomorrows	tonneau	toothy
togs	toll	tompion	tonneaus	tooting
togt	tollbooth	tompions	tonnes	tootle
tohubohu	tolled	toms	tonometer	tootled
toil	tolling	tomtit	tonoplast	tootles
toile	tolls	tomtits	tons	tootling
toiled	tollway	ton	tonsil	toots
toiler	tollways	tonal	tonsillar	tootsie
toilers	tolu	tonalite	tonsils	tootsies
toiles	toluene	tonalitic	tonsorial	tootsy
toilet	tom	tonality	tonsure	top
toileted	tomahawk	tonally	tonsured	topaz
toileting	tomahawks	tondi	tonsures	topazes
toilets	tomalley	tondo	tonsuring	topcoat
toilette	tomalleys	tone	tontine	topcoats
toiling	tomatillo	toneburst	tontines	tope
toils	tomatin	toned	tonus	toped
toilsome	tomatine	toneless	tony	topee
toilworn	tomato	toneme	too	topees
tokamak	tomatoes	tonemes	took	toper
tokamaks	tomatoey	tonemic	tool	topers
tokay	tomb	tonepad	toolbar	topes
tokays	tombola	tonepads	toolbars	tophi
toke	tombolas	toner	toolbox	tophus
toked	tombolo	toners	toolboxes	topi
token	tombolos	tones	tooled	topiarian
tokenism	tomboy	tong	tooler	topiaries
tokens	tomboyish	tonga	toolers	topiarist
toker	tomboys	tongas	tooling	topiary

topic	torchère	torrid	tossers	tottering
topical	torchères	torridity	tosses	totters
topically	torches	torridly	tossing	tottery
topics	torching	tors	tosspot	totties
toping	torchlit	torsade	tosspots	totting
topis	torchon	torsades	tostada	totty
topknot	torcs	torse	tostadas	toucan
topknots	tore	torsel	tostado	toucanet
topless	toreador	torsels	tostados	toucanets
toplofty	toreadors	torses	tostone	toucans
topman	torero	torsi	tostones	touch
topmast	toreros	torsion	tosyl	touchable
topmasts	toreutic	torsional	tosylate	touchback
topmen	toreutics	torsk	tot	touchdown
topminnow	torgoch	torsks	total	touché
topmost	torgochs	torso	totaled	touched
topo	tori	torsos	totaling	toucher
topoi	toric	tort	totalise	touchers
topology	torii	torte	totalised	touches
toponym	torment	tortelli	totalises	touchier
toponymic	tormented	torten	totality	touchiest
toponyms	tormentil	tortes	totalize	touchily
toponymy	tormentor	tortilla	totalized	touching
topos	torments	tortillas	totalizer	touchline
topped	torn	tortious	totalizes	touchwood
topper	tornadic	tortoise	totalled	touchy
toppers	tornado	tortoises	totalling	tough
toppie	tornadoes	tortrices	totally	toughed
toppies	tornados	tortricid	totals	toughen
topping	toroid	tortrix	totara	toughened
toppings	toroidal	torts	totaras	toughener
topple	toroids	tortuous	tote	toughens
toppled	torpedo	torture	toted	tougher
topples	torpedoed	tortured	totem	toughest
toppling	torpedoes	torturer	totemic	toughie
tops	torpefied	torturers	totemism	toughies
topsail	torpefies	tortures	totemist	toughing
topsails	torpefy	torturing	totemists	toughish
topside	torpid	torturous	totems	toughly
topsides	torpidity	torula	toter	toughness
topsoil	torpidly	torulae	toters	toughs
topspin	torpor	torulosis	totes	toupee
topstitch	torque	torus	tother	toupees
topwater	torqued	toruses	toting	toupet
toque	torques	tosa	tots	toupets
toques	torquey	tosas	totted	tour
tor	torquing	tosh	totter	touraco
torc	torr	toss	tottered	touracos
torch	torrent	tossed	totterer	toured
torched	torrents	tosser	totterers	tourer

tourers	towlines	toyon	tractable	trainable
touring	town	toyons	tractably	trainband
tourism	townee	toys	tractate	trained
tourist	townees	toytown	tractates	trainee
touristed	townie		traction	trainees
touristic	townies		tractive	trainer
tourists	townish	**T R**	tractor	trainers
touristy	townland	trabeated	tractors	training
tournedos	townlands	trabecula	tractrix	trainload
tourney	townlet	trace	tracts	trains
tourneyed	townlets	traceable	trad	trainsick
tourneys	towns	traced	tradable	traipse
tournois	townscape	traceless	trade	traipsed
tours	townsfolk	tracer	tradeable	traipses
tourtiere	township	traceried	traded	traipsing
tousle	townships	traceries	trademark	trait
tousled	townsite	tracers	trader	traitor
tousles	townsites	tracery	traders	traitors
tousling	townsman	traces	trades	traits
tout	townsmen	trachea	tradesman	tram
touted	townward	tracheae	tradesmen	tramcar
touter	townwards	tracheal	trading	tramcars
touters	towpath	tracheas	tradition	tramlines
touting	towpaths	tracheate	traduce	trammel
touts	towplane	tracheid	traduced	trammeled
tovarich	towplanes	trachoma	traducer	trammels
tovarish	tows	trachyte	traducers	tramp
tow	towy	trachytes	traduces	tramped
towable	toxaemia	trachytic	traducing	tramper
towage	toxaemic	tracing	traffic	trampers
towai	toxaphene	tracings	traffics	tramping
towais	toxemia	track	tragedian	trampish
toward	toxic	trackage	tragedies	trample
towards	toxically	trackball	tragedy	trampled
towed	toxicant	trackbed	traghetti	trampler
towel	toxicants	trackbeds	traghetto	tramplers
toweled	toxicity	tracked	tragi	tramples
toweling	toxics	tracker	tragic	trampling
towelled	toxigenic	trackers	tragical	tramps
towelling	toxin	tracking	tragopan	trams
towels	toxins	trackless	tragopans	tramway
tower	toxocara	trackman	tragus	tramways
towered	toxocaras	trackmen	trail	trance
towering	toxoid	tracks	trailed	tranced
towers	toxoids	trackside	trailer	trancedly
towery	toxophily	tracksuit	trailered	trances
towhee	toy	trackway	trailers	tranche
towhees	toyed	trackways	trailing	tranches
towing	toying	trackwork	trails	trancing
towline	toylike	tract	train	trank

tranked	trapesed	travesty	trecento	trench
tranks	trapeses	travois	tree	trenchant
trannie	trapesing	trawl	treed	trenched
trannies	trapeze	trawled	treeing	trencher
tranny	trapezes	trawler	treeless	trenchers
tranquil	trapezia	trawlers	treeline	trenches
trans	trapezii	trawling	treelines	trenching
transact	trapezium	trawls	treen	trend
transacts	trapezius	tray	treenail	trended
transaxle	trapezoid	trayf	treenails	trendier
transcend	trapline	trayful	treens	trendies
transcode	traplines	trayfuls	trees	trendiest
transduce	trapped	trays	treetop	trendify
transect	trapper	treachery	treetops	trendily
transects	trappers	treacle	trefa	trending
transept	trapping	treacly	trefid	trendoid
transepts	trappings	tread	trefoil	trendoids
transfect	traprock	treader	trefoiled	trends
transfer	traps	treaders	trefoils	trendy
transfers	trash	treading	trehalose	trepan
transfix	trashed	treadle	trek	trepang
transform	trashes	treadled	trekked	trepangs
transfuse	trashier	treadles	trekker	trepanned
tranship	trashiest	treadling	trekkers	trepans
tranships	trashily	treadmill	trekking	trephine
transient	trashing	treads	treks	trephined
transire	trashy	treason	trellis	trephines
transires	trass	treasure	trellised	treponema
transit	trattoria	treasured	trellises	treponeme
transited	trauma	treasurer	trem	trespass
transits	traumas	treasures	trematode	tress
translate	traumata	treasury	tremble	tressed
transmit	traumatic	treat	trembled	tresses
transmits	travail	treatable	trembler	tressing
transmute	travailed	treated	tremblers	tressure
transom	travails	treater	trembles	tressures
transomed	travel	treaters	trembling	tressy
transoms	traveled	treaties	tremblor	trestle
transonic	traveler	treating	trembly	trestles
transpire	travelers	treatise	tremolite	tret
transport	traveling	treatises	tremolo	trevally
transpose	travelled	treatment	tremolos	trews
transude	traveller	treats	tremor	trey
transuded	travels	treaty	tremored	treys
transudes	travers	treble	tremoring	triable
trap	traversal	trebled	tremors	triac
trapball	traverse	trebles	trems	triacs
trapdoor	traversed	trebling	tremulous	triad
trapdoors	traverser	trebly	trenail	triadic
trapes	traverses	trebuchet	trenails	triads

triage	trice	tried	trihedron	trines
trial	triceps	triene	trihydric	trining
trialed	trichina	trienes	trike	trinities
trialing	trichinae	triennia	triked	trinity
trialist	trichome	triennial	trikes	trinket
trialists	trichomes	triennium	triking	trinketry
trialled	trichroic	trier	trilbied	trinkets
trialling	trichrome	triers	trilbies	trinomial
triallist	trick	tries	trilby	trio
trialogue	tricked	trifa	trilinear	triode
trials	tricker	trifecta	trilith	triodes
triangle	trickers	triffid	trilithon	triolet
triangles	trickery	triffids	triliths	triolets
triathlon	trickier	trifid	trill	trios
triatomic	trickiest	trifle	trilled	triose
triaxial	trickily	trifled	triller	trioses
triazine	tricking	trifler	trilling	trioxide
triazines	trickish	triflers	trillion	trioxides
triazole	trickle	trifles	trillions	trip
triazoles	trickled	trifling	trillium	tripe
tribade	trickles	trifocal	trilliums	triplane
tribades	trickling	trifocals	trills	triplanes
tribadism	tricks	triforia	trilobite	triple
tribal	tricksier	triforium	trilogies	tripled
tribalism	tricksily	triform	trilogy	triples
tribalist	trickster	trig	trim	triplet
tribally	tricksy	trigamies	trimaran	triplets
tribals	tricky	trigamist	trimarans	triplex
tribasic	triclad	trigamous	trimer	triplexed
tribe	triclads	trigamy	trimeric	triplexes
tribes	triclinia	trigemini	trimerous	tripling
tribesman	triclinic	trigged	trimers	triploid
tribesmen	tricolor	trigger	trimester	triploids
triblet	tricolors	triggered	trimeter	triploidy
triblets	tricolour	triggers	trimeters	triply
tribology	tricorn	trigging	trimetric	tripmeter
tribrach	tricorne	triglyph	trimix	tripod
tribrachs	tricornes	triglyphs	trimly	tripodal
tribunal	tricorns	trigon	trimmed	tripods
tribunals	tricot	trigonal	trimmer	tripoli
tribunate	tricuspid	trigone	trimmers	tripolis
tribune	tricycle	trigones	trimmest	tripos
tribunes	tricycled	trigons	trimming	triposes
tributary	tricycles	trigram	trimmings	trippant
tribute	tricyclic	trigrams	trimness	tripped
tributes	tridactyl	trigraph	trimpot	tripper
tricar	trident	trigraphs	trimpots	trippers
tricars	tridents	trigs	trims	trippier
tricast	triduum	trihedra	trine	trippiest
tricasts	tridymite	trihedral	trined	tripping

tripple	trivet	troopie	trout	trudging
trippled	trivets	troopies	trouting	true
tripples	trivia	trooping	trouts	trued
trippling	trivial	troops	trouvère	trueing
trippy	trivially	troopship	trouvères	trueness
trips	trivium	trope	trove	truer
triptych	trocar	tropes	trover	trues
triptyque	trocars	trophic	trovers	truest
tripwire	trochaic	trophies	troves	truffle
tripwires	trochaics	trophy	trow	truffled
triquetra	trochee	tropic	trowed	truffles
trireme	trochees	tropical	trowel	truffling
triremes	trochlea	tropics	troweled	trug
tris	trochleae	tropism	troweling	trugs
trisect	trochlear	tropology	trowelled	truing
trisected	trochoid	tropolone	trowels	truism
trisector	trochoids	troponin	trowing	truisms
trisects	trod	troppo	trows	truistic
trishaw	trodden	trot	troy	trull
trishaws	trog	troth	truancies	trulls
trismus	trogged	trots	truancy	truly
trismuses	trogging	trotted	truant	trumeau
trisomy	trogon	trotter	truanted	trumeaux
tristesse	trogons	trotters	truanting	trump
tritanope	trogs	trotting	truants	trumped
trite	troika	trouble	truce	trumpery
tritely	troikas	troubled	truces	trumpet
triteness	troilism	troubler	truck	trumpeted
triter	troll	troublers	truckage	trumpeter
tritest	trolled	troubles	trucked	trumpets
tritheism	troller	troubling	trucker	trumping
tritheist	trollers	troublous	truckers	trumps
tritiated	trolley	trough	truckie	truncal
triticale	trolleys	troughs	truckies	truncate
tritium	trolling	trounce	trucking	truncated
triton	trollius	trounced	truckle	truncates
tritone	trollop	trouncer	truckled	truncheon
tritones	trollops	trouncers	truckler	trundle
tritons	trolls	trounces	trucklers	trundled
triturate	trombone	trouncing	truckles	trundles
triumph	trombones	troupe	truckling	trundling
triumphal	trommel	trouper	truckload	trunk
triumphed	trommels	troupers	trucks	trunkfish
triumphs	trona	troupes	truculent	trunkful
triumvir	tronc	troupial	trudge	trunkfuls
triumviri	troncs	troupials	trudged	trunking
triumvirs	troop	trouser	trudgen	trunkless
triune	trooped	trousered	trudger	trunks
triunity	trooper	trousers	trudgers	trunnel
trivalent	troopers	trousseau	trudges	trunnels

trunnion
trunnions
truss
trussed
trusser
trussers
trusses
trussing
trust
trustable
trusted
trustee
trustees
truster
trusters
trustful
trustier
trusties
trustiest
trustily
trusting
trusts
trusty
truth
truthful
truths
try
trying
tryingly
trypsin
tryptic
trysail
trysails
tryst
trysted
tryster
trysters
trysting
trysts

| T | S |

tsamma
tsammas
tsantsa
tsantsas
tsar
tsardom
tsardoms
tsarevich

tsarina
tsarinas
tsarism
tsarist
tsarists
tsars
tsatske
tsatskes
tsessebe
tsessebes
tsessebi
tsessebis
tsetse
tsetses
tsimmes
tsotsi
tsotsis
tsuba
tsubas
tsubo
tsubos
tsukemono
tsunami
tsunamis

| T | U |

tuan
tuans
tuatara
tuataras
tub
tuba
tubal
tubas
tubbable
tubbed
tubbier
tubbiest
tubbiness
tubbing
tubby
tube
tubectomy
tubed
tubeless
tuber
tubercle
tubercles
tuberose

tuberoses
tuberous
tubers
tubes
tubesnout
tubful
tubfuls
tubifex
tubifexes
tubing
tubs
tubular
tubulars
tubule
tubules
tubulin
tuck
tuckahoe
tuckahoes
tucked
tucker
tuckered
tuckering
tuckers
tucket
tuckets
tucking
tucks
tucuxi
tufa
tufaceous
tuff
tuffet
tuft
tufted
tufting
tufts
tufty
tug
tugboat
tugboats
tugged
tugger
tuggers
tugging
tugrik
tugriks
tugs
tui
tuile

tuiles
tuis
tuition
tuitional
tularemia
tule
tules
tulip
tulips
tulipwood
tulle
tullibee
tullibees
tulp
tulps
tulsi
tulsis
tum
tumbaga
tumble
tumblebug
tumbled
tumbler
tumblers
tumbles
tumbling
tumbrel
tumbrels
tumbril
tumbrils
tumefied
tumefies
tumefy
tumefying
tumescent
tumid
tumidity
tumidly
tummies
tummler
tummlers
tummy
tumor
tumorous
tumors
tumour
tumours
tump
tumpline
tumps

tums
tumuli
tumult
tumults
tumulus
tun
tuna
tunable
tunas
tundish
tundishes
tundra
tundras
tune
tuneable
tuned
tuneful
tunefully
tuneless
tuner
tuners
tunes
tunesmith
tungstate
tungsten
tungstite
tunic
tunica
tunicae
tunicate
tunicated
tunicates
tunicle
tunicles
tunics
tuning
tunned
tunnel
tunneled
tunneling
tunnelled
tunneller
tunnels
tunnies
tunning
tunny
tuns
tup
tupelo
tupelos

tupik
tupiks
tupped
tuppence
tuppences
tuppenny
tupping
tups
tuque
tuques
tur
turaco
turacos
turban
turbaned
turbanned
turbans
turbaries
turbary
turbid
turbidite
turbidity
turbidly
turbinal
turbinals
turbinate
turbine
turbines
turbit
turbits
turbo
turbofan
turbofans
turbojet
turbojets
turboprop
turbos
turbot
turbots
turbulent
turd
turds
tureen
tureens
turf
turfed
turfing
turfman
turfmen
turfs

turfy
turgid
turgidity
turgidly
turgor
turion
turions
turista
turkey
turkeys
turlough
turloughs
turmeric
turmoil
turn
turnabout
turnback
turnbacks
turncoat
turncoats
turncock
turncocks
turndown
turndowns
turned
turner
turneries
turners
turnery
turning
turnings
turnip
turnips
turnipy
turnkey
turnkeys
turnout
turnouts
turnover
turnovers
turnpike
turnpikes
turnround
turns
turnsick
turnsole
turnsoles
turnspit
turnspits
turnstile

turnstone
turntable
turpitude
turps
turquoise
turret
turreted
turrets
turron
turs
turtle
turtles
turves
tush
tushes
tushies
tushy
tusk
tusked
tusker
tuskers
tusks
tusky
tussah
tussive
tussle
tussled
tussles
tussling
tussock
tussocks
tussocky
tussore
tut
tutee
tutees
tutelage
tutelar
tutelary
tutor
tutorage
tutored
tutorial
tutorials
tutoring
tutors
tutorship
tuts
tutsan
tutsans

tutti
tuttis
tutu
tutus
tux
tuxedo
tuxedoed
tuxedoes
tuxedos
tuxes
tuyère
tuyères

T W

twaddle
twaddled
twaddler
twaddlers
twaddles
twaddling
twain
twang
twanged
twanging
twangs
twangy
twat
twats
twatted
twatting
twayblade
tweak
tweaked
tweaking
tweaks
twee
tweed
tweedier
tweediest
tweedily
tweeds
tweedy
tweely
tweeness
tweenies
tweeny
tweer
tweest
tweet

tweeted
tweeter
tweeters
tweeting
tweets
tweeze
tweezed
tweezers
tweezes
tweezing
twelfth
twelfthly
twelve
twelvemo
twelvemos
twenties
twentieth
twenty
twerp
twerps
twibill
twibills
twice
twiddle
twiddled
twiddler
twiddlers
twiddles
twiddling
twiddly
twig
twigged
twigging
twiggy
twigs
twilight
twilights
twilit
twill
twilled
twilling
twin
twine
twined
twiner
twiners
twines
twinge
twinged
twingeing

twinges
twinging
twining
twinkie
twinkies
twinkle
twinkled
twinkler
twinklers
twinkles
twinkling
twinkly
twinned
twinning
twins
twinset
twinsets
twinspot
twinspots
twirl
twirled
twirler
twirlers
twirling
twirls
twirly
twirp
twirps
twist
twisted
twister
twisters

twistier
twistiest
twisting
twistor
twistors
twists
twisty
twit
twitch
twitched
twitcher
twitchers
twitches
twitchier
twitching
twitchy
twite
twites
twits
twitted
twitten
twittens
twitter
twittered
twitterer
twitters
twittery
twitting
twittish
twizzle
twizzled
twizzles

twizzling
two
twoc
twocced
twoccer
twoccers
twoccing
twocs
twofold
twoness
twopence
twopences
twopenny
twosome
twosomes

| T | Y |

tychism
tycoon
tycoons
tying
tyke
tykes
tylopod
tylopods
tympan
tympana
tympani
tympanic
tympanies
tympans

tympanum
tympanums
tympany
typal
type
typecast
typed
typeface
typefaces
types
typeset
typesets
typhlitic
typhlitis
typhoid
typhoidal
typhonic
typhoon
typhoons
typhous
typhus
typical
typically
typified
typifier
typifiers
typifies
typify
typifying
typing
typist
typists

typo
typology
typos
tyramine
tyrannies
tyrannise
tyrannize
tyrannous
tyranny
tyrant
tyrants
tyre
tyres
tyro
tyros
tyrosine
tystie
tysties

| T | Z |

tzar
tzarina
tzarinas
tzars
tzatziki
tzedakah
tzigane
tziganes
tzimmes
tzimmis

U

| U | A |

uakari
uakaris

| U | B |

ubac
ubacs
ubieties

ubiety
ubiquitin
ubiquity
ubuntu

| U | D |

udal
udals
udder

uddered
udders
udon

U F

ufologist
ufology

U G

ugali
ugh
uglier
ugliest
uglified
uglifies
uglify
uglifying
uglily
ugliness
ugly

U H

uh
uhlan
uhlans

U J

ujamaa

U K

ukase
ukases
uke
ukes
ukulele
ukuleles

U L

ulama
ulamas
ulcer
ulcerate
ulcerated
ulcerates
ulcered
ulcerous
ulcers
ulema
ulemas

ulexite
ullage
ulmo
ulmos
ulna
ulnae
ulnar
ulnas
ulster
ulsters
ulterior
ultimacy
ultimata
ultimate
ultimates
ultimatum
ultimo
ultisol
ultisols
ulto
ultra
ultracold
ultradian
ultraism
ultraist
ultraists
ultras
ulu
ululant
ululate
ululated
ululates
ululating
ululation
ulus

U M

um
umbel
umbellate
umbels
umber
umbers
umbilical
umbilici
umbilicus
umbles
umbo
umbonal

umbonate
umbones
umbos
umbra
umbrae
umbrage
umbral
umbras
umbrella
umbrellas
umfaan
umfaans
umiak
umiaks
umlaut
umlauted
umlauting
umlauts
umma
ummah
ump
umph
umphs
umpirage
umpire
umpired
umpires
umpiring
umps
umpteen
umpteenth
umu
umus

U N

unabashed
unabated
unable
unadopted
unadorned
unafraid
unaided
unaligned
unalike
unalloyed
unaltered
unamiable
unamused
unaneled

unanimity
unanimous
unapt
unaptly
unaptness
unarmed
unary
unashamed
unasked
unaudited
unavowed
unaware
unawares
unawed
unbacked
unbalance
unban
unbanned
unbanning
unbans
unbar
unbarred
unbarring
unbars
unbeaten
unbeknown
unbelief
unbeloved
unbelt
unbelted
unbelting
unbelts
unbend
unbending
unbends
unbent
unbiased
unbiassed
unbidden
unbind
unbinding
unbinds
unblended
unblessed
unblest
unblind
unblinded
unblinds
unblock
unblocked

unblocks
unblown
unbolt
unbolted
unbolting
unbolts
unbookish
unborn
unbosom
unbosomed
unbosoms
unbound
unbounded
unbowed
unbrace
unbraced
unbraces
unbracing
unbranded
unbridled
unbroken
unbruised
unbuckle
unbuckled
unbuckles
unbuild
unbuilds
unbuilt
unbundle
unbundled
unbundler
unbundles
unburden
unburdens
unburied
unburies
unburned
unburnt
unbury
unburying
unbutton
unbuttons
uncaged
uncalled
uncannier
uncannily
uncanny
uncap
uncapped
uncapping

uncaps	unclosed	unctions	undergo	undertook
uncared	uncloses	unctuous	undergoes	undertow
uncaring	unclosing	uncurbed	undergone	undertows
uncase	unclothe	uncured	undergrad	underuse
uncased	unclothed	uncurl	underhand	underused
uncases	unclothes	uncurled	underhung	underuses
uncashed	unclouded	uncurling	underlaid	undervest
uncasing	unco	uncurls	underlain	underwear
unceasing	uncoated	uncut	underlay	underwent
uncertain	uncoil	undamaged	underlays	underwing
unchain	uncoiled	undated	underlet	underwire
unchained	uncoiling	undaunted	underlets	underwood
unchains	uncoils	undead	underlie	underwork
unchancy	uncolored	undecagon	underlies	undesired
unchanged	uncombed	undeceive	underlife	undid
uncharged	uncomely	undecided	underline	undies
uncharted	uncomfy	undee	underling	undiluted
unchaste	uncomment	undefiled	underlip	undine
unchecked	uncommon	undefined	underlips	undines
unchosen	unconcern	undelete	underman	undivided
unchurch	uncooked	undeleted	undermans	undo
uncial	uncool	undeletes	undermine	undock
uncials	uncork	undented	undermost	undocked
unciform	uncorked	under	underpaid	undocking
uncinate	uncorking	underact	underpart	undocks
uncivil	uncorks	underacts	underpass	undoes
uncivilly	uncos	underarm	underpay	undoing
unclad	uncounted	underbid	underpays	undone
unclaimed	uncouple	underbids	underpin	undoubted
unclasp	uncoupled	underbite	underpins	undrained
unclasped	uncouples	underbody	underplay	undraped
unclasps	uncourtly	underbred	underplot	undrawn
uncle	uncouth	undercard	underprop	undreamed
unclean	uncouthly	undercast	underrate	undreamt
uncleaner	uncover	undercoat	undersea	undress
uncleanly	uncovered	undercook	underseal	undressed
unclear	uncovers	undercool	undersell	undresses
uncleared	uncreate	undercut	underset	undue
unclearer	uncreated	undercuts	undersets	undulant
unclearly	uncreates	underdamp	undershot	undulate
unclench	uncropped	underdog	underside	undulated
uncles	uncross	underdogs	undersize	undulates
unclimbed	uncrossed	underdone	undersoil	unduly
uncloak	uncrosses	underfed	undersold	undutiful
uncloaked	uncrowded	underfelt	undersow	undy
uncloaks	uncrown	underflow	undersown	undyed
unclog	uncrowned	underfoot	undersows	undying
unclogged	uncrowns	underfund	undertake	undyingly
unclogs	uncrushed	underfur	undertint	unearned
unclose	unction	undergird	undertone	unearth

unearthed	unfitter	ungloved	unheeding	unicuspid
unearthly	unfittest	unglued	unhelpful	unicycle
unearths	unfitting	ungodly	unheroic	unicycles
unease	unfix	ungreen	unhinge	unideal
uneasier	unfixed	ungreenly	unhinged	uniface
uneasiest	unfixes	ungroup	unhinges	unified
uneasily	unfixing	ungrouped	unhinging	unifier
uneasy	unfledged	ungroups	unhitch	unifiers
uneatable	unfleshed	ungual	unhitched	unifies
uneaten	unfocused	unguard	unhitches	uniflow
unedited	unfold	unguarded	unholier	uniform
unelected	unfolded	unguards	unholiest	uniformed
unending	unfolding	unguent	unholy	uniformly
unendowed	unfolds	unguents	unhood	uniforms
unengaged	unforced	ungues	unhooded	unify
unenvied	unformed	unguided	unhooding	unifying
unequal	unfounded	unguis	unhoods	unimodal
unequaled	unframed	ungulate	unhook	unimpeded
unequally	unfree	ungulates	unhooked	uninjured
unerring	unfreedom	unguled	unhooking	uninsured
unethical	unfreeze	unhand	unhooks	uninvited
uneven	unfreezes	unhanded	unhoped	uninvoked
unevenly	unfrock	unhandily	unhorse	union
unexpired	unfrocked	unhanding	unhorsed	unionise
unexposed	unfrocks	unhandled	unhorses	unionised
unfading	unfroze	unhands	unhorsing	unionises
unfailing	unfrozen	unhandy	unhoused	unionism
unfair	unfunded	unhang	unhuman	unionist
unfairer	unfunnier	unhanging	unhung	unionists
unfairest	unfunnily	unhangs	unhurried	unionize
unfairly	unfunny	unhappen	unhurt	unionized
unfancied	unfurl	unhappens	unhusk	unionizes
unfasten	unfurled	unhappier	unhusked	unions
unfastens	unfurling	unhappily	unhusking	uniparous
unfazed	unfurls	unhappy	unhusks	uniped
unfed	unfussily	unharmed	uni	unipeds
unfeeling	unfussy	unharmful	uniaxial	uniplanar
unfeigned	ungainly	unharness	unibodies	unipod
unfelt	ungallant	unhasp	unibody	unipods
unfenced	ungeared	unhasped	unica	unipolar
unfertile	ungenial	unhasping	unicities	unipotent
unfetter	ungentle	unhasps	unicity	unique
unfetters	ungently	unhatched	unicolor	uniquely
unfilial	ungifted	unhealed	unicolour	unironed
unfilled	ungird	unhealthy	unicom	unis
unfit	ungirded	unheard	unicoms	uniserial
unfitly	ungirding	unheated	unicorn	unisex
unfitness	ungirds	unhedged	unicorns	unisexual
unfits	ungiving	unheeded	unicum	unison
unfitted	unglazed	unheedful	unicursal	unisonous

unisons	unkindly	unlighted	unmapped	unpack
unissued	unking	unlikable	unmarked	unpacked
unit	unkinged	unlike	unmarried	unpacker
unitard	unkinging	unlikely	unmask	unpackers
unitards	unkings	unlimber	unmasked	unpacking
unitarily	unkink	unlimbers	unmasker	unpacks
unitarist	unkinked	unlimited	unmaskers	unpaid
unitarity	unkinking	unlined	unmasking	unpainted
unitary	unkinks	unlink	unmasks	unpaired
unite	unknit	unlinked	unmatched	unpaved
united	unknits	unlinking	unmatured	unpeeled
unitedly	unknitted	unlinks	unmeaning	unpeg
unites	unknot	unlisted	unmeant	unpegged
unities	unknots	unlit	unmelted	unpegging
uniting	unknotted	unlivable	unmerited	unpegs
unitise	unknowing	unlived	unmet	unpeople
unitised	unknown	unload	unmindful	unpeopled
unitises	unknowns	unloaded	unmixed	unpeoples
unitising	unlabeled	unloader	unmoor	unperson
unitive	unlabored	unloaders	unmoored	unpersons
unitize	unlace	unloading	unmooring	unpick
unitized	unlaced	unloads	unmoors	unpicked
unitizes	unlaces	unlock	unmoral	unpicking
unitizing	unlacing	unlocked	unmounted	unpicks
units	unlade	unlocking	unmourned	unpin
unity	unladed	unlocks	unmovable	unpinned
univalent	unladen	unlooked	unmoved	unpinning
univalve	unlades	unloose	unmoving	unpins
univalves	unlading	unloosed	unmown	unpitied
universal	unlaid	unloosen	unmuffle	unpitying
universe	unlash	unloosens	unmuffled	unplaced
universes	unlashed	unlooses	unmuffles	unplanned
univocal	unlashes	unloosing	unmusical	unplanted
unjoin	unlashing	unlovable	unmuzzle	unplowed
unjoined	unlatch	unloved	unmuzzled	unplucked
unjoining	unlatched	unlovely	unmuzzles	unplug
unjoins	unlatches	unloving	unnamable	unplugged
unjoint	unlawful	unluckier	unnamed	unplugs
unjointed	unlay	unluckily	unnatural	unplumbed
unjoints	unlaying	unlucky	unneeded	unpoetic
unjust	unlays	unmade	unnerve	unpointed
unjuster	unleaded	unmake	unnerved	unpolitic
unjustest	unlearn	unmakes	unnerves	unpolled
unjustly	unlearned	unmaking	unnerving	unpopular
unkempt	unlearns	unman	unnoticed	unposed
unkemptly	unlearnt	unmanaged	unoiled	unpowered
unkept	unleash	unmanly	unopened	unpressed
unkind	unleashed	unmanned	unopposed	unpriced
unkinder	unleashes	unmanning	unordered	unprimed
unkindest	unless	unmans	unowned	unprinted

unproud	unriper	unsays	unshod	unsteady
unproved	unripest	unscaled	unshorn	unstep
unproven	unripped	unscarred	unsighted	unstepped
unquiet	unripping	unscathed	unsightly	unsteps
unquietly	unrips	unscented	unsigned	unstick
unquote	unrisen	unscrew	unsized	unsticks
unquoted	unrivaled	unscrewed	unskilful	unstinted
unquotes	unrivet	unscrews	unskilled	unstirred
unquoting	unriveted	unseal	unsliced	unstitch
unrated	unrivets	unsealed	unsling	unstop
unravel	unrobe	unsealing	unslings	unstopped
unraveled	unrobed	unseals	unslung	unstopper
unravels	unrobes	unseat	unsmiling	unstops
unreached	unrobing	unseated	unsmoked	unstrap
unread	unroll	unseating	unsnap	unstraps
unready	unrolled	unseats	unsnapped	unstring
unreal	unrolling	unsecured	unsnaps	unstrings
unrealism	unrolls	unseeable	unsnarl	unstrung
unreality	unroofed	unseeded	unsnarled	unstuck
unreally	unroot	unseeing	unsnarls	unstudied
unreason	unrooted	unseemly	unsocial	unstuffed
unreel	unrooting	unseen	unsoiled	unstuffy
unreeled	unroots	unseens	unsold	unstylish
unreeling	unrope	unselfish	unsolved	unsubdued
unreels	unroped	unserious	unsorted	unsubtle
unreeve	unropes	unserved	unsought	unsubtly
unreeves	unroping	unsettle	unsound	unsuccess
unreeving	unrounded	unsettled	unsounded	unsugared
unrefined	unrove	unsettles	unsoundly	unsuited
unrelated	unruffled	unsex	unsoured	unsullied
unrelaxed	unruled	unsexed	unsown	unsung
unrenewed	unrulier	unsexes	unsparing	unsure
unreserve	unruliest	unsexier	unspent	unsurely
unrest	unruly	unsexiest	unspilled	unswayed
unrested	unsaddle	unsexing	unspilt	unswept
unresting	unsaddled	unsexy	unspoiled	unsworn
unrevised	unsaddles	unshackle	unspoilt	untack
unrevoked	unsafe	unshaded	unspoken	untacked
unrhymed	unsafely	unshaken	unspool	untacking
unridable	unsafer	unshaped	unspooled	untacks
unridden	unsafest	unshared	unspools	untainted
unriddle	unsaid	unsharp	unspotted	untaken
unriddled	unsalable	unshaved	unsprayed	untamable
unriddles	unsalted	unshaven	unsprung	untamed
unrig	unsaved	unsheathe	unstable	untangle
unrigged	unsavory	unshed	unstabler	untangled
unrigging	unsavoury	unshelled	unstably	untangles
unrigs	unsay	unship	unstained	untanned
unrip	unsayable	unshipped	unstamped	untapped
unripe	unsaying	unships	unstated	untasted

untaught
untaxed
untenable
untenably
untended
untenured
untested
untether
untethers
unthanked
unthaw
unthawed
unthawing
unthaws
unthought
unthread
unthreads
unthrifty
unthrone
unthroned
unthrones
untidier
untidiest
untidily
untidy
untie
untied
unties
until
untilled
untimely
untinged
untiring
untitled
unto
untold
untoned
untouched
untoward
untraced
untracked
untrained
untreated
untrendy
untried
untrimmed
untrodden
untrue
untruly
untrussed

untruth
untruths
untuck
untucked
untucking
untucks
untuned
untuneful
unturned
untutored
untwine
untwined
untwines
untwining
untwist
untwisted
untwists
untying
untypical
unusable
unused
unusual
unusually
unuttered
unvalued
unvaried
unvarying
unveil
unveiled
unveiling
unveils
unversed
unviable
unvisited
unvoiced
unwaged
unwalled
unwanted
unwarily
unwarlike
unwarned
unwary
unwashed
unwatched
unwatered
unweaned
unwearied
unwed
unwedded
unweight

unweights
unwelcome
unwell
unwept
unwhipped
unwieldy
unwilling
unwind
unwinding
unwinds
unwinking
unwisdom
unwise
unwisely
unwished
unwitting
unwomanly
unwonted
unwooded
unworked
unworldly
unworn
unworried
unworthy
unwound
unwounded
unwrap
unwrapped
unwraps
unwritten
unyoke
unyoked
unyokes
unyoking
unzip
unzipped
unzipping
unzips

U P

up
upas
upases
upbeat
upbeats
upbraid
upbraided
upbraids
upbuild

upbuilds
upbuilt
upcast
upcasting
upcasts
upchuck
upchucked
upchucks
upcoast
upcoming
upcountry
updatable
update
updated
updates
updating
updoming
updraft
updrafts
updraught
upend
upended
upending
upends
upfield
upflung
upfront
upgrade
upgraded
upgrades
upgrading
upgrowth
upgrowths
uphaul
upheaval
upheavals
upheave
upheaved
upheaves
upheaving
upheld
uphill
uphold
upholder
upholders
upholding
upholds
upholster
upkeep
upland

uplands
uplift
uplifted
uplifter
uplifters
uplifting
uplifts
uplight
uplighter
uplights
uplink
uplinked
uplinking
uplinks
upload
uploaded
uploading
uploads
upmarket
upmost
upon
upped
upper
uppercut
uppercuts
uppermost
uppers
upping
uppish
uppishly
uppity
upraise
upraised
upraises
upraising
uprate
uprated
uprates
uprating
upright
uprightly
uprights
uprise
uprisen
uprises
uprising
uprisings
upriver
uproar
uproars

uproot
uprooted
uprooter
uprooters
uprooting
uproots
uprose
uprush
uprushes
ups
upscale
upset
upsets
upsetter
upsetters
upsetting
upshift
upshifted
upshifts
upshot
upside
upsides
upsilon
upsilons
upslope
upslopes
upstage
upstaged
upstages
upstaging
upstair
upstairs
upstand
upstart
upstarts
upstate
upstater
upstaters
upstream
upstroke
upstrokes
upsurge
upsurges
upswell
upswells
upswept
upswing
upswings
uptake
uptakes

uptempo
upthrew
upthrow
upthrown
upthrows
upthrust
upthrusts
uptick
upticks
uptight
uptime
uptown
uptowner
uptowners
uptrend
uptrends
upturn
upturned
upturning
upturns
upward
upwardly
upwards
upwarp
upwarped
upwarping
upwarps
upwelling
upwind

U R

uracil
uraei
uraemia
uraemic
uraeus
uraninite
uranium
uranyl
urate
urates
urban
urbane
urbanely
urbanise
urbanised
urbanises
urbanism
urbanist

urbanists
urbanite
urbanites
urbanity
urbanize
urbanized
urbanizes
urbs
urchin
urchins
urea
ureide
ureides
uremia
ureter
ureteral
ureteric
ureters
urethane
urethra
urethral
urethras
urge
urged
urgencies
urgency
urgent
urgently
urger
urgers
urges
urging
urial
uridine
urinal
urinals
urinary
urinate
urinated
urinates
urinating
urination
urine
urn
urned
urnfield
urnfields
urning
urns
uroboric

uroboros
urodele
urodeles
urogram
urograms
urography
urokinase
urolagnia
urologic
urologist
urology
urophilia
uropod
uropods
uropygial
uropygium
uroscopy
urostyle
urostyles
ursine
urtext
urtexte
urticaria
urticate
urticated
urticates
urus
urushiol

U S

us
usability
usable
usage
usages
usance
use
useable
used
useful
usefully
useless
uselessly
user
username
usernames
users
uses
ushabti

ushabtis
usher
ushered
usherette
ushering
ushers
using
ustad
ustads
usual
usually
usualness
usucapion
usufruct
usurer
usurers
usurious
usurp
usurped
usurper
usurpers
usurping
usurps
usury

U T

ute
utensil
utensils
uteri
uterine
uterus
utes
utile
utilise
utilised
utilises
utilising
utilities
utility
utilize
utilized
utilizer
utilizers
utilizes
utilizing
utmost
utricle
utricles

utricular
utriculus
utter
utterable
utterance
uttered

utterer
utterers
uttering
utterly
uttermost
utters

U V

uvarovite
uvea
uveal
uveas

uveitis
uvula
uvulae
uvular
uvulars

U X

uxorial
uxoricide
uxorious

V

V A

vac
vacancies
vacancy
vacant
vacantly
vacate
vacated
vacates
vacating
vacation
vacations
vaccinate
vaccine
vaccines
vaccinia
vacillate
vacs
vacua
vacuities
vacuity
vacuolar
vacuole
vacuoles
vacuous
vacuously
vacuum
vacuumed
vacuuming
vacuums
vada

vadas
vadose
vagabond
vagabonds
vagal
vagaries
vagarious
vagary
vagi
vagina
vaginae
vaginal
vaginas
vaginitis
vaginosis
vagotomy
vagrancy
vagrant
vagrantly
vagrants
vague
vaguely
vagueness
vaguer
vaguest
vaguish
vagus
vail
vailed
vailing
vails
vain

vainer
vainest
vainglory
vainly
vair
vairy
vajra
vajras
valance
valanced
valances
vale
valence
valences
valencies
valency
valentine
valerate
valerates
valerian
valerians
vales
valet
valeta
valetas
valeted
valeting
valets
valgus
valguses
valiant
valiantly

valid
validate
validated
validates
validity
validly
valine
valise
valises
vallecula
valley
valleys
vallum
valonia
valonias
valor
valorise
valorised
valorises
valorize
valorized
valorizes
valorous
valour
valproate
valse
valses
valuable
valuables
valuably
valuate
valuated

valuates
valuating
valuation
valuator
valuators
value
valued
valueless
valuer
valuers
values
valuing
valuta
valvate
valve
valved
valveless
valves
valvular
vambrace
vambraces
vamoose
vamoosed
vamooses
vamoosing
vamp
vamped
vampier
vampiest
vamping
vampire
vampires

vampiric
vampirism
vampish
vampishly
vamplate
vamplates
vamps
vampy
van
vanadate
vanadates
vanadium
vanaspati
vandal
vandalise
vandalism
vandalize
vandals
vandyke
vandykes
vane
vaned
vanes
vannesid
vanessids
vang
vanga
vangs
vanguard
vanguards
vanilla
vanillas
vanillin
vanish
vanished
vanishes
vanishing
vanitas
vanities
vanity
vanquish
vans
vantage
vantages
vapid
vapidity
vapidly
vapor
vaporable
vapored

vaporetti
vaporetto
vaporing
vaporise
vaporised
vaporises
vaporize
vaporized
vaporizer
vaporizes
vaporous
vapors
vaporware
vapour
vapoured
vapourer
vapouring
vapourish
vapours
vapoury
vaquero
vaqueros
varactor
varactors
varda
vardas
vardo
vardos
varec
variable
variables
variably
variance
variant
variants
variate
variates
variation
variceal
varicella
varices
varicose
varicosed
varied
variedly
varies
varietal
varietals
varieties
varietist

variety
varifocal
variform
varimax
variola
variolar
varioloid
variolous
variorum
various
variously
varistor
varistors
varix
varlet
varletry
varlets
varmint
varmints
varna
varnas
varnish
varnished
varnisher
varnishes
varroa
varroas
varsities
varsity
varus
varuses
varve
varved
varves
vary
varying
varyingly
vas
vasa
vasal
vasbyt
vasbyted
vasbyting
vasbyts
vascula
vascular
vasculum
vase
vasectomy
vaseful

vasefuls
vaseline
vaselined
vaselines
vases
vasomotor
vasovagal
vassal
vassalage
vassals
vast
vastation
vaster
vastest
vastly
vastness
vat
vatic
vaticinal
vats
vatted
vatting
vatu
vault
vaulted
vaulter
vaulters
vaulting
vaults
vaunt
vaunted
vaunter
vaunters
vaunting
vaunts
vavasory
vavasour
vavasours

V E

veal
vector
vectored
vectorial
vectoring
vectorise
vectorize
vectors
vedette

vedettes
vee
veejay
veejays
veena
veenas
veep
veeps
veer
veered
veering
veers
veery
vees
veg
vega
vegan
vegans
vegas
vegetable
vegetal
vegetate
vegetated
vegetates
vegged
vegges
veggie
veggies
vegging
vegie
vegies
vehemence
vehement
vehicle
vehicles
vehicular
veil
veiled
veiling
veilings
veilless
veils
vein
veined
veinier
veiniest
veining
veinless
veinlet
veinlets

veinous	vendeuses	ventral	verdant	vermicide
veins	vendible	ventrally	verdantly	vermiform
veinstone	vending	ventricle	verderer	vermifuge
veiny	vendor	vents	verderers	vermilion
vela	vendors	venture	verdict	vermin
velamen	vends	ventured	verdicts	verminate
velamina	vendue	venturer	verdigris	verminous
velar	vendues	venturers	verdin	vermis
velaria	veneer	ventures	verdins	vermouth
velarise	veneered	venturi	verditer	vernaccia
velarised	veneering	venturing	verdure	vernal
velarises	veneers	venturis	verdured	vernalise
velarium	venerable	venue	verdurous	vernalize
velarize	venerably	venues	verge	vernally
velarized	venerate	venule	verged	vernation
velarizes	venerated	venules	vergence	verneuk
velars	venerates	venus	vergences	verneuked
veld	venerator	venuses	verger	verneuker
veldskoen	venereal	veracious	vergers	verneuks
veldt	venery	veracity	verges	vernicle
veleta	venetian	veranda	verging	vernicles
veletas	venetians	verandaed	verglas	vernier
veliger	vengeance	verandah	veridical	verniers
veligers	vengeful	verandahs	veriest	vernix
velleity	venial	verandas	verified	vernixes
vellum	veniality	verapamil	verifier	veronal
velocity	venially	veratrine	verifiers	veronica
velodrome	venison	veratrum	verifies	veronicas
velour	vennel	veratrums	verify	veronique
velours	vennels	verb	verifying	verruca
velouté	venogram	verbal	verily	verrucae
velum	venograms	verbalise	verism	verrucas
velvet	venom	verbalism	verismo	verrucose
velveted	venomed	verbalist	verist	verrucous
velveteen	venomous	verbalize	veristic	versal
velvety	venosity	verballed	verists	versant
venal	venous	verbally	veritable	versants
venality	venously	verbals	veritably	versatile
venally	vent	verbascum	vérité	verse
venation	vented	verbatim	verities	versed
vend	venter	verbena	verity	verselet
vendace	ventiduct	verbenas	verjuice	verselets
vendaces	ventifact	verbiage	verkramp	verses
vendange	ventil	verbless	verkramps	verset
vended	ventilate	verbose	verlig	versets
vender	ventils	verbosely	verligs	versicle
venders	venting	verbosity	verligte	versicles
vendetta	ventless	verboten	verligtes	versified
vendettas	ventouse	verbs	vermeil	versifier
vendeuse	ventouses	verdancy	vermian	versifies

versify
versin
versine
versines
versing
versins
version
versional
versions
verso
versos
verst
versts
versus
vert
vertebra
vertebrae
vertebral
vertex
vertexes
vertical
verticals
vertices
vertigo
vertisol
vertisols
verts
vertu
vervain
verve
vervet
vervets
very
vesicae
vesical
vesicant
vesicants
vesicate
vesicated
vesicates
vesicle
vesicles
vesicular
vesper
vespers
vessel
vessels
vest
vesta
vestal

vestals
vestas
vested
vestee
vestees
vestiary
vestibule
vestige
vestiges
vestigial
vesting
vestiture
vestment
vestments
vestries
vestry
vestryman
vestrymen
vests
vesture
vestures
vet
vetch
vetches
vetchling
veteran
veterans
vetiver
vetivers
vetivert
vetkoek
vetkoeke
vetkoeks
veto
vetoed
vetoer
vetoers
vetoes
vetoing
vets
vetted
vetting
vex
vexation
vexations
vexatious
vexed
vexedly
vexer
vexers

vexes
vexilla
vexillum
vexing
vexingly

V I

via
viability
viable
viably
viaduct
viaducts
vial
vials
viand
viands
viatica
viaticum
vibe
vibes
vibist
vibists
vibracula
vibrancy
vibrant
vibrantly
vibrate
vibrated
vibrates
vibratile
vibrating
vibration
vibrato
vibrator
vibrators
vibratory
vibrio
vibrios
vibrissae
viburnum
viburnums
vicar
vicarage
vicarages
vicarial
vicariate
vicarious
vicars

vicarship
vice
viceless
viceregal
vicereine
viceroy
viceroyal
viceroys
vices
vici
vicinage
vicinages
vicinal
vicinity
vicious
viciously
vicomte
vicomtes
victim
victimise
victimize
victims
victor
victoria
victorias
victories
victors
victory
victrices
victrix
victual
victualed
victualer
victuals
vicuña
vicuñas
vicus
vid
vide
videlicet
video
videodisc
videoed
videoes
videofit
videofits
videogram
videoing
videos
videotape

videotex
videotext
vidicon
vidicons
vidiot
vidiots
vids
vie
vied
vielle
vielles
vies
view
viewable
viewdata
viewed
viewer
viewers
viewgraph
viewing
viewings
viewless
viewpoint
viewport
viewports
views
viff
viffed
viffing
viffs
vig
viga
vigesimal
vigil
vigilance
vigilant
vigilante
vigils
vigneron
vignerons
vignette
vignetted
vignettes
vigor
vigorish
vigoro
vigorous
vigour
vihara
viharas

vihuela	vinery	violists	viroids	visitable
vihuelas	vines	viologen	virology	visitant
vilayet	vineyard	viologens	viropexis	visitants
vilayets	vineyards	violone	virtu	visited
vile	vinier	violones	virtual	visiting
vilely	viniest	viols	virtually	visitor
vileness	vinified	vipassana	virtue	visitors
viler	vinifies	viper	virtues	visits
vilest	vinify	viperfish	virtuosi	visna
vilified	vinifying	viperine	virtuosic	visor
vilifier	vining	viperish	virtuoso	visored
vilifiers	vino	viperous	virtuosos	visors
vilifies	vinos	vipers	virtuous	vista
vilify	vinosity	viraemia	virulence	vistas
vilifying	vinous	viraemic	virulent	visual
vill	vinously	virago	virus	visualise
villa	vint	viragoes	viruses	visuality
village	vintage	viragos	visa	visualize
villager	vintager	viral	visage	visually
villagers	vintagers	virally	visaged	visuals
villages	vintages	virelay	visages	vital
villagey	vinted	virelays	visagiste	vitalise
villain	vinting	virement	visas	vitalised
villains	vintner	viremia	viscacha	vitalises
villainy	vintners	vireo	viscachas	vitalism
villas	vints	vireos	viscera	vitalist
villein	viny	virescent	visceral	vitalists
villeins	vinyl	virga	viscid	vitality
villi	vinyls	virgae	viscidity	vitalize
villous	viol	virgate	viscose	vitalized
villus	viola	virgates	viscosity	vitalizes
vim	violable	virger	viscount	vitally
vin	violas	virgers	viscounts	vitals
vina	violate	virgin	viscounty	vitamin
vinaceous	violated	virginal	viscous	vitamins
vinas	violates	virginals	viscously	vitelli
vinca	violating	virginity	viscus	vitellin
vincas	violation	virgins	vise	vitelline
vincible	violator	virgule	vises	vitellus
vincula	violators	virgules	visible	vitiate
vincular	violence	viridian	visibles	vitiated
vinculum	violent	virile	visibly	vitiates
vindaloo	violently	virilism	vision	vitiating
vindaloos	violet	virility	visional	vitiation
vindicate	violets	virilocal	visionary	vitiator
vine	violin	virino	visioned	vitiators
vinegar	violinist	virinos	visioning	vitiligo
vinegary	violins	virion	visions	vitreous
vineries	violist	viroid	visit	vitrified

vitrifies
vitriform
vitrify
vitrine
vitrines
vitriol
vitriolic
vitta
vittae
vittle
vittles
viva
vivace
vivaces
vivacious
vivacity
vivaed
vivaing
vivaria
vivarium
vivas
vivat
viverrid
viverrids
vivers
vivianite
vivid
vivider
vividest
vividly
vividness
vivified
vivifies
vivify
vivifying
vivisect
vivisects
vixen
vixenish
vixens
vizard
vizards
vizier
vizierate
vizierial
viziers
vizor
vizors
vizsla
vizslas

V L

vlast
vlei
vleis

V O

vobla
vocable
vocables
vocal
vocalese
vocalic
vocalise
vocalised
vocalises
vocalism
vocalisms
vocalist
vocalists
vocality
vocalize
vocalized
vocalizer
vocalizes
vocally
vocals
vocation
vocations
vocative
vocatives
vocoder
vocoders
vodka
vodkas
vodun
voe
voes
voetsak
vogue
vogues
voguish
voice
voiced
voiceful
voiceless
voicemail
voicer
voicers

voices
voicing
void
voidable
voidance
voided
voiding
voidness
voids
voila
voile
volant
volar
volatile
volatiles
volcanic
volcanism
volcano
volcanoes
volcanos
vole
voles
volet
volets
volition
volitive
volk
volke
volkisch
volley
volleyed
volleyer
volleyers
volleying
volleys
volplane
volplaned
volplanes
volt
voltage
voltages
voltaic
volte
volted
voltes
volting
voltmeter
volts
voluble
volubly

volume
volumes
volumise
volumised
volumiser
volumises
volumize
volumized
volumizer
volumizes
voluntary
volunteer
volupté
volute
voluted
volutes
volution
volutions
volva
volvas
volvox
volvoxes
volvuli
volvulus
vomer
vomers
vomit
vomited
vomiter
vomiters
vomiting
vomitoria
vomitory
vomitous
vomits
vomitus
voodoo
voodooed
voodooing
voodooism
voodooist
voodoos
voracious
voracity
vortex
vortexes
vortical
vortices
vorticity

vorticose
votaries
votarist
votarists
votary
vote
voted
voteless
voter
voters
votes
voting
votive
votives
vouch
vouched
voucher
vouchers
vouches
vouching
vouchsafe
voulu
voussoir
voussoirs
vow
vowed
vowel
voweled
vowelise
vowelised
vowelises
vowelize
vowelized
vowelizes
vowelled
vowelless
vowelly
vowels
vowing
vows
voxel
voxels
voyage
voyaged
voyager
voyagers
voyages
voyageur
voyageurs
voyaging

voyeur
voyeurism
voyeurs

V R

vroom
vroomed
vrooming
vrooms
vrouw
vrouws

vrow
vrows

V U

vug
vuggy
vugs
vugular
vulcanise
vulcanism
vulcanite

vulcanize
vulgar
vulgarian
vulgarise
vulgarism
vulgarity
vulgarize
vulgarly
vulgate
vulgates
vuln

vulned
vulnerary
vulning
vulns
vulpine
vulture
vultures
vulturine
vulturish
vulturous
vulva

vulval
vulvar
vulvas
vulvitis

V Y

vygie
vygies
vying

W A

wabbit
wabi
waboom
wabooms
wack
wacke
wacked
wackes
wackier
wackiest
wackily
wackiness
wacko
wackoes
wackos
wacks
wacky
wad
wada
wadable
wadas
wadcutter
wadded
waddies
wadding

waddle
waddled
waddler
waddlers
waddles
waddling
waddy
wade
wadeable
waded
wader
waders
wades
wadi
wadies
wading
wadis
wads
wady
wafer
wafered
wafering
wafers
wafery
waffle
waffled

waffler
wafflers
waffles
waffling
waffly
waft
wafted
wafting
wafts
wag
wage
waged
wager
wagers
wages
wagged
waggeries
waggery
wagging
waggish
waggishly
waggle
waggled
waggler
waggles
waggling

waggly
waggon
waggoner
waggoners
waggons
waging
wagon
wagoner
wagoners
wagonette
wagonload
wagons
wags
wagtail
wagtails
wah
wahey
wahine
wahines
wahoo
wahoos
waiata
waiatas
waif
waifish
waifs

wail
wailed
wailer
wailers
wailful
wailing
wailingly
wails
wain
wains
wainscot
wainscots
waist
waistband
waistcoat
waisted
waistless
waistline
waists
wait
waited
waiter
waiters
waiting
waitress
waitron

waitrons	wall	wanderoo	warblers	warmonger
waits	wallabies	wanderoos	warbles	warms
waitstaff	wallaby	wanders	warbling	warmth
waive	wallah	wands	warbonnet	warn
waived	wallahs	wane	ward	warned
waiver	wallaroo	waned	warded	warner
waivers	wallaroos	wanes	warden	warners
waives	wallboard	waney	wardens	warning
waiving	wallchart	wangle	warder	warningly
waka	walled	wangled	warders	warnings
wakame	wallet	wangler	warding	warns
wakas	wallets	wanglers	wardress	warp
wake	walleye	wangles	wardrobe	warpage
wakeboard	walleyes	wangling	wardrobes	warpaint
waked	wallies	waning	wardroom	warpath
wakeful	walling	wank	wardrooms	warped
wakefully	wallop	wanked	wards	warper
waken	walloped	wanker	wardship	warpers
wakened	walloper	wankers	wardships	warping
wakening	wallopers	wanking	ware	warplane
wakens	walloping	wanks	wared	warplanes
waker	wallops	wanly	warehou	warps
wakers	wallow	wanna	warehouse	warragal
wakes	wallowed	wannabe	wares	warragals
waking	wallower	wannabes	warfare	warrant
wakizashi	wallowers	wanner	warfarin	warranted
waldo	wallowing	wanness	warhead	warrantee
waldoes	wallows	wannest	warheads	warranter
waldrapp	wallpaper	want	warhorse	warrantor
waldrapps	walls	wanted	warhorses	warrants
wale	wally	wanting	warier	warranty
wales	walnut	wanton	wariest	warred
wali	walnuts	wantoned	warily	warren
walis	walrus	wantoning	wariness	warrener
walk	walruses	wantonly	waring	warrens
walkable	waltz	wantons	warlike	warrigal
walkabout	waltzed	wants	warlock	warrigals
walkathon	waltzer	wapentake	warlocks	warring
walked	waltzers	wapiti	warlord	warrior
walker	waltzes	wapitis	warlords	warriors
walkers	waltzing	waqf	warm	wars
walkies	wambenger	war	warmblood	warship
walking	wampum	waragi	warmed	warships
walkout	wan	waratah	warmer	wart
walkouts	wand	waratahs	warmers	warthog
walkover	wander	warbird	warmest	warthogs
walkovers	wandered	warbirds	warming	wartier
walks	wanderer	warble	warmish	wartiest
walkway	wanderers	warbled	warmly	wartime
walkways	wandering	warbler	warmness	warts

warty
wary
was
wasabi
wash
washable
washbag
washbags
washbasin
washboard
washcloth
washday
washdays
washdown
washdowns
washed
washer
washeries
washers
washery
washes
washier
washiest
washiness
washing
washland
washout
washouts
washrag
washrags
washroom
washrooms
washstand
washtub
washtubs
washy
wasp
waspie
waspies
waspish
waspishly
wasps
wassail
wassailed
wassailer
wassails
wast
wastage
waste
wasted

wasteful
wastegate
wasteland
waster
wasters
wastes
wasting
wastrel
wastrels
watch
watcha
watchable
watchdog
watchdogs
watched
watcher
watchers
watches
watchfire
watchful
watching
watchman
watchmen
watchword
water
waterbed
waterbeds
waterbird
waterbody
waterbuck
watercock
waterdog
waterdogs
watered
waterer
waterers
waterfall
waterfowl
watergate
waterhen
waterhens
waterhole
watering
waterleaf
waterless
waterline
waterman
watermark
watermen
watermill

waters
watershed
waterside
waterski
waterskis
waterway
waterways
waterweed
watery
watt
wattage
wattle
wattled
wattles
wattling
wattmeter
watts
waul
wauled
wauling
wauls
wave
waveband
wavebands
waved
waveform
waveforms
wavefront
waveguide
waveless
wavelet
wavelets
waver
wavered
waverer
waverers
wavering
wavers
wavery
waves
wavetable
wavicle
wavicles
wavier
waviest
wavily
waviness
waving
wavy
wax

waxberry
waxbill
waxbills
waxcloth
waxed
waxen
waxer
waxers
waxes
waxier
waxiest
waxily
waxiness
waxing
waxings
waxpod
waxpods
waxwing
waxwings
waxwork
waxworks
waxy
way
wayang
waybill
waybills
waybread
wayfarer
wayfarers
wayfaring
waylaid
waylay
waylayer
waylayers
waylaying
waylays
waymark
waymarked
waymarker
waymarks
waypoint
waypoints
ways
wayside
waysides
wayward
waywarder
waywardly
wayzgoose
wazir

wazirs
wazzock
wazzocks

W E

we
weak
weaken
weakened
weakener
weakeners
weakening
weakens
weaker
weakest
weakfish
weakish
weaklier
weakliest
weakling
weaklings
weakly
weakness
weal
wealed
wealing
weals
wealth
wealthier
wealthily
wealthy
wean
weaned
weaner
weaners
weaning
weanling
weanlings
weans
weapon
weaponed
weaponry
weapons
wear
wearable
wearer
wearers
wearied
wearier

wearies
weariest
weariless
wearily
weariness
wearing
wearingly
wearisome
wears
weary
wearying
weasel
weaseled
weaseling
weaselled
weaselly
weasels
weather
weathered
weatherly
weathers
weave
weaved
weaver
weavers
weaves
weaving
web
webbed
webbing
weber
webers
webmaster
webs
webwork
webworks
webworm
webworms
wed
wedded
wedding
weddings
wedge
wedgebill
wedged
wedges
wedgie
wedgies
wedging
wedlock

weds
wee
weebill
weebills
weed
weeded
weeder
weeders
weedgrown
weedicide
weedier
weediest
weediness
weeding
weedless
weeds
weedy
weeing
weejuns
week
weekday
weekdays
weekend
weekended
weekender
weekends
weeklies
weekly
weeks
weel
ween
weened
weenie
weenier
weenies
weeniest
weening
weens
weeny
weep
weeper
weepers
weepie
weepier
weepies
weepiest
weepily
weepiness
weeping
weepingly

weeps
weepy
weer
wees
weest
weever
weevers
weevil
weevils
weevily
weft
wefts
weigela
weigelas
weigh
weighable
weighed
weigher
weighers
weighing
weighs
weight
weighted
weightier
weightily
weighting
weights
weighty
weir
weird
weirded
weirder
weirdest
weirdie
weirdies
weirding
weirdly
weirdness
weirdo
weirdos
weirds
weirdy
weirs
weka
wekas
welch
welched
welches
welching
welcome

welcomed
welcomely
welcomer
welcomers
welcomes
welcoming
weld
weldable
welded
welder
welders
welding
weldmesh
welds
welfare
welfarism
welfarist
welkin
well
welled
wellie
wellies
welling
wellness
wells
welly
wels
welsh
welshed
welsher
welshers
welshes
welshing
welt
welted
welter
weltered
weltering
welters
welting
welts
wen
wench
wenched
wencher
wenchers
wenches
wenching
wend
wended

wendigo
wendigoes
wendigos
wending
wends
wens
went
wept
were
werewolf
werf
werfs
wert
werven
west
westbound
westering
westerly
western
westerner
westerns
westing
westings
westward
westwards
wet
weta
wetas
wetback
wetbacks
wether
wethers
wetland
wetlands
wetly
wetness
wets
wetsuit
wetsuits
wettable
wetted
wetter
wettest
wetting
wettish
wetware
wey
weys

W H			
whack	whatnot	wheezes	whicker	whinier
whacked	whatnots	wheezier	whickered	whiniest
whacker	whatsit	wheeziest	whickers	whining
whackers	whatsits	wheezily	whidah	whiningly
whackier	whatso	wheezing	whidahs	whinnied
whackiest	whaup	wheezy	whiff	whinnies
whacking	whaups	whelk	whiffed	whinny
whacko	wheal	whelks	whiffier	whinnying
whackoes	whealed	whelm	whiffiest	whinstone
whackos	whealing	whelmed	whiffing	whiny
whacks	wheals	whelming	whiffle	whip
whacky	wheat	whelms	whiffled	whipbird
whale	wheatear	whelp	whiffles	whipbirds
whaleback	wheatears	whelped	whiffling	whipcord
whalebird	wheaten	whelping	whiffs	whipcords
whaleboat	wheatgerm	whelps	whiffy	whiplash
whalebone	wheatmeal	when	while	whipless
whaled	whee-	whence	whiled	whipped
whaler	wheech	whenever	whiles	whipper
whalers	wheeched	whenua	whiling	whippers
whales	wheeches	where	whilom	whippet
whaling	wheeching	whereas	whilst	whippets
wham	wheedle	whereat	whim	whipping
whammed	wheedled	whereby	whimbrel	whippings
whammies	wheedler	wherefore	whimbrels	whippy
whamming	wheedlers	wherefrom	whimper	whips
whammo	wheedles	wherein	whimpered	whipsaw
whammy	wheedling	whereof	whimperer	whipsawed
whams	wheel	whereon	whimpers	whipsawn
whanau	wheelback	whereto	whims	whipsaws
whang	wheelbase	whereupon	whimsey	whipstock
whanged	wheeled	wherever	whimseys	whiptail
whanging	wheeler	wherewith	whimsical	whiptails
whangs	wheelers	wherries	whimsies	whipworm
whap	wheelie	wherry	whimsy	whipworms
whapped	wheelies	wherryman	whin	whir
whapping	wheeling	wherrymen	whinchat	whirl
whaps	wheelless	whet	whinchats	whirled
whare	wheelman	whether	whine	whirler
whares	wheelmen	whets	whined	whirlers
wharf	wheels	whetstone	whiner	whirligig
wharfage	wheelsman	whetted	whiners	whirling
wharfie	wheelsmen	whetter	whines	whirlpool
wharfies	wheelspin	whetters	whinge	whirls
wharfs	wheen	whetting	whinged	whirlwind
wharves	wheesht	whew	whingeing	whirr
what	wheeze	whey	whinger	whirred
whatever	wheezed	which	whingers	whirring
	wheezer	whichaway	whinges	whirrs
	wheezers	whichever	whingy	whirs

whisht
whisk
whisked
whisker
whiskered
whiskers
whiskery
whiskey
whiskies
whisking
whisks
whisky
whisper
whispered
whisperer
whispers
whispery
whist
whistle
whistled
whistler
whistlers
whistles
whistling
whit
white
whitebait
whitebeam
whitecoat
whited
whiteface
whitefish
whitefly
whitehead
whitely
whiten
whitened
whitener
whiteners
whiteness
whitening
whitens
whiter
whites
whitest
whitetail
whitewall
whitewash
whitewood
whitework

whitey
whiteys
whither
whiting
whitish
whitlow
whitlows
whittle
whittled
whittles
whittling
whiz
whizes
whizz
whizzed
whizzes
whizzing
whizzo
whizzy
who
whoa
whodunit
whodunits
whodunnit
whoever
whole
wholefood
wholemeal
wholeness
wholesale
wholesome
wholism
wholly
whom
whomever
whomp
whomped
whomping
whomps
whomso
whoomp
whoomph
whoomps
whoop
whooped
whoopee
whooper
whoopers
whooping
whoops

whoopsie
whoopsies
whoosh
whooshed
whooshes
whooshing
whop
whopped
whopper
whoppers
whopping
whops
whore
whored
whoredom
whores
whoreson
whoresons
whoring
whorish
whorishly
whorl
whorled
whorling
whorls
whose
whosever
whoso
whosoever
whump
whumped
whumping
whumps
whup
whupped
whupping
whups
why
whyda
whydah
whydahs
whydas
whys

wibble
wibbled
wibbles
wibbling

wibbly
wick
wicked
wickeder
wickedest
wickedly
wicker
wicket
wickets
wicking
wickiup
wickiups
wicks
widdle
widdled
widdles
widdling
wide
wideawake
widebody
widely
widen
widened
widener
wideners
wideness
widening
widens
wideout
wideouts
wider
wides
widest
widgeon
widgeons
widger
widget
widgets
widish
widow
widowbird
widowed
widower
widowers
widowhood
widowing
widows
width
widths
widthways

widthwise
wield
wielded
wielder
wielders
wielding
wields
wieldy
wiener
wieners
wienie
wienies
wife
wifehood
wifeless
wifely
wifey
wifeys
wifie
wifies
wig
wigeon
wigeons
wigged
wiggier
wiggiest
wigging
wiggings
wiggle
wiggled
wiggler
wigglers
wiggles
wiggling
wiggly
wiggy
wight
wights
wigless
wigs
wigwag
wigwagged
wigwags
wigwam
wigwams
wilco
wild
wildcat
wildcats
wilded

wilder	willy	windgall	wingding	winterer
wildered	wilt	windgalls	wingdings	winterers
wildering	wilted	windhover	winged	wintering
wilders	wilting	windier	winger	winterise
wildest	wilts	windiest	wingers	winterize
wildfire	wily	windigo	winging	winterly
wildfires	wimmin	windigoes	wingless	winters
wildfowl	wimp	windigos	winglet	wintery
wilding	wimped	windily	winglets	wintrier
wildings	wimpier	windiness	wingman	wintriest
wildish	wimpiest	winding	wingmen	wintrily
wildlife	wimping	windings	wingover	wintry
wildling	wimpish	windlass	wingovers	winy
wildlings	wimpishly	windless	wings	wipe
wildly	wimple	windmill	wingspan	wipeable
wildness	wimpled	windmills	wingspans	wiped
wilds	wimples	window	winier	wiper
wildwood	wimps	windowed	winiest	wipers
wildwoods	wimpy	windowing	wining	wipes
wile	win	windows	wink	wiping
wiled	wince	windpipe	winked	wire
wiles	winced	windpipes	winking	wired
wilful	wincer	windrow	winkle	wireframe
wilfully	wincers	windrows	winkled	wireless
wilga	winces	winds	winkler	wireline
wilgas	wincey	windsail	winklers	wireman
wilier	winceys	windsails	winkles	wiremen
wiliest	winch	windslab	winkling	wirer
wilily	winched	windsock	winks	wirers
wiliness	wincher	windsocks	winless	wires
wiling	winchers	windstorm	winnable	wiretap
will	winches	windsurf	winner	wiretaps
willed	winching	windsurfs	winners	wireworm
willemite	wincing	windswept	winning	wireworms
willer	wincingly	windward	winningly	wirier
willers	wind	windwards	winnings	wiriest
willet	windage	windy	winnow	wirily
willets	windbag	wine	winnowed	wiriness
willful	windbags	wineberry	winnower	wiring
willie	windbound	wined	winnowers	wiry
willies	windbreak	winemaker	winnowing	wis
willing	windburn	wineries	winnows	wisdom
willingly	windburnt	winery	wino	wise
williwaw	windchest	wines	winos	wiseacre
williwaws	winded	wineskin	wins	wiseacres
willow	winder	wineskins	winsome	wisecrack
willows	winders	winey	winsomely	wised
willowy	windfall	wing	winter	wisely
wills	windfalls	wingbeat	wintered	wisent
		wingbeats		wisents

wiser
wises
wisest
wish
wishbone
wishbones
wished
wisher
wishers
wishes
wishful
wishfully
wishing
wising
wisp
wispily
wispiness
wisps
wispy
wissed
wisses
wissing
wist
wistaria
wistarias
wisteria
wisterias
wistful
wistfully
wit
witan
witans
witblits
witch
witched
witchery
witches
witchetty
witching
witchlike
witchweed
witchy
with
withal
withdraw
withdrawn
withdraws
withdrew
withe
wither

withered
withering
witherite
withers
withes
withheld
withhold
withholds
withies
within
without
withstand
withstood
withy
witless
witlessly
witling
witlings
witloof
witness
witnessed
witnesses
wits
witted
witter
wittered
wittering
witters
witticism
wittier
wittiest
wittily
wittiness
witting
wittingly
wittol
wittols
witty
wivern
wiverns
wives
wiz
wizard
wizardly
wizardry
wizards
wizen
wizened
wizzo

W O

wo
woad
wobbegon
wobbegong
wobbegons
wobble
wobbled
wobbler
wobblers
wobbles
wobblier
wobblies
wobbliest
wobbling
wobbly
wodge
wodges
woe
woebegone
woeful
woefully
woes
wog
woggle
woggles
wogs
wok
woke
woken
woks
wold
wolds
wolf
wolfed
wolfhound
wolfing
wolfish
wolfishly
wolfram
wolfs
wolfsbane
wolfskin
wolfskins
wolverine
wolves
woma
woman
womanhood

womanise
womanised
womanises
womanish
womanism
womanist
womanists
womanize
womanized
womanizer
womanizes
womankind
womanless
womanlike
womanly
womas
womb
wombat
wombats
wombs
women
womenfolk
womyn
won
wonder
wondered
wonderer
wonderers
wonderful
wondering
wonders
wondrous
wonga
wonk
wonkier
wonkiest
wonkily
wonkiness
wonks
wonky
wont
wonted
wonting
wonton
wontons
wonts
woo
wooable
wood
woodbine

woodblock
woodchat
woodchats
woodchip
woodchips
woodchuck
woodcock
woodcraft
woodcut
woodcuts
wooded
wooden
woodenly
woodentop
woodgrain
woodier
woodiest
woodiness
woodland
woodlands
woodlark
woodlarks
woodless
woodlice
woodlouse
woodman
woodmen
woodnote
woodnotes
woodpile
woodpiles
woodrat
woodrats
woodruff
woodruffs
woodrush
woods
woodscrew
woodshed
woodsheds
woodsia
woodsias
woodsier
woodsiest
woodsman
woodsmen
woodsmoke
woodstar
woodstars
woodsy

woodwasp
woodwasps
woodwind
woodwinds
woodwork
woodworm
woodworms
woody
woodyard
woodyards
wooed
wooer
wooers
woof
woofed
woofer
woofers
woofing
woofs
woofter
woofters
wooing
wool
woolen
woolens
woollen
woollens
woollier
woollies
woolliest
woolly
woolman
woolmen
woolpack
woolpacks
wools
woolshed
woolsheds
woomera
woomeras
woomph
woonerf
woonerfs
woonerven
woopie
woopies
woopy
woos
woosh
wooshed

wooshes
wooshing
woozier
wooziest
woozily
wooziness
woozy
wop
wops
word
wordage
wordages
wordbook
wordbooks
worded
wordier
wordiest
wordily
wordiness
wording
wordings
wordless
wordplay
words
wordsmith
wordy
wore
work
workable
workably
workaday
workalike
workbench
workboat
workboats
workbook
workbooks
workbox
workboxes
workday
workdays
worked
worker
workers
workfare
workflow
workflows
workforce
workhorse
workhouse

working
workings
workless
workload
workloads
workman
workmate
workmates
workmen
workout
workouts
workpiece
workplace
workroom
workrooms
works
worksheet
workshop
workshops
worksite
worksites
workspace
worktop
worktops
workweek
workweeks
world
worldlier
worldling
worldly
worlds
worldwide
worm
wormed
wormer
wormeries
wormers
wormery
wormfish
wormhole
wormholes
wormier
wormiest
worminess
worming
worms
wormseed
wormwheel
wormwood
wormwoods

wormy
worn
worried
worriedly
worrier
worriers
worries
worriment
worrisome
worrit
worrited
worriting
worrits
worry
worryguts
worrying
worrywart
wors
worse
worsen
worsened
worsening
worsens
worship
worshiped
worshiper
worships
worst
worsted
wort
worth
worthier
worthies
worthiest
worthily
worthless
worthy
worts
wot
wotcha
wotcher
would
wouldst
wound
wounded
wounding
woundings
woundless
wounds
woundwort

wove
woven
wow
wowed
wowee
wowing
wows
wowser
wowsers
woylie
woylies

| W | R |

wrack
wracked
wracking
wracks
wraith
wraiths
wrangle
wrangled
wrangler
wranglers
wrangles
wrangling
wrap
wrapped
wrapper
wrappers
wrapping
wraps
wrasse
wrasses
wrath
wrathful
wrathy
wreak
wreaked
wreaker
wreakers
wreaking
wreaks
wreath
wreathe
wreathed
wreathes
wreathing
wreaths
wreck

wreckage
wrecked
wrecker
wreckers
wreckfish
wrecking
wrecks
wren
wrench
wrenched
wrenches
wrenching
wrens
wrentit
wrentits
wrest
wrested
wresting
wrestle
wrestled
wrestler
wrestlers
wrestles
wrestling
wrests
wretch
wretched

wretches
wrier
wriest
wriggle
wriggled
wriggler
wrigglers
wriggles
wrigglier
wriggling
wriggly
wright
wrights
wring
wringer
wringers
wringing
wrings
wrinkle
wrinkled
wrinkles
wrinklie
wrinklier
wrinklies
wrinkling
wrinkly
wrist

wristband
wristlet
wristlets
wrists
wristwork
wristy
writ
writable
write
writer
writerly
writers
writes
writhe
writhed
writhen
writhes
writhing
writing
writings
writs
written
wrong
wrongdoer
wronged
wronger
wrongers

wrongful
wronging
wrongly
wrongness
wrongs
wrot
wrote
wroth
wrought
wrung
wry
wrybill
wrybills
wryer
wryest
wryly
wrymouth
wrymouths
wryneck
wrynecks
wryness
wrythen

W U

wuff
wuffed

wuffing
wuffs
wulfenite
wunnerful
wurst
wurtzite
wushu
wuss
wussies
wussy
wuz

W Y

wye
wyes
wyn
wynd
wynds
wyns
wysiwyg
wyvern
wyverns

X A

xanthan
xanthate
xanthene
xanthine
xanthoma
xanthomas

X E

xebec
xebecs

xenocryst
xenogamy
xenograft
xenolith
xenoliths
xenon
xenophobe
xenotime
xeric
xeriscape
xeroderma
xerophile

xerophyte
xerox
xeroxed
xeroxes
xeroxing

X I

xi
xis

X O

xoana
xoanon

X U

xu

X Y

xylem
xylene

xylitol
xylophone
xylose
xysti
xystus

Y A

ya
yaar
yabber
yabbered
yabbering
yabbers
yabbie
yabbies
yabby
yacht
yachted
yachtie
yachties
yachting
yachts
yachtsman
yachtsmen
yack
yacker
yacks
yaffle
yaffles
yag
yagé
yagés
yagna
yagnas
yags
yah
yahoo
yahoos
yahrzeit
yahrzeits
yajna
yajnas
yak
yakitori
yakka
yakked
yakking
yaks

yakuza
yam
yammer
yammered
yammerer
yammerers
yammering
yammers
yams
yandied
yandies
yandy
yandying
yang
yank
yanked
yanking
yanks
yantra
yantras
yap
yapok
yapoks
yapp
yapped
yapper
yappers
yappier
yappiest
yapping
yappy
yaps
yarak
yard
yardage
yardages
yardang
yardangs
yardarm
yardarms
yardbird
yardbirds

yarded
yarding
yardman
yardmen
yards
yardstick
yare
yarmulka
yarmulkas
yarmulke
yarmulkes
yarn
yarned
yarning
yarns
yarraman
yarramans
yarramen
yarran
yarrans
yarrow
yarrows
yashmak
yashmaks
yataghan
yataghans
yatra
yatras
yatter
yattered
yattering
yatters
yaupon
yaupons
yautia
yautias
yaw
yawed
yawing
yawl
yawls
yawn

yawned
yawner
yawners
yawning
yawningly
yawns
yawp
yawped
yawper
yawpers
yawping
yawps
yaws
yay

Y C

yclept

Y E

ye
yea
yeah
yean
yeaned
yeaning
yeans
year
yearbook
yearbooks
yearling
yearlings
yearly
yearn
yearned
yearner
yearners
yearning
yearnings
yearns
yeast

yeastier
yeastiest
yeastily
yeasty
yecch
yech
yechy
yeehah
yeehaw
yegg
yeggs
yeh
yell
yelled
yelling
yellow
yellowed
yellower
yellowest
yellowfin
yellowing
yellowish
yellowly
yellows
yellowy
yells
yelp
yelped
yelper
yelpers
yelping
yelps
yen
yenned
yenning
yens
yenta
yentas
yeoman
yeomanly
yeomanry
yeomen

yeow
yep
yer
yerba
yes
yeses
yeshiva
yeshivas
yesses
yessir
yessired
yessiring
yessirs
yessum
yesterday
yet
yeti
yetis
yeuch
yew
yews
yez

Y I

yi
yield
yielded
yielder
yielders
yielding
yields
yikes
yin
yip
yipped
yippee
yippie

yippies
yipping
yips

Y L

ylem
ylid
ylide
ylides
ylids

Y O

yo
yob
yobbery
yobbish
yobbishly
yobbo
yobboes
yobbos
yobby
yobs
yock
yocks
yod
yodel
yodeled
yodeling
yodelled
yodeller
yodellers
yodelling
yodels
yods
yoga
yogh
yoghourt

yoghourts
yoghs
yoghurt
yoghurts
yogi
yogic
yogis
yogurt
yogurts
yohimbe
yohimbes
yohimbine
yoicks
yok
yoke
yoked
yokel
yokels
yokes
yoking
yokozuna
yoks
yolk
yolked
yolkless
yolks
yolky
yomp
yomped
yomping
yomps
yon
yonder
yoni
yonis
yonks
yoof
yore

york
yorked
yorker
yorkers
yorking
yorks
you
young
younger
youngest
youngish
youngling
youngster
younker
younkers
your
yourn
yours
yourself
yous
youse
youth
youthful
youths
yow
yowl
yowled
yowling
yowls

Y T

ytterbium
yttrium

Y U

yuan
yuca

yucca
yuccas
yuck
yuckier
yuckiest
yucky
yuga
yugas
yuh
yuk
yukata
yukatas
yukkier
yukkiest
yukky
yulan
yulans
yum
yummier
yummiest
yummy
yup
yuppie
yuppiedom
yuppies
yuppified
yuppifies
yuppify
yuppy
yups
yurt
yurts
yus

Z

Z A

zaffer
zaffre
zaftig
zag
zagged
zagging
zags
zaibatsu
zaire
zakat
zakouska
zakouskas
zakouski
zakuska
zakuskas
zakuski
zambra
zambras
zami
zamia
zamindar
zamindari
zamindars
zamindary
zamis
zander
zanders
zanier
zanies
zaniest
zanily
zaniness
zany
zap
zapateado
zapped
zapper
zappers
zappier
zappiest
zapping

zappy
zaps
zarda
zareba
zarebas
zari
zariba
zaribas
zarzuela
zarzuelas
zax
zaxes
zazen

Z E

zeal
zealot
zealotry
zealots
zealous
zealously
zebec
zebecs
zebra
zebras
zebrawood
zebu
zebus
zed
zedoaries
zedoary
zeds
zee
zeera
zees
zein
zeitgeber
zeitgeist
zemindari
zenana
zenanas
zenith

zenithal
zeolite
zeolites
zeolitic
zephyr
zephyrs
zero
zeroed
zeroes
zeroing
zeros
zeroth
zest
zester
zesters
zestful
zestfully
zestier
zestiest
zesty
zeta
zetetic
zeugma
zeugmas
zeugmatic

Z H

zho
zhos

Z I

ziff
ziffs
zig
zigged
zigging
ziggurat
ziggurats
zigs
zigzag
zigzagged

zigzags
zilch
zilla
zillah
zillahs
zillas
zillion
zillions
zillionth
zinc
zinced
zincing
zincite
zinco
zincos
zincs
zindabad
zineb
zing
zinged
zinger
zingers
zingier
zingiest
zinging
zings
zingy
zinnia
zinnias
zip
zipless
ziplock
zipped
zipper
zippered
zippering
zippers
zippier
zippiest
zippily
zippiness
zipping

zippo
zippy
zips
zircalloy
zircaloy
zircon
zirconia
zirconium
zit
zither
zitherist
zithers
ziti
zits
zizz
zizzed
zizzes
zizzing

Z L

zloties
zloty
zlotys

Z O

zodiac
zodiacal
zoetrope
zoetropes
zoftig
zoisite
zokor
zokors
zol
zolle
zols
zombie
zombies
zombified
zombifies
zombify

zonal
zonally
zonation
zone
zoned
zones
zoning
zonk
zonked
zonking
zonks
zonule
zonules
zonure

zonures
zoo
zooid
zooidal
zooids
zookeeper
zoolatry
zoologist
zoology
zoom
zoomed
zooming
zooms
zoonoses

zoonosis
zoonotic
zoophyte
zoophytes
zoos
zoospore
zoospores
zori
zorilla
zorillas
zoris
zorro
zorros
zouaves

zouk
zounds
zowie

Z U

zucchetto
zucchini
zucchinis
zugzwang

Z Y

zydeco
zygoma

zygomata
zygomatic
zygospore
zygote
zygotene
zygotes
zygotic
zymase
zymogen
zymogens
zymurgy

COUNTDOWN PUZZLER SUPPLEMENT

C OUNTDOWN was the first programme on Channel 4 (on Tuesday 2 November 1982) and Richard Whiteley's was the first face to be seen. Countdown was initially contracted for 27 shows over seven weeks. In March 2001 the 3,000th show was recorded, part of the 44th series.

The Countdown final at 4.55pm on Christmas Day 1999 had more viewers (3.5 million) than BBC2, Channel 4, Channel 5, or GMTV, and attracted the eleventh highest audience of the day on any channel. All five shows regularly feature in Channel 4's weekly top ten programmes, with audiences ranging from 2.5 to 5 million. From Thursday to Monday Countdown is repeated at 5.30 in the morning, and the Saturday morning show regularly attracts around 100,000 viewers.

Over the years there have been several embarrassing mistakes: once, the mixed-up version of the conundrum was P A R T Y D O E R , with the expected answer being P O R T R A Y E D . One of the contestants buzzed and said P R E D A T O R Y , and was disallowed ... but of course he was correct – you can get both words out of P A R T Y D O E R .

For the 1,000th show someone came up with the idea of using M I L L E N N I U M as the conundrum. Unfortunately, they misspelled it M I L L E N I U M (the word should not have been used at all, as it has ten letters). M I L L E N N I U M was guessed by one contestant, but the losing contestant had to be given a compensatory set of dictionaries.

Several conundrums have been used more than once over the years: the two champions are P R O B A T I O N and T U R B U L E N T , which have both been used four times.

Over the years other 'disasters' have included the clock going backwards, the clock starting but not the music, one of the overhead lights bursting into flames, heavy snow which meant that there was an audience of six people, contestants who have dropped out on the morning of their recordings ... and an elusive cat which miaowed its way through the latter part of a show without being discovered – it was eventually found wandering the gantry thirty feet above the studio floor!

C O U N T D O W N R U L E S

Since July 2000 Countdown has used the *New Oxford Dictionary of English* (NODE) as its 'Bible'. So, to be allowed in the game, a word must either be in NODE or be a legitimate inflection of one that is.

All permissible words are in the dictionary section of this book.

☑ Words which are allowed

Inflections

e.g. **knighted** and **fought** are fine, but **fighted** isn't.

Plurals

Think carefully whether a noun can logically have a plural, e.g. **elements** is fine, but **hydrogens** isn't.

You should take particular care when pluralizing words ending in:

- **-ness/-less**
  Many words ending in '-ness' do not have a plural: **fitnesses** is not allowed, although **illnesses** is fine; **witnesses** and **harnesses** are of course also fine.

- **-age**
  Words in this category that you can pluralize are those which indicate an action (e.g. **breakage**), the result of an action (e.g. **dosage**), or a place (e.g. **anchorage**, **orphanage**). Most others can't logically be pluralized (e.g. **dotage**, **parentage**).

- **-ing**
  You can only pluralize a word ending in '-ing' if it is a noun, and one that can logically have a plural, e.g. **endings** is fine, but **bakings** isn't.

Comparatives and superlatives

Providing they are logically possible, comparative and superlative adjectives (ending in –er and –est respectively) can be made from any adjectives of one syllable (except adjectives formed from verbs, e.g. **pleased**) or from two-syllable words ending in '-y', '-ow', '-le', or '-er' (e.g. **tinier**, **tiniest**, **fickler**, **ficklest**).

Accented words

Words that normally have accents are allowed without them, e.g. **fiance** and **senor** are fine, even though they are entered in the dictionary as *fiancé* and *señor*.

American spellings

e.g. **color** or **traveling** are fine.

Other variant spellings

e.g. **horsey** and **horsy**, **matins** and **mattins** are all fine, even though in NODE one of each pair is considered to be the main one.

Problem categories

With some types of word, you just have to use your knowledge to gauge how likely they are to exist. All those that are at all common are allowed:

- **'-er' nouns**
  ('agent nouns' meaning 'a person or thing that does something'): e.g. **walker** and **curer** are fine, but **cheeper** and **trogger** aren't.

- **'-ly' words**
  (adverbs): e.g. **quickly** and **stubbily** are fine, but **mootly** and **mankily** aren't.

- **'-less' words**
  e.g. **earless** and **guileless** are fine, but **boatless** and **moodless** aren't.

- **'-ness' words**
  e.g. **greenness** and **bushiness** are fine, but **beigeness** and **gabbiness** aren't.

- **'un-' words**
  e.g. **unhinge** and **untaken** are fine, but **unwrite** and **ungobbled** aren't.

- **'re-' words**
  e.g. **remount** and **reword** are fine, but **rewatch** and **reknow** aren't.

- **'-ish' words**
  e.g. **yellowish** and **newish** are fine, but **maroonish** and **directish** aren't.

☒ Words which are not allowed

Hyphenated words

e.g. **check-up** and **waist-deep** aren't allowed.

Part-words

Affixes such as **non-** and **-arium** aren't allowed, nor are parts of combinations that aren't words in their own right, e.g. **mistle**, from *mistle thrush*, and **mecum**, from *vade mecum*.

Words beginning with a capital letter

e.g. **Hibernian**, **Martello**, and **Samson** aren't allowed.

Abbreviations

e.g. **NATO** and **OED** aren't allowed.

Words containing apostrophes

e.g. **whene'er** and **howsoe'er** aren't allowed.

COUNTDOWN TIPS

■ Letters games

- Look for common endings such as **-ing**, **-ed**, **-iest**, and **-er**, and for common beginnings such as **pre-**, **un-**, **sub-**, etc.

- If there is a choice between an unusual word and a common word of the same length, go for the common one.

- Remember the 's'. It's annoying to be beaten because you forgot to pluralize your word.

■ Numbers games

- Try to write your solution down, or you may forget exactly how you reached the target.

- It often helps to add or subtract one or more small numbers from the larger number before multiplying or dividing.

- Learn the 75 times table off by heart – there is often more chance of reaching the target using this than by using 50 or 25.

> You can increase your word power and your ability to see words by practising; you can increase your speed and ability at the numbers by practising ... but when it comes to the conundrum you either see it or you don't – so don't worry about it!

■ Distribution of consonants and vowels in Countdown

Consonants (66)				Vowels (65)	
2 ×	B	3 ×	P	15 ×	A
3 ×	C	1 ×	Q	20 ×	E
5 ×	D	6 ×	R	14 ×	I
2 ×	F	7 ×	S	11 ×	O
4 ×	G	7 ×	T	5 ×	U
2 ×	H	2 ×	V		
1 ×	J	2 ×	W		
1 ×	K	1 ×	X		
5 ×	L	2 ×	Y		
3 ×	M	1 ×	Z		
6 ×	N				

The producers always have two sets of letters – and numbers – available in case some are damaged or go missing.

There is also a separate set of letters for compiling the conundrums.

After every round, the letters used are set aside in piles – in case of retakes – and are shuffled back into the pack at the end of the show. After every three shows the whole pack is reshuffled.

THE GAMES

■ Letters games

A contestant selects nine letters one by one (consonants and vowels, in any order). The two contestants then have 30 seconds in which to make the longest word they can from those letters, using each letter only once.

Scoring: 1 point per letter in the winning word – unless a contestant gets a nine-letter word, in which case the score is doubled and they get 18 points.

Only the longest word scores: e.g. if contestant A gets a seven-letter word and contestant B gets a six-letter word, then the score is contestant A 7, contestant B 0. However, if both contestants get seven-letter words then the score is 7 points each.

> **Only words contained in the dictionary (the *New Oxford Dictionary of English*, or the *Official Countdown Dictionary*) are allowed.**

Try the following letters games: test yourself and then check your words against those on p. 343.

1. L Y T A N M E L S
2. I T M A O C R A B
3. M T O C U V I N S
4. O N U F M A R I L
5. D A R I O L T A E
6. W N T U O N A R E
7. F I D F E H S W I
8. C O N V E L A T E
9. S O N O D I L E F
10. T O C K Y P O S E

11. N E T W U T R I N
12. A T E D L U L U S
13. P I L O F E R U W
14. B N A C E L I M A
15. Y I R W A H T O E
16. G U H E T S R A L
17. G E R G O D U S H
18. U R S E Q I L R Y
19. R I T E R S U S O
20. L E N P A Y F O M

21. C A R L N O V I C
22. O O N A N C I V E
23. H Y S G U N D O L
24. B O N E Y A R D I
25. M U L I O S E D O
26. C R A W S I V E T
27. P A S O L D E S I
28. N A H I M E C T A
29. Y E L A M I T R I
30. B A W O K R E L E

■ Numbers games

Numbers cards are arranged face-down in four rows. The top row has the numbers 25 50 75 100 in random order; the other three rows consist of the numbers 1 - 10 twice, also in random order.

After the contestant has selected a combination of six numbers (e.g. 'one from the top row and any five from the other three rows') an electronic random number generator produces a three-figure target between 100 and 999.

The contestants then have 30 seconds to reach the target by using the six selected numbers (each number may be used only once – but you don't have to use them all) and the four basic methods of arithmetic: addition, subtraction, multiplication and division ... no square roots, powers, or fractions.

Scoring:
• 10 points for getting the target spot on
• 7 points for being within 5 of the target
• 5 points for being within 10 of the target.

Only the contestant nearest to the target scores – but if both get it exactly right, or are equidistant, then both score.

One of the problems that can arise with the numbers comes when a very easy target comes up, e.g. 408 for the selected numbers 3 4 5 8 6 100.
It's been decided that it's unfair to change the target, so it is left as it is and both contestants score an easy 10 points.

Try the following numbers games, then check your answers on page 344. Remember that in some cases there may be more than one solution!

		Target				Target
1.	75 2 3 4 6 9	889	11.	75 7 3 6 9 10	402
2.	9 5 6 4 7 3	764	12.	25 8 9 5 5 2	381
3.	25 7 3 1 2 3	897	13.	50 25 7 2 8 6	590
4.	50 10 10 8 4 6	742	14.	25 50 8 4 3 6	776
5.	50 7 6 5 6 7	539	15.	100 4 7 9 9 6	548
6.	100 1 1 2 2 8	511	16.	10 5 10 3 4 6	727
7.	75 3 8 9 7 1	321	17.	50 75 9 6 6 9	397
8.	50 100 75 3 6 7	367	18.	75 2 6 8 5 5	699
9.	25 2 2 3 5 7	756	19.	50 75 100 25 10 3	284
10.	100 50 6 9 6 5	206	20.	25 3 4 3 2 5	755

■ Conundrums

The conundrum is a nine-letter word which is displayed on two parallel flip-boards (one for the jumbled-up version and one for the answer). The top board initially displays the word COUNTDOWN and the bottom board displays the word CONUNDRUM.

The presenter starts the 30-second clock and the top board is flipped to reveal a jumbled-up nine-letter word. For example, METALWORK might be mixed up as TOMWALKER, and ENGROSSED as GREENSODS.

The contestants can buzz at any time during the 30 seconds if they think that they have recognized the word. If a contestant buzzes and is correct then the bottom board is flipped to reveal the word and they are awarded 10 points. However, if they are incorrect then the clock – which stopped when they buzzed – is restarted and their opponent has the rest of the 30 seconds to work out the correct solution.

If the scores are tied after all nine rounds then we stop the tape and put in another conundrum, continuing until someone wins. However, any points gained from an 'extra' conundrum do not count towards contestants' points totals for the quarter-finals.

All the conundrums listed below have appeared in past programmes. Test yourself, and check the answers on page 345.

The five most difficult conundrums – maybe

1. SOCCERDEN
2. TOPGARDEN
3. RAVENSOUP
4. DOESAFARI
5. MOONSLICE

Some unusual mixed-up conundrums

1. TADCASTER
2. PEPSICOLA
3. TOMCRUISE
4. LETISSIER
5. LIAMBRADY
6. ORCHESTRA
7. SECTIONAL
8. SUPERDIET
9. RAREDIETS
10. EATINGTOE
11. LANCASTER

50 more Countdown conundrums

1. M O C F R I E N D
2. C I G A R E T T S
3. A L P I N E T O T
4. S E A D I N E R S
5. R U N S A L I V E
6. R I P E B E R C S
7. B O O M T E N T S
8. L O U S Y R I S E
9. G O N I F T R I P
10. T H I N G L O O M
11. E T T A D I D E M
12. D R A M A T R E K
13. T E N D E I G H T
14. S P E E D I F I C
15. R U I N E D M A C
16. A G R E E N C O U
17. W O K L E G E N D
18. R A P D E S I G N
19. O U M A N T R A P
20. M I N G Y P O L E
21. G I A N T D I N N
22. R I N G M A K E R
23. A T A R T S D U E
24. L U G A B L I N I
25. D R E E M S H O T

26. R A C E C H A R T
27. T I N Y G L O V E
28. N E I L Y U N G E
29. R E D P A R E N T
30. O M I N G H O S T
31. N E D R E D A M E
32. P R E D A T E U R
33. I N A P O O T E R
34. P U R E L Y T E D
35. V I C S I N G E R
36. D R E A D B O N E
37. L U N A H I P P Y
38. I T O U R S O O N
39. P U N I C M A I L
40. L Y R E S P I C E
41. T I D I C L E A N
42. N U R S E L E F T
43. S P O I L T M E N
44. A D E D I C A N T
45. O P I E R R O T S
46. N E X T D I N G E
47. E I G H T M I L L
48. I L L E S T A T E
49. T I G H T E N E R
50. S O M B R E N I T

UNUSUAL WORDS

In the eighteen years of Countdown there have been some amazing words, many of them from Dictionary Corner, but even more from contestants. Here are a few examples just from series 29:

APOMIXIS
asexual reproduction in plants.

ATLANTES
plural form of 'atlas', a Greek pillar in the form of a male figure.

BIOME
a large naturally occurring community of flora and fauna occupying a major habitat, e.g. a forest.

CARYATIDS
Greek pillars in the form of draped female figures.

CETANE
a colourless liquid hydrocarbon of the alkane series, present in petroleum spirit.

DUPION
a rough silk fabric woven from the threads of double cocoons.

ELUTION
the action of removing an adsorbed substance by washing with a solvent.

ESPALIER
a fruit tree or ornamental shrub whose branches are trained to grow flat against a wall.

GALIPOT
hardened resin deposits formed on the stem of the maritime pine.

GAMELAN
a traditional instrumental ensemble in Java and Bali, including many bronze percussion instruments.

HALITE
sodium chloride as a mineral; rock salt.

HOPLITE
a heavily armed foot soldier of ancient Greece.

LAZARET
the rear part of a ship's hold, used for stores.

MANGONEL
a former military device for throwing stones and other missiles.

MOREEN
a strong ribbed cotton fabric, used chiefly for curtains.

SANGAREE
a cold drink of wine, water, and spices.

SARDELLE
a sardine, anchovy, or other small fish similarly prepared for eating.

TEAZELS
dried heads from the teazel, a tall prickly plant with spiny purple flower heads.

TENACE
a pair of cards in one hand in bridge, whist, etc. which rank immediately above and below a card held by an opponent.

TOROID
a geometric figure having the shape of a torus (rather like a ring doughnut).

VELAMEN
an outer layer of empty cells in the exposed roots of some orchids and plants of the arum family.

VERONAL
a sedative and sleep-inducing drug.

VESICANT
a substance that causes blistering.

C O U N T D O W N   C H A M P I O N S

1982
Series 1   Joyce Cansfield

1983
Series 2   Ash Haji
Series 3   Andrew Guy

1984
Series 4   Brian Hudson
C of C I   Mark Nyman
Series 5   Peter Evans

1985
Series 6   Darryl Francis
Series 7   Ian Bebbington

1986
Series 8   Clive Spate
C of C II   Clive Freedman
Series 9   David Trace
Series 10   Harvey Freeman

1987
Series 11   John Clarke
Series 12   Stephen Balment
C of C III   Harvey Freeman
Series 13   Hilary Hopper
Series 14   Nic Brown

1988
Series 15   Dick Green
Series 16   Tony Vick

1989
C of C IV   Nic Brown
Series 17   Lawrence Pearse
Series 18   Rajaretnam Yogasagarar

1990
Series 19   Michael Wareham
Series 20   Liz Barber

1991
C of C V   Tim Morrissey
Series 21   Barry Grossman
Series 22   Chris Waddington

1992
Series 23   Gareth Williams
Series 24   Wayne Summers

1993
C of C VI   Wayne Summers
Series 25   Don Reid
Series 26   Andy Bodle

1994
Series 27   David Elias
Series 28   Damian Eadie

1995
C of C VII   Don Reid
Series 29   Darren Shacklady
Series 30   Verity Joubert

1996
Series 31   David Acton
Series 32   Alan Sinclair
Cof C VIII   Chris Rogers
Series 33   (SC) Harvey Freeman

1997
Series 34   Huw Morgan
Series 35   Peter Cashmore
Series 36   Tony Baylis
Series 37   Ray McPhie

1998
C of C IX   Natascha Kearsey
Series 38   John Ashmore
Series 39   Kate Ogilvie

1999
Series 40   Terence English
Series 41   Scott Mearns
C of C X   Scott Mearns

2000
Series 42   Michael Calder
Series 43   Graham Nash

C of C = Champion of Champions
SC = Supreme Champion

The scores are given in brackets (remember that a nine-letter word scores double, i.e. 18 points).

1. LAMENT (6), AMNESTY (7), MENTALLY (8)

2. COMBAT (6), ACROBAT (7), AROMATIC (8)

3. INMOST (6), SUCTION (7), VISCOUNT (8)

4. OILMAN (6), UNIFORM (7), INFORMAL (8)

5. LARIAT (6), RADIATE (7), IDOLATER (8)

6. TOWER (5), NATURE (6), NEUTRON (7)

7. WIDISH (6), WHIFFED (7), FISHWIFE (8)

8. ALCOVE (6), ENCLAVE (7), COVALENT (8)

9. FOOLED (6), EIDOLON (7), SOLENOID (8)

10. STOKE (5), POCKET (6), COYOTES (7)

11. NUTTIER (7), NUTRIENT (8), UNWRITTEN (18)

12. LASTED (6), DULLEST (7), ULULATED (8)

13. FLOWER (6), PROFILE (7), POWERFUL (8)

14. MANACLE (7), AMICABLE (8), IMBALANCE (18)

15. WATER (5), THEORY (6), HAYWIRE (7)

16. HURTLES (7), LAUGHTER (8), SLAUGHTER (18)

17. GOURDS (6), SOUGHED (7), SHRUGGED (8)

18. SLURRY (6), SURLIER (7), SQUIRREL (8)

19. RUSSET (6), SERIOUS (7), TROUSERS (8)

20. FOAMY (5), FELONY (6), MAYPOLE (7)

21. CALICO (6), CLARION (7), VOLCANIC (8)

22. VOICE (5), CONNIVE (7), NOVOCAINE (18)

23. GHOUL (5), SHOULD (6), UNGODLY (7)

24. BEYOND (6), BANDIER (7), DEBONAIR (8)

25. MUESLI (6), MOODIES (7), MELODIOUS (18)

26. CRAVE (5), WAIVER (6), VISCERA (7)

27. LAPSED (6), ADIPOSE (7), DISPOSAL (8)

28. ANAEMIC (7), HAEMATIC (8), MACHINATE (18)

29. TAMELY (6), REALITY (7), MILITARY (8)

30. WARBLE (6), BLEAKER (7), WORKABLE (8)

1. $(4 \times 3) \times 75 = 900$
    $900 - (9 + 2) = 889$

2. $(3 \times 9) \times 5 = 135$
    $(135 - 7) \times 6 = 768$
    $768 - 4 = 764$

3. $(3 \times 2) \times (7 - 1) = 36$
    $(36 \times 25) - 3 = 897$

4. $50 + 4 - (10/10) = 53$
    $8 + 6 = 14$
    $53 \times 14 = 742$

5. $50 - (7/7) = 49$
    $(6 + 5) \times 49 = 539$

6. $(100/2) + 1 = 51$
    $(8 + 2) \times 51 = 510$
    $510 + 1 = 511$

7. $75 + 9 = 84$
    $84 \times (3 + 1) = 336$
    $336 - (8 + 7) = 321$

8. $(3 \times 75) + 100 = 325$
    $325 + (7 \times 6) = 367$

9. $2 \times 2 \times 25 = 100$
    $100 + 5 + 3 = 108$
    $108 \times 7 = 756$

10. $9 - 5 = 4$
    $(4 \times 50) + 6 = 206$

11. $(75 - 10) \times 6 = 390$
    $9 + 3 = 12$
    $390 + 12 = 402$

12. $2 \times 8 \times 25 = 400$
    $5 + 5 + 9 = 19$
    $400 - 19 = 381$

13. $2 \times 6 \times 50 = 600$
    $25 - (8 + 7) = 10$
    $600 - 10 = 590$

14. $(8 \times 25) - 6 = 194$
    $194 \times 4 = 776$

15. $7 + (9/9) = 8$
    $(100 - 8) \times 6 = 552$
    $552 - 4 = 548$

16. $(10 + 4) \times 10 = 140$
    $(140 + 6) \times 5 = 730$
    $730 - 3 = 727$

17. $6 \times 75 = 450$
    $50 + 9 - 6 = 53$
    $450 - 53 = 397$

18. $75 + 2 = 77$
    $8 + (5/5) = 9$
    $(77 \times 9) + 6 = 699$

19. $(75 - 50) + 3 = 28$
    $28 \times 10 = 280$
    $280 + (100/25) = 284$

20. $(3 \times 2) + 4 = 10$
    $(10 \times 3) \times 25 = 750$
    $750 + 5 = 755$

The five most difficult conundrums – maybe

1. CRESCENDO
2. GODPARENT
3. SUPERNOVA
4. AFORESAID
5. SEMICOLON

Some unusual mixed-up conundrums

1. CASTRATED
2. EPISCOPAL
3. COSTUMIER
4. STERILISE
5. ADMIRABLY
6. CARTHORSE
7. COASTLINE
8. DISREPUTE
9. DREARIEST
10. NEGOTIATE
11. ANCESTRAL

50 more Countdown conundrums

1. CONFIRMED
2. STRATEGIC
3. POTENTIAL
4. READINESS
5. UNIVERSAL
6. PRESCRIBE
7. TOMBSTONE
8. SERIOUSLY
9. PROFITING
10. MOONLIGHT
11. MEDITATED
12. TRADEMARK
13. TIGHTENED
14. SPECIFIED
15. MANICURED
16. ENCOURAGE
17. KNOWLEDGE
18. SPREADING
19. PARAMOUNT
20. EMPLOYING
21. INDIGNANT
22. REMARKING
23. SATURATED
24. BILINGUAL
25. SMOTHERED
26. CHARACTER
27. LONGEVITY
28. GENUINELY
29. PARTNERED
30. SMOOTHING
31. MEANDERED
32. DEPARTURE
33. OPERATION
34. REPUTEDLY
35. SERVICING
36. BROADENED
37. UNHAPPILY
38. NOTORIOUS
39. MUNICIPAL
40. PRECISELY
41. IDENTICAL
42. RESENTFUL
43. SIMPLETON
44. CANDIDATE
45. POSTERIOR
46. EXTENDING
47. LIMELIGHT
48. SATELLITE
49. TETHERING
50. BRIMSTONE